WORKERS OF THE WORLD

WORKERS OF THE WORLD: AFRICAN AND ASIAN MIGRANTS IN ITALY IN THE 1990S

Steven Colatrella

Africa World Press, Inc.

P.O. Box 1892
Trenton, NJ 08607

P.O. Box 48
Asmara, ERITREA

Africa World Press, Inc.

P.O. Box 1892
Trenton, NJ 08607

P.O. Box 48
Asmara, ERITREA

Cover Design: Ashraful Haque

Library of Congress Cataloging-in-Publication Data

Colatrella, Steven
   Workers of the world : African and Asian migrants in Italy in the
1990s / by Steven Colatrella.
      p. cm.
Includes bibliographical references and index.
   ISBN 0-86543-920-6 (hardcover) – ISBN 0-86543-921-4 (pbk.)
   1. Alien labor, African--Italy--Veneto. 2. Alien labor,
Asian--Italy--Veneto. 3. Immigrants--Italy--Veneto. I. Title.
   HD8488.A2 C65 2001
   331.6'2'0945--dc21
                                    2001005059

For my mother, Betty Colatrella

CONTENTS

ACKNOWLEDGMENTS

This study has been a more collective endeavor than most, and I am deeply grateful to the many, many people without whose efforts, assistance, patience and kindness I could never have gotten very far in completing it. First and foremost I must thank all of the immigrants who gave me their time, who answered my questions, who explained their life's choices and aspirations to me, extending a graciousness, patience and willingness to help which is astounding to recall, and which even now many months later remains with me as one sign of the possibilities of a new basis for civilization in the making. It is my greatest hope that this work will help to change the conditions which they face everyday and be a tool in their struggles. The rest is, as they say, academic.

Ferruccio Gambino helped to make this study possible, enabling me to work in Padua with access to the resources of the Dipartimento di Sociologia there; he constantly encouraged me at moments when it seemed most difficult to carry through the research project.

My dissertation chair Jim Geschwender has been the Joe Torre of this research, and it needed one. Martin Murray probably did more actual work on this project than he finds for his own work, reading and re-reading, providing me with methodological critiques and questions, sending me comments on every written page month after month. Phil Kraft gave me very positive feedback at an important stage.

Silvano Cogo literally shared his life and work with me after the strange day in late 1994 when a left-wing American former union organizer turned sociologist showed up in his office at the

CGIL union to ask about contacting immigrant workers. That the world still holds dedicated individuals like Silvano is a great cause for hope—a man who thinks nothing of spending his Sundays off driving for hours to meet Senegalese or Nigerian workers in trouble and calling up his American friend to come with him. He and his wife Donatella have so graciously extended hospitality to myself and my family that I can never sufficiently express my gratitude.

Michele Fassina found time to work with me on my questionnaire, introduced me to countless people, befriended me and included me as an equal in the activities of Associazione Immigrati Extracomunitari.

Enzo Mingione never once flinched when I asked him for help in his capacity as chair of the Dipartimento di Sociologia at the University of Padua, and I asked him often. He and the entire staff, faculty and doctoral student body of the department never treated me as other than one of their own department's graduate students. In doing so, they have set an example of how academics should act in relation to guests, and if I am ever in a position to reciprocate for any of them I will model my actions after their own. The staff of the department—Marzia, Roberta, Daniela and Giovanni have done so much to make my stay in Italy and my work possible that I can never thank them enough.

I would also like to thank: Grazia Bellini of the Ufficio Immigrati of the CGIL in Padua, Mortesà, Gabrielle and the rest of the staff of the Municipal Ufficio Accoglienza Immigrati of Vicenza and the staff of the immigrant office of the CGIL of Montebelluna (whom I leave unnamed for reasons they will understand); Marco Paggi explained labor and immigration law to me, Guido Negrin helped me unravel some of the history of immigrants in Italy, and he and Michele Fassina helped me understand the links to Italian colonialism.

My thanks to Rick Sprout, Dario Padovan, Dario Da Re, Rossana Mungiello, Devi Sacchetto, Valter Zanin, Silvia Federici and George Caffentzis, Mariarosa Dalla Costa, Dario De Bortoli, Giovanna Franca Dalla Costa and her husband ,the staffs of the libraries at Binghamton University and at the Institute of Political

Science at the University of Padua, and at Loyola University's Rome Center,Valerio Belotti ,Ilvo Diamanti.

Hillary Creek and Enzo Dimassi and their son Thomas, Mariarosa and Franca Dalla Costa and their families, my mother Betty Colatrella, Silvia Federici and George Caffentzis, Silvano Cogo and his wife Donatella., Dan Karan and Gillian Kaye, my brother Paul Colatrella and my sister Elizabeth Colatrella all came through with at times desperately needed material aid in one form or another without which this study would never have been completed.

I am very grateful to Binghamton University, and the taxpayers of New York State for a Dissertation Year Fellowship which first enabled me to go to Italy and commence this research, and to my faculty who nominated me for the award. This study was partially funded by a Fulbright Award, for which I am very grateful.

Dario Da Re hosted me for an entire year in his living space and acted as if it was something that could be taken for granted. It isn't, and I will always be grateful. Dario Padovan heard every idea in this dissertation a thousand times, and critiqued them, corrected them and was my most continual comrade and co-thinker on social questions for three years.

Finally, the lives and work of E. P. Thompson, C.L.R. James, Walter Rodney and George Rawick permeate every page of this study. I cannot fully express how much I miss these four men, inspirations to me everyday; nor can I fully admit that they have left us alone to face an ever more arrogant capitalism without their wise counsel and their sharp insight. They would have known what to make of this world market, and they would have understood the capabilities of these at times bedraggled and wretched Senegalese, Moroccans, Filipinas, Romanians, Albanians, Nigerians and others whose stories I have tried to tell - and I daresay they would have told them far better than I have. I hope to have accomplished something useful in these pages, for the world outside academe and not only for sociological understanding, but my whole life development is impossible to understand without reference to their life work. Like the medieval scholars, if we see as far as we do today, it is because we stand on the shoulders of giants.

1

INTRODUCTION

Across our planet today, tens of millions of people live and work as immigrants. Peoples that have not migrated in large numbers for decades or centuries are now found in the farthest reaches of the world. Places such as Senegal, Nigeria, and the Mayan regions of the Americas, which have never before been sources of emigration (or not since the forced migration of the Atlantic slave trade), today send hundreds of thousands of their citizens to live and work overseas. Countries that have never before received large numbers of immigrants, such as Italy, Japan, South Korea, and Spain, are today the destinations for millions of the world's workers. Stephen Castles and Mark Miller have called this century the advent of an "Age of Migration."[1] Simultaneously, in some parts of the planet, new forms of work and new markets for products and money have developed. In other places, the centuries-old process of the separation of workers from land and the means of production and subsistence has accelerated, uprooting tens of millions from their communities and their way of life. The uprooted are becoming a new planetary proletariat, which has led to new political movements and demands. Migration is an activity as ancient as our species, but in the modern, capitalist era migration has been associated with expropriation of land, labor markets, state policies and the rise of the working class. Today's migration is reshaping the face of the world. What is the relationship between these varied and vast processes? What links migrants from the remotest regions of the world to new forms of work and global markets at the dawn of a new century? This book is an attempt to answer these questions.

This is a study of immigrants in a particular region, the Veneto region of northeastern Italy. I wanted to find out more about how recent transformations in the global North and South are related. I chose to study a region which receives immigrants, and which is also a site of new market possibilities and innovative organizations of work. Any number of regions of the world economy fit these criteria. Newly industrialized countries of East Asia, which have seen heavy immigration, include Malaysia, and South Korea. Parts of Japan and the United States have also become new destinations for migrants.[2] The Iberian Peninsula and even Ireland might also fit these criteria. Similar studies of these regions will further our understanding of the profound changes discussed here.

Thousands of immigrants, from Africa, Asia, and Eastern Europe, live and work in the northeast of Italy. They are there as a result of planetary social conflicts and a worldwide web of contacts, which are reshaping the labor market and the working class in Europe and throughout the world. Economic changes in recent years in both the North and South of our planet involve common economic strategies by elites, common proletarian experiences of expropriation and work, and social networks of transnational communities of migrants. Elites around the world have developed a more-or-less common strategy known by such terms as neoliberalism, structural adjustment, privatization, and globalization. This strategy depends on production for the market and export, decreasing social services, and reducing wages. It also means loss of access to land and other means of subsistence as well as to any guaranteed employment and wages which workers had won in previous generations through social struggle. In order to survive these transformations, communities in many of the poorer countries have expanded their family and community networks by sending members of their families and communities as migrants to other cities, regions, and countries. Doing so has expanded their access to economic and other resources. This strategy has fostered complex, widespread communications, and transportation networks and moved people, goods and money, so that the community can maintain its material and cultural life. At the same time, the migrant community has transformed cultural and community life in the regions where they have arrived, as well as among their own ranks. They have transformed the working class in many wealthier countries, including Italy. In many areas, including the Veneto, they have entered workplaces that are closely linked to the world market and to export. Some of these workplaces are part of local economies of flexible production and small-scale industry, replacing mass production and large cities as engines for the creation of wealth. The migrants link the restructuring of the North with that of the South, and in so doing, tie the respective communities closer together. They do so through an increasingly planetary exchange of people, information, goods, money, cultural forms, and organization. They connect the working class of their own regions with that in their areas of destination; as well as with other parts of the planet when they come in contact with people from other regions.

One of the ways in which social science understands human mobility is through the metaphor of the labor market. Indeed, the concept of the labor market is the principal way in which the separation of working people from the means of production and subsistence, and their subsequent availability to work for capitalist enterprises has been theorized. In the case of international migration for work, this metaphor becomes the "world," "international," or "global" labor market. This metaphor of the market has in turn been treated either as an objective reality or as a goal for economic policy makers. This study however, finds that the world labor market does not exist as an entity as such, but rather is being made by migrants themselves. If they didn't make it, it wouldn't exist at all. The presence of Bangladeshi men in northern Italian factories and Filipina women in New Jersey hospitals might imply a worldwide market for labor power exists. However this appearance is only superficial. Instead, the worldwide links between areas of migrant origin and those of destination depend upon two conflicting sets of institutions: the forces of structural adjustment and flexible work on the one hand,

and autonomous transnational migrant communities on the other. Migrant networks have brought together labor, capital, needs, resources, and cultural wealth. The phrase "labor market" barely scratches the surface as a description of what is going on. For, despite the common class interest which has restructured the First, Second, and Third worlds in recent decades, such changes would not have automatically led to available workers for the new industries and forms of work. The assumptions of free market thinkers and neoclassical economists are not sustained by the real workings of planetary inter-relations.

The world migrations of today are not a result of structural adjustment and other neoliberal policies, though to be sure these policies are in part meant to create a pool of available labor power throughout the world. Rather, the migrations, and the social networks which have organized and initiated them, are a response to these policies and an attempt to resolve the problems that global economic policies have brought their communities. They must be understood in part as a form of opposition and resistance to structural adjustment and to the neoliberal form of capitalist globalization. They are also a continuation of the social conflicts, previously local, which preceded the economic re-structurings. In organizing migrations, communities have created an increasingly planetary web of communications; information flow; mutual aid; transfer of people; goods and money; and local and international forms of organization and mobilization. These increasingly widespread and dense contacts provide a means not only for transforming the community and enabling it to survive under the conditions of neoliberal society, but for mobilizing it for political, economic, and cultural objectives. These webs of migrant knowledge are valuable resources, and they become the sites of struggles for control by states, networks of organized crime, and by the same international agencies which fostered structural adjustment in the first place. These forces seek to undermine the autonomy of migrant communities and to profit from the flow of people, wealth, and information that follow the migrant web lines of social contact.

Each moment in the expropriation and migration process is contested and conflictual, with an indeterminant outcome. The result of these conflicts at any given moment is what we call the "world labor market." The appearance of immigrants from Senegal, Morocco, or Albania in the factories and construction sites of northern Italy is the result of these conflicts. These migrant workers provide solutions to local economic problems faced by Italian businessmen; these workplaces then become loci of new or wider conflicts. Thus class conflicts, which were previously only hypothetically or ideally related (the great accomplishment and limit of international socialist theory and practice), are now materially linked by the social networks and mobilizations of migrant communities. The networks, having reshaped the world labor market, play a central role in the remaking of the working class in First World countries as well, as new alliances and mobilizations take place around new demands.

This work is thus both anti-neoliberal and anti-postmodern. Neoliberal thought takes for granted the existence and desirability of a worldwide labor market, and views wage levels as having a gravitational effect of attracting workers from locales of lower wages to those with higher levels of pay. On the contrary, the world labor market is a contingent and necessarily incomplete project. This project is struggled over, as governments, corporations, and international agencies seek to bring it into being, while various communities around the world, as well as migrant networks, resist this project and seek to counter it with their own projects, which often involve goals that are not strictly economic in motivation. Where postmodernists see the various moments in this process of worldwide struggle as representing an integral and fundamental "difference," and observe problems of "incommunicability," in fact, extremely varied cultural and political movements in today's world are linked. The experiences of expropriation, mobility, social networks, work, and political mobilization among diverse nationalities of immigrants in Italy—and elsewhere—show remarkable commonalities. Indeed, immigrants in the Veneto have demonstrated a practical unity among different nationalities with regard to common goals, views, and demands that suggests that class relations, and not merely market relations, are becoming planetary in form and content.

The extreme emphases of neoliberalism on economic

explanations, and of postmodernism on cultural ones both miss the real news: the self-activity of ordinary people has expanded the site of class conflicts in some regions to the larger world, and has thereby incorporated the class conflicts of still other regions into an ever more planetary and integrated set of social relations. The working class of the world is remaking itself—this time on a planetary basis. Yet this incorporation is not reducible to that theorized by world systems thinkers and others for whom regions lie relatively or wholly within or without the world capitalist system and are gradually incorporated into an increasingly complete capitalism. Rather, it is precisely the opposition to capitalist integration on its own terms that is linking regions more closely. Furthermore, it is not only economies that are more closely related, but movements and social struggles. It is with this active, conflictual, and indeterminate process in mind that we must attempt to explain the creation of a planetary labor market. For the abstract logic of capital, which assumes that the expropriation of people in one place will lead to their being available as labor power in another, cannot cause even one person to set foot over a national boundary unless an alternative social order exists capable of carrying out migrations. Ironically, such social orders organize migrations only for objectives that contradict and conflict with the interest of capital. One current view, which connects neoliberal and postmodern thought, sees capitalism today as lacking regulation, and as "disorganized." This view misses the point. The question today is whether the social order regulating world economic relations will be that represented by international financial and planning agencies (the IMF and World Bank, the WTO, the UN), states and multinational corporations or will instead be based upon the informal webs of working class communities, increasingly planetary in scope, which have their own objectives both material and extraeconomic.

THEORETICAL APPROACHES TO MIGRATION

Until the 1970s, studies of migration were dominated by two main approaches: neoclassical economic models and studies of assimilation. The first approach was concerned with the labor market and sought to describe the laws that governed the migration of workers—a process which was seen as largely determined by relative wage levels. The latter was more interested in cultural questions of how immigrants adapted themselves to their new home and consisted overwhelmingly of studies of immigration to the United States. Where neoclassical models assumed that migrant populations acted out of exclusively economic motivations, assimilation theorists often treated migrants as primarily cultural beings, torn between two cosmological settings—the peasant community from which they had been uprooted (to use Oscar Handlin's excellent title) and the vibrant, open but often frightening and hostile environment of the new world.[3] In neoclassical models, theorists assumed the existence of a perfectly functioning self-regulating market. Such theorists perceived as imperfections, external to the model itself, such factors as state policies, limited access to transport or information, self-organized migrant community structures and cultural practices, and labor market segmentation by race, gender, nationality, or ethnicity. The result was that immigrants were viewed as acting out of narrowly economic motivation, even to the point of constituting "an unlimited supply of labor" that could be called upon at will.[4]

During the 1970s and early 1980s, various Marxist theorists emphasized how international inequalities in the distribution of wealth and local capitalist labor market structures determined the life chances and opportunities available to immigrants, or called migrations into being in the first place. Such theories stressed how capital made use of migrant labor power to weaken working class organization and to lower production costs.

More recently studies of migrant social networks have argued that human agency needs to be "brought back in" and that migration studies focus on migrant networks which organize migrations collectively. Some theoretical innovations are however, needed to more fully describe the planetary character of contemporary migration. In particular, the labor market for flexible production, though it has many continuities with that for mass production, also differs from that which filled jobs at large assembly plants in previous migrations. Thus the migration which today results in Senegalese working in very small furniture shops, or Filipina women cleaning Italian homes, is very different from that which in the post-World War II era saw East Indians working for Ford in Britain, and Mozambiquans flowing into the mining districts of South Africa.

Assimilation studies have also come under considerable criticism in the past two decades. Assimilationist work has been challenged for assuming that assimilation is a one-way process in which the dominant culture of the receiving country does not also undergo change as a result of the migration process. Furthermore, a multiculturalist approach has questioned whether assimilation even necessarily takes place, arguing instead that contemporary immigrants tend keep their own languages and cultures and that this maintaining of autonomous cultures has been historically important. More recently, a number of transnationally oriented works, mostly in the social network tradition, have focused on the process by which transnational communities are created. These works transcend the previous debate between assimilationists and multiculturalists by demonstrating how communities and cultures now increasingly live, work and move about simultaneously in two locales. As members of migrant communities circulate increasingly rapidly between points of "origin" and "destination," living their lives in both places while fostering this same circulation in other community members, the issue of assimilation fades in importance. The nature and practice of these new kinds of communities requires study.

Though challenged in the 1970s and early '80s by Marxian and social network approaches, neoclassical explanations and descriptions of migration have recently come back into fashion, due more, one suspects, to political reasons than to any improvement in their explanatory power. For as free market ideology has increasingly come to hold a near monopoly on public decision-making and intellectual discourse concerning global economics, migrants have again appeared in the writings and arguments of prominent theorists and politicians as homo economicus, acting in a narrowly rationalistic fashion to maximize economic advantage. Tied closely to conservative opposition to increased migration to the U.S., some writers have turned to human capital theory[5] arguing that current immigrants are less skilled compared with their predecessors of different national origin. These studies rely on many of the same methods that were painstakingly criticiqued a generation ago. The Marxist-influenced critics of free market models developed several counter arguments in the 1970s and early '80s. Portes and Walton, for instance, criticized the argument that higher wage levels act like gravity to attract workers as immigrants by citing the empirical reality that even the largest migrations involve only a minority of the population of impoverished areas. Migration from say, India to England, or Mexico to the U.S. does not continue until the sending countries are empty, nor have wages between the two areas ever equalized.[6] Aristide Zolberg argued that, far from an imperfection in the market, state policy lay at the very center of the migration process, shaping and defining it.[7] Robin Cohen criticized the individualism of free market approaches, arguing that the decision to migrate is taken in the context of family, village, culture, government regulation, educational level, and other factors.[8]

In place of free market and neoclassical models, such theorists developed an alternative approach to the study of migration based upon the Marxist concept of the reserve army of labor and on diverse understandings of imperialism or world systems theory. A literature describing and theorizing the uses of migrant labor by capital arose,[9] of which three early and influential works were those by Castles and Kosack, by Castells, and by Piore.[10] All three argued for a model that stressed the capitalist need for cheaper, more politically compliant labor power in the industrialized countries of the United States and Western Europe, resulting in the migrations of the postwar period. For each, the state played a key role in recruitment and encouragement of migration, representing the interests of capital. Further, each study found labor market stratification in which immigrant workers played the role of a reserve army of labor, essentially available to capital whenever needed. Castles and Kosack saw the business cycle as determining the flow of migration, based upon the needs of French employers.[11] Piore also saw capitalist business needs as controlling the migration process.

Recruitment by employers and government was so effective that the supply of labor available to employers should be assumed to be unlimited, a view further confirmed for Piore by the fact that even when recruitment stopped, the flow of migrants continued.[12] Piore argued that migrants systematically ended up in the lowest paying and most insecure jobs in a segmented labor market. Castells stressed the political motivations behind capitalist sponsorship of immigration, and came to somewhat different conclusions about the nature of the labor market. For Castells, the immigrant workers were a tool by which capital could overcome the declining rate of profit through substitution of non-unionized immigrant workers for the organized workers who had imposed full employment and higher wages on capital. Since immigrants were to be used to undermine union organization and working conditions, their labor power would be used throughout the economy, and not only in the low paying, precarious sectors of the economy; the immigrants would rather be placed in direct competition with the locally born working class.[13] Further elaborations included those of Saskia Sassen, and Edna Bonacich and Lucy Cheng, all of whom stressed the impact of capitalist development on the places of immigrant origin in creating and maintaining migration flows. Sassen, in particular, stressed the role of the U.S. military presence and direct investment in regions of migrant origin as a vital material link leading to migration. Bonacich and Cheng emphasized the distortion of local subsistence economies by colonialism, leading to a workforce needing to work for wages and a petite bourgeoisie that recruits labor and mobilizes an immigrant enclave under its own ethnically based hegemony, thus guaranteeing a cheap labor force to capital.[14] These approaches have the advantage of helping to explain a paradox of neoclassical economics: why migrants flow to the U.S. from, say, South Korea, but not from, for instance, Mali, which is much poorer, but which has seen far less direct US economic or military intervention. Such analyses led to works that argued that the areas of migrant origin and those of destination should not be treated separately, but rather understood as two sites in the same global process and economic system.[15]

For all of their insights, however, these analyses and studies all treated migration not as something that people and groups of people organize and do, but rather as something which happens, or rather is made to happen, when capitalist interests require it. The Marxist works on migration, while providing some needed alternative explanations to the facile abstractions of neoclassical theories, were all heavily structuralist. Granted, the empirical conditions of the postwar period provided ample evidence that capital needed labor power for expansion, and later for access to cheap labor given the wage and welfare victories of First World workers. The turn by many states toward restricting immigration in the mid-'70s seemed to be explained by the economic crisis following the oil price rises and the Yom Kippur War. But by the mid-'80s it was clear that migration had far from halted, despite a lack of apparent interest in new immigrant labor power by business. Were the continuing flows into the U.S. and Western Europe and the new flows into Japan, the Persian Gulf, and East Asia to be understood as merely a manifestation of Piore and Lewis' unlimited labor supply? Some migration scholars, notably the MacDonalds, Tilly and Portes and Bach, believed that the structuralist Marxists and the neoclassical free marketeers had both been looking at the wrong subject of study.[16] They argued that the proper unit of study of migration is the social networks of migrant communities. Migration is a process of social transformation organized by the social networks of migrant communities themselves. These networks mobilize the decision to migrate, develop niches and enclaves, and provide accurate information to would-be emigrants. They transcend national borders. Thus, to understand the migration process in any locale, we must be aware of the international context and dimension of migration choices. For Tilly, migration organized by social networks is "collective transformation involving the use of old social networks and categories to produce new ones."[17] Networks in an increasingly global economy, use contemporary communications and transportation, according to Portes and Bach, to make possible the circulation of information and people with a velocity such that migrant communities can be said to exist in at least two places at once: "Villages in Mexico today," they write, "maintain regular contact with ethnic communities in Chicago.

Remote towns in the mountains of the Dominican Republic are accurately informed about labor market conditions in Queens and the Bronx."[18]

The long term impact of this coordinated existence of communities in multiple geographic locales will be greater than the much heralded new global markets and communications technologies such as the internet, important as these are and will remain. For the transnational communities are learning to use the communications and transportation technologies for their own projects, enabling them to take greater advantage of the global markets or to resist the encroachments of these markets. They are thereby able to maintain social and cultural relations irreducible to economics. For instance, anthropologist Jack Weatherford has argued recently that the much commented upon revival of tribal identities is made possible by the use of new technologies—television, telephones, fax machines, internet, cassette and video recorders, cheap air travel—to open up the possibility of participating in one's tribal or village identity or language or religious group, even while overseas.[19] Events like relative's weddings or the celebration of a local holiday, or cultural developments in music or changes in leadership are now accessible to migrants outside their home area in a way which was not possible for the European immigrants of the turn of the century.

STRUCTURAL ADJUSTMENT AND FLEXIBLE PRODUCTION

Since the mid-1970s, economic restructuring has transformed the World's North and South. A neoliberal regime of less regulated markets, emphasis on export production, elimination of social guarantees, and open access for multinational corporations characterizes both regions, though with great disparities in material life. The rise of flexible production, based upon small-batch, export-oriented work using temporary, part-time labor, and so-called globalization in the United States, Japan, and Western Europe, and structural adjustment in Africa, Asia, Eastern Europe, the Middle East, and Latin America are linked in many ways. The most obvious similarity is the overall tendency of both processes to move towards a neoliberal regime. The agents which impose these processes are international in character in both cases: the G-7 governments and transnational planning agencies such as the IMF, the World Bank, and the WTO. Less obvious is that the two processes are connected by migration. Indeed, without migration structural adjustment and flexible production could not be made to function as a world labor market, the former expropriating potential workers from land and social guarantees, the latter organizing the exploitation of their labor power for the world market. In Marxist terms, these involve the creation of abstract labor power and the exploitation of concrete labor. They are always contingent processes, whose success is never to be taken for granted.

PRIMITIVE ACCUMULATION: THE EXPROPRIATION OF SMALL PRODUCERS, THE NEW ENCLOSURES OF THE COMMONS, AND THE DISEMBEDDING OF WORKERS FROM THE SOCIAL FABRIC

Abstract labor is not a natural phenomenon, but the result of expropriation. In *Capital*, Marx traced the origins of capital accumulation to the enclosures movement in England and argued that extra-economic coercion and expropriation from land and other means of subsistence and production were essential preconditions for capitalist development.[20] But enclosure is not necessarily a one-time historical event; expropriation of proletarians from land and social guarantees is essential to capitalist survival at certain historical periods, including the current one.[21] Caffentzis writes, "Whenever the profit rate tendentially falls and workers' power over the means of production and reproduction rises, the launching of a new phase of the primitive accumulation process is potentially at hand."[22] Today a new proletariat is being formed as a result of new expropriations. Like the expropriations of the 16th to the 18th centuries, which involved not only the clearance of the Scottish Highlands[23] and the English enclosures, but also genocide in the

Americas and the African slave trade,[24] these actions seek to privatize common land, separate small producers from the means of production, and, as Polanyi so strongly reminded us, separate workers from the dense fabric of social relations in which their work was previously embedded.

At least three different approaches to expropriation, past and present, stress the separation of workers from the social relations that had previously constituted a cosmology within which their work activity took place and a means of limiting exploitation by strictly economic forces. The first of these focuses on the results of the uprooting of Africans by the slave trade. It emphasizes their subsequent exploitation as labor power in the plantation system of the New World as having been made possible by the loss of local African community relations, which made resistance difficult. This literature also stresses the resiliance of African culture and its transmutation in the Americas into new forms of community and resistance.[25]

The second approach is that of Austrian economist Karl Polanyi.[26] For Polanyi, the transformation to a self-regulating market is possible only when land, labor, and money, are torn from the community relations protecting society and nature from destruction by sheer, unadorned economic forces.[27] Polanyi, like Marx, sees the labor market as something "unnatural" which must be created and working people as not only economically oriented actors, but also members of communities. Communities of working people involve informal relations and contacts, sometimes based upon family affiliations, usually involving at least initially geographic proximity or cultural, ethnic, or religious homogeneity. Mutual social reproduction, the continuation of everyday life for community members is organized through their cooperation or interaction with one another. Communities, are complex systems, and initial conditions can prove to be of great influence over time as communities develop, grow, or change. Migrant networks are communities in the process of change and geographic movement. The relationships, commitments and responsibilities which were most significant before the migration (family, religious association, to neighborhood or extended kin network, values such as land or home ownership, helping family members, or saving money to marry) become the objectives around which the migrant communities organize themselves. The creation of a world labor market involves a struggle between such working class communities and capital in various places. This results, under contemporary conditions of transport, communications and migrant organization, in the transposition of these communities and changes in their social organization. Migrant social networks are based on the reality that the separation of workers from the social context in which they are embedded is no longer complete under contemporary conditions (if it ever was—the African slavery literature argues the opposite). Rather, migrant social networks consist of these communities' efforts to maintain social control over market forces and work conditions to the extent possible during and after the "great transformation."

This is the viewpoint of the third approach to the separation of workers from the means of production. The journal Midnight Notes[28] has recently revived the study of the enclosures of the commons, defining commons not only as communal land, but more broadly as all social guarantees won in struggles with capital over previous generations. The commons—communal land and tribal or village relations, unionized or guaranteed workplaces, informal urban neighborhood networks, socialized services and income transfers and subsidies for basic needs—are understood as both results of and bases of class power and conflict. Their existence as a result of previous struggles provides a base for further resistance to capitalist exploitation. The resistance to their "enclosure," therefore, becomes an important moment in the making of a planetary working class.

The most obvious forms of resistance to expropriation thus far have been the revolts, strikes and coups which have occured in dozens of countries in opposition to Structural Adjustment Programs (SAP) imposed by the International Monetary Fund (IMF), along with the Zapatista movement in southern Mexico.[29] These revolts and the opposition to World Bank and IMF programs are of directly related to the presence of immigrants in the Veneto. There is evidence that specific immigrations follow specific expropriations and episodes of resistance. The Moroccan presence in Italy, for instance, rapidly increased following the anti-SAP revolts in June 1981 and January 1984; the Ghanaian migration began after the collapse of oil prices in 1986 and the subsequent expulsion of hundreds of thousands of Ghanaians from Nigeria. Their presence in Nigeria had itself been a partial result of the post-1983 structural adjustment program in Ghana itself; The Filipino presence in Italy (based on the Philippine state's use of migrant remittances for debt payment) grew after the mass expulsion of workers from the Gulf states during the 1991 Gulf War; and the Yugoslavian presence grew in the wake first of the IMF devaluations and then the civil war which itself is arguably a result of this SAP.[30] The full nature of SAPs cannot be understood except through the concept of primitive accumulation. This accumulation in turn, should be understood as "accumulation of the proletariat." The debt mechanism is used to force a transformation of the conditions of social reproduction in the countries that undergo SAPs, and to expropriate workers. These workers link expropriations to the flexible production sites of northern Italy, and in the process construct the world labor market, and their own class.

FLEXIBLE WORK AND THE VENETO

Expropriation creates what Marx called "abstract labor": the theoretical availability of workers for work in the capitalist economy. But abstract labor must be converted to "concrete labor": actual work performance in specific jobs producing surplus value and profit. The Veneto, and rest of the so-called "Third Italy," are crucial sites for new strategies in the exploitation of concrete labor. The Third Italy consists of the central and northeast part of the country comprising the regions of Emilia-Romagna, Tuscany, Umbria, and the Marche in central Italy, and the regions of Veneto, Trentino-Alto-Adige, and Friuli-Venezia-Giulia in the northeast. The name was coined by Arnaldo Bagnasco, who claimed that Italy consists of three distinct social formations: the industrial northwest (including Milan, Genoa, and Turin); the underdeveloped south; and the Third Italy which traditionally consists of small-scale sharecroppers and artisanal producers.[31] The central regions have long been characterized by left wing regional and local governments, while the Veneto and its neighboring regions have long been "white" regions characterized by a very powerful Catholic influence and until recently by strong Christian Democratic Party rule.[32]

Two books have in recent years elevated the Third Italy to the position of a model of both production relations and democracy: Piore and Sabel's *The Second Industrial Divide* and Putnam's *Making Democracy Work.*[33] Both argue that the current production relations reinforce democratic and egalitarian relations. In addition, both claim that the regional economy and its political structure are based on a particular social capital in the form of long-standing social traditions in social life of the regions.

A number of writers have discussed the reorganization of global production relations as a move away from mass production and from the so-called Fordist regime of mass assembly-line production and labor organization.[34] Others have described a new international division of labor in which industrial production is restructured along global lines—semi-skilled production work is done in the Third World by people of color and women. Such workers play the predominant role in new workplaces whose production process spans national boundaries.[35] A debate has ensued over the meaning of the new production relations in the Third Italy, one of the world's faster growing economic regions and now one of the richest in Europe.[36] While some thinkers, following Bagnasco and Piore and Sabel, have described flexible work as a renewal of craft work and a generalization of high wage levels,[37] others have found a wide disparity of conditions among workers in the region based upon skill level, gender, degree of employment security, employment status, firm size, and nationality.[38] These production relations have become increasingly widespread globally, and so have come to constitute both a nationwide economic strategy and an international phenomon, as other countries and regions attempt to copy the success of the Third Italy.

Piore and Sabel launched an international debate over the rise of small-scale production in central Italy oriented towards specialized global markets. They argue that the crisis in large-scale mass production factories caused by mass market saturation and working class struggles in the 1970s has put an end to mass production and ushered in a new era of small-scale craft production. This new era is the result of the decentralization of production by capitalists eager to escape union power and regulation and workers anxious to escape the exploitation of the factory by seeking the independence of craft work and self-employment. These phenomena created niches for the production in small batches of highly specialized products for export, while production shifted geographically toward central and northeast Italy.[39] In their view, flexible specialization, as Piore and Sabel called it, constitutes the world-historical revival of craft production and is less alienating, more community-oriented, and conducive to more democratic and regionally based politics. Hierarchies between employers and workers are less rigid.[40] Other writers have been sceptical about these claims, seeing flexible specialization as an anti-union strategy and a new hierarchical division of labor. The debate over this question is testimony to how much Italian society has been transformed in recent decades. It supersedes the earlier debate on the nature of the Italian economy and its role in the world division of labor.[41] Italy was until recently, seen as a society midway between the advanced capitalist states and the Third World, characterized by a combination of development and underdevelopment. Today, Italy's integration into the world market and its status as a wealthy capitalist country are taken for granted.

In opposition to Piore and Sabel's theses, Anna Pollert and John Tomaney both stress that worker flexibility in production and the labor market has always been a capitalist demand, and they see flexible specialization as anything but a new mode of production.[42] However, they do not adequately address the role of the state in organizing and defining the workers' relation to the labor market and its guarantees. Zolberg and others have stressed the relation between immigrant status, citizenship and unfree labor, and have emphasized the importance of unfree labor in capitalist production.[43] During 1990–1998, the period studied here, Italian immigration law, in a variety of ways, limited considerably the status of so-called "extracomunitarians" (immigrants from outside the European Community) as free workers. The very word extracomunitarian reminds us of the historical origin of unfree labor in conquest and the unfree workers' lack of membership in the community. The relation between citizenship status, legal and illegal working conditions, and flexible production suggests that flexible production requires stratification by legal status, organization of production, type of contract, and work conditions.[44] The workers of the world in Italy work under conditions of inequality.

CIVIC ASSOCIATIONISM AND THE VENETO MORAL ECONOMY

Another issue that has arisen regarding this region of Italy is that of associational democracy, civic culture, and social capital based on civic and participatory traditions. Robert Putnam's comparative study of regional governments in northern and southern Italy argues that a long-standing tradition of civic associations in northern Italy has led to more responsive government institutions and a higher level of democractic practice. Putnam links these civic traditions with the social networks that underly the regional economy and sustain small industrial zones, flexible production, and cooperative rather than competitive between local firms.[45]

Putnam is too sweeping in his generalizations. The Veneto is characterized by a Catholic moral economy, which has often restrained the worst excesses of capitalism, but in a different manner than has the alternative left wing tradition in Emilia-Romagna, the region immediately to the south. Both traditions shape the flexible production economy and the political conditions in which immigrant workers find themselves. While much has been written on the Red Zones such as Emilia-Romagna and other areas with leftwing local and regional governments, the Veneto has been neglected. Though its social structure is similar to that of Emilia-Romagna (artisan production, small farmers, and small industrial zones based on small-to-medium size firms), Veneto's cultural tradition is very different. Veneto is where the Christian Democratic Party (DC) was born, and it was, until recently (when that party collapsed at the national level as a result of the Tangentopoli scandal), the White Zone par excellence. The party developed a dense network of community and social organizations linked to the Church and a political regime more benign than that which dominated the South during the postwar period when Christian Democrats governed.[46] Indeed, the DC held onto power in the Veneto in part because of its ability to project itself as an anti-capitalist defender of a Catholic moral economy against the abuses of an unrestrained market.[47] Aided by local government, businesses cooperate and share technology and market information. A dense social network of business, government and religious affiliations has for decades gradually shaped the local economy, and maintained community standards, such as limited inequality and widespread private property. The local moral economy of the Veneto has had an impact on industrial relations, but the growth of an export-oriented economy is eroding it, changing working conditions and the context in which immigrant organization takes place. The differences between regional cultures are also important in shaping work conditions. Bagnasco found in his study of Bassano, a small industrial city in the Veneto (province of Vicenza), that union membership was lower, that courts tended to find in favor of employers over workers more often. He also found that social services were less developed than in Emilia-Romagna.[48]

Thus, the sweeping generalizations made by writers such as Putnam, regarding civic culture and associationism in "the north" must be specified more carefully by taking into account the difference between Catholic and Marxist cultures. The Veneto can be described as both export-oriented for many centuries (Venice was, after all, a major economic power until the rise of the Atlantic economies)[49] and insular and inward-looking.[50] This historical contradiction is today a major theme in the life of the Veneto. The fastest growing export region in Europe is also the region where the local dialect is most commonly used instead of the national language.[51] Export and immigration are shaped by the local social networks, and the Catholic ideology and moral economy of the region. But precisely because of export and the presence of immigrants, the Veneto is increasingly integrated into the world division of labor and the world market. And both of these have undergone epic changes in recent years.

These changes in the world market and division of labor include the shift of much production work and especially assembly work (the global assembly line) to Third World countries; the predominance of female labor; and the use of export zones from the Maquiladoras in Mexico to Taiwan and Singapore. In these export zones, transnational corporations take advantage of low wages, tax incentives, and a low level of unionization and enforcement of workers' rights.[52] Recent studies indicate a significant variation in such export zones in terms of work conditions, forms of work organization and levels of resistance on the part of women workers, based on a complex interplay of class, gender, local culture and social organization.[53] Such studies, like the present one, stress the inter-relation of global economic transformations and the pressures of export production on the one hand, and the particular social relations found in specific locales on the other, as forces shaping workers' conditions and capacities for organization. Saskia Sassen, has emphasized the growth of services and contemporaneous "consolidation of a new kind of economic center from where the world is managed and serviced."[54] This servicing occurs in "global cities" where financial services, immigrant workers, and communications nodes are concentrated such as New York, London, and Tokyo; such cities are characterized by aggregations of immigrants who carry out both service and lower skilled manufacturing work.[55]

The changes shaping the Veneto in recent years are part and parcel of such transformations. Yet the conditions in the Veneto, both for Italians and immigrants, don't seem to fit the same pattern. While the Veneto is undoubtedly an export zone, and a site of the transfer of production from traditional industrial areas, it is a very different kind of export zone than those studied in Third World countries: It is characterized by the virtual absence of multinational corporations, relatively higher wages than in other parts of the industrialized world, small-scale, mostly local ownership, and a continuing relative predominance of male workers in local industry. And, while it is undoubtedly a part of the same transformations affecting all First world countries, it has seen a shift from services to industrial growth in the last twenty years, unlike much of the rest of the regions of G7 countries. Finally, it a zone of concentrated industry—and now of immigrant labor—without any large metropolitan area, let alone a "global city." Worldwide transformations, however, do shape the context in which the world labor market is manifested in the Veneto.

WORKERS OF THE WORLD

In studying the lives and work of the immigrant workers in the Veneto, we can find out much about how the conflict between workers and capital has re-structured both the North and South simultaneously, and how transnational migrant networks link the two parts of the planet. We can better understand how capital and workers function as worldwide actors as well as local ones. It seems that rumors of the death of the world working class have been greatly exaggerated. Indeed, in recent years there has been a growth of new expropriations of workers from land and social guarantees, as well as new forms of exploitation, class composition, and organization. It is essential to find the connections between structural adjustment, immigration, the creation of a world market for labor power, flexible forms of exploitation, and new forms of worker mobilization. Unlike much of the recent social history of the working class, which has focused on the class as a strictly local political subject, and unlike world system theory which sees capital as a worldwide force but the working class as virtually wholly dependent, I see working-class people as active agents in the current struggles over structural adjustment (expropriation) as well as over conditions within the global assembly line (exploitation), and so as actors on the worldwide stage.

In doing so, I treat the categories "working class" or "workers" and "capital" heuristically, as adding insight to a wide range of types of organization of work and forms of social conflict. In this, I follow Marx who structured Chapter 14 of Volume 1 of *Capital* around an analysis of the variety of forms of work and degrees of capitalist supervision involved in handicrafts, guild organization, manufacturing, putting-out and the factory system. In "The Results of the Immediate Process of Production,"[56] Marx distinguished between the formal and real subsumption of labor to capital. The formal subsumption exists where forms of work remain under worker or other, often traditional, organization, but where production is of commodities to be sold by a merchant, who increasingly is able to dictate the amounts of production needed, while lacking control over the process itself.[57] The real subsumption involves direct organization of the process of work itself by the capitalist. Well into the factory era, much organization of work was based upon workers' control of tools and knowledge. The overall trend over recent centuries is toward real subsumption to capital. In reality of course, there are significant gray areas between formal and real subsumption. The form of the wage may vary as much as the forms of work, reflecting customary usages (as Peter Linebaugh has recently demonstrated in, The London Hanged),[58] continuing worker attachment to the soil, access to the materials of production, benefits which are socialized by state policies, room and board and other means of guaranteeing the reproduction of labor power (to use Marx's term). The reproduction of labor power refers to both the biological reproduction of living workers and to all of the work and material means which maintain workers in condition to continue working. Following Marx, and utilizing the insights of feminist writers who have underlined the importance of reproductive work in capitalist economies, I define workers as all those whose work, regardless of the form of wage, produces and reproduces commodities (including labor power itself), or contributes to producing commodities to be sold for profit by an individual or collective capitalist. Ghanaian cocoa farmers, Senegalese peanut growers, Veneto self-employed financial service providers, Filipina women performing domestic work within or outside their own families, 18th and 19th century African slaves, European and Asian indentured servants, prostitutes forcibly brought to Italy from Albania, craft workers who alternate self-employment with working for money wages in small factories and employing others in their own workshops, and Moroccan street sellers can all be considered workers. While it is important to keep in mind the differences in work culture, community life and specificities of social interaction that are distinct for each of these types of worker, it is their conflictual relation with capital that defines them as part of the working class. Indeed, the form of conflict and of the wage differs considerably for each type of worker listed above. But we must recall that the wage is, as Marx argued, a relation of struggle and not a sum of money. Wages can include scrip paid to West Virginia miners, cash payments, paychecks, annual salaries, hourly wages, or piece rates. Social security payments to the state on the employee's behalf forms a large part of labor costs in Italy. In other situations the wage has taken the form of a plot of land,[59] a share of a crop, access to common land, gleaning and gathering rights, payment for a service to a freelance worker (increasingly common in northern Italy today), housing and food, a share of the waste of the product's raw material in an industrial or manufacturing process, health care benefits, access to the commodities purchased by a husband's wage, student stipends, or the G.I. Bill. The wage is the share of social production which goes to the worker and is therefore the basis of working class power and organization. Treating these classical categories with some degree of flexibility and openness will aid us in understanding the transformations wrought by the making of today's planetary labor market.

The experience of immigrants in northeastern Italy is part of the larger problems of contemporary worldwide social and economic change. The specific character of the local Veneto society seems to overdetermine much of the immigrant experience in the Veneto. Yet the Veneto itself seems to be in transformation as a result of the forces of the world market and of the migrant networks that carry out migrations. In explaining these contradictions, I have emphasized the social construction, or rather the making of the world labor market and the planetary working class through social conflicts. The "making" because as E.P. Thompson argued, the working class is present at its own birth. Like the working class, the world market is made by those who enter it and those who attempt to plan it. It is a contingent, not a structural relation. This very contingency makes it the result of various actions and conflicts in various specific places. Yet as David Harvey has argued, the many transformations of modes of production in the last twenty years have sped up the velocity of capitalist value production and profit realization, resulting in what he calls a "time-space compression."[60] The control over space has reached new levels, as the world market appears to dominate every specific locale. This is at least as true of the labor market as of any other. Yet precisely this renewed dominance of time over space, and of the capitalist control of space over the class compositions in specific places, leads to a renewed importance in the world market of the advantages of particular locales based on their local character, as each region competes for markets, workers, investments, and the division of profits.

This new situation requires us to move from the global to the local and back again. On the one hand we find that structural adjustment and flexible production result in the linking of diverse capitalist modes of production and class compositions in the world market; on the other we find that these are brought into contact only by the web of migrant communities' autonomous networks. This autonomy is what actually results in the labor power created by structural adjustment programs becoming concrete labor, that is in that meeting of labor and capital in particular places that is necessary for value production. Further, this autonomy by migrants has accomplished this making of the world labor market by expanding the geographic dimension of class conflicts. In doing so, they integrate the local class conflicts found in their migratory destination with the larger international class conflicts. They make the working class truly universal in a way only predicted by Marx and Engels. In this way, the labor power created by expropriation has not ceased to be a working class in the process of migration. Rather, the project of migration remains a strategy for addressing the problems encountered in the place of origin. Deterministic or monocausal explanations are not appropriate here. The possible and actual responses to structural adjustment, to the migration process, to work and community experience in the Veneto, are quite varied. Migrant self-organization makes the telling of this possible; it is a contingent intervening factor. The capitalist responses, themselves contingent, have consisted of various attempts to subordinate these migratory projects to the needs of value production either by state, international agency, by organized criminal control of the migratory process itself, or by various methods of social control in migrant destinations.

It remains to be seen whether these strategies can be successful. Already Nestor Rodriguez has questioned U.S. ability to even maintain a border, let alone control it, in the face of growing migrant autonomy from Mexico and Latin America. Italy has recently headed an international military mission to Albania in large part to defend its own border from migrants and to restore control in Albania itself of value production for Italian firms. Increasingly, state agencies are preoccupied with how to contend with the new capacities and resources of migrant networks. We are looking at, here, the contemporary making of the world labor market and working class through the geographical expansion of class conflict by both labor and capital. The immigrant workers in the Veneto are a part of that making. Their very presence is a sign of the Veneto's further integration into the world market. But their own self-activity has in part created that market and is now transforming the Veneto and the world.

Notes

1. Stephen Castles and Mark Miller, *The Age of Migration* (New York: Guilford, 1993).
2. See, for instance, the excellent study of Vietnamese meat packers in Garden City, Kansas in Louise Lamphere et al., eds., *Newcomers in the Workplace*.
3. See the classic, Oscar Handlin, *The Uprooted* (New York: Grosset & Dunlap, 1951).
4. I.S. Lowry, *Migration and Metropolitan Growth: Two Analytical Models* (San Francisco: Chandler, 1966), p. 156. Einstein had viewed gravity as the universal force which bound all coordinate systems. See Gary Zukav, *The Dancing Wu Li Masters* (New York: Bantam, 1979), p. 175. Lowry goes so far as to treat the migrant as an individual, sovereign consumer, ibid., p. 158. See also J.R. Hicks, *The Theory of Wages* (London: MacMillan Press, 1932), p. 76; George Borjas, "Economic Theory and International Migration," *International Migration Review* 23:3 (Fall 1989). See W.R. Bohning, "Elements of a Theory of International Economic Migration to Industrial Nation States," in Kritz, Keely and Tomasi, eds., *Global Trends in Migration: Theory and Research on*

International Population Movements (Staten Island, NY: Center for Migration Studies, 1981) for both a discussion of this assumption and for an attempt to rework the theory to include cost of transport, flow of information and the role of the state in introducing non-economic criteria into the migration decision, which may be based upon economic, social or psychological needs. Ironically, in an earlier theorizing of migration, that of Ravenstein, distance and transport cost plays a crucial role. Bohning, pp. 31-36; E.G. Ravenstein, "The Laws of Migration," *Journal of the Royal Statistical Society* 48:2 (June 1885); and Ravenstein, "The Laws of Migration," *Journal of the Royal Statistical Society* 52 (June 1889). See also Everett Lee, "A Theory of Migration," in J.A. Jackson, *Migration* (Cambridge, England: Cambridge University Press 1969); Siegried Berninghaus and Hans Gunther Seigert-Vogt, *International Migration under Incomplete Information: A Micro-Economic Approach* (New York: Springer-Verlag, 1991) for an attempt to develop an equilibrium model of international migration with an assumption of incomplete information. see also Bohning, op. cit. on this point. Bohning calls for recognizing the usefulness of equilibrium and push-pull factors as heuristic tools if the attempt at generalizing theory is dropped. This is in effect, the early post-modernism of the approach notwithstanding, the type of defense which leaves a model secure while surrending all of its components. However, as we shall see below, the strength of equilibrium theory is precisely its unempirical assumptions; on development and migration see W.A. Lewis, "Economic Development with Unlimited Supplies of Labour," in *Manchester School of Economic and Social Studies* (Manchester: University of Manchester Press, 1954); see also J. Fei, and G. Ramis, "A Theory of Economic Development," *American Economic Review* (Sept. 1961); M. Todaro and J. Harris, "Migration, Unemployment and Development: A Two-Sector Analysis," *American Economic Review* (March 1970).

5. Such as George Borjas, see for instance.
6. Alejandro Portes and John Walton, *Labor, Class and the International System* (New York: 1981), pp. 27-28.
7. Aristide Zolberg, "International Migrations in Political Perspective," in M. Kritz, C. Keely and S. Tomasi, eds., *Global Trends in Migration* (Staten Island, NY: Center for Migration Studies, 1981), p. 5.
8. Robin Cohen, *The New Helots: Migrants in the International Division of Labor* (Brookfield, Vermont: Gower, 1987), p. 36. This argument has found support in several empirical studies of migrant social networks: see Alejandro Portes and Julia Sensenbrenner, "Embeddedness and Im-migration: Notes on the Social Determinants of Economic Action," *Journal of American Sociology* no. 987 (May 1993); Douglas Massey, Rafael Alarcon, Jorge Durand and Humberto Gonzales, *Return to Aztlan: The Social Process of International Migration from Western Mexico* (Berkeley Los Angeles and London: University of California Press, 1987); Grace Anderson, *Networks of Contact: The Portugese and*

28   WORKERS OF THE WORLD

Toronto (Waterloo, Ontario: Wilfred Laurier University Press, 1974).

9. See the synthesis of this literature in Alejandro Portes and Robert Bach, *Latin Journey* (Berkeley, California: University of California Press, 1985), pp. 11-20.

10. Stephen Castles and G. Kosack, *Immigrant Workers and Class Structure in Western Europe* (London: Oxford University Press, 1973); Manuel Castells, "Immigrant Workers and Class Struggles in Advanced Capitalism: The Western European Experience," in R. Cohen, P. Gutkind and P. Brazier, eds., *Peasants and Proletarians* (New York: Monthly Review Press, 1979); Michael Piore, *Birds of Passage: Migrant Labor and Industrial Societies* (New York: Cambridge University Press, 1980).

11. Castles and Kosack, *Immigrant Workers*, p. 98.

12. Piore, *Birds*, pp. 16-17.

13. Castells, "Immigrant Workers," pp. 356-63.

14. Saskia Sassen, *The Mobility of Labor and Capital* (New York: Cambridge University Press, 1988); Lucy Cheng and Edna Bonacich, *Labor Migration under Capitalism* (Berkeley, California: University of California Press 1984), pp. 3, 9-10; see also Edna Bonacich, "A Theory of Middleman Minorities," *American Sociological Review* 37:5 (1973).

15. Portes and Bach *Latin Journey*, p. 26; Portes and Walton, *Labor*, p. 29. These works were heavily influenced by the world systems analysis found in Immanual Wallerstein, *The Modern World System*, Vol. 1 (Orlando, Florida: Academic Press 1974).

16. Charles Tilly, "Transplanted Networks," in V. Yans-McLaughlin, ed., *Immigration Reconsidered* (New York: Oxford University Press, 1990); see also J.S. MacDonald and Leatrice D. MacDonald, "Chain Migration, Ethnic Neighborhood Formation and Social Networks," *The Millbank Memorial Fund Quaterly* 42 1964; and Douglass Massey, Rafael Alarcon, Jorge Durand and Humberto Gonzales, *Return to Aztlan: The Social Process of International Migration from Western Mexico* (Berkeley, Los Angeles and London: University of California Press 1987); Grace Anderson, *Networks of Contact: The Portugese and Toronto* (Waterloo, Ontario: Wilfred Laurier University Press 1974).

17. Tilly, "Transplanted Networks," p. 83.

18. Portes and Bach, *Latin Journey*, p. 10.

19. Jack Weatherford, "Tribal Technology in Weatherford," *Savages and Civilization* (New York: Ballantine, 1994), pp. 242-56; Benjamin R. Barber, though posing an ultimate contradiction between tribal and tribalish identities on the one hand, and global cultural and technological homogeneity on the other, also sees the latter contributing to the growth of the former in the short-term in his *Jihad vs. McWorld:How Globalism and Tribalism are Re-Shaping the World* (New York: Ballantine Books, 1996).

20. Karl Marx, *Capital*, part VIII.

21. Midnight Notes, "Introduction to the New Enclosures," *The New Enclosures*.

22. Caffentzis, "The Fundamental Implications of the Debt Crisis for Social Reproduction in Africa," in Mariarosa Dalla Costa and Giovanna F. Dalla Costa, eds., *Paying the Price: Women and International Economic Strategy*, (Atlantic Highlands, NJ: Zed), p. 18.
23. On the clearance of the Scottish Highlands, see George C. Caffentzis, "On the Scottish Origins of Civilization," in Silvia Federici, ed., *Enduring Western Civilization: The Construction of the Concept of Western Civilization and its Others* (Westport, Connecticut: Praeger, 1995).
24. There is of course an enourmous literature on these struggles. See, among others, Walter Rodney, *How Europe Underdeveloped Africa* (London: Bogle-L'Ouverture Publications, 1972); C.L.R. James, *The Black Jacobins* (New York: Vintage, 1970); W.E.B. DuBois, *Black Reconstruction in America*, op.cit.; Ronald Wright, *Time Among the Maya* (London: Abacus, 1997); *Popul Vuh*, translated by Dennis Tedlock (New York: Simon and Schuster, 1985); George W. Lovell, *Conquest and Survival in Colonial Guatemala* (Montreal: McGill-Queen's University Press, 1985); George W. Lovell, "Rethinking Conquest: The Colonial Experience," in *Latin America Journal of Historical Geography*, Vol. 12; Frances Jennings, *The Invasion of America* (New York: Norton, 1988); Dee Brown, *Bury My Heart at Wounded Knee* (New York, 1969); Lydia Potts, *Labour Market*; Jack Weatherford, *Native Roots* (New York: Fawcett 1992); Rigoberta Menchu, *I, Rigoberta Menchu* (New York: Verso, 1984); Eric Williams, *From Columbus to Castro: A History of the Caribbean* (New York: Random House, 1984).
25. See among a vast literature, George Rawick, *From Sundown to Sunup: The Making of the Black Community* (Westport, Connecticut: Greenwood, 1972); Cedric Robinson, *Black Marxism* (Atlantic Highlands, NJ: Zed, 1980); Eugene Genovese, *Roll Jordan Roll: The World the Slaves Made* (New York: Random House, 1976); Dee Brown, *Bury My Heart at Wounded Knee: An Indian History of the American West* (New York: H. Holt & Co., 1971); Frances Jennings, *The Invasion of America: Indians, Colonialism and the Cant of Conquest* (New York: Norton, 1976); Walter Rodney, *A History of the Upper Guinea Coast* (New York: Monthly Review, 1980); C.L.R. James, *Jacobins*; Karl Marx, *Capital*, Vol. 1, part VIII; *Popul Vuh: The Sacred Book of the Quiché Maya* (Norman: University of Oklahoma Press, 1950); Rigoberta Menchu, *I, Rigoberta*; Eric Williams, *Capitalism and Slavery: The Caribbean* (London: Trafalgar Square-David & Charles, 1964); Eric Williams, *Columbus to Castro*.
26. Polanyi's most succinct synthesis of his view of the development of the autonomy of economic relations as a contingent historical act is in his still classic *The Great Transformation* (Boston: Beacon Press, 1944).
27. Ibid., p. 249.
28. Midnight Notes is the product of a group of writers and activists, including the author, who have worked together since 1979. It is

published in Jamaica Plain, Massachusetts.

29. For a description of the widespread analysis of the anti-IMF struggle see Midnight Notes, *Midnight Oil*, op. cit. pp. 17-20; Midnight Notes, *Auroras of the Zapatistas* (Brooklyn: Autonomedia, forthcoming) esp. "Chronology of Anti-Structural Adjustment Struggles." For an analysis of the Zapatista revolt in its relation to primitive accumulation and the IMF/World Bank programs, see also Silvia Federici, "Chiapas and the New World Order," in Midnight Notes, *Auroras*; see also Kevin Danaher and Muhammad Yunus, eds., *50 Years is Enough: The Case against the World Bank and the International Monetary Fund* (Boston: South End Press, 1994).

30. Chapter Three discusses these links between immigrants in the Veneto and the effects of structural adjustment in some depth. For now, on Morocco's anti-IMF revolts see Kevin Dwyer, Arab Voices: *The Human Rights Debate in the Middle East* (New York and London: Routledge, 1994); on the relationship between oil prices, oil workers and the Gulf War on the one hand, and structural adjustment, see Midnight Notes, *Midnight Oil*; on Ghana, see Ross Hammond and Lisa McGowan, "Ghana: The World Bank's Sham Showcase"; and on the Philippines, "The International NGO Forum, World Bank and IMF Lending in the Philippines," both in Danaher and Yunus, *50 Years*; on the relationship between debt, structural adjustment, and the migration of women from the Philippines, see Bridget Anderson, *Britain's Secret Slaves: An Investigation into the Plight of Overseas Domestic Workers in the United Kingdom with contributions from Anti-Slavery International and Kalayaan and the Migrant Domestic Workers* (London: Anti-Slavery International, 1993); and Milton Meltzer, *Slavery: A World History* (updated edition) (New York: DaCapo Press, 1993), pp. 297-98.

31. Arnaldo Bagnasco, *Tre Italie* (Bologna: Il Mulino, 1977).

32. For an excellent overview see Paul Ginsborg, *A History of Contemporary Italy: Society and Politics 1943–1988* (London: Penguin, 1985), pp. 201-02.

33. See Michael Piore and Charles Sabel, *The Second Industrial Divide: Prospects for Prosperity* (New York: Basic Books, 1984); Robert Putnam, *Making Democracy Work: Civic Traditions in Modern Italy* (Princeton: Princeton University Press, 1993).

34. See Michael Piore and Charles Sabel, *The Second Industrial Divide: Prospects for Prosperity* (New York: Basic Books, 1984); Michel Aglietta, *A Theory of Capitalist Regulation* (London: New Left Books 1979); David Harvey, *The Condition of Postmodernity* (Cambridge, MA: Blackwell, 1989). See also Alvin Toffler, *Powershift* (New York: Bantam, 1991).

35. See Katherine Ward, ed., *Women Workers and Global Restructuring* (Ithaca: ILR Press 1992); Michael Blim and A. Rothstein, eds., *Anthropology and the Global Factory* (New York: Cambridge University Press, 1992); June Nash and M.P. Fernandez-Kelly, *Women, Men and the*

International Division of Labor (Albany: SUNY Press, 1983); Barbara Ehrenreich and A. Fuentes, *The Global Assembly Line* (New York: Monthly Review, 1983). See also Midnight Notes, *Midnight Oil*; and Mariarosa Dalla Costa and Giovanna Franca Dalla Costa, eds., *Paying the Price.*

36. *Il Gazzettino* (Padua), 25 June 1995, p. 1.
37. Notably, Sebastiano Brusco, "The Emilian Model: Productive Decentralization and Social Integration," *Cambridge Journal of Economics* no. 6 (1982); Marco Bellandi, "The Role of Small Firms in the Development of Italian Manufacturing Districts," in Goodman and Bamford, eds., *Small Firms and Industrial Districts in Italy* (New York: Routledge, 1989); Jonathan Zeitlin, "The Third Italy: Inter-firm Cooperation and Technological Innovation," paper given at Brighton Technology Conference March 12, 1987, Brighton, England; Sebastiano Brusco and Ezio Righi, "Local Government, Industrial Policy and Social Consensus: The case of Modena (Italy)," *Economy and Society* 18:4 (Nov. 1989); Richard M. Locke, "The Resurgence of the Local Union: Industrial Restructuring and Industrial Relations in Italy," *Politics and Society* 18:3 (Sept. 1990); Mark Lazerson, "Organizational Growth of Small Firms: An Outcome of Markets and Hierarchies," *American Sociological Review* 53 (June 1988); Charles Sabel, "Flexible Specialization and the Re-Emergence of Regional Economics," in Hirst and Zeitlin, eds., *Reversing Industrial Decline* (UK: Oxford University Press Berg, 1988); Richard Locke, *Remaking the Italian Economy* (Ithaca: Cornell University Press, 1995).
38. Michael Blim, *Made in Italy:Small-Scale Industrialization and its Consequences* (New York: Praeger, 1990), p. 150; Mark Lazerson, "Organizational Growth of Small Firms," *American Sociological Review* 53 (June 1988); Fergus Murray, "Flexible Specialization in the Third Italy," *Capital and Class* 33 (Winter 1987); Philip Mattera, "Small Is Not Beautiful: Decentralized Production and the Underground Economy in Italy," *Radical America* 14:5 (Sept.-Oct. 1980).
39. Piore and Sabel, *Industrial Divide*, pp. 151-56.
40. Ibid., pp. 205-08, 214-16.
41. For this earlier debate, centered around the theme of dualism in the Italian economy, see Ginsborg, op.cit., is a brillant historical overview of postwar Italy which sees duality in terms of a gap between economic growth and the failure to adopt reforms of the political structure; Adrian Nicola Carello, *The Northern Question: Italy's Participation in the European Community and the Mezzogiorno's Underdevelopment* (Newark, Delaware: University of Delaware Press, 1989) sees the North's geographic and economic proximity as threatening yet wider north-south disparities; Antonio Gramsci, *Selections from the Prison Notebooks* (New York: International Publishers, 1989) is the classic formulation of the failure of the Risorgimento to involve the southern masses via land reform; Ray Hudson and Jim Lewis, eds., *Uneven*

Development in Southern Europe: Studies of Accumulation, Class, Migration and the State (New York: Metheun, 1985); Giovanni Arrighi, ed., *Semiperipheral Development: The Politics of Southern Europe in the Twentieth Century* (Beverly Hills: Sage, 1985) discusses the role of southern Europe as a whole in the global economy's southern periphery and Italy's arrival as an advanced capitalist state with a peripheral south: Luciano Cafagna, *Dualismo e sviluppo nella storia d'Italia* (Milan: Einaudi, 1989) is a straightforward history of the use of tariffs to draw resources from southern agriculture to advance northern industry after unification; Russell King, *The Industrial Geography of Italy* (London: Croom & Helm, 1985); Giorgio Mori, *Il capitalismo industriale in Italia* (Rome: Editori Riuniti, 1977) stresses the lateness of Italy's industrial revolution; Massimo Paci, *Capitalismo e classi sociali in Italia* (Bologna: Il Mulino, 1978) emphasizes that southern underdevelopment is no longer a question of agriculture but of industrial unemployment; Diana Pinto, ed., *Contemporary Italian Sociology: A Reader* (New York: Cambridge University Press, 1981); Frederic Spotts and Theodor Wieser, *Italy: A Difficult Democracy* (New York: Cambridge University Press, 1986); Andrew Schonfield, *Modern Capitalism: The Changing Balance of Public and Private Power* (New York: Oxford University Press, 1965) emphasizes the role of state enterprises in Italian postwar development as well as the lack of a single unified plan on the French model; Allan Rodgers, *Economic Development in Retrospect: The Italian Model and its Significance for Regional Planning in Market-oriented Economies.* (Washington: V.H. Winston, 1979).

42. Brusco, *Emilian Model*; Anna Pollert, "Dismantling Flexibility," *Capital and Class* (Winter 1989).

43. See Zolberg, "International Migrations"; Thomas Hammar, "Dual Citizenship and Political Integration," *International Migration Review* 19:2 (Fall 1985); Thomas Hammar, *Democracy and the Nation-State: Aliens, Denizens and Citizens in a World of International Migration* (Aldershot: Averbury Press, 1990). Hammar, recalling the relation between free and unfree labor in the ancient world, has called for the revival of the ancient status of denizen used by the Greek polis for foreigners. Hammar is not the only thinker who sees parallels between the current world division of labor and the ancient categories: see Robin Cohen, *The New Helots*; Ellen Mieksins Wood, *Peasant, Citizen, Slave* (New York: Verso, 1988); see also Zig Henry-Layton, *The Political Rights of Migrant Workers in Western Europe* (London: Sage, 1990); Castles and Miller, *Age of Migration*; P. Corrigan, "Feudal Relics or Capitalist Monuments? Notes in the Sociology of Unfree Labor," *Sociology* no. 11 (1977); W.E:B: DuBois, *Black Reconstruction in America* (New York: Harcourt Brace, 1937); B.B. Ferencz, *Less Than Slaves: Jewish Forced Labor and the Quest for Compensation* (Cambridge: Harvard University Press, 1979); N. Harris, "The New Untouchables: The International Migration of Labour," *International*

Socialism 2:8 (1980); Ulrich Herbert, *A History of Foreign Labor in Germany, 1880-1980: Seasonal Workers/Forced Laborers/Guest Workers* (Ann Arbor: University of Michigan Press, 1990); B. Hindess and P.Q: Hirst, *Modes of Production and Social Formation* (London: MacMillan, 1977); E.L. Homse, *Foreign Labor in Nazi Germany* (Princeton: Princeton University Press, 1967); Sasha Lewis, *Slave Trade Today: America's Exploitation of Illegal Aliens* (Boston: Beacon Press, 1979); E. Maldonado, Contract Labor and the Origin of the Puerto Rican Communities in the United States, *International Migration Review* no. 13 (1979); Midnight Notes, *Midnight Oil*; Robert Miles, *Capitalism and Unfree Labor: Anomaly or Necessity?* (New York: Tavistock Publishers, 1987); Immanual Wallerstein, *World System*, Vol. 1; Lydia Potts, *Labour Market*; R. Baubock, Migration and Citizenship, *New Community* 18:1 (1991). The most useful recent analysis of forced labor in the contemporary world economy is Rossana Mungiello's study of Brazil, Saudi Arabia, India and China in Rossana Mungiello, Lavoro coatto a fine secolo in quattro grandi aree economiche in *Altreragioni* (Milano) no. 6 (1997).

44. See regarding legal conditions and flexible production, Mattera, op. cit.; Sergio Bruno, "The Industrial Reserve Army, Segmentation and the Italian Labour Market," *Cambridge Journal of Economics* no. 3 (1979); see also Vittorio Capecchi, "The Informal Economy and the Development of Flexible Specialization," in Emilia Romagna, *Industrial Restructuring and the Informal Sector*, for a study of subcontracting and differing conditions of formality in Veneto's most famous firm, see Fi Belussi, "New Technologies in a Traditional Sector: The Benetton Case," BRIE Working Paper, October 1986, unpublished; see also Ian Taplin, "Segmentation and the Organization of Work in the Italian Apparel Industry," *Social Science Quarterly* 70:2 (June 1989).

45. Robert Putnam, *Making Democracy Work: Civic Traditions in Modern Italy* (Princeton: Princeton University Press, 1993); see also studies which support Putnam's thesis, Richard Locke, *Remaking the Italian Economy*; Raffaella Y. Nanetti, *Growth and Territorial Policies: The Italian Model of Social Capitalism* (New York: Pinter, 1988).

46. See Robert Leonardi and Douglas A. Wertman, *Italian Christian Democracy: The Politics of Dominance* (London: MacMillan, 1989); Judith Chubb, *Patronage, Power and Poverty in Southern Italy a Tale of Two Cities* (New York: Cambridge University Press, 1982).

47. See Linda Weiss, *Creating Capitalism: The State and Small Business since 1945* (New York: Basil Blackwell 1988), pp. 106-13.

48. A. Bagnasco and C. Trigilia, eds., *Società e politca nelle aree di piccola imprese: Il caso di Bassano* (Venice: Arsenale Editrice, 1984).

49. On the demise of the Venetian commercial economy see the summary of the debate in Vera Zamagni, *The Economic History of Italy 1860–1997* (London: Leicester University Press, 1992); Wallerstein, *World System*; and the essays in Arrighi, ed., *Semi-Peripheral*.

34   WORKERS OF THE WORLD

. Peter Musgrave, *Land and Economy in Baroque Italy:Valpolicella 1630–1797* (London: Leicester University Press, 1992) argues against the viewpoints expressed in the debate over Venetian decline (see footnote directly preceding this one) that in fact the 17th century was not characterized by any overall decline in the Venetian economy from the point of view of material well being and growth, but rather by a retreat from world commerce to an expansion of the local economy based upon the land empire of Venice—the Terra Firma which today comprises the Veneto and parts of Lombardy. This locally based economy thus became economy well-off until the late 18th century but increasingly culturally inward-looking and parochial.

51. See Fondazione Corrazzin, *La Società Veneta 1991* (Venice: CEDAM, 1992) for a general overview of cultural and economic changes in the Veneto in recent years; see also Paul Ginsborg, ed., *Stato dell'Italia* (Milan: Il Saggiatore, 1994); Fondazione Corrazin, *La Società Veneto 1992* (Venice: CEDAM, 1993).

52. Frobel et.al., *The New International Division of Labour* (Cambridge: Cambridge University Press, 1980); Katherine Ward, ed., *Women Workers and Global Restructuring* (Ithaca: ILR Press, 1992); Michael Blim and A. Rothstein, eds., *Anthropology and the Global Factory* (New York: Cambridge University Press, 1992); June Nash and M.P. Fernandez-Kelly, *Women, Men and the International Division of Labor* (Albany: SUNY Press, 1983); Barbara Ehrenreich and A. Fuentes, *The Global Assembly Line.*

53. See the collection of essays in Kathryn Ward, ed., *Women Workers and Global Restructuring* (Ithaca: ILR Press Cornell University, 1990); see also, Lourdes Beneria and Marta Roldan, *The Crossroads of Class and Gender* (Chicago: University of Chicago Press, 1987).

54. Saskia Sassen, "The New Labor Demand in Global Cities," in M.P. Smith, ed., *Cities in Transformation* (Beverly Hills: Sage, 1984), p. 140.

55. Saskia Sassen, *The Global City* (New York: 1992); see also Manuel Castells, *The Information City* (Berkeley: University of California Press, 1994).

56. Karl Marx, *Capital,* Vol. 1, Appendix: Results of the Immediate Process of Production, pp. 943-1084.

57. For a wealth of detail into this relation, see Fernand Braudel, *The Wheels of Commerce,* Vol. 2 of *Civilization and Capitalism* (New York: Harper & Row, 1979).

58. Peter Linebaugh, *The London Hanged* (New York: Cambridge University Press, 1992).

59. Such as among the forest workers whom Lenin included in his chapter on machine workers in *The Development of Capitalism in Russia* because they produced the source of energy, wood, used to fuel the machines. In that remarkable section Lenin, as usual less doctrinaire than most Leninists, described the employment of serf labor in industry, the efforts of mine-owners to tie workers down to the land, and wrote of the lumber

workers: "Thus the lumber workers constitute *one of the big sections of the rural proletariat, who have tiny plots of land* and are compelled to sell their labour-power on the most disadvantageous terms." V.I. Lenin, *The Development of Capitalism in Russia* (Moscow: Foreign Languages Publishing House, 1956), pp. 513, 541-42, 575-85; the passage quoted on lumber workers appears on page 579.

60. David Harvey, *The Condition of Postmodernity* (Cambridge: Blackwell, 1989).

2

A HISTORICAL TYPOLOGY
OF MIGRATIONS: THE MAKING OF
THE WORLD LABOR MARKET

INTRODUCTION

The contemporary migrations into Italy and elsewhere are best understood in historical context. Through a discussion of previous migration experiences in the creation of a world labor market, we may better understand the continuities between today's and previous migrations as well as the unique characteristics of current movements. In analyzing historical migrations, both forced and voluntary, I argue for a typology of migrations that distinguishes between historical experiences based on the sources of emigration, the role of the state, and the migrants' degree of autonomous organization. Each large-scale migration in the past 500 years has been linked to the rise of new forms of work organization. However, the argument is not deterministic. The relation of migration to new labor markets and types of work has changed with each new migration experience. The need for labor power automatically does not automatically lead to a migration, forced or otherwise, in a functional manner. Rather, two processes mediate between potentially available labor power: expropriation, itself a locus of struggle whose outcome is never predetermined; and the organization of migration, which can be initiated by the state or employers of labor, or by migrant communities. Each moment in the migration process is a site of struggle. The labor market that is created and feeds new forms of exploitation results from this multiplicity of struggles. This typology will enable us to weigh the relative roles of capital and labor in the construction of the world labor market. Concretely, this allows us to discuss the question of agency in a more nuanced way, as the role of, say, the state or of migrant autonomy has varied with each new migration.

Historical changes in this labor market have been linked to the rise of various modes of capitalist production, such as the plantation, the factory, large-scale industry, and mass assembly production. However, markets or structural needs for labor power have not always been equally important in creating migrations in each case. In most of these historical moments, the state played an important role in organizing or facilitating the mass migration of labor power on a world scale. Private or semi-private recruitment or seizure of labor power also played an important role in the creation of both labor power (expropriation) and concrete labor (exploitation). These two social conflicts, over expropriation from the means of production and subsistence, and over exploitation at work, are the twin pillars of what economists describe using the metaphor of a market. Flexible production and small scale export industry today are forms of work which the Veneto region of Italy exemplifies. These will be understood as part of changing production needs that involve particular types of labor power linked to a particular cycle of world migration. Migrants have played different roles in the organization of migrations: they have engaged in highly self-organized processes of mass geographical mobility; they have found themselves the objects of well-organized recruiting systems by states or employers; they have been forcibly transported across borders, continents and oceans. If there is a secular trend, however, it is toward an increasing capacity by migrants collectively for autonomous organization of and use of migration. There is also a counter-trend by states, employers, international agencies and organized crime networks to submerge this autonomy and channel migration into forms that will primarily benefit these diverse capitalist actors.

After a discussion of the historical labor markets for Native
American forced, African slave, European indentured, Asian
indentured, and European free wage labor power, the chapter will
then examine the state-organized migrations from certain Third
World countries to post-World War II Europe, the Persian Gulf,
South Africa, and the United States. These postwar migrations
were the immediate precursor to the current migrations to Italy. A
common misconception is to see migration patterns over the past
10 or 15 years as a continuation of these postwar experiences.
The diversity of countries of origin in today's migrations and the
level of self-organization by migrant social networks is similar to
that which mobilized the Atlantic migrations of European peoples
in the nineteenth and early twentieth centuries. These factors
make the contemporary worldwide migrations quite different from
those which immediately preceded them. There are however,
many important continuities among all of the historical migrations
discussed below. The expropriation of labor power from the
means of production, the forms of recruitment and physical
transportation, and even certain forms of exploitation and forced
labor are remarkably similar over time. Indeed, as forms of unfree
labor make a resurgence at the dawn of a new century, it becomes
crucial to understand the relation between these forms of work,
migration, and the world market.

This chapter argues that the migration trend is toward an
increasing autonomy on the part of the migrant communities and
networks in initiating and sustaining migrations. Migrations are
therefore increasingly *less functional* to production needs, and
their relation to the rise of new forms of work should be
understood as a spatial expansion of class conflicts. Put differently, many areas of emigration, forced or otherwise, remained
outside the world economic system and outside of a money-based
production system. As Immanual Wallerstein and others have
argued, this outsideness of labor in part enabled capital to make
use of "free" labor power—labor power, that is, which had been
reproduced outside the sphere of capitalist social relations and
whose cost to capital was very low.[1] With each cycle of
migrations, however, this outsideness was reduced, gradually
altering the capitalist control of space and its use in dominating

particular places. This reduced capital's ability to use the inside/outside dichotomy. Our own times are characterized instead by an unprecedented control over a space which is seemingly all "inside" the capitalist world market. It was largely due to the self-organization of struggles by slaves, indentured servants, anti-colonial movements and immigrants—the social subjects who had made up the previous sources of labor power—that capital was denied use of such "costless" labor power.

Today, migrants leave areas where they require money to live, but often to accomplish goals that are not strictly economic in nature. The contemporary migrations are arguably the first based primarily on the initiative of migrant communities and on their effort to have access to more money income; this income covers their own money-based reproduction costs in the areas of origin and of arrival. It is, in short, a migration which can be and is used by capitalist forces, but which is not entirely wanted by these same forces inasmuch as they did not initiate it nor do they control it. A world market for labor, new forms of work, and mass migrations of some peoples and the destruction of others are the elements of the history of migration in a capitalist world. It has been a long march from the slave trade and European conquest to the rise of flexible production and globalization, and in examining it we shall find surprising continuities and crucial differences.

SLAVERY AND EUROPEAN INDENTURED SERVITUDE 1492–1888

With European expansion in the early 16th century, the indigenous peoples of the Americas became a new source of labor power for the predominantly extractive industries in the New World. The Spanish Conquistadors' control and exploitation of this source of labor power took two forms: wholesale genocide and forced labor. These twin aspects of early colonialism were seemingly contradictory for a number of reasons. First, the destruction of indigenous communal and community forms of social reproduction as well as of political structures was necessary to "free" the labor power for exploitative use by the colonial power. Indeed, the reproduction of labor power—which requires above all making that labor power available to capital for exploitation—should not be confused with the reproduction of human beings and their communities; the Nazi program in Eastern Europe and in the death camps should make the distinction apparent. Second, much of the subsequent annihilation of whole peoples, even that attributable to disease, stemmed at least equally from murderous levels of overwork. Las Casas was aware of this in his descriptions of how the indigenous Hispaniola population of three million was reduced to 200 in 40 years. The indigenous peoples of Puerto Rico, Jamaica, Cuba, the Bahamas and other areas met similar fates. Overall, Las Casas estimated that between 12 million and 15 million people were slaughtered by overwork, disease and war in four decades.[2] The third reason why extermination and forced labor were only seemingly in contradiction is because both settlement and, more importantly, the creation of a plantation economy required eliminating a pattern based upon dense population in settled communities. Once the previously mined gold and silver was exhausted, the need for surplus value production led to the development of accumulation in the New World. Extermination of the local population and with it its capacity for resistance against this process of accumulation was thus not so much a policy of *lebensraum*, of territorial conquest, so much as an *arbeitsraum* policy, one of territorial control for exploitation of labor.[3]

But this policy of accumulation by production required labor power, and so the state began to play a larger role to more securely guarantee reproduction of the workforce. In 1511 the Spanish crown even banned slavery temporarily to increase the labor force. In 1513 it imposed slavery on any Indians not recognizing the Pope and the Spanish king as their sovereigns.[4] Eventually the state became more concerned about the increasingly real contradiction between extermination and the need to guarantee a labor force—in 1526 it decreed that only the royal governor or the king could declare Indians enslaved, and in 1542 it declared that no Indians could be enslaved. Soon the *encomienda* and *mita* labor forms replaced slavery as methods of exploiting the remaining indigenous communities.

In the meantime, however, the need for labor power in the plantation economy had increasingly given rise to the African slave trade. The Africans, separated from their homes, family networks and communities, initially lacked means of resistance on the same scale as indigenous peoples struggling in their own land and still embedded within their own communal relations. The separation of working people from their cultural and social relations, and the juridical forms by which slavery was instituted, suggest continuities with both ancient slavery and modern immigration. Historically the degree to which political communities recognize obligations toward and respect for rights of their residents has been closely related to the extent to which the diverse categories of residents have origins within that same community or remain embedded within their own social network however external it may be to that of their residence. Ancient Athens recognized a category of foreign residents whose degree of community membership was higher than that of slaves, who were perceived as having been seperated from their own community by war or similar cause. Unlike slaves, denizens were understood to be members of *some* community, and therefore to have some degree of protection and recognition by their host society. Slaves lacked rights throughout the ancient and medieval world since sparing their life and enslaving them—an act of mercy—eliminated their "host" community's obligations to them. Slavery was a form of "social death", as Orlando Patterson puts it.[5] David Brion Davis has demonstrated the historical continuity of slavery in Western history, both in the legal forms and the uses to which slave labor power has been put: "There was more institutional continuity between ancient and modern slavery than has generally been supposed."[6] This continuity includes the continuation of slavery on the edges of medieval Europe, in Spain and the medieval Muslim world, in Byzantium and Kievan Russia. However, it is perhaps with the Venetian slave trade and use of slave labor to grow sugar in the Mediterranean that slavery was first linked to the development of the world labor market. This trade, according to Davis, was crucial to both the Genoan and Venetian economies. By 1300, the Venetians purchased slaves on the Dalmatian coast and sold them to Syria and Egypt, and had established joint stock companies that used African slaves to grow sugar cane on Cypress. At least 10,000 slaves were sold in Venice itself between 1414 and 1423, for example. "Long before Columbus," comments Davis, the Venetian and Genoan merchants invented the distinctive institutions that later characterized the West Indies and African trade.[7]

Thus the African trade began well before 1550, the date at which it is usually considered to have begun in earnest. Certainly by that time, the Spanish and Portugese states had been involved for some time in the enslavement and transportation of Africans to New World colonies. Potts writes, "During the first half of the 16th century the crown repeatedly granted licenses allowing several hundreds or even several thousands of African slaves to be brought to America," though Indians were for a time still cheaper and Africans showed a capacity to resist and rebel as early as 1526 in Puerto Rico, 1531 in Panama and 1537 in Mexico. This labor power was primarily for use in the plantation economies, where, over centuries, it would produce the major commodities of capitalist world trade—sugar, coffee, tobacco, and later cotton. Potts writes, "By 1600 Portugal had transformed Brazil into one huge sugar plantation." By 1850, when slave importations to Brazil were finally banned, from 3 to 9 million Africans arrived there as slaves.[8]

All told, between ten and twenty million persons were transported from Africa as slaves.[9] Potts estimates that between 40 and 200 million Africans were affected, including those killed in slave raids, those who died in transport, and those transported. Between 1580 and 1680 over 1.5 million were carried away from Angola and the Congo, though some estimates place the number from Angola alone at 4 million.[10] Peter Stalker claims that 15 million were transported in all, of which 13 percent died en route.[11] The abstract labor power intended for work on the plantations of the Americas and West Indies was created by what Basil Davidson describes as three distinct phases of recruitment: (1) piracy; (2) warlike ventures in agreement with local chieftans; (3) partnerships in which African polities carried out expeditions specifically for sale to Europeans.[12] The prime age group sought was 15–25 years old, and the price fell by a third for ages 5–15 or

25–35. The price of men was 25 percent higher. Most of the enslaved Africans left from 20 or so principal slave markets along the 3,000 mile coastline stretching from Senegal to Angola.[13] There were "tight packer" and "loose packer" schools of thought, with the former usually having the upper hand on the slave ships. That the British government, also attempting to limit the losses of labor power, passed a 1788 law limiting slave ships to carrying no more than 454 persons, gives some idea of conditions.

Two important changes transformed the slave system dramatically, one, the decline of European indentured servitude, begun in earnest in the plantation colonies of North America in the 17th century; the other, the suppression of the slave trade, which grew out of a widespread trans-Atlantic opposition that blossomed in the late 18th century and was finally realized in the nineteenth. In keeping with the continuum of forms of unfree labor, in the first half of the 17th century there was no clear line distinguishing indenture from slavery, nor was it yet codified that African workers were condemned to hereditary slavery for life while European workers were only indentured for a fixed number of years. It was only after Bacon's rebellion, as Edmund Morgan has shown, that fear of an alliance between white and black workers and of the growth of a steadily increasing free population of poor whites led the ruling class of Virginia to decrease the influx of white indentures and to codify into law the subsequently permanent and hereditary character of slavery on a racial basis.[14] Before this, the majority of Europeans arriving in the North American colonies were indentured. Conservatively, Richard Morris estimates that one half of the total white immigration to the 13 American colonies arrived as bound labor.[15] This European bound labor took three main forms: redemptions, also called "free willers"; convicts whose death sentences had been commuted in transportation to the colonies with indentures, and those who were kidnapped. The redemptioners were bound by a contract to work between two and seven years in exchange for having transit paid either by an employer in America or a shipping agent who upon arrival sold the contract to a local employer. Until the end of the seventeenth century the tobacco colonies of Virginia, Maryland and the Carolinas were the main recipients of bound European labor; afterwards the main flow was toward Pennsylvania, as the southern colonies switched to African slave labor. Most of these workers came from the British Isles, though a substantial number came from various German states. German workers often arrived without written terms of contract, and upon arrival sold themselves into an indenture to pay for the cost of passage. The latter in the seventeenth century averaged about £5 to £6 sterling, or £10-£12 where clothing and paying the middleman's fee were included. By the late eighteenth century this rose to about £20.[16]

As with the slave trade, private interests initiated the trade in indentured servants, and the state later stepped in to regulate it. Transportation was underwritten by planters, or "by merchants specializing in the sale of servants' indentures."[17] The latter were the historical ancestors of both the recruiting agents who encouraged nineteenth-century European immigrants and who transported Chinese and Indian indentured servants, and also of those who today, more carefully hidden from the light of day, carry immigrants from Asia and Africa to the coast of Italy and across the borders of European states. Morris describes how these agents operated in the seventeenth century:

> Recruiting agents employed by merchants and called "Crimps" in England and "Newlanders" on the Continent, hired drummers to go through the various inland towns in England or along the Rhineland areas devastated by years of warfare publicly crying the voyage to America. They also arranged for the distribution of extravagant literature at annual fairs with the help of a piper to draw the crowd. The bulk of the contemporary descriptive material relating to the colonies may be viewed as optimistic sales propaganda to be placed in the hands of the credulous prospects.[18]

Fraud was common, as agents misled workers as to conditions they would find on arrival. Ships were overcrowed in comparison with anything short of the slave ships: The "White Guineamen," as the ships were called, carried 300 passengers on ships of 200 tons, not dramatically more humane than the slave ships themselves, and 50 percent mortality rates were not unknown. These conditions led the state to step in. For instance, Pennsylvania, whose economy depended on the health of this labor force, set minimum deck space per passenger. Families were divided and young girls often found themselves sold into an indenture ostensibly for domestic work, but which in reality involved sexual activity. Despite these conditions, with the redemptioner system, for the first time, there's an element of autonomy on the part of migrant workers themselves—one recognized in their appellation as "free willers." Despite the decidedly unfree form of labor services upon arrival, and the fact that the demand for labor was decisive in creating the market for indentures, the voyage itself, even if at times based on misleading information, was their own activity and founded on their own goals and life projects. This autonomy was later manifested upon arrival in efforts to escape the indenture, in staking out an independent position or in wage demands after the indenture ended, in extralegal activity, and in open, organized revolt.

Lacking this voluntary element were the convicts who were also transported as indentured workers. At the end of the 17th century, given the perpetual labor shortage in the colonies and the lack of enough skilled workers to spare in England after the Plague and London Fire of 1666, British authorities encouraged the slave trade and the British courts began to commute death sentences in favor of terms of service in the colonies for convicts.[19] By 1718 the British Parliament authorized transportation for seven years for lesser crimes and fourteen for death penalty offenses. Estimates suggest that at least 50,000 convicts were shipped to America, over 10,000 between 1717 and 1775 from London's Old Bailey alone. One source claims that in Maryland, which received 20,000 convicts, over half after 1750, convicts constituted fully half of all 18th-century indentured servants. Morris tells us that the transportation of convicts was extremely profitable, though it made the merchants who engaged in the activity widely unpopular in the colonies. In Ireland, Sheriffs were paid £5 for each convict transported, while the law around 1740 provided for paying contractors £3 per convict for transportation. But these same contractors were able to sell the convicts for between £9 10s. for unskilled workers and £25 for artisans.[20] The colonies attempted to suppress the trade however, finding that large numbers of the runaway servants were convicts, and often fearing violence on their part and participation in revolts. Maryland unsuccessfully sought to ban the importation of convicts in 1676, while Pennsylvania after 1722 imposed a duty of £5 per convict imported as well as a steeply priced bond. But merchants thereafter brought convicts to nearby colonies and smuggled them into Pennsylvania by land. The British government yielded consistently to the interests of contractors and merchants, and even overruled colonial government limitations and duties involving importation of convicts. Thus state and private interests combined to form this part of the labor market.

Beyond this concert of private and state interests, however, was private coercion of migration. The word kidnapping was invented in the 1670s to describe certain practices attributed to recruiting agents of indentured servants. Press gang-like practices seem to have been common enough as were a simple blow to the head or a seemingly friendly plying with whiskey of the intended migrant. While the British state officially opposed kidnapping as a private practice, it encouraged the forcible transportation of workers and even minors to an astounding degree. In 1670 Parliament rejected the death penalty for those found guilty of kidnapping workers, though it did set up a registry office to record the names of all departing indentured servants. In 1619 the City of London chose one hundred children for transportation bound as apprentices to Virginia (where, as Morgan tells us the mortality rate was astronomical). Many of the children were opposed to going there. Faced with the city's lack of authority to transport persons against their will, the Privy Council ordered that any children found "obstinat to resist" were to be imprisoned or punished until they agreed to be transported to Virginia. The state's main concern regarding kidnapping was with the potentially autonomous use of it on the part of workers. Many a runaway servant escaping an indenture, wife deserter, or escaped convict managed to sign up for transportation to escape unfavorable conditions. Others enticed agents by agreeing to an indenture and then charged them with kidnapping. The state's fear was that the private side of the trade might be used to favor workers' own projects instead of the labor market that nascent capitalist interests and the British government wanted to develop. As we shall see in chapter four, this theme of control over migrant autonomy, and the effort of state, capital and workers to control the use of space and migration has become only more important with time.

Gradually, the system was suppressed: the demand for labor declined in the tobacco plantation states, German states denied permission for their subjects to work as indentured servants, in 1785 England prohibited the use of British ships for transport of indentures, and there was some regulation in post-revolutionary America. By about the 1830s the indentured labor system had died a lingering death. Its decline had coincided, however, first in late 17th century Virginia, with a growth in the African slave trade. And that preference for African slave labor, coincided with fears of the potential political threat of white indentured labor, especially when allied with African labor. The creation of abstract labor power and the creation of concrete labor—the availability of labor to capital and then the actual meeting of capital and labor for production—were both seemingly accomplished by the indenture through the merchant contractors and the indenture contract. However, these social forms allowed for dangerous moments of potential autonomy which limited the functionality of indentured servants to the world labor market, and the American Revolution showed that this autonomy could produce results of an international, revolutionary nature.[21]

Thus, even under conditions where workers were already linked to bonded labor by contract, migration was not always functional to capitalist needs. There remained room for the autonomy, however minimal, of working-class subjects. The limits to this autonomy derived from both the unfree nature of the work upon arrival and the separation of the worker from the community at home in which he or she had previously been "embedded." Abstract labor power is created by the separation of workers from various types of communities, but many indentured workers clearly preferred to leave the limited possibilities for autonomy in England and Europe and to take their chances in America and the Caribbean. For African slaves, there was no choice involved, and therefore one cannot speak of autonomy in the actual leaving of their homeland. However, historians of the black community have taught us not to underestimate the autonomous organizational ability of Africans even under these conditions. Autonomy took three forms: communication and even revolt on the slave ship itself; the formation of the African American and African Caribbean communities on the plantations; and open and organized revolt, including the creation of maroon communities, revolutionary movements, and an abolitionism led by free black communities.

As Linebaugh points out, despite the well known use of linguistic difference to make organization difficult, the slave ship plan illustrated in figure 1 can also be seen as a communication device and as a carrier of ideas.[22] The fact that there were revolts on the ships indicates that some communication was possible, perhaps using pidgins or even fully developed creoles from coastal areas long used to the slave trade. Individual revolt, in the form of suicide and infanticide on board, horrific as these were under the circumstances, indicate that the human subjects did not remain strictly functional as abstract labor power, but remained cultural beings with their own priorities. Even under the most terrible conditions imaginable, they were agents and not just objects of history. But it was upon arrival that the full flowering of autonomy could take place. As George Rawick tells us, from sundown to sunup organization could take place, and a black community could be formed.[23] Such communities were able to organize strikes, create the makings of the black church, lay the basis for maroon communities, and organize open revolts such as those of Nat Turner, Denmark Vesey, and many others throughout the Caribbean and Brazil. In Santo Domingo this organizational capacity led to the Haitian Revolution, which brought into being the modern nation of Haiti and which C.L.R. James credited with ending the Mercantile Age.[24] In the U.S., through what DuBois called a general strike, and through enlistment in the Union Army, the black community played a key role in the destruction of U.S. slavery.[25]

Once in place, and despite the forced mobility of many enslaved individuals, the African diaspora was able to turn its own forced migration against capital. As the Haitian Revolution showed, the mass concentration of enslaved workers in one locale could be dangerous, as slave-owning interests were often quite aware. Less obvious, though in the long run perhaps more decisive, was the geographic dispersion and mobility of the Atlantic pan-African community, which made possible the circulation of news, ideas, revolts, and organized campaigns around the whole Atlantic basin. Denmark Vesey was a seaman for part of his working life, as was Olaudah Equiano. Several southern states in the United States tried to restrict the movement of black seamen in their port cities, or exclude them altogether in the nineteenth century, even accusing them, perhaps not without foundation, of circulating David Walker's *Appeal* and other abolitionist literature. It was while working outside his owner's plantation, on the Baltimore docks, that Frederick Douglass first learned of freedom in the North from Irish seamen. Indeed, one unintentional side effect of the massive transportation of enslaved labor power across the ocean was the creation of a vast diaspora of free black workers also capable of linking various points of struggle and of challenging authority even on shipboard itself: both were threats to the capitalist monopoly over control of space used in controlling labor in specific locales on a worldwide scale. Linebaugh tells us:

Shipboard communication was decisive to the formulation of the eighteenth-century pan-Africanism—it was an American mariner who taught Olaudah Equiano to read *Paradise Lost* on shipboard during the 1760's. . . . Sailors were among the first to study slavery and abolition. . . . Such pan-Atlantic interchanges, and the communities built upon them on ship and in port, are often regarded as "marginal". The contrary may be true: they were the essence of the proletariat of merchant capital, and they were the basis of the circulation of rebellion in widely differing geographical and cultural settings. The New York insurrection of St. Patrick's Day 1741 was the work of Africans, Irishmen, a Londoner, North American Indians and Spaniards.[26]

Equiano, himself a former plantation slave and then a mariner, was the leader of the London black community's movement against the slave trade. As shoemaker Thomas Hardy's roommate, Equaino linked Hardy's London Corresponding Society to the Sheffield abolitionist and Corresponding Society activists, a moment considered by E.P.Thompson the first working class organization in England.[27] The first organizational victory of this diaspora was the abolition of the slave trade, first in the British colonies, then to the United States. The leaders of the movement for abolition were the trans-Atlantic free black community. In March 1807, both the United States and Great Britain banned the African slave trade, though the U.S. act, according to DuBois, "came very near to being a dead letter."[28] The abolition of the slave trade, and later of slavery, which took varied forms in diverse areas and states, were complex affairs with multiple causes. Economic interest, morality, concern for the condition of white workers, and slave resistance have all been put forward as causes of abolition. Eric Williams famously posed the declining profitability of England's sugar plantations against French and Spanish competition—particularly Saint Domingue and Cuba - as decisive.[29] But his view that Jamaica was declining is doubtful, with sugar production peaking at 100,000 tons of exports in 1805, a 67 percent increase over the 1791 level.[30] It is likely that a long-range sense of where British interests eventually lay was a significant motive behind parliamentary efforts to abolish the trade. But value and values are often linked in both thought and activity and the distinction between economics and philosophical concerns may be an artificial one. DuBois linked the two, though he, as does Hugh Thomas gave prominence to the moral aspect of abolition.[31] C.L.R. James and recently Robin Blackburn laid emphasis on the self-activity of slaves as the decisive factor, mediated through the political struggles consequent upon the French Revolution.[32] Indeed, these factors could be intermixed in such a way as to give greater weight to slave and free black community resistance through its impact on economic profitability and moral concerns. Thomas comments on the April 1792 resolution that the slave trade would gradually be abolished, the first bill ever to pass British parliament recognizing abolition as a legislative goal (even if the eventuality might be indefinitely postponed):

The votes on these· motions, if inadequate for Wilberforce, Fox, Burke and Pitt, constituted a remarkable change from what had happened the previous year. Yet the main event in recent politics was the revolution in Saint-Domingue, an occurrence which was already causing a real shortage of sugar, and not just in France. Perhaps the impact of that terrible event was to make the members realize that an end had to come one day to the system of slave plantations. Of course Saint-Domingue was referred to in the debate.[33]

Legal abolition, regardless of the motives that brought it, did not end the trade. U.S.-based ships traded slaves to Cuba on a large scale until the 1840s. Private traders brought slaves in over land from Florida, still under Spanish control. The U.S. federal government turned a blind eye, refusing to impose the death penalty for engaging in the trade, in part because northern merchant interests and southern planters found common cause. "I cannot believe," said one Rhode Island member of Congress, "that a man ought to be hung for only stealing a Negro."[34] The illegal importation of labor power is a recurring theme in the history of modern migrations, both forced and voluntary; the slave trade lay at one extreme end of a long continuum of forms of unfree work. With the British abolition of slavery in 1838, and the American Civil War, brought on in large part through the self-activity of slaves, slavery itself was on the agenda for abolition. After Brazilian abolition in 1888, the institution as a legal structure was dead. But by the time of the British abolition, the need for labor power had already altered the world market for labor through a new institution, or rather the revival of an old one with new subjects as workers—indentured work, in the form of the coolie system.

ASIAN INDENTURED LABOR

The use of indentured laborers from Asia in significant numbers dates from the 1830s and the abolition of slavery in the British colonies. Asian labor was used on a worldwide basis for plantation production of trade commodities such as tea, coffee, and sugar, as well as in construction and railroad work including in the United States. Lydia Potts estimates that between 12 million and 37 million workers were coolies between 1834 and 1916, when the practice was abolished.[35] China and India were the largest suppliers of workers in the coolie system. State intervention was crucial to the coolie system at least in the initial phases. First and foremost, the system *presupposed colonial control* by the British state of the regions of indentured workers' origin. Further, not unlike the prelude to today's migrations to Italy and other countries, *the coolie system presupposed a series of enclosures*—that is a series of transformations separating potential workers from their access to the means of production and subsistence, or at least reducing or devalorizing these in such a way that they would no longer be sufficient for self-reproduction by persons, families, villages. The contemporary enclosures and their role in fostering current migrations to Italy are dealt with extensively in the following chapter. As for those of the nineteenth century in Asia, Potts writes,

The British colonial rulers had begun to prepare the ground for a massive liberation of workers back in the 17th century, yet in the 19th century many of these workers still had to be forced by means of direct compulsion to offer their labour as "coolies" on the world market for labor power.[36]

Here is one of the limitations of the argument that capital always benefits from the incomplete integration of workers into the money wage system since it keeps reproduction costs and therefore wages low.[37] The ability to reproduce themselves and their families or social contexts allows workers to refuse to make themselves available as labor power on the world market. State or colonial power serve precisely to overcome this refusal to enter the market. Under such circumstances, primitive accumulation or enclosures become necessary, where possible, to eliminate such independent access to the means of life. Thus in the 18th and 19th century, India was bankrupted and disrupted by wholesale British looting, war, the break-up of village communities by force, the dismantling of social structures, neglect of public works such as irrigation, and by the elimination of traditional handicraft industries by both cheap British imports and armed force.[38] Linebaugh recounts the means by which labor power in Bengal was captured, so as to be available for exploitation on the world market:

The Battle of Plassey (1757) was the turning point in the transition from merchant trading to the direct command over Bengali labour. In 1761 Pondicherry surrendered. In 1763 Mir Kasim was defeated. In 1764 Hector Munro suppressed a strike among sepoys by setting four 6-pounders on them. Twenty-four were killed. In 1765 the East India Company obtained the diwan, enabling it to gather directly the Bengal revenues, thus replacing the Mogul Empire as the supreme sovereignty. In the same year Robert Clive instituted the "cruelties that hitherto stand perhaps unparalleled in the records of nations". The husbandmen in this "paradise of India" paid half their crop in rents. The castes of weavers and winders of silk suffered a fall in wages and incarceration in the "factories" of Dacca and Murshidabad, as well as imprisonment, flogging and bond slavery, against which sometimes the only form of resistance was self-mutilation of thumbs and fingers.

The Company's policies caused the first imperialist famine in 1769; a third of the population perished. In the same year the amounts of raw silk imported into England from Bengal reached about 700,000 lbs., almost double the average imports of any previous year. . . . After 1766 Bengal replaced Italy and Turkey as the main source of raw silk.[39]

In about one hundred years from 1834 on, over 30 million Indians went overseas as indentured laborers. They worked in Mauritius and in Australia, in Ceylon and Jamaica, in Kenya and Guyana. From 1838 to 1918, 430,000 Indians were sent to seven British Caribbean colonies; from 1879 to 1916, 61,000 went to Fiji; five million went to Malaya over 100 years up to 1930; from 1913 to 1929, 4,580,730 Indians, of whom 311,400 were women and another 201,944 were children arrived in Burma. From 1834 to 1867 366,000 Indians went to Mauritius; as late as 1924 there were still 255,000 Indians on Mauritius, of whom 10 percent were indentured. In In addition, 700–750,000 Indians worked the tea plantations of Assam from 1870–1900.

The other major source for indentured labor power was China. From 1847–1874, half a million workers left China to work abroad under indentures. From 1888–1931, 305,000 Chinese were brought to the plantations of Eastern Sumatra; nearly three million went to work in Malaya in a nine-year period from 1928–1937. By 1855 there were 36,557 Chinese workers on the Pacific Coast of the United States, of whom 20,000 went to work in the California gold mines.[40] Mining and railroad work were the main tasks reserved for Chinese indentured labor. From 1866–1869, 10,000 worked for the Central Pacific Railroad, boring the Sierra tunnel and laying track across Nevada and Utah.[41] Though these later workers had been recruited directly by the railroad's agents in China,[42] they were exceptions among the Chinese who went to the United States. In an extraordinary work of 1909, Dr. Mary Roberts Coolidge painstakingly presented the evidence that no coolies were ever transported to the West Coast of the United States.[43] The word coolie came from a Chinese verb usually used to denote unskilled, as opposed to skilled labor, and meaning to rent out strength or muscle—that is, almost literally to sell labor power. Whatever the later meaning based upon the experience of indenture under the coolie system, its meaning in Chinese society implied some kind of wage labor relation.[44] Whereas the indentured labor trade was based in the Portugese port of Macao and the Chinese city of Whampoa, the migration to California went through Hong Kong. The prepaid tickets and readily available jobs characteristic of Chinese workers in California were phenomena of social network activity, not, as opponents of Chinese migration so often thought, evidence of unfree status.[45] Even among the labor recruiters for the coolie system, links of family, friendship, neighborhood, or common secret-society membership between the latter and the overseas indentured workers were common, indicating an aspect of self-organization within an overall structure of unfree labor contracts.[46] Indeed, these social networks which had resulted in the far-flung Chinatowns of North America, were also utilized much later for raising material aid and activists for Dr. Sun Yat-Sen's Nationalist Revolution of 1911.[47] One group of Chinese workers that did arrive under largely unfree conditions, however, were prostitutes. The reproduction of the male labor power embodied in the Chinese community in North America required female company and labor, like the male migrant communities which today produce, process, and transport oil in the Middle East today. Thus, seven of ten women in San Francisco's Chinatown were prostitutes in 1870, and by 1907 prostitutes were 22.5 percent of the Chinatown population in that city.[48] As alarmingly as the press in Veneto cities decries Nigerian or Chinese or Albanian slave trading and prostitution today, the American press often published alarmist tales with titles like "Confessions of a Slave Dealer," "Her Back Was Burnt With Iron," and "Stories of Girls Shows Working of a Chinese Ring,"[49] Like today's "traffic in women," as one recent study has termed the international migratory sex trade,[50] the nineteenth-century female Chinese migration to the United States was a complex combination of forced migration, voluntary mobility and the efforts of profiteers to subordinate the geographical mobility and aspirations of women to their own projects.[51]

Alexander Saxton reports that with regard to other fields of work in post-Civil War California, the extent to which Chinese could move into trades was determined by whether the product was sold on a local or national market. Chinese workers all but took over cigar-making, a national market product, while they were (literally) driven from construction work by white workers in an 1867 attack in San Francisco.[52] Eventually, the anti-Chinese movement among white workers in California succeeded in expelling most Chinese from the state—in 1868 40,000 Chinese miners were driven out of California, and Chinese workers were massacred in Los Angeles three years later. In 1882, Congress passed the Chinese Exclusion Act, which remained in effect until the Second World War. In 1885, in part to eliminate the padrone system of Italian migrant communities, the U.S. government banned all forms of contract labor. Several hundred thousand Japanese, and some Micronesians and Melanesians also worked as indentured workers during the nineteenth and early twentieth centuries.

Although state power was instrumental in organizing the availability of indentured Asian workers, the methods by which they arrived at their destinations were private and involved some measure of self-organization. The voyage itself resembled little so much as the slave's Middle Passage. Indeed, in Calcutta to Jamaica or the China to Peru runs, it could be a much longer voyage—four months instead of four to six weeks for the Africa to Caribbean voyage. A ship of four hundred people (see figure 2) could expect seven or eight dead after the first few days.[53] In 1856–1857 the death rate was 17 percent. Sailing ships were used for indentured workers well past the start of widespread use of steamships. One important difference between this voyage and that of the slaves was that the *indentured workers paid their own fare*: about $75 each, according to Potts. Carrying 1.4 Asian workers per register ton compared with 2-3 African slaves per register ton, one ship carried 500 Chinese to the United States and took in $37,000 in fares. Another difference was that the return rate was very high, whereas the slaves obviously did not return.[54]

While 2.8 million Chinese were sent to Malaya, 2.4 million returned; rates of return over any given period were similar for most indentured Asian worker destinations. These return rates could indicate that the same workers returned at the end of the contract (usually of 5 years' duration) or it could indicate in at least some cases that children returned in place of parents. The latter seems unlikely to have been a majority however. The return rate, nearly always around three-fourths or more, as well as the fact that a certain minority remained in spite of British interest in shipping them back, indicate a certain autonomy on the part of Chinese workers within the migration process. (see Table 1 below for the return and settlement numbers for India).

Two important aspects of the transportation of indentured workers were the role of private merchants from the same countries as the workers, and the fact that such workers often arrived in groups. The Chinese in California arrived in groups, and were received by the Six Companies, a group of Chinese merchants who acted as employment brokers between the workers in their home countries and overseas employers. Saxton describes the system: "At the bottom of this organization structure were the laborers. Above them was an assortment of gang foremen, agents and interpreters. At the top were the Chinese merchants of San Francisco who, as directors of the Six Companies, represented or were associated with even wealthier merchants and businessmen in China."[55]

These merchants were able to arrange contracts with railroads, industries, California farmers, Southern planters, New England shoe manufacturers, and even a New Jersey laundry operator. Such a capacity for supplying labor power, for turning the abstract indentured labor power into concrete labor by arranging the meeting of labor and capital, involved both hierarchy and the Chinese community's remarkable for self-organization. The system provided not only employment for Chinese workers but also protection to some extent from hostile outside forces, an organized social life to make the sojourn bearable, and even women for the mostly male workers. Its basis, however, was a vertical system within the Chinese community and an arrangement with the state:

Table 1. Estimated Total Migration to and from India 1834–1937

	Emigrants	Returned	Net
1834-35	62,000	52,000	10,000
1836-40	188,000	142,000	46,000
1841-45	240,000	167,000	73,000
1846-50	247,000	189,000	58,000
1851-55	357,000	249,000	108,000
1856-60	618,000	431,000	187,000
1861-65	793,000	594,000	199,000
1866-70	976,000	778,000	197,000
1871-75	1,235,000	958,000	277,000
1876-80	1,505,000	1,233,000	272,000
1881-85	1,545,000	1,208,000	337,000
1886-90	1,461,000	1,204,000	257,000
1891-95	2,326,000	1,536,000	790,000
1896-00	1,962,000	1,268,000	694,000
1901-05	1,428,000	957,000	471,000
1906-10	1,864,000	1,482,000	382,000
1911-15	2,483,000	1,868,000	615,000
1916-20	2,087,000	1,867,000	220,000
1921-25	2,762,000	2,216,000	546,000
1926-30	3,298,000	2,857,000	441,000
1931-35	1,940,000	2,093,000	-162,000
1936-37	815,000	755,000	59,000
Total	30,192,000	24,104,000	6,088,000

Source: Lydia Potts, *The World Labour Market* 1990 p.71

Essential to such a system of recruitment and employment was strict internal discipline. Contracts had to be honored and advances of passage money repaid. Yet any legal machinery for the enforcement of contracts was lacking. The Chinese organization therefore enforced its own regulations, adjudicated disputes, punished transgressors. While all this was, in terms of American law, not only extra-legal but illegal, the American courts and police authorities actually served as bulwarks for the entire structure. For many years the Six Companies kept a special Chinatown contingent of San Francisco policemen on their payroll. They also retained competent lawyers who were frequently in court seeking the apprehension of runaway laborers or sing-song girls on complaints of petty theft which would later be withdrawn. As final capstone to this structure, the Six Companies maintained an unwritten protocol with shipping lines to the effect that no Chinese would be booked passage *out* of California unless he carried a clearance from the Six Companies. It was a tight system.[56]

Railroads procured Chinese workers from agents such as the Dutchman Cornelius Koopmanschap who brought 30,000 Chinese workers into California. Chinese workers engaged in at least some strikes in the U.S. and elsewhere. These may have been a factor in the ultimate ending of the practice, though it would seem that the decline of colonialism itself dried up the supply of ready labor power in a more decisive fashion. Thus, the system of Asian indentured labor depended upon state sponsorship, and on private transportation whose cost was paid ultimately by the workers themselves. The return rate was very high among workers, but we may interpret this rate in more than one way. Labor power was used in a functional way by capital—workers were transported, worked out their contract, and were returned home. But the same numbers indicate that Chinese, Indian, and other Asian workers also used the coolie system in their own way, to realize some of their own aspirations. They took advantage of it to the extent possible, returning home after having accumulated a bit of money to use at home where its value was greater, or staying on if possible and constructing one of the new Chinatowns or other Asian communities in the New World. In this way, they are the first precursors of today's planetary migrants. As permanent settlers in countries ranging from Malaysia to the United States, from South Africa to Trinidad, and from Kenya to Guyana, ex-coolie workers came to constitute important ethnic minorities in societies where they had arrived as indentured workers.

THE GREAT EUROPEAN MIGRATIONS

From 1820 to 1914, 25.5 million people emigrated from Europe to the United States. There are important similarities between these historical migrations and the migrations which today criss-cross our planet. First, the migrations of the 19th and early 20th century were not a state-centered process. While states mildly encouraged migration at times, and did nothing to hinder them, these policies hardly constitute initiative on the part of governments. Zolberg, who has done so much to point out the importance of the state in migration processes, is right to point out that even the absence of passport requirements is a state policy decision. In such a case, however, it is a decision by the state to not put itself at the center of a migration process, if indeed it had any choice in the matter. Second, though there was some recruiting of workers—early on in Ireland to work on the Erie Canal, for example, or in Eastern Europe toward the end of the nineteenth century—the flow either was self-organized from the start or became so as a result of the so-called chain migration phenomenon—that is, the organization of migration by migrant transnational social networks. Third, the migrations were a response to structural transformations in the economic life of the sending countries. In particular, dramatic changes in agricultural life and rural social relations, along with the effects of these (such as the Irish Famine of 1847–49), led to the use of migration as a response to resolve the problems faced in the country of origin. For many millions this meant permanent settlement in North or South America. For others, it meant a long period of work in the Western Hemisphere, sending money home to help the family survive or bringing back resources with which to begin other projects. For yet others, savings were used to bring over relatives. The process of autonomous use of migration, begun in the most unfree conditions of indenture, first by seventeenth- and eighteenth-century Europeans, then by the free African diaspora and by Asian indentured workers, flowered in the nineteenth and early twentieth centuries, as millions challenged in a more complete way the previous capitalist monopoly over geographic mobility to resolve problems of class relations.

With only some exaggeration, Maldwyn Allen Jones has described the nineteenth-century European immigration as one of maximum autonomy on the part of the migrants and their communities:

The mass immigration of the nineteenth century originated as a self-directed, unassisted movement. . . . Here lies a key to the patterns both of distribution and of adjustment. That immigrants moved entirely as individuals or in family groups, that they received virtually no aid or direction, and that they were subject to control neither by European nor by American agencies or governments would largely determine their destination in the New World and the nature of their reaction to it.[57]

Jones leaves out here the role of labor recruiters, who were at times important in various countries, and the more important roles of those who transported and those who organized job searches for the immigrants upon their arrival. Shipping companies in particular were active, though mainly to publicize their ever cheaper fares. Railroad companies, anxious to encourage settlement along their lines in the American West, likewise encouraged migrants, as did, at times, employers building canals and roads.[58] Nevertheless, the basic argument, that the migrant chains were fundamentally self-organized on the basis of their own needs remains accurate. With few exceptions, historians of the European migrations of the mid-19th to early 20th century have downplayed the role of recruiters. At most, they directed, not initiated, the migratory flow, and in the case of every national group, only in the early stages, before the autonomous networks of family and neighborhood were able to substitute themselves for labor recruiters.[59]

Many, perhaps most, of the immigrants throughout the nineteenth and early twentieth century were encouraged and helped to arrive by others, friends and relatives, who sent money, bought tickets, and often found jobs for newcomers before their departure from the country of origin. On the whole, the family and social network organization of the departure and arrangements upon arrival are the main defining feature of the great European migrations. This social network activity was itself a response to changing agricultural conditions, brought on by the influx of cheap American grain on the world market and the enclosure of common lands or the outright expropriation of smallholders in various countries. The mechanisms of these expropriations were many: the unification of Italy (the first measure of the new Kingdom was abolition of common lands in the South); Russian anti-Jewish pogroms; the Irish Famine resulting from British colonialism and rising land prices due to the growth of linen profits; and the elimination of many customary peasant land uses in the German countryside, including the abolition of gathering rights to wood in the forest which first propelled the young Karl Marx into political activity and economic studies.[60] Yet the increasing integration of industrial and handicraft production into the world market could also lead to structural changes in the life chances of migrants. Artisans likewise utilized networks of family, neighborhood or religion to migrate, even before the mass migrations of the mid-19th century and beyond.

In Ulster, for instance, the growth of the world linen industry led to higher prices for land rents and the buying of land; these, combined with a farming crisis, led to emigration in the early nineteenth century. The passenger trade from Derry to Philadelphia grew out of the existing commercial links, as flax seed ships returned from Derry to Philadelphia with passengers. Local shipping firms like J&J Cooke controlled much of the emigrant trade.[61] Such firms, writes one historian, "Relied considerably on passenger bookings made by Irish people who wished to bring out their friends and relatives. The importance of pre-paid bookings in Irish emigration had always been considerable and the practice was most prevalent in Ulster."[62] The emigrants themselves were generally not the poorest of the regions of emigration, nor predominantly from the poorest areas, but were rather those who, while not affluent, were able to pay part of the voyage's expense. This was true even during the Famine, though local church-sponsored emigration and the use of the cheaper passage by sail later enabled poorer families to join the emigration, especially with the help of those already in the United States. After the Famine, women were predominant in the Irish emigration. Mageean shows that in 1850 in some quarters of Philadelphia four-fifths of the men performed unskilled labor for a railroad, while in other neighborhoods the majority were skilled workers. That the majority of the arriving families had their passages pre-paid, and that in the mid-19th century Philadelphia was a textile center made emigration and finding work more possible in jobs for which immigrants from a linen center were qualified.

The movements of people to the United States reached mass proportions from the middle of the century on, when agricultural populations were uprooted in one country after another by changes in land tenure, enclosures, and land clearances. Regarding the Irish famine-era emigration, Kerby Miller writes,

> For thirty years prior to the Famine, Irish landlords had striven against popular opposition to rationalize their estates by consolidating farms and evicting insolvent or "superfluous" tenants; the potato blight now provided unique opportunities and added incentives to carry out their designs. By mid-1846, thousands of tenants were in arrears; middling and small farmers could stave off hunger by consuming grain and livestock formerly sent to market, but then they had no money to pay their rent. . . . In general, landlords refused to give abatements, responding instead with distraining orders and eviction notices.[63]

The Irish situation was tied up with particular issues of colonial domination as well, but the seeming specificity of the Irish Famine, an unparalleled catastrophe, hides *the commonality of the process of land clearance throughout Europe.* Oscar Handlin's discussion of the process of enclosure, which provided the title for his classic work, *The Uprooted*, remains the most moving and insightful overview of these sweeping changes as a whole. Despite the fact that migration studies have in recent years deemphasized studies of assimilation, one of Handlin's other themes, the book's description of the vast changes in world history wrought by the expropriations of this period in Europe remains unsurpassed:

> By the beginning of the nineteenth century the effects were noticeable in almost every part of Europe. As landlords, eager to consolidate their holdings, combined the old strips into contiguous plots, the peasant suffered. . . .
>
> Only the power of government could effect the transition, for the dissolution of vested rights, centuries old, called for the sanctions of law. From England to Russia, in the century or so after 1750, a series of enactments destroyed the old agricultural order. The forms were varied, there were statutes by parliaments, decrees from the Crown. The terms varied— enclosure, reform, liberation. But the effect did not vary. . . .
>
> The communal holdings were to dissapear; every plot would be individual property, could be fenced around and dealt with by each as he liked.
>
> Whether or not strict justice was done the peasant depended upon local circumstances and the conscience of the executing officials; it was not always possible to supply precise legal proof for property traditionally held. But in every case, the change undermined the whole peasant position. They were

indeed now owners of their own farms; but they were less able than ever to maintain their self-sufficiency. The cost of the proceedings, in some places the requirement of fencing, left them in debt; they would have to find cash to pay. When the wastes disappeared there disappeared also the free wood for fire or building; there would have to be cash now to buy. If there were no longer common meadows, where would the cows graze? . . .

The change, which wakened all, desolated those whose situation was already marginal. The cottiers, the crop-sharers, the tenants on short-term leases of any kind could be edged out at any time. They had left only the slimmest hopes of remaining where they were. . . .

So Europe watched them go—in less than a century and a half, well over thirty-five million of them from every part of the continent. In this common flow were gathered up people of the most diverse qualities, people whose rulers had for centuries been enemies, people who had not even known of each others' existence. Now they would share each other's future.[64]

Kerby Miller stresses that at times of economic downturn in the United States, already arrived immigrants would write to their relatives in Ireland to convince them not to emigrate, sometimes with effect, but in the 1840s and 1850s to no avail at all. He concludes:

Although remittances and favorable reports from North America, coupled with the ease of transatlantic travel, made possible and encouraged departures, the fact that most emigrants' letters written in the post-Famine decades contained not flattering but cautionary or negative information about New World conditions indicated the primacy of Irish over American stimulants to emigration.[65]

This was undoubtedly so, but we must add that it was precisely the remittances, low transportation fees, and presence of even dissuading relatives and friends in the New World that made the migration feasible and possible. These conditions were similarly reproduced, with specifically local variations, in each of the subsequent migrations from Europe.

Italian migration took off within a decade of the establishment of the Italian state. Enclosures of common lands in the South, the increasing conversion to cash crops and the consolidation of large estates,[66] trade war with France and high tariffs that wrecked southern textiles, as well as wheat, fig and olive exports, combined to devastate southern farmers and agricultural workers.[67] Similarly to the Irish pre-Famine Ulster migration, the earliest migrants, likewise affected by the specific impacts of economic changes, were relatively well-off groups of workers and artisans. At first the migrants were northerners, and the first destinations were Argentina, where in fact land was to some extent available, and Brazil, which was abandoned after a yellow-fever epidemic killed nine thousand Italians. The United States became the destination of choice. By the 1880s, following the privatization of land in the South and the elimination of its previously subsidized industry, southerners became the vast majority of emigrants. By the end of the nineteenth century more than 5.3 million Italians had emigrated. Padrones, who often served as labor recruiters, would often lend passage money to the prospective emigrant at high interest rates, and navigation companies would send recruiters around the countryside. But the extent of self-organization of emigration must not be underestimated. Both the Italian state and the local landowners were uneasy with the massive exodus, if not downright opposed. When authorities delayed passports to prospective emigrants in Lombardy, the latter set fire to a number of dairy farms, shouting, "to America, to America!"[68] Conditions on board ships were crowded, and in 1902 Congress enacted the Passenger Act requiring that chairs and tables be provided for every passenger in every class, though a study a few years later showed 90 percent of all passenger ships carrying emigrants to be in violation of the Act.[69] Many immigrants were instructed to lie to immigration officials upon arrival and deny that they had had their ticket prepaid and a job offer already awaiting them since these were grounds for deportation, in violation of the U.S. 1885 law outlawing contract labor (originally meant to exclude Chinese). The questions were asked to put limits on the padrone system. Soon the padrone system fell into disuse as employers began to use their already employed migrant workers to find other available laborers.

Donna Gabaccia has convincingly argued that this Italian labor power was an international proletariat "as one part of a segmented international market for labor." "Internationally," she writes, "the largest group of Italian migrants provided muscle power for the creation of capitalist infrastructure. Tunnels, railroads, streets, canals, skyscrapers, municipal buildings and elevated subway tracks were built by this labor. Northern Italians tended to go to European or South American destinations, southerners to north Africa, America or Australia."[70] But the main segmentation, according to Gabaccia, was occupational, and it involved self-organization and perpetuation of migration:

> Wheat growing Sicilian peasants became cane harvesters in Louisiana while their shoemaker paesani plied their trade in Tunis or New York; northern Italian villages even developed occupational specializations, training each new generation for the work and trades needed abroad. Scholars have long argued that foreign workers entered segmented labor markets at their destinations; in fact, they moved through an international market thoroughly segmented from top to bottom by region, ethnicity, occupation, and gender.
>
> The creation of an international market for unskilled gang labor was also in part the creation of Italian skilled workers and rural entrepreneurs eager to expand their own horizens and influence.[71]

Women made up one-quarter to one-third of the emigrants. But often the more male-dominated Italian role in this international labor market depended upon subsistence agricultural production by women who remained in the area of origin. Indeed, for millions of families this combination of peasant-migrant worker prevented the wholesale proletarianization of the local population. It was a strategy to confront the transformations at the international level, which had in turn transformed local rural conditions. "Migration guaranteed that Italy's peasant economy was as dynamic as the capitalist world it confronted," writes Gabaccia.[72] The social networks of family and village organized the mass migrations; their objective was to limit the family's integration into the labor market and avoid complete dependence upon that market. This objective was accomplished through a strategy of selectively participating in the market—part of the family worked for wages while another part remained attached to and working on the land.

Word of mouth, as Suzanne W. Model has put it, was the primary means of finding a job for most European immigrants, and as we shall see in chapters 4 and 8, this is true also of the immigrants in Italy today. Migrants established what Model calls the family economy. It was this family economy that enabled the migration to take place and allowed for settlement in the new country, or for return based on the accumulation of wealth earned as immigrants and on the "enormous amounts of money they sent to their hometowns."[73] This family economy and its extension to village and neighborhood networks was the means by which the job market was organized not only for the immigrants, but by them. Their arrival accomplished, abstract labor power was potentially available to employers; but to create concrete labor, that is to bring about the meeting of employers and workers, required contacts. At first, as we have seen, labor recruiters and agencies mostly carried this out, and it is from such activity that the padrone system in the Italian migrant community was born. Eventually this work fell instead to previously arrived migrant workers themselves, leading to three results: a largely autonomous organization of the labor market by migrant communities; an ethnic segmentation of various industries, companies and departments of workplaces based on such recruitment practices; and the relative re-embeddedness of the worker in a network of family and village or neighborhood social relations that tended to minimize the former's exposure to strictly market forces. The exploitation of the labor force under capital is facilitated by the expropriation of workers from the social relations that aid them and enable them to survive. Expropriation from the means of production and subsistence makes more difficult the realization of life projects that are not strictly economic in nature. This expropriation remained partial in the case of many European immigrants.

There were many advantages to worker-organized recruitment, both for the worker and employers. For one thing it eliminated the need for outside agencies and the related expense for both contacts and interpreting. Model explains:

Once a given nationality had established an industrial beachhead, the need for formal intermediaries in the hiring process evaporated. Each worker was actually and potentially in touch with a reservoir of untapped labor in his homeland, fact that did not take long for employers to appreciate. Thus foremen, supervisors, and other gatekeeping figures turned increasingly to their existing labor force in the search for additional labor.

Reliance on worker intermediaries was a cheap way of procuring labor: it was also more efficient than recruiting outsiders. When existing employees sponsored new workers, the ties between the two simplified on-the-job training and socialization. Even though skill demands were low, some orientation remained necessary and was facilitated by a shared linguistic background between sponsor and protégé. Employers likely also noticed that when newcomers entered the workplace via personal sponsorship, they felt an obligation not to let the sponsor down, an obligation that motivated them to greater diligence than they might otherwise display.[74]

We might add that it would also, in the long run, make worker organization at the workplace and in the neighborhood easier, though a diversity of nationalities at any given workplace could militate against this tendency. Indeed, these enormous migrations were finally shut off by the First World War and U.S. fears of spreading international radicalism after the Russian Revolution. These fears were not unfounded, since migrants from Italy, Russia and elsewhere had engaged in labor militancy, formed or joined anarchist and socialist organizations, played a key role in several IWW supported strikes, and unionized several industries such as New York's garment trade. As the autonomy of social networks, which had created a mass migration and an international proletariat, gradually transformed itself into a self-organized working class doors that had once been wide open to migrants began to shut. Once again, state action was more oriented toward preventing the autonomous use of migration than toward encouraging or discouraging migration per se. Indeed, the 1920s saw the European migration flow to the United States replaced in part by a large influx from the Caribbean, which, among other things, led to the huge mass movement of black workers behind Marcus Garvey and to the Pan-African Congresses. Limiting autonomous immigration became a state obsession in the twentieth century. By World War II passports, which before the First World War had been almost unknown, became a universal feature of nation-states policies towards entry and exit.

The mass European migrations are the most similar to the migrations of our own day of any historical precedents. First, these migrations were primarily self-organized, rather than state-centered; through geographically disperse family networks, they linked the waged work experience at an international level with agriculture; they constituted a response to structural changes in

the local economy brought on in turn by worldwide transformations; and finally they were primarily a search for access to
wages in order to realize the immigrants' own autonomous
projects. Through each of these activities, European immigrants a
century ago had much in common with the exodus which today
brings Nigerians, Moroccans, Filipinas, Senegalese and Yugoslavs to the Veneto, as we shall see in subsequent chapters. Yet
there are also important differences. For one thing, though the
states in question did little to organize the migrations of the
nineteenth and early twentieth century, they did little to hinder
them. The same cannot be said of today's migration, as chapters 4
and 6 will illustrate. For another, though recruitment may have
been only a trigger launching the early migrations, there was a
huge demand for labor power in an industrializing United States,
a demand which grew for decades. There were times therefore
when employment agents provided needed services. Today the
migrants may be creating the demand, and therefore the labor
market itself, where it otherwise would not have existed. Two
other differences which represent significant novelties in
migration history are the use of transportation and communications technology to maintain an even closer link to home
base than the European migrants were able to do using steamships
and telegrams and letters, and the geographical origins of the
migrants themselves. With the post-World War II migrations, the
peoples of the former colonies of the Third World re-entered the
history of migration as its principal actors. This time, however,
they did not enter as slaves and indentured servants, at least not
the vast majority, but rather as migrants seeking access to wages,
using methods similar to those of 19th-and early 20th-century
European migrants. By now, these migrations are fully self-
organized, as chapter 4 will show. But the initial migrations from
ex-colonies after the Second World War took a form which was
perhaps the extreme opposite of that of the European exoduses.
They were almost completely organized by state-to-state
agreements and on behalf of specific needs for labor power during
the postwar boom.

THE POST WAR MIGRATIONS TO EUROPE, THE GULF STATES, AND SOUTH AFRICA, AND THE BRACERO PROGRAM IN THE UNITED STATES: THE STATE-CENTERED MODEL OF MIGRATION

The organization of the major post-World War II labor migrations was virtually colonial in form, inasmuch as it involved state-to-state contracts between former colonies and former colonial powers whereby the former provided the latter with labor power on demand. Indeed, there had already been, before and after the war, a large migration of workers in the African colonies under conditions of forced labor or of waged work necessitated by taxes and other polices created to impose waged work in the mineral extraction industries and settler economies of the continent. After independence, particularly in West Africa, borders were open enough that a certain regular movement of workers took place. By the 1950s, for example, an estimated 300,000 people moved annually between the Gold Coast (Ghana) and the French colonies, 60,000 into the cocoa regions of Nigeria for seasonal work, and 40-55,000 between Senegal and Gambia and other regional areas. After colonialism, it was estimated that at least 300,000 West Africans moved across national borders annually, mostly for agricultural work.[75] These population movements are very relevant to the growth of the current migrations to Italy. The general migration trend in this region was until recently north to south, towards the peanut regions of Senegal, the cocoa areas of Ghana and the Ivory Coast and later the oil producing regions of southern and eastern Nigeria. At times of economic crisis, both Ghana in 1965 and Nigeria in 1983 have expelled each others' nationals, the latter during a decline in oil prices—an expulsion involving 1.5 million workers.

But the population movements towards the more industrialized world after the Second World War took place under conditions that at first all but reproduced the previously colonial conditions. The German Gastarbeiter (guest worker) program, the U.S. Bracero program, the movement from the ex-colonies to France, Britain and other European countries, the labor migration to work in the extractive industries of apartheid-era South Africa, and the vast flows of workers to the Persian Gulf states during oil booms were all organized on the basis of formal agreements between states to provide workers. By 1975, more than one quarter of the work force of Jordan, Oman and Yemen were working in the Gulf, largely as a result of state-to-state recruitment.[76] In South Africa "prohibited immigrants"—that is, immigrant workers from countries like Malawi and Mozambique—were not allowed to settle in South Africa, but could enter the country only under the terms of an inter-governmental treaty or approved program of labor recruitment.[77] The South African example, of course, also included the project of creating artificial "homelands" within the country's boundaries so as to create a "foreign workforce". In the United States, the 1942 Bracero agreement, was originally intended as a wartime emergency program but it was extended until 1964 under pressure from the California agricultural lobby. The system involved periodic expulsions of workers from the United States. And in the Middle East, entry and exit were thoroughly restricted, though labor recruitment was handled, at least among Arab workers, as much by private recruiters as by states. But workers to this day in countries like Saudi Arabia and Kuwait are unable to change jobs or quit before the end of their contract. The postwar migrations were above all governed by the principle that the state could both restrict entry and expel workers on a regular basis.

This form of labor migration organization placed the burden for reproduction of the labor force on the country of origin, as Burawoy[78] argues, and specifically on the agricultural subsistence work of women who remain in the rural areas of origin. There is a great deal of truth to this argument, which sees such an arrangement as completely functional to capital. But the maintenence of access to land or other means of subsistence always means that survival is possible even when access to wages is limited, at least for some. Nevertheless, this organization of reproduction of labor power can be functional to capital if the state is able to maintain control of when and how many migrants enter the country of migrant destination. The history of postwar migrations has been a history of state-to-state agreements on supplying workers, the closing of border to prevent entry, and expulsions of those who do not fit into state migration policies. But it has also been the story of long-term settlement of ethnic minorities based on these migrations, state policies notwithstanding (especially in Europe, but also in the United States on the part of undocumented workers), and therefore of the autonomous self-activity of the migrant communities themselves, who at least in Europe and the United States have used family reunion legislation, often won by years of struggle, to create full-scale communities and permanent residence.

The Bracero system ended almost simultaneously with the change in United States migration legislation of 1965 which officially opened the U.S. more widely to migration from Asia and the Western Hemisphere. That the Bracero program involved at least an attempt to maintain strict control of the border, not to prevent entry, but to prevent settlement, and therefore autonomous use of entry by migrants, is shown by the figures in Table 2 which illustrates the numbers of migrants who entered from Mexico as Bracero labor and the numbers expelled.

The migrations to the Middle East have been necessary to the production of oil, and to the work of construction, transport and reproduction of the labor force (cooking, cleaning, sex) which produces this crucial commodity. Wages are determined by nationality, with Americans and Europeans paid the most, followed by Arab nationals, then Asians. There is also a hierarchy of nationality based wages within this regional hierarchy. For instance, wages for a Thai can be four times as much as for a Bangladeshi worker.[79] Before the Gulf War there were 5.2 million migrant workers in the Gulf (see Tables 3 and 4).

Domestic workers, usually Asian women, have the most precarious contracts, and often the most oppressive working conditions, including physical violence. The largest group comes from Sri Lanka, and many are Filipinas. In 1983, 200,000 Sri Lankans, mostly women, were working in the Gulf region, and migration has continued.[80] Filipina women occupied their embassy in Kuwait after the Gulf War to protest sexual harassment, rape and beatings suffered at the hands of their

Table 2. Contract labor under the Bracero Program and arrests of undocumented workers

	Number of contract workers	Arrests of undocumented workers
1942	4,203	
1943	52,098	
1944	62,170	
1945	49,454	
1946	32,043	
1947	19,632	
1948	33,288	
1949	143,455	
1950	76,519	
1951	211,098	500,628
1952	187,894	543,538
1953	198,424	875,318
1954	310,476	1,075,168
1955	390,846	242,608
1956	444,581	76,442
1957	450,422	44,451
1958	418,885	37,242
1959	447,535	30,196
1960	427,240	29,651
1961	294,149	29,877
1962	282,556	30,272
1963	195,450	39,124
1964	181,738	43,844
1965	103,563	
1966	18,544	
1967	7,703	
1968	6,127	
Total	5,050,093	3,584,359

Source: Cohen (1987) pp. 50, 52.

Table 3. Immigrant workers in the Gulf 1975-1990: numbers and percentage of labor force (in thousands)

	1975	%	1980	%	1990	%
Saudi Arabia	475	32	1,734	59	2,878	60
AUR	234	84	471	90	805	89
Kuwait	218	70	393	78	731	86
Oman	103	54	171	59	442	70
Qatar	57	83	106	88	230	92
Bahrain	39	46	78	57	132	51
Total	1,125	47	2,953	65	5,218	68

Source: Stalker (1994), p. 241.

Table 4. Migrant Workers in Iraq and Kuwait before the Gulf War

Country of Origin

Egypt	1,115,000
Jordan/Palestine	537,000
Other Arabs	188,000
Sudan	200,000
India	181,000
Sri Lanka	101,000
Pakistan	95,000
Bangladesh	90,000
Philippines	55,000
Thailand	13,000
Other Asians	92,000
Others	47,000
Total	2,714,000

employers. In the United Arab Emirates, 2,600 complaints of servants fleeing were registered with a government agency in 1991.[81] Pakistan, Bangladesh and India have effectively banned the emigration of women to the Gulf as domestic workers. But remittances from domestic workers are crucial to some states, including the Philippines, a case which I will examine in detail in chapter 3, and so in practice the state does little to protect these workers and continues to encourage their emigration. For instance, in 1988 the Philippine government had banned agencies from recruiting domestic workers to go to Kuwait, but workers are recruited for Qatar and Bahrain instead and promptly sent to Kuwait.[82] Workers are recruited to contracts based upon nationality, and host states have been careful to avoid a concentration of workers who have too much in common culturally or politically so as to prevent organization and revolt.[83] This concern increased after the Iranian revolution of 1979, and the subsequent seizure of Mecca by Shi'ite Muslims during the Haj that same year. The Gulf War was, among other things, an opportunity for a tremendous expulsion.

Over 5 million workers were expelled from the Gulf states in one form or another during and after the Gulf War, and recruitment targets changed, with Arab workers, such as Yemeni and Palestinians, replaced by workers from India, Pakistan and Bangladesh. Over one million Yemeni were expelled, and around half a million Palestinians and Jordanians. For workers from countries like the Philippines, the Gulf War also signalled a change of destination for many using the information on work conditions available through social networks. Among other destinations, Italy became a site of Filipina arrival after the Gulf War (see chapters 3 and 4). Recruitment continues, using private agencies in the home countries that often charge an exorbitant amount. In Sri Lanka there were already 500 such agencies operating in 1980, and as many as 1,000 in the Philippines by 1982.[84] An Indian expecting to make a $175 base salary a month might pay an agent's fee of around $1,500-$2,000. If the worker uses one-third of his or her salary to live and one-third to send home in remittances, such a fee would be paid off only after three years of work. Yet the flow to the Gulf continues, though as the next chapter will show, under conditions in which workers, when possible, attempt to use a variety of possible destinations, or a frequent change of country of work, to impose their own projects to a greater extent on the labor market.

After the Second World War, and especially after the 1950s, every major industrialized country in Europe experienced large-scale migrations of workers from other lands. These migrant workers played a central role in the restructuring of the economy: first, as semi-skilled labor power for the generalization of mass assembly production until about 1973; and second, as a sector of the working class set apart to absorb a disproportionate share of unemployment during the more recent tranformation into flexible forms of production. Migrant communities and ethnic minorities have become indispensible to the economic lives of European countries and to some extent are present in almost every sphere of life. In the process of migration they have created communities that are by now considered permanent ethnic minorities in many European societies. To some extent Italy was an exception to this trend. It received virtually no foreign-born workers before 1980, but rather used its own south as its pool of migrant semi-skilled labor for mass assembly work. Indeed, it is precisely the arrival of migrants in areas *which previously have not received them*, and under conditions which *do not include a growth of mass industry*, that make the current migrations far from merely an extention of the previous migration to Europe. Most other European countries had banned new immigration around or shortly after 1973, though migrants have used family reunion and, in certain countries like Germany, refugee protocols to enter Europe. The permanent settlement of ethnic minorities from largely Third World countries was a consequence unintended by the countries that had encouraged immigration.

Over 30 million workers born in other countries entered European states as migrants between 1945 and 1973, and the net population increase in Western Europe from migration was 10 million.[85] Three million of the permanent resident migrants are women.[86] Originally, the majority of the migrants were from Southern Europe—Italians, Spaniards, Portugese and Greeks. But in every country that received migrants, the percentage of and the absolute numbers of southern Europeans arriving as migrants has fallen off, while the percentage of arrivals from outside Europe increased (see Tables 5 and 6). Most of the non-European migrants have come from the greater Mediterranean—Turkey and North Africa—but many arrived from the Indian sub-continent and other Asian, African and Caribbean countries.

Table 5. Foreign Resident Population in Western Europe 1950-1990 (in thousands with % of population)

Country	1950	%	1970	%	1982	%	1990	%
Austria	323	4.7	212	2.8	303	4.0	512	6.6
Belgium	368	4.3	696	7.2	886	9.0	905	9.1
Denmark	—	—	—	—	102	2.0	161	3.1
Finland	11	0.3	6	0.1	12	0.3	35	0.9
France	1,765	4.1	2,621	5.3	3,680	6.8	3,608	6.4
Germany (W.)	568	1.1	2,977	4.9	4.667	7.6	5,242	8.2
Greece	31	0.4	93	1.1	60	0.7	70	0.9
Ireland	—	—	—	—	69	2.0	90	2.5
Italy	47	0.1	—	—	312	0.5	781	1.4
Liechtenstein	3	19.6	7	36.0	9	36.1		—
Luxembourg	29	9.9	63	18.4	96	26.4	109	28.0
Netherlands	104	1.1	255	2.0	547	3.9	692	4.6
Norway	16	0.5	—	—	91	2.2	143	3.4
Portugal	21	0.3	—	—	64	0.6	108	1.0
Spain	93	0.3	291	0.9	418	1.1	415	1.1
Sweden	124	1.8	411	1.8	406	4.9	484	5.6
Switzerland	285	6.1	1,080	17.2	92	14.7	1,100	16.3
U.K.	—	—		—	2,137	3.9	1,875	3.3
Total	**5,100**	**1.3**	**10,200**	**2.2**	**15,000**	**3.1**	**16,600**	**4.5**

Source: Stalker, *The Work of Strangers* (Geneva International Labor Organization, 1994), p. 190.

Looking at Table 5, we note that the foreign resident population has fallen or stagnated in many countries. With the exception of Finland, where foreign resident numbers remain miniscule, Italy is the only country where the foreign-born resident population as a percentage of the population rose substantially from 1982 to 1990—indeed, it virtually tripled. Furthermore, only Germany had a higher increase in absolute numbers of foreign residents during that period. We should note that the numbers for three countries—France, Sweden and the United Kingdom—are somewhat reduced, in the former two because of their relatively high naturalization rates, and in the latter because many immigrants were citizens of either colonies or commonwealth member states and therefore already British citizens.

Table 6. Sources of Foreign Residents in Selected European Countries 1990 (thousands)

Sending Country	Receiving Country				
	Belgium	France	Netherlands	Germany	U.K.
Algeria	10.7	619.5	—	6.7	—
Greece	20.9	—	4.9	315.5	—
India	—	—	—	—	155.0
Iran	—	—	—	89.7	—
Italy	241.1	253.7	16.9	548.3	75.0
Morocco	141.6	584.7	156.9	67.5	—
Pakistan	—	—	—	—	55.0
Poland	—	46.3	—	241.3	—
Portugal	16.5	645.7	8.3	84.6	21.0
Spain	52.2	216.0	17.2	134.7	24.0
Tunisia	6.3	207.5	2.6	25.9	—
Turkey	84.9	201.5	203.5	1,675.0	—
Yugoslavia	5.8	51.7	13.5	652.5	—
Others	312.8	781.0	257.3	1,401.1	1,443.0
Total	904.5	3,607.6	692.4	5,241.8	1,875.0
non EC	354.1	2,298.7	524.0	3,916.4	986.0

Source: Stalker (1994), p. 191.

The migrations were largely organized by states, though to varying degrees, with the German and Swiss "Guestworker" programs the most heavily state-centered, and the U.K. migration probably the least state-organized. The most direct way in which states organized migrations was by state-to-state agreements. France, for instance, signed bilateral agreements with Italy (1946), Spain (1961), Portugal and Morocco (1963), Turkey and Yugoslavia (1965), and Algeria (1962). Often the receiving states carried out recruitment themselves, especially West Germany, which set up recruitment offices in Naples, Istanbul, and elsewhere. The German state had a monopoly on recruitment, following agreements with businesses and labor unions. In a sense, the various European states had already played a role in the migrations by colonial conquest and social transformation of the countries of migrant origin. Many of the migrants came to France, Holland and Great Britain. from former colonies, and even in the case of Germany, many migrants followed paths first traced by

Nazi-era foreign-worker conscription. These state-centered migrations to Europe reversed the trend of colonialism which sent settler populations out of Europe to the colonies. No European country claimed to encourage permanent settlement by migrants.[87] They were seeking labor power for the mass production industries of the so-called Fordist era. Human beings came instead. In Germany, official pronouncements that "Germany is not a country of immigration" continue despite the relatively high numbers of foreign residents. The Gastarbeiter program in Germany was used to fine tune the number of entries and expulsions according to the needs of German industry.[88] This attempt to fully govern the mobility of workers was thwarted, however. Further, though attempts were made to keep migrants in certain sectors of the economy, and to some extent such segmentation is a reality, the contradictory tendency of the labor market is such that the effort to divide workers by segmentation also gives way in part to the attempt to lower wages and working conditions throughout the economy. This strategy in turn provides an opening for the invasion by migrant workers into all sectors of economic life.

Migrants workers have been heavily represented in shift work, foundries, and work that is dangerous, heavy, or unpleasant, work that locally born labor sought to escape doing.[89] Nevertheless, it is far from clear that the division of labor in European economies has been qualitatively stratified according to national origin. Migrants constituted 13 percent of the workers in manufacturing in Germany as of 1981, and 12 percent of building workers. (They were 7.6 percent of the population, though a higher percentage of the workforce.) Fifty-seven percent of all foreign workers were in manufacturing, compared with 41 percent of all workers. The percentage of migrants working in the building trades was 10 percent as opposed to the national percentage of 8 percent. Foreigners were overrepresented in German foundries in 1978 (27 percent of total employment in that industry), in hotels and catering (22 percent), and textiles (20 percent), and underrepresented in self-employment (3.8 percent of foreigners, 9.1 percent of Germans) and non-manual workers (37.5 percent of Germans, only 14.5 percent of foreigners).[90]

These figures do reflect a substantial stratification of the labor market, but they also show a considerable overlap between German and foreign workers. For instance, 73 percent of foundry workers and 78 percent of hotel and catering workers are Germans. Such a presence of both locally and foreign born workers in the same industries means interaction on a daily basis between Germans and other workers.

Such communication and interaction between workers may have helped fuel the strike waves that swept Western Europe in the late 1960s and early 1970s. Migrant workers played important roles in strike activity in several countries, and by the early '60s had already established autonomous class-based organization in Great Britain. Migrant workers were active in the strike and factory occupations movement in France in May 1968. In the fall of 1973 a wave of strikes led by Turkish women hit German factories. Shortly afterwards but before the October price increases that ushered in the Energy Crisis of the mid-'70s, Germany banned all new immigration. France followed less than a year later, and by 1975, every other industrialized Western European society had officially followed suit.[91]

The timing is important because it indicates that it was migrant worker militancy, and not the economic pressures of the Energy Crisis, that led European states to ban new immigration. The state-centered migrations had resulted in autonomous migrant class organization and militancy. Thus, following the pattern of previous migrations analyzed in this chapter, the postwar state-organized migrations to Europe were eventually blocked by the state because of the development of autonomous activity by migrants. The ending of new immigration, as noted however, has failed to shut off the flow completely. Since 1973 an entirely new migration has begun, even if in many cases, and especially in certain countries, it takes the form of family reunion. Since 1973, however, the self-organization of the contemporary world migrations has been its principal characteristic. The source of migrant origins has become dramatically more varied. The same is true of migrants' choice of destinations. The latter is determined by social networks now spanning the planet utilizing an unprecedented amount of information to choose destinations based on the most favorable conditions. These include availability of work, wage levels and working conditions, established presence of friends and relatives, and state entry and residence policies, among other factors. Most of the European countries during the mass assembly boom received migrants from two or three major points of origin, at a certain point making a shift from southern European origin countries to Third World ones. This was a logical result of the state organization of the migrations, and the use of migration agreements with specific states to do so. Thus, in West Germany, in 1984 there were 1.5 million Turks, 600,000 Yugoslavs, 545,000 Italians and 287,000 Greeks—these four groups accounting for about two-thirds of all migrants. More recently, the main flow has been from East Europe, with 370,000 Poles arriving in 1988 and 1989 alone.[92] In the Netherlands, Turks, Moroccans and Spaniards were the main early groups of migrants; later former colonial peoples arrived from the Dutch Antilles, Indonesia and Surinam. In Belgium, Turks and Moroccans were the main migration groups. In the United Kingdom, Ireland and the former colonies of the Caribbean and the Indian subcontinent were the main points of emigration. In France, Algerians, Moroccans and Tunisians replaced Italians, Portugese and Spaniards as the largest groups. Indeed, as late as 1990, as a result of the largely bilateral migration process, a few national groups dominated the migrant population of most European countries. However, recent arrivals, as a result of the newer, more autonomous post-1973 migrations have made the migrant population somewhat more heterogeneous (see Table 6).

We see from Table 6 that the Mahgreb countries account for nearly two-thirds of all non-European Community residents in France; that Turks and Yugoslavs make up a large majority of the same category of residents in Germany; that Moroccans and Tunisians account for a solid majority of non-EC residents in the Netherlands. Although the United Kingdom appears the exception to the rule of having one or two national groups dominate the non-European migrant communities, in 1990 there were 584,000 people of Indian descent, 457,000 Pakistanis and 109,000 Bangladeshis, leaving the descendents of the subcontinent just shy of half the entire ethnic minority population of 2,614,000. Another 474,000 were of Afro-Caribbean descent. Thus, even in the relatively diverse Great Britain, a few groups make up a significant majority of the Third World-descended population.[93] Thus, until recently, the flows of migrants, based upon the earlier paths originally organized by the state, were substantially from a few countries to a limited number of destinations, of which one or two were predominant.

THE CONTEMPORARY, SELF-ORGANIZED MIGRATIONS: SOME SIGNS OF CHANGE IN MIGRATION PATTERNS

This tendency toward fairly homogenous flows of migrants to a relatively limited number of destinations has changed dramatically in the past ten years or so. In looking at recent arrivals to Europe and the United States, we find an almost bewildering diversity of national origin on the part of migrant communities, and the emergence of destinations that had not been large recipients of migrants. Among the latter, we may count Italy, which has shifted in net annual terms from being a long-time country of emigration to one of immigration in the late 1980s and 1990s, though the large numbers of Italian nationals living abroad (as for example in Table 6) continue to dwarf the numbers of immigrants living in Italy in gross terms. To better understand the change in terms of the migration patterns, let us take two examples. Table 7 shows the net immigration to the Netherlands for 1991.

Here we find that the category "All others," reflecting a vast diversity of national origins whose numbers for any particular nationality are relatively small, has become nearly 40 percent of the total migration flow. We note further that women have become more than two-fifths of the newly arriving migrant population. Moroccans and Turks, the two largest groups, would seem to account for less than a quarter of the incoming population—though we must underline that since the left hand column tells us only the last country of residence it is reasonable to assume that a large percentage of the people coming into the

Netherlands from other European states, and perhaps also some from the United States, are non-European citizens.

Looking at the recent migration to the United States, we find an increasing diversity in national origin since the 1960s which is in large part attributable to the changes in immigration law in 1965 that opened spaces for larger quotas from non-European populations (see Table 8).

Table 7. Net immigration to the Netherlands 1991

Last Residence	Male	Female	Total
Turkey	8,070	4,306	12,376
Morocco	5,487	3,408	8,895
Germany	3,724	3,115	6,839
Suriname	2,986	3,685	6,671
U.K.	3,758	2,209	5,976
United States	1,406	1,209	2,615
Belgium	1,284	1,076	2,360
Yugoslavia	1,252	935	2,187
France	990	713	1,703
Ghana	1,076	580	1,656
All others	18,346	14,722	33,068
Total	**48,379**	**35,958**	**84,337**

Source: Stalker (1994), p. 203.

Table 8. Where U.S. legal immigrants came from 1951–1985 (%)

Country of Birth	1951–60	1961–70	1971–80	1981–85
Europe and Canada	70.0	45.9	20.4	14.8
Latin America and Caribbean	22.5	39.0	40.3	32.0
Asia	6.2	13.4	36.4	48.4
Other	1.1	1.8	2.8	4.8

Source: David Simcox ed., *U.S.Immigration in the 1980's: Reappraisal and Reform* (London: Westview Press, 1988), p 17.

We see in Table 8 an increasing diversity of migrant origin, such that no one continent dominates U.S. migration. These categories account for a vast variation of national origin, of course. While changes in immigration law can partially account for the increased flow of migrants from Latin America and Asia as opposed to Europe, they cannot, despite a certain "common sense" view to the contrary, account for the increase in the overall numbers of arrivals. Let us examine the absolute numbers of legal immigrants arriving in the U.S. since 1956 (see Table 9).

The years 1966 to 1969, which we might have expected to show large increases in immigration, instead show rather modest annual increases over the previous period, and rather low figures compared with the numbers for the 1980s. Indeed, since by the mid-1990s U.S. annual immigration reached one million legal arrivals, we must assume that the 1968 figure, which is larger than those for preceding and subsequent years, represents a good part of the pressure for entry that had presumably built up in anticipation of the change in U.S. immigration law. Indeed, until 1977 the figure remains below 400,000 per year, and is not qualitatively larger than the figures for years preceding 1965. Only in the 1980s does the number of arriving immigrants stabilize above 500,000, and only in the 1990s did it double that figure. This suggests that whatever the effect of the immigration law in making possible the arrival of legal immigrants from new areas of the world, it did not cause the numerical increase in absolute numbers, which did not occur until about 15 years or more after passage of the 1965 legislation. In short, some other factor or factors must account for these increases. Most of the immigrants in the United States in the past two decades have entered under family reunion preference provisions of the post-1965 immigration legal system, which were left largely intact by the 1986 and 1990 reforms.[94] This would seem to indicate that the law has been the decisive factor, after all, but merely required a decade or so for the first arrivals to activate the family reunion provisions. This begs the question as to why more family reunions didn't take place earlier, since they were legally possible some years before 1975. One study in 1973-74 showed that 70 percent

Table 9. Legal Immigration to the U.S. 1956-1986

Year	Number of Persons	Year	Number of Persons
1956	321,625	1972	384,685
1957	326,867	1973	400,063
1958	253,265	1974	394,861
1959	260,686	1975	386,194
1960	265,398	1976	398,613
1961	271,344	1977	462,315
1962	283,763	1978	601,442
1963	306,260	1979	460,348
1964	292,248	1980	530,639
1965	296,697	1981	596,600
1966	323,040	1982	594,131
1967	361,972	1983	559,763
1968	454,448	1984	543,903
1969	358,579	1985	570,009
1970	373,326	1986	601,700
1971	370,478		

Source: Simcox, ed. (1988), p. 17.

of Mexicans legally arriving during that period had already lived in the United States for at least six months, and subsequent studies have indicated that this high percentage remains roughly constant.[95] In other words, regardless of the legal structure, immigrants have arrived and often only later taken advantage of, or gained through pressure, legal sanction to legitimize their condition. The laws may place obstacles to, or may facilitate entry, legalization of status, employment, family reunion, but do not create or sustain the migrations, and these would occur, albeit under altered conditions, even under different legal mechanisms. I will argue in the next two chapters, using Italy as the example, that the current migration flows are organized by recently created self-organized networks of migrant communication based on transnational communities and that they are a response to the social changes brought about by Structural Adjustment Programs in the countries of immigrant origin.

Before turning to these themes and to Italy, it is worth mentioning one other aspect of the changes in the composition of immigrant destinations. This is the rise of countries such as Ireland,[96] South Korea,[97] and Italy, as destinations for immigrants. A recent study estimates there are 150,000 immigrant workers in South Korea, previously strictly a country of emigration, as of December 1995.[98] Table 10 shows the number of legal and illegal migrants from Asia, according to the South Korean Ministry of Justice, in South Korea as of the end of 1995.

Though we do not know to what extent this number represents an increase in recent years, we know that apprehensions of illegal foreign workers in South Korea has risen from about 1,000 in 1990 to 82,000 in 1995, indicating that the flow, in any case a recent one, may be increasing.[99] Another study found the number of foreign training workers to have risen from 10,000 in 1992 to 57,000 in June 1996, and the total number of foreign workers in South Korea from 100,000 to 160,000 in the same period.[100] No single country or group of countries dominates the migration flow into Korea. Rather, the diversity of national origin is staggering. Many of these nationalities, arrive as migants to many other destinations as well. In chapter 4 we will examine more closely the increasing integration of migrant flows and destinations by transnational migrant communities. Using greater access to information than ever before, these are able to choose between different potential destinations, in an increasingly independent way.

CONCLUSIONS

We have examined a number of major migration flows over the past five centuries in the formation of a worldwide labor market. We have found that each—slavery, European indentured servitude, Asian indentured labor, European migrations of the 19th and early 20th century, and postwar migrations to Europe, the United States (the Bracero program), South Africa and the Persian Gulf states—was linked to the rise of a particular mode of capitalist production. We have seen that the role of the state was a source of continuity in migrations, but the European migrations of

Table 10. Legal and Illegal Migrants in South Korea,
December 1995, with country of origin:

Legal Migrants		Illegal Migrants	
China	11,742	Korean-Chinese	17,093
Philippines	6,426	Philippines	7,614
Vietnam	9,122	Bangladesh	5,244
Myanmar	1,000	Pakistan	2,276
Bangladesh	5,848	Nepal	2,072
Pakistan	1,200	China	2,056
Sri Lanka	2,500	Thailand	1,305
Indonesia	8,485	Myanmar	979
Nepal	1,045	Japan	902
Iran	500	Taiwan	815
Thailand	750	Sri Lanka	802
Uzbekistan	1,200	Iran	749
		India	565
		Vietnam	130
		Indonesia	127
		Mongolia	124
		Singapore	69
		Malaysia	69
		Uzbekistan	13
Total Asia	49,818	**Total Asia**	49,496

Source: Su Dol Kang, *Globalization of the Labor Market: Foreign Labor Issue in Korea* (Seoul, Korea: Labor Institute, 1996), pp. 28, 35.

the last century were similar to those of today in being largely self-organized. We have found another continuity in every period, except for the post-World War II state-centered migrations, of private transport and labor recruitment agents. And we have found that each migration was eventually blocked by the state because migrant communities had found ways to develop autonomous control or use of the migration process, thus challenging the capitalist use of space to control labor forces concentrated in particular places. Finally, we have seen that while the post-World War II migrations were perhaps the most thoroughly state-organized migrations ever, they have given way to a new migration regime in which many of the previous centers of immigration have officially closed their borders and in which new destinations have emerged receiving migrants from both old and new countries of origin.

Italy is a prototype of the immigrant destination of the present period. By analyzing first the composition of migrants in Italy and their points of origin, and how they arrive in the context of the world labor market, which migrants are creating through their own self-activity, I will show why this is so. Italy is one of the new sites of immigrant arrival in the world today, and its rate of growth of immigrant population far surpasses any other European country. Having received large numbers of immigrants only after the post-1973 closing of borders and transformation of industrial structures, it has received migrants from an extraordinary variety of origin countries. These migrations can be explained only as responses to Structural Adjustment Programs in the countries of origin, thus locating them as a new phenomenon, and not as merely a continuation of the previous European migrations of the pre-1973 period. In short, the migrations across the planet since the early 1980s, as the example of Italy will help to demonstrate, are an entirely new phenomenon that does not fit neatly into any of the previous typology of historical migrations. That typology we may summarize as follows:

Origin	Recruitment	State Role	Destination	Agent
Indenture (1)				
Europe	Private, Contract	Initiation	America	State, Employers
Slave Trade				
Africa	Forced	Initiate, Sustain	Americas	Slavers, Masters
Indenture (2)				
Asia	State, Private	Colonialism	British Empire	State, Empoyers
European Migration				
Europe	Private/Family	Minimal	Americas	Migrants, Employers
Post-WWII				
N.Africa, Turkey	State Recruit	Expel	Europe, U.S., S. Europe, Africa, Gulf, S. Africa, Mexico	State
Contemporary				
Many countries	Self-Organized	Prevention, Social Control	Many Countries: Third World and E. Europe	Migrant Networks

We are currently witnessing a migration experience which, despite its superficial appearances, is a sharp departure from every previous migration. The most similar historical migration is the European migration of the 19th and early 20th century. The differences are four: (1) the previous migrants were European instead of from the former colonies—that is, white people; (2) the states of that time made little attempt to block this migration, whereas today most states are attempting to restrict migration which continues despite these efforts; (3) the means of transport and communication and therefore the possibilities of frequent return and of maintenence of community, while not qualitatively different, are today qualitatively faster and cheaper; and (4) migration recruitment does not take place today under conditions of growth of new industries which openly seek workers; rather, the migration is linked to a transformative restructuring of work relations in both the countries of origin and that of destination.

Notes

1. Wallerstein, *World System.*
2. Lydia Potts, *The World Labour Market: A History of Migration* (Atlantic Highlands, New Jersey: Zed 1990), pp. 10-12.
3. For a useful discussion of the relation between space and capital accumulation and class organization, see two works by the Midnight Notes Collective: *Space Notes* (Jamaica Plain, Massachusetts: 1982) and *The New Enclosure* (Jamaica Plain, Massachusetts: 1990).
4. Potts, *Labour Market*, p. 13.
5. Orlando Patterson, *Slavery and Social Death: A Comparative Study* (Cambridge: Harvard University Press, 1982).
6. David Brion Davis, *The Problem of Slavery in Western Culture* (Ithaca: Cornell University Press, 1966), p. 30.
7. Ibid., pp. 41-42.
8. Potts, *Labour Market*, p. 32. Potts writes that up to 18 million arrived in Brazil, but given the numbers mentioned in footnote 9 below, this number seems too high. If two-thirds of all captured Africans were transported to Brazil, then given Inikori's higher estimates, this would total a maximum of 9 million brought to Brazil.
9. Philip Curtin estimated the total number of persons traded as slaves from the 15th to the 19th century at no less than 8 million, but not much more than 10 million. Philip Curtin, *The Atlantic Slave Trade: A Census* (Madison: University of Wisconsin Press, 1969), p. 268; J.E. Inikori argued in 1982 that "there is now some consensus among specialists that

Curtin underestimated the volume of the Atlantic exports," revising Curtin's figure upwards to 15,400,000, in part based upon Curtin's leaving out the related Muslim slave trade. J.E. Inikori, "Introduction" in Inikori ed., *Forced Migration* (London: Hutchinson University Library for Africa, 1982), pp. 20-21; Hugh Thomas has recently revisited the question, finding that "some of Curtin's detailed country-by-country estimates, especially by his own admission those in the Spanish Empire, were full of uncertainties," and that Curtin's estimates of illegal slave trading to the United States after abolition of the trade were also low. But, while admitting the Inikori's criticisms regarding Curtin's uncertain figures for Cuba and Brazil in the 19th century are somewhat valid, Thomas concludes by revising the estimates for the total slave trade at around 11 million "give or take 500,000." Hugh Thomas, *The Slave Trade: The Story of the Atlantic Slave Trade 1440-1870* (New York: Simon & Schuster, 1997), pp. 861-62.

10. Ibid., p. 43.
11. Peter Stalker, *The Work of Strangers: A Survey of International Labor Migration* (Geneva: International Labour Office, 1994), p. 9.
12. Cited in Potts, *Labour Market*, p. 43.
13. Stalker, *Work*, p. 9.
14. Edmund Morgan, *American Slavery, American Freedom* (New York: Norton, 1975), pp. 307-08.
15. Richard B. Morris, *Government and Labor in Early America* (New York: Harper & Row, 1946), p. 315.
16. Ibid., p. 319.
17. Ibid., p. 320.
18. Ibid., p. 320.
19. Ibid., p. 324.
20. Ibid., p. 336.
21. For a fuller description of the role of seventeenth century and eighteenth century workers, indentured, enslaved and otherwise in the diffusion of a trans-Atlantic opposition and later revolutionary activity, see Peter Linebaugh, "All the Atlantic Mountains Shook," *Labour/Le Travail* (Winter 1982) and Peter Linebaugh, *The London Hanged.*
22. Linebaugh, "All the Atlantic Mountains."
23. George Rawick, *From Sundown to Sunup*, pp. 11-12.
24. C.L.R. James, *The Black Jacobins.*
25. W.E.B. DuBois, *Black Reconstruction in America 1860-1880* (New York: Atheneum, 1973).
26. Linebaugh, *The London Hanged*, p. 136.
27. Ibid., p. 415.
28. Footnote Quote from DuBois
29. Eric Williams, *Capitalism and Slavery.*
30. Hugh Thomas, *The Slave*, p. 531.
31. W.E.B. DuBois, *The Suppression of the African Slave Trade to the United States of America 1638-1870* (New York: Shocken Books, 1969),

p. 109; Hugh Thomas, *The Slave Trade*, p. 507.

32. C.L.R. James, *The Black Jacobins*; Robin Blackburn, *The Overthrow of Colonial Slavery* (New York: Verso, 1990).
33. Thomas, *Slave Trade*, pp. 529-30.
34. DuBois, *The Suppression of the African Slave Trade*, pp. 103, 109.
35. Potts, *Labour Market*, p. 71.
36. Ibid., p. 65.
37. Immanual Wallerstein, *Historical Capitalism and Capitalist Civilization* (London: Verso, 1996), pp. 32-33.
38. Ibid., p. 66.
39. Linebaugh, *The London Hanged*, p. 272.
40. Potts, *Labour Market*, pp. 65-71.
41. Alexander Saxton, *Indispensible Enemy:Labor and the Anti-Chinese Movement in California* (Berkeley: University of California Press, 1971), p. 4.
42. Mary Roberts Coolidge, *Chinese Immigration* (New York: Arno Press and New York Times, 1969), p. 52.
43. Ibid., pp. 41-54.
44. Ibid., pp. 41-42. There is no consensus on the meaning and derivation of the word, though this interpretation has scholarly support. I thank Professor Robert Culp for his aid in researching this question. For a study of the policy of the Chinese government towards its subjects working overseas as coolies from 1845–1874 see Yen Ching-Hwang, *Coolies and Mandarins China's Protection of Overseas Chinese during the Late Ch'ing Period (1851–1911)* (Kent Ridge, Singapore: Singapore University Press, 1985), pp. 32-134.
45. Coolidge, *Chinese Immigration*, pp. 45-46.
46. Ching-Hwang, *Coolies and Mandarins*, p. 39.
47. Lynn Pan, *Sons of the Yellow Emperor* (Boston-Toronto-London: Little, Brown and Company, 1990), pp. 126-27.
48. Ibid., p. 123.
49. Ibid., p. 123; compare these headlines with those from Veneto newspapers described in chapters 4 and 7 below.
50. Siriporn Skrobanek, Nattaya Boonpakdi, Chutima Janthakeero, *The Traffic in Women: Human Realities of the International Sex Trade* (London and New York: Zed, 1997).
51. Ibid., p. 98. The authors conclude in terms that are very much in agreement with the conclusions of the present work: "The trade in human beings is an outcrop of international labour migration, and cannot be seperated from it. Millions of people seek to migrate temporarily to work in richer countries in order to improve their economic standing at home. For men . . . opportunities still exist. For women migrants, apart from domestic labor (itself often subject to conditions of virtual captivity), prostitution is one of the few options. The traffickers, with their extensive networks, move in on the voluntary movement of women, and divert them into forced labour", p. 98.

52. Saxton, *Indispensible Enemy*, p. 6.
53. Potts, *Labour Market*, p. 71.
54. Excepting of course, those of African descent who settled Liberia and Sierra Leone, and rare individual cases of escape or liberation and return.
55. Saxton, *Indispensible Enemy*, p. 8.
56. Ibid., p. 8.
57. Maldwyn Allen Jones, *American Immigration* (Chicago: University of Chicago Press, 1992), pp. 98-99.
58. Ibid., p. 100.
59. Jones op. cit. states this explicitly; Marcus Lee Hansen concludes with respect to German migration and the activity of labor recruiters and shipping agents, "many mistakenly saw in their activities the principal cause of the exodus." *The Atlantic Migration 1607–1860* (Cambridge: Harvard University Press, 1945), p. 198. In discussing the Irish migration in the wake of the potato famine, Hansen does discuss shipping agents, "Certainly no one could escape the ever present reminders: handbills of the shipping agents distributed wherever crowds assembled, notices of sailings on the billboards, personal letters that kept the interest alive." Ibid., p. 283. But here the role of personal letters from family and friends is stressed at least as of equal weight in whetting the apetite for migration; similarly, Kerby Miller, in his opus on the Irish migrations, lays emphasis throughout on the role of presentations of American life and conditions by letters from family members." After 1815, new emigrants' letters enhanced the New World's already glowing reputation and convinced increasing numbers of Irishmen that "independence" could best be achieved in what one Ulsterman called 'the land of freedom and no oppression'" *Emigrants and Exiles: Ireland and the Irish Exodus to North America* (New York and Oxford: Oxford University Press, 1985), p. 203. His mention of recruiting and advertizing on the same page is much more muted in its emphasis:"Likewise, the lower classes received encouragement from advertisements of work on American roads and canals." Ibid. Donna Gabaccia, in her study of Sicilian migration, found that agenti played a role only in the migration of peasants, and again, only in the very early stages. This role was superseded by a growing peasant autonomy from local notables, which, as she argues, may have been a major objective of the migration in the first place. Among artisans from the region she studied, no agents were used, but the entire migration from the first was self-financed by remittances. *Militants and Migrants: Rural Sicilians Become American Workers* (New Brunswick, New Jersey and London: Rutgers University Press, 1988), pp. 84-92; Brinley Thomas, though he is critical of a strictly supply-and-demand explanation for the Atlantic migrations of the nineteenth century, sees the migration flows as following the cycles of export capital flows, but does not indicate how one led to another—in keeping with the neo-classical assumption of perfectly available information. Such a viewpoint has no need of recruiting agents either, but neither proves nor disproves their role. Brinley Thomas, *International Migration and Economic Develop-*

ment (Paris: Unesco, 1961), p. 11; Lastly, Oscar Handlin in the classic, *The Uprooted*, stressed movement of peoples resulting from enclosure and land clearance throughout the continent, and assigned to shipping agents and their advertizing efforts the role of spreading information about the increasing cheapness of travel:"The shipping lines had also the means and the interest to spread information. In distant villages the placards went up at the chapel gate or by the side of the inn. . . . For the first time, transportation was available at a price the emigrants could pay and that undoubtedly made them more willing to travel long distances to the great ports." *The Uprooted: The Epic Story of the Migrations that Made the American People* (Boston: Little, Brown and Co., 1952), p. 42.

60. See Deirdre M. Mageean, "From Irish Countryside to American City: The Settlement and Mobility of Ulster Migrants in Philadelphia," in Colin G. Pooley and Ian D. Whyte eds., *Migrants, Emigrants and Immigrants: A Social History of Migration* (London: Routledge, 1991), p. 43; Peter Linebaugh, Karl Marx and the Theft of Wood; Humbert S. Nelli, *Italians in Chicago 1889–1930* (New York: Oxford University Press, 1971).

61. Mageean, "Irish Countryside," p. 44.

62. Ibid., p. 46.

63. Kerby Miller, *Emigrants and Exiles*, p. 287.

64. Handlin, *Uprooted*, pp. 21-35.

65. Miller, *Emigrants and Exiles*, p. 358.

66. Pino Arlacchi, *Mafia, Peasants and Great Estates: Society in Traditional Calabria* (London and New York: Cambridge University Press, 1980), has warned us against generalizing too much concerning the Italian South. Responses to cash or market agriculture were diverse even in neighboring regions, though the international economic transformations and the processes of land consolidation more less held everywhere. But where some areas made the transition to surviving with at least some small-scale market farmers, other, like the Cosenza area, used emigration as the solution to impossibility of shifting from self-sufficient production to market farming, p. 57.

67. Frank Sturino, *Forging the Chain: A Case Study of the Italian Migration to North America 1880–1930* (Toronto: Multicultural History Society of Ontario, 1990), pp. 50-55.

68. Jerry Mangione and Ben Morreale, *La Storia: Five Centuries of Italian-American Experience* (New York: HarperCollins, 1992), p. 70.

69. Ibid., p. 104.

70. Donna Gabaccia, "Worker Internationalism and Italian Labor Migration 1870–1914," *International Labor and Working Class History* 45 (Spring 1994): 64.

71. Ibid., p. 65.

72. Ibid., p. 67.

73. Suzanne W. Model, "Work and Family: Blacks and Immigrants from South and East Europe," in Virginia Yans-McLaughlin, *Immigration Reconsidered: History, Sociology and Politics* (New York: Oxford

University Press, 1990), p. 134.
74. Ibid., p. 133.
75. Douglas Rimmer, *The Economies of West Africa* (London: Weidenfeld and Nicolson, 1984), p. 13.
76. Midnight Notes, *Midnight Oil*, p. 26.
77. Cohen, *The New Helots*, p. 88.
78. Michael Burawoy, "The Functions and Reproduction of Migrant Labor: Comparative Material from Southern Africa and the United States," *American Journal of Sociology* 81 (March 1976).
79. Stalker, *Work*, p. 244.
80. Midnight Notes, *Midnight Oil*, p. 32.
81. Ibid., p. 33.
82. Stalker, *Work*, p. 245.
83. Midnight Notes, *Midnight Oil*, p. 25.
84. Ibid., p. 27.
85. Stephen Castles, *Here for Good: Western Europe's New Ethnic Minorities* (London: Pluto Press, 1984), p. 1.
86. Mirjana Morokvasic, "Birds of Passage Are Also Women," *International Migration Review* 18 (Winter 1984): 887.
87. Stephen Castles, *Migrant Workers and the Transformation of Western* (Ithaca: Cornell University Press, 1989), p. 1.
88. Ulrich Herbert, *A History of Foreign Workers in Germany 1880–1980 Seasonal Workers/Forced Laborers/Guest Workers* (Ann Arbor: University of Michigan Press, 1990), p. 211.
89. Castles (1984) op. cit., p. 140; Race Today Collective, *The Struggles of Asian Workers in Britain* (Pamphlet) (London, 1983).
90. Castles, *Here for Good*, pp. 132-33.
91. Herbert, *Foreign Workers*, p. 234.
92. Zig Layton-Henry, *The Political Rights of Migrant Workers in Western Europe* (London: Sage, 1990), p. 32; John Borneman, *After the Wall: East Meets West in the New Berlin* (New York: Basic Books, 1991), p. 227.
93. Stalker, *Work*, p. 198.
94. Alejandro Portes and Rubén G. Rumbaut, *Immigrant America*, 2nd ed. (Berkeley and Los Angeles: University of California Press, 1996), p. 15.
95. Ibid., p. 15.
96. "Immigrants Turn Tables on Ireland," *International Herald Tribune*, June 16, 1997, p.1
97. Su Dol Kang, Globalization of the Labor Market: Foreign Labor Issue in Korea (Seoul: Korea Labor Institute, September 1996).
98. Ibid., p. 1.
99. Ibid., p. 39.
100. Hye-kyung Lee, "The Employment of Foreign Workers in Korea: Issues and Policy Suggestions," *International Sociology* 12 (September 1997): 353-71, 353.

3

STRUCTURAL ADJUSTMENT AND IMMIGRANTS IN THE VENETO: NEW ENCLOSURES AND WORLDWIDE MIGRATION

INTRODUCTION: MIGRATION AND STRUCTURAL ADJUSTMENT

This chapter examines the relationship between migration and the experience of, and struggles against, structural adjustment in the immigrants' country of origin. This constitutes a mere opening of discussion on this relation, since the literatures on structural adjustment and on world migration have largely ignored each other. But the connection became apparent from the responses by immigrants in the Veneto to questions regarding their regions of origin, family background, work experience and reasons for migrating. Whether migration was a consciously sought result of International Monetary Fund, World Bank and various states' policies, or an unexpected consequence of these, such policies have created crises of social reproduction in many regions. Local working people have responded to these crises by organizing migrations. This has not been the only nor even the dominant response to structural adjustment. Others have included undergoing greater exploitation and increased work in order to survive, anti-IMF riots, support for revolutions, guerrilla movements or populist coup d'etats, resignation, despair and death. But in at least the cases of the communities from which the immigrants in the Veneto have come, migration has been one attempted solution to the problems posed by structural adjustment. Obviously, the various strategies mentioned above are not mutually exclusive. Migration may be understood as a form of resistance to structural adjustment by community networks. Migration, whatever else it is, is also collective action—it is movement, both figuratively and literally, and may be seen among other things as "voting with one's feet." Migration may be an intended consequence of policies meant to develop increasingly marketized social relations, or it may be a means of avoiding participation in such relations. It is therefore possible to see migration as an unintended consequence of structural adjustment; it is just as plausible to migration as no consequence of the latter at all, but rather as its antithesis.

THE IMMIGRANTS IN ITALY AND THE VENETO

An examination of the regions of origin of immigrant workers in the Veneto region of Italy reveals a close relationship between the migrants and the effects of Structural Adjustment Programs imposed in their various countries of origin by the International Monetary Fund and the World Bank. Notwithstanding a pre-occupation with overpopulation or underdevelopment in general in the sociological literature, reflecting neo-classical conceptions of causes of migration (or even racist conceptions of overpopulation), there are very specific links between certain migrations—their timing, choice of occupation and forms of organization and destination—and specific experiences of expropriation from land, occupation, neighborhood, social guarantees, and legal rights resulting from structural adustment programs. Let's begin with a look at the immigrant populations in Italy and in the Veneto. The category, "extracomunitarian" is an official title referring to citizens of non-European Union countries, and therefore includes non-Third World nations such as the United States, Australia and Canada. Table 11 lists the main nationalities of extracomunitarian immigrants in Italy in possession of a permesso di soggiorno (resident permit), according to the national Italian statistical bureau ISTAT.

Table 11. Extracomunitarian Immigrants in Italy in possession of resident permits 1991–1994— 20 leading nationalities

Country	1991 #	1991 %	1992 #	1992 %	1993 #	1993 %	1994 #	1994 %
Morocco	89,005	10.3	95,741	10.4	97,604	9.9	92,617	10.0
ex-Yugoslavia	33,928	3.9	44,650	4.8	72,377	7.3	89,444	9.7
United States	59,728	6.9	62,112	6.7	63,960	6.5	56,714	6.1
Tunisia	46,393	5.4	50,405	5.4	44,505	4.5	41,105	4.4
Philippines	40,965	4.7	44,155	4.8	46,332	4.7	40,714	4.4
Albania	26,381	3.0	28,628	3.1	30,847	3.1	31,926	3.5
Senegal	27,119	3.1	27,572	3.0	26,368	2.7	24,615	2.7
Egypt	22,406	2.9	23,515	2.5	24,555	2.5	21,230	2.3
Romania	13,548	1.6	16,443	1.8	19,385	2.0	20,220	2.2
Brazil	16,939	2.0	18,751	2.0	21,075	2.1	19,589	2.1
China	20,632	2.4	21,417	2.3	22,875	2.3	19,485	2.1
Poland	19,098	2.2	21,221	2.3	21,075	2.1	18,929	2.0
Sri Lanka	14,545	1.7	17,242	1.9	19,722	2.0	18,689	2.0
Somalia	11,853	1.4	14,973	1.6	19,553	1.9	16,325	1.8
India	12,115	1.4	13,382	1.5	14,303	1.4	13,336	1.4
Ghana	12,782	1.5	14,216	1.6	14,021	1.4	12,646	1.4
Russia	9,245	1.1	10,048	1.1	11,947	1.2	11,158	1.2
Argentina	14,837	1.7	14,871	1.6	13,978	1.4	10,681	1.2
Ethiopia	12,566	1.5	13,001	1.4	14,016	1.4	9,819	1.1
Peru	6,396	0.7	7,493	0.8	8,879	1.0	8,721	0.9
Total	717,551		778,459		834,451		781,129	

The numbers in Table 11 are to be taken with a grain of salt, since official statistics in Italy often vary widely with one another from ministry to ministry (the numbers cited above are the "cleaned up" version, adjusted for a miscount of fully one-third by the Interior Ministry). Further, the number of immigrants who remain clandestine is difficult to determine, with estimates ranging from 250,000 to over half a million.[1] Beyond this, it is quite common for resident permits to expire, while the immigrant remains in Italy. We shall have a further look at these numbers in subsequent chapters, and explore more fully their limits as a guide to the absolute quantitative presence of immigrants in Italy. However, they still serve to give us a sense of the dimensions of the immigrant presence and of the relative proportions between nationalities. As such, an examination of them leads us to certain observations. The first thing that impresses one is the enormous variety of countries that the immigrants have come from. Keeping in mind the previous discussion of immigrant populations in European countries resulting from the post-World War II migration, we find that the degree of diversity of national origins is vastly greater in Italy. The 20 leading countries of emigration account for only 62.5 percent of the extracomunitarian population according to these numbers, while no single source country accounts for over 10 percent. When we examine the Veneto, we find an equally impressive diversity of national origins of immigrants (see Table 12).

Table 12. Extracomunitarian Immigrants in the Veneto 1990–1991 by national origin

Country	Dec. 1990	%	Dec. 1991	%	% increase 1990-91
Morocco	5,205	22.5	7,884	24.5	51.5
ex-Yugoslavia	3,807	16.5	4,503	14.0	18.3
Ghana	2,170	9.4	2,874	8.9	32.4
Senegal	1,352	5.9	2,164	6.7	60.1
Albania	103	0.4	1,525	4.7	1,380.5
Tunisia	642	2.8	1,204	3.7	87.5
Philippines	711	3.1	825	2.6	16.0
China	825	3.6	813	2.5	-1.5
Nigeria	545	2.4	761	2.4	39.6
Romania	337	1.5	649	2.0	92.6
Argentina	474	2.1	598	1.9	26.2
Brazil	471	2.0	562	1.7	19.3
Poland	424	1.8	547	1.7	29.0
Colombia	349	1.5	512	1.6	46.7
Sri Lanka	324	1.4	494	1.5	52.5
Iran	465	2.0	411	1.3	-11.6
Dominican Republic	262	1.1	379	1.2	44.7
Vietnam	400	1.7	357	1.1	-10.8
India	189	0.8	254	0.8	34.4
Somalia	196	0.8	248	0.8	26.5
Jordan	221	1.0	242	0.8	9.5

Table 12 (cont.)

Country	Dec. 1990	%	Dec. 1991	%	% increase 1990-91
Lebanon	223	1.0	234	0.7	4.9
Algeria	155	0.7	231	0.7	49.0
Czechoslovakia	146	0.6	215	0.7	47.3
ex-Soviet Union	134	0.6	209	0.6	56.0
Egypt	203	0.9	201	0.6	-1.0
Bulgaria	95	0.4	191	0.6	101.1
Pakistan	146	0.6	180	0.6	23.3
Hungary	184	0.8	169	0.5	-8.2
Peru	135	0.6	167	0.5	23.7
Venezuela	150	0.6	142	0.4	-5.3
Syria	134	0.6	141	0.4	5.2
Turkey	130	0.6	134	0.4	3.1
Chile	123	0.5	130	0.4	5.7
Ethiopia	129	0.6	130	0.4	0.8
Ivory Coast	103	0.4	126	0.4	22.3
Thailand	86	0.4	125	0.4	45.3
Mexico	85	0.4	98	0.3	15.3
South Korea	71	0.3	91	0.3	28.2
Panama	21	—	84	0.3	200.0
Iraq	81	0.4	80	0.2	-1.2
Cameroon	40	0.2	75	0.2	87.5
Guinea	59	0.3	74	0.2	25.4
Bangladesh	29	0.1	71	0.2	373.3
Uruguay	56	0.2	71	0.2	26.8
Zaire	52	0.2	69	0.2	32.7
Burkina Faso	45	0.2	66	0.2	46.7
Togo	52	0.2	62	0.2	19.2
Ecuador	45	0.2	53	0.2	17.8
Benin	43	0.2	51	0.2	18.6
Others	625	2.7	738	2.3	18.1
Total	**23,094**	**100.0**	**32,214**	**100.0**	**39.5**

Source: E. Bisogno, C. Gatto & F. Neri, *L'immigrazione straniera in Veneto e Friuli-Venezia Giulia* Padua CEDAM (1993), p 94.

Again, I stress both the relative inaccuracy of these figures in and of themselves and their incompleteness: The full statistical breakdown by national origin for the region as a whole beyond 1991 was not available as of the writing of this study, but the total of extracomunitarian immigrants with resident permits in the

Veneto had officially risen to 64,179 by 1995, and the national total to over one million.[2] The two largest national groups in the Veneto remained Moroccans at 11,437, and those from the ex-Yugoslavia, now including 5 different nation states, at 16,800; the two combined now account for well over 40 percent of the Veneto's immigrant population (I will use the term immigrant only for non-EC and non-G7 nationals, except where referring to official statistical methods, as the term extracomunitarian has political overtones and is best avoided). However, they together account for only about half of the increase in the immigrant total since 1991. Indeed, most groups would seem to have steadily increased in size, judging from the tables above and extrapolating from local figures (see chapter 8). If anything, the amount of diversity has increased.

Ironically, this diversity of national origin masks a striking commonality behind the experiences of the countries of origin listed above. For this could as easily be a list of the countries which have undergone significant economic changes toward privatization of land and enterprises, neo-liberal export policies, the cutting of public sector expenditures and economic regulation and the elimination of guarantees of subsidies, employment, land access or income. In short, virtually everyone of these has undergone a Structural Adjustment Program (SAP). This might seem merely fortuitous, given that nearly all of the Third World and the former "socialist" countries have implemented such policies in the course of the 1980s and 1990s. Thus, one might merely conclude that it is a list of Third World and former "socialist" countries, the link with SAPs being merely a function of the former. Perhaps drawing attention to the extent to which the countries of migrant origin are countries where SAP's have been imposed is like saying that they are "developing countries," or "underdeveloped countries," or merely "poor countries." Yet the distinction is important.

As Larry Lohmann has recently argued, categories such as "poor" and "underdeveloped," which grew out of the modernization theories of the 1950s, serve to mask the transformations of social relations that are brought about by privatization, enclosure, structural adjustment, and neo-liberal market policies.[3] Further, the category "poor" is too often used to cover vastly divergent conditions. In some cases it refers to social contexts in which working people maintain control of or access to means of production and subsistence and/or sustain well-integrated community, tribal or village structures; in other cases it can mean instead the conditions facing those whose lack of material wealth is based upon landlessness, below-subsistence wages, or forced labor. Examining the effects of specific transformations of conditions provides us with a less vague means of addressing changes in the local environment of migrant origin. It is striking how virtually silent the migration literature is on the question of structural adjustment even where changes in local social conditions are taken into account.

Field research, by bringing out certain background information in the immigrants' life histories, drew my attention to the often very close link between the migrant communities in the Veneto and specific structural adjustment programs. While the common experience of structural adjustment linking the various countries of migrant origin leads us to the surprising (in these allegedly postmodern times) *homogeneity of experience of working people on a worldwide scale* as they enter and create a labor market, it is only by examining specific migrations and their backgrounds that we can more fully understand the relationships between social actors.

In the course of field research, 250 immigrant workers were interviewed in three provinces of the Veneto—Padua, Vicenza and Treviso (the Treviso interviews were all conducted in the city of Montebelluna). The national origins of the interviewees can be found in Table 13.

There is a considerably greater concentration of certain nationalities at the regional level in the Veneto than at the national Italian level, reflected in both the official numbers cited in Table 12, and in the subjects of my field research in three locales. On the other hand in the case of certain nationalities, there is a significant variation in the percentages found by counting official resident permits and those found in my interviewee numbers. This is primarily true of the numbers for Moroccans, who were interviewed proportionally less than their regional percentage of

Table 13. National Origins and Gender of Interviewees
in three Veneto provinces, 1996–1997

Country	Padova		Vicenza		Treviso		Total		% total
	All	F	All	F	All	F	All	F	Interviewed
Senegal	33	0	7	0	7	0	47	0	18.8
Morocco	14	1	11	0	16	2	41	3	16.4
Ghana	0	0	41	3	0	0	41	3	16.4
ex-Yugoslavia:	7	0	19	5	10	1	36	6	14.4
Yugoslav	1	0	6	0	4	0	12	0	4.8
Serbian	0	0	7	3	4	0	13	3	5.2
Bosnian Serb	3	0	4	1	0	0	4	1	1.6
Croatian	3	0	1	1	2	1	6	2	2.4
Macedonian	0	0	1	0	0	0	1	0	0.4
Philippines	11	10	5	0	0	0	16	10	6.4
Albania	4	0	7	0	5	1	16	1	6.4
Nigeria	12	6	3	1	0	0	15	7	6.0
Tunisia	4	0	1	0	4	1	9	1	3.6
Romania	5	3	2	2	0	0	7	5	2.8
India	0	0	4	0	0	0	4	0	1.6
Ivory Coast	0	0	3	0	0	0	3	0	1.2
Bangladesh	0	0	3	0	0	0	3	0	1.2
Pakistan	1	0	1	0	0	0	2	0	0.8
Others	4	2	6	3	0	0	10	5	4.0
Totals	95	22	113	14	42	6	250	42	100.0

the migrant population, though within reasonable range of their national percentage, and Senegalese, who were interviewed in numbers considerably higher than both their regional and national percentage. The latter outcome is attributable to the addition of thirty interviews conducted using the questionnaire I had developed, which were carried out with the help of two friends, a local union organizer and a local Italian woman. Though I was often present during these interviews, these constitute the few interviews with research subjects which I did not carry out myself. Of these, twenty of the thirty were with Senegalese men, part of a community with whom both my friends had a long-standing relationship. Since the conclusions to be drawn here are largely of a qualitative rather than statistical nature, and since my research approach was designed to overcome a general lack of both information and knowledge about the immigrant communities in the Veneto, I see the additional information gathered by these interviews as a useful means to deepen our understanding of the communities examined in this study.

The other group significantly under-interviewed are women, who accounted for 16.8 percent of the total interviewees, but who constitute 43.5 percent of the immigrants in Italy with resident permits at the start of 1995.[4] This percentage however, hides drastic gender variation within different nationalities: women were 11 percent of the offically counted Tunisian population, 11.5 percent of the Moroccan, but 69 percent of the Filipino population and 87 percent of those from the Cape Verde Islands. Only adults were interviewed for this study. Children of less than 18 years consist of only 3.1 percent of the total immigrant population in Italy.[5] However, the more full-length interviews, participant observer activities, and informal contacts which were part of my research for this study, as well as a separate research on the immigrant family in the Veneto which I carried out for a research institute in Rome, all served to at least partially make up for these gaps in the materials gathered through questionnaire-based interviews. This is true not only for some understanding of the conditions of immigrant women in the study, but also to obtain information in general which was not obtainable by means of the questionnaire research.

Women constituted significant percentages of four groups of interviewees: Romanians (71 percent); Filipinas (63 percent); Nigerians (47 percent) and ex-Yugoslavs (17 percent). Italy recognizes a right of family reunion, but unlike most other countries in Europe, very few people of either sex enter under this category. Thus in 1995, only 174,993 resident permits, out of an official Italian national total of 991,419, were for family reunion. Just under 350,000 were for waged employment ("dependent work" in Italian bureaucratic language); 108,373 for legally unemployed immigrants; 7,000 for training for waged work; and 38,431 resident permits were for self-employment (only about 4 percent of the entire immigrant total). Over 10,000 immigrants were officially political exiles, another 55,000 had resident permits for "humanitarian reasons," and 163,000 had permits for religious, educational or "elective residence." Though this last covers mostly non-Third World citizens, the former two categories constitute the means by which many immigrants initially enter Italy, often staying beyond the expiration of their permit. A further 48,000 had tourist permits, but again, this is a category which includes many who will attempt to stay. The remainder of the total of nearly a million consists of people waiting to adopt children, missionaries, the 5,500 immigrants in prison or awaiting trial, and those in Italy for health reasons. Regarding undocumented immigrants, we should keep in mind the incomplete nature of these official figures.

To understand the migration process, and the presence of these diverse nationalities in Italy, we must examine the regions of origin of the migrants, and the social transformations which in part led to the migrations. To do so requires that we look at forms of work, changes in social policy and land use, and cuts in social services. At the base of the migrations we find expropriation—from small landholdings, stable or guaranteed employment, small petty trade, subsidies on basic consumption goods. In investigating the social transformations in Senegal, Ghana, the Philippines, the ex-Yugoslavia, Morocco, Romania, Nigeria and Albania, we open questions of primitive accumulation of abstract labor and of capital, of forms of resistance and working class formation and of an increasingly worldwide imposition of structural adjustment, privatization and world market incorporation of local economies. In investigating the origins of the migrants in the Veneto, in short, we find class conflicts, which though at one time were isolated in their specific locales, have by means of migration, expanded to take on a worldwide presence. In toto, these origins tell a story of a new planetary enclosures movement, de-stabilizing local economies and giving rise to strategies of migration in certain locales and sectors around the planet.

THE MIGRANTS AND STRUCTURAL ADJUSTMENT

Taking only those groups that are more numerous in the Veneto, their family histories are linked to forms of work impacted by SAPs, and the timing of their migration is linked to cycles of SAPs, the resistance to them, and to movements of certain commodity prices. Most of the Ghanaians are children of cocoa farmers and market women, and many were themselves cocoa farmers before migrating. Almost two-thirds, 26 of the 41 Ghanaians interviewed reported having parents or brothers and sisters who had been cocoa farmers, and 14 described their mothers or sisters as market traders. One other responded that his father worked for the Cocoa Marketing Board. Another five had themselves farmed, at least in part cocoa, before migrating. Small shop owners, mechanics, and teachers are also well represented.

The overwhelming majority of Senegalese in Veneto come from the peanut producing regions of central Senegal, especially near the holy Muslim city of Touba. No fewer than 34 of the 47 interviewed reported being the children of peanut farmers, or 72 percent of all respondents.[6] All Senegalese respondents were Wolof, and all were Mouride Muslims, largely reflecting both the ethnic and religious composition of the Senegalese population in Italy as a whole. Of the 15 Nigerians interviewed using question-naires, all but one were originally from a crescent of southern Nigeria running along highways A122 and A2 from Owo to the Port Harcourt region, a center of oil production. Eleven described their mothers as market traders or businesswomen. Three other Nigerians interviewed in more in-depth fashion were also from this region.

The Moroccan migration dates on a large-scale from the early to mid-1980s structural adjustment and the repression of anti-SAP demonstrations. While, one-third responded that their families had been involved in small scale food sales—mostly butchers and bakers—a majority had been either students or unemployed. Well over half came from cities, especially from Casablanca, original home to 23 of 41 interviewees.

The collapse of Albanian socialism speaks for itself as an example of the New Enclosures, while the flow from Romania likewise dates from privatization policies. The large majority of respondents from both countries—all but two of the Romanians and all but three of the Albanians—were from urban working-class backgrounds. Five of the seven Romanians came from families of factory workers, while thirteen of the sixteen Albanians had parents who had worked either in transport, shoe factories, leather tanneries, or, in the case of fully half of all Albanian respondents, the building trades. The war in Yugoslavia was largely attributable to an IMF adjustment plan; as one of its effects, it has led to a migration of thousands, which in part based itself on previously established migration routes. The continuing policy of the Phillipine government to earn hard currency to pay its foreign debt, a SAP priority, through the remittances of migrant nationals leads to its encouragement of female migration as domestic workers or nurses to every corner of the world.

These origins are important because they reveal just how homogeneous the experience of migration has become. Put differently, they indicate the presence of a planetary working class, expropriated from differing methods of work and subsistence, but by instruments—debt and restructuring, adjustment and privatization, physical repression and war—which are roughly similar. Yet the differences in these experiences are also important for understanding the political resources, experience, and alternatives available to these workers of the world.

To understand these experiences, we must see what migration has to do with export production. Ghana (cocoa), Senegal (peanuts) and Nigeria (oil) are all highly dependent on the sale of a single commodity. The southern and central zones of these West African countries, which previously received migrants to work in these industries, are now the zones of migrant origin. Capital has begun to abandon its dependence for certain commodities on the formal subsumption of labor to capital embodied in small farmers and traders, and to develop agribusiness on a larger scale in such regions, freeing these workers up as available labor power in cities or in the richer countries.

Ghana

In Ghana, cocoa accounts for more than 60 percent of the total export earnings, and the SAP program, lauded as an IMF showcase, has brought about both a considerable increase in cocoa production and a serious crisis in agriculture. Domestic food production plummeted and food imports rose 400 percent in the decade up to 1984 (only about 20 percent of the arable land is under cultivation).[7] Greater emphasis on export cocoa production has meant a further dependence on the world market for cocoa prices, something utterly outside the control of the Ghanaian farmers. This has been especially so since 1966 when the overthrow of the Nkrumah government in a coup just days after refusing to agree to IMF terms led to abandonment of the main point of disagreement: Nkrumah's plans to build state-run cocoa warehouses to enable farmers to withhold cocoa from the market when prices were too low.[8] Further, a significant concentration of holdings has occured under the SAP in the cocoa sector, which, combined with the collapse of urban real wages also resulting from the IMF plan, has led to the decision to emigrate for thousands of Ghanaians. While there is no doubt that the Ghanaian economy was characterized in 1966 by indebtedness, export dependence on a very few products, and budget deficits, the IMF-imposed solutions appear to have dealt irreparable harm to the economic life of Ghana. To be sure, the difficulty farmers faced in social reproduction had already, under Nkumah, led to the use of migration to Nigeria as a means to ensure community survival.[9] In 1983, with the decline of oil prices, Nigeria evicted at least one million Ghanaians. Subsequent IMF policies re-inforced Ghana's dependence on export of raw materials and crops.

Projects that under the Nkrumah government had been financed with the help of "socialist"-bloc countries with an eye toward establishing more self-sufficiency in the processing of the country's raw materials, were eliminated under the military regime and under IMF tutelage. The Tarkwa Gold Refinery, which was nearly completed at the time of the coup, was cancelled because, as the World Bank report put it, it was "understood that the ore could be refined more cheaply abroad." This ended the Nkrumah government's plans for self-sufficiency in gold ore processing. Today, Ghanaians and other West Africans work in the Veneto's gold jewelry workshops near the city of Vicenza. Similarly, and perhaps more importantly, the state cocoa silos which were planned to give the country more control over the world market price—one of the culprits in Ghana's economic troubles both before and after the IMF-supported policies—were never completed The IMF-planned devaluation of the *cedi*, the Ghanaian currency, led to little improvement during the 1970s, since the prices of cocoa and coffee, two important Ghanaian exports, are determined by world marketing agreements that are expressed in dollars. By 1983, the economy was in real trouble. Faced with declining cocoa prices and $1.5 billion in loan repayments, which had been rescheduled in 1974 and now fell due, as well as the return of one million migrants from Nigeria, the Rawlings government turned to the IMF. As a result, the government instituted a structural adjustment program involving cutting the public sector, devaluing the currency, investing in natural resource export, and opening the economy to foreign investors. This program led to an emphasis on renewed cocoa export and on the export of natural resources such as timber.

By the 1890s, following the drop in world market prices for palm oil, cocoa had become the main export crop of the Gold Coast colony. Sharecropping arrangements were organized in the wet soils of the Ghanaian rain forest, a type of terrain which no longer exists in Ghana due to deforestation resulting from both extensive cocoa production and the emphasis on timber exports following the structural adjustment policies of the 1980s.[11] Based on a somewhat reckless frontier approach to extensive farming of cocoa—the average life of a cocoa farm is about 40 or 50 years— Ghana was able to maintain a price advantage on the world market after independence. Most production was by smallholders with some sharecropping.[12] The results of structural adjustment on this economy have led to a crisis of the social relations of land ownership and concentration of wealth in cocoa production and have increased inequality among traders, which disproportionately affects Ghanaian women.

The volume of Ghana's cocoa exports rose more than 70 percent from 1983 to 1988.[13] But the world market price of cocoa has fallen during the subsequent period. By 1990 world cocoa prices were 54 percent lower than in 1986, wiping out the 33 percent increase in cocoa production since that year. This flew in the face of World Bank estimates in 1987 projecting only a 14 percent decline in cocoa prices.[14] For a country deriving 70 percent of its export earnings by the early 1990s from cocoa, this meant serious damage to the social fabric involved in producing cocoa. Yet these results followed logically from the entire approach of the structural adjustment program. For as Mihevc charges, the IMF and World Bank policy of encouraging the revival of cocoa production was based upon the idea that Ghana could increase prices to the producer and thereby increase overall cocoa production "*without having any impact on the world price of cocoa*" (italics in original).[15] In keeping with the neoliberal world market policies that the World Bank and the IMF espouse, production of export crops was encouraged in many countries at the same time. Thus, world production increased by up to 7 percent, while consumption rose only 2 percent from the mid-80s to the mid-1990s.[16] The international financial agencies had encouraged production of cocoa in Brazil and Southeast Asia, and had evidence of falling demand and prices: A 1983 World Bank report forecast declines in coffee and cocoa prices and stagnant demand, and called on producers to diversify and reduce production. But the World Bank's Ghana program has emphasized increased cocoa production.[17] Yet the end of frontier space in the rapidly diminishing rain forest has eliminated the basis of Ghana's price advantage in the world market. Meanwhile, competitors like Brazil and Malaysia, using Green Revolution hybrids and production methods in large-scale production sites, have increasingly captured market share. Output per hectare in Malaysia, for instance, is up to six times greater than in Ghana, which has seen its market share of cocoa drop from 27 percent in 1970 to only 10 percent in 1990 (see Table 14).[18] Biotechnologically developed products such as higher-yield cocoa plants and cocoa butter—the result of collaboration between U.S. universities and chocolate multinationals such as Hershey's, Cadbury-Schweppes, and Nestlé—are expected to raise cocoa production from the 150-200 kilograms per acre, which is the level at which Ghana currently produces, to over 1,400 kilograms per acre.[19] In addition, laboratory-produced cocoa butter and the production of cocoa from vegetable oils and microorganisms is considered imminent—developments that will effectively eliminate the production of cocoa plants.

Table 14. Cocoa Production and Export Dependency

	Production 1987*	% Change 1980–87	Yield (KG/HA) 1987	Exports 1987	Cocoa as % agric. exports
Cameroon	120	0	267	237	52
Ghana	210	-22	175	489	99
Ivory Coast	570	21	543	1,084	57
Nigeria	130	-23	186	168	73
Brazil	405	23	622	606	7
Malaysia	175	361	1,072	344	9
Other Third World	392	32	308	867	1
Third World Total	2,002	18	369	3,795	5

*1000s milletons
Source: Mihevc (1995), p. 215.

The two countries whose agricultural exports are most dependent upon cocoa, Ghana and Nigeria, are also the only two to have seen decreasing production in the period from 1980–1987. These two countries are also the only two on the list to have sent large numbers of emigrants to Italy from their agricultural export-producing regions in southern West Africa. Along with the declining market share, cocoa producers in Ghana facing the need to market their product with considerably less state regulation and help, due to the massive layoffs of Cocoa Marketing Board in 1983 imposed by the SAP, have seen a disasterous decline in the percentage of the export price which they receive as their income, as Table 15 illustrates.

Put simply, Ghanaian farmers, despite receiving a higher nominal price in devalued cedis, have been receiving an increasingly lower percentage of the wealth that they have produced. But this migration is not merely a response to declining regional income per se. For the results of structural adjustment for cocoa production, as well as for small-scale trade in West Africa, have been to increase inequality and concentrate landholdings and market control. Landholdings in cocoa and agricultural export earnings are increasingly concentrated in a few hands. By the mid-1990s, the top 7 percent of Ghana's cocoa producers own almost half of all cocoa-producing land, while 70 percent of cocoa producers farm less than six acres.[20]

Table 15. Producer Price of Cocoa as percent of Export Price
(in Ghanaian Cedis)

Year	Production Tons	Exports Tons	Producer Price Per Ton	Export Price Per Ton	Product Price as % of Export Price
1980–81	257,974	200,251	4,000	5,975	66.9
1981–82	224,882	201,200	12,000	4,946	242.6
1982–83	178,626	162,122	12,000	4,149	289.2
1983	158,956	140,549	20,000	59,130	33.8
1984–85	174,813	162,122	30,000	108,700	27.6
1985–86	219,044	193,170	56,600	208,000	27.2

Source: Jonah, "The Social Impact of Ghana's Adjustment Program 1983–86," in Onimode (1989), p. 147.

Therefore, while cocoa has been highly favored over food production all along by the IMF-World Bank economic program, only a small group of cocoa farmers have benefited. A study of one region revealed that only 32 percent of cocoa farmers received 94 percent of all gross income, leaving the remaining 6 percent for the other 68 percent of farmers.[21] The structural adjustment program has included World Bank projects favoring agribusiness, a trend that also has struck Senegal's economy. Cocoa farmers constitute 18 percent of all agricultural households in Ghana, but it is the minority of this minority that have reaped the benefits of the SAP, while the majority of Ghanaians have seen a decline in conditions and, perhaps just as importantly, a rending of the social fabric due to rising inequality and the loss of control over subsistence.

Food production has been driven into deep crisis in Ghana throughout the SAP period. This is due to the unswerving commitment of the structural adjustment program to favor cocoa production over food production, even though the devaluations of the cedi, while not helping exports, nevertheless raise the prices of food imports. Small-scale food producers have increasingly lost the competition over land use to large-scale cocoa production. Producer prices for food have plummeted relative to cocoa and non-food consumer goods since the 1983 advent of the SAP, as Table 16 shows.

**Table 16. Relative Producer Prices: Ghana
1977–1987 (1977=100)**

	1977	1981	1983	1984	1987
Terms of Trade food/non food consumer goods	100	91	138	86	55
Relative prod. price food/cocoa	100	92	184	136	42

Source: Mihevc, p. 158.

Marketed food production fell by over 20 percent from 1984–1986 after the introduction of structural adjustment. The SAP impacted women and children disproportionally. It is a long-standing West African practice for women to market their own food production as a basis of their own income and to meet their children's needs. We recall that one-third of the Ghanaians interviewed for this study described their mothers or sisters as market traders. This category of working person, often linked to subsistence food production and a cocoa-growing household, is also in deep crisis as a result of the SAP. Recent studies have found increasing inequality between rich and poor traders, and the movement of many small traders into other fields in order to survive. Since the Ghanaian community in the Veneto is characterized by one of the highest percentages of women of any immigrant group, it is likely that migration abroad has also become a strategy for survival. Given that women often have independent sources of income in West African family and household organization, and recalling the predominance of women's agricultural and trade activities for family subsistence, the crises giving rise to the strategy of migration affect women as well as men. Subsistence itself has become difficult for many Ghanaians as a direct result of SAP policies.

The structural adjustment program has promoted the export of timber. As a result, timber exports have increased both in volume and in value, rising from $16 million at the start of the SAP in 1983 to $99 million in 1988.[22] Deforestation, already a serious problem due to the extension of cocoa farming, has reached disastrous proportions: Between 1981 and 1985, the annual rate of deforestation was 1.3 percent, and some estimates

Padua

Either

Tuesday Sept 29
& Wed   Sept 30

(or)

& Wed Sept 30
& Thurs ~~Sept~~ Oct 1

indicate that this rate has more recently risen to over 2 percent per year.[23] The country's forest cover has declined from 8.2 million square kilometers at the start of the twentieth century, to 1.9 million square kilometers in 1987, and some estimates claim that by the year 2000 the forest cover will be completely removed. This level of deforestation has had a serious impact upon living standards in Ghana. Not only does deforestation contribute to soil erosion, drought, and regional climate change, conditions which Kojo Sebastian Amanor verified in his study of the Volta Lake region.[24] This deforestation has worsened the food crisis, because 75 percent of Ghanaians depend on wild game for protein, a food source which is in turn dependent on the existence of the forest. [25] For women, this also means a loss of income from harvesting of food, fuel, and medicine from the forest. Ironically, a substantial part of the export of wood arrives in the Veneto as raw material for the important furniture industry: In 1995, Ghana exported 8,630 tons of wood to the Veneto, at a value of 19 billion Italian lire, or about $12 million—a sum equal to 75 percent of the entire 1983 (hence pre-SAP) revenue of Ghanaian timber exports. The Veneto's wood furniture exports totaled 2.5 trillion lire, or about $1.7 billion.[26] Though Ghanaian workers in the Veneto are more heavily represented in tanneries and foundry work, four of the Ghanaians interviewed, or roughly 10 percent, worked in the furniture industry in the province of Vicenza. Nkrumah's hope that Ghanaian workers could increasingly process the raw materials produced in their own country has perhaps come to pass—but in the factories and workshops of the Veneto!

The SAP in Ghana, as in the rest of Africa, has also hit intellectual and professional workers hard. Thousands of government jobs were eliminated, including 30,000 jobs at the Cocoa Marketing Board; one of the Ghanains interviewed reported that his father had worked for the CMB.[27] The introduction of user services for education have also placed a serious burden on students, teachers and their families. Two of the Ghanaians interviewed were students, and three had been teachers in Ghana. Four others reported that they had hoped to study in Italy, but had so far found that impossible and were instead working in industrial jobs. Such people would have been hit hard by cutbacks, inflation that reduced teachers' salaries in some cases below subsistence levels, the 100-percent devaluation of the cedi between 1983 and 1992 in a country increasingly dependent on food imports, and by user fees and the transformation of education implied by such a policy in a Third World country. We are not necessarily speaking of a privileged middle class, disconnected from farming and working families. Rather, as the Committee for Academic Freedom in Africa and Professor Silvia Federici have pointed out, education in Africa often involves contributions and sacrifices by many relatives, especially the student's mother, and is linked to both extended household and family networks and to the continued possibility of subsistence food production and the marketing of household products, which stem from communal land relations.[28]

These very relations are what are most under attack. Indeed, given inadequate wages in the public sector, access to the village or family land for subsistence to supplement urban income becomes crucial to survival strategies, along with what Ghanaians call "chopping for the work side"—using the facilities and materials of the workplace for subsistence, by selling paper, making photocopies for pay, using an office car as a moonlight taxicab and so forth.[29] Any access to income is made available to a large extended family, a practice common to the African migrant communities in Italy. One Ghanaian man told me, "When you ask me how many brothers and sisters I have, that's one thing, but when you ask how many people are in my family, it's about 100." Thus the combination of access to wages and the maintenence of subsistence structures at the village level become a comprehensive strategy for family survival, just as the income from communal land was previously used to help advance education and careers in exchange for help by the employed family member to pay for schooling and other expenses for relatives.[30] An average of fifteen people are estimated to be dependent on the wages of a single Ghanaian wage earner.[31] While nearly all of the Ghanaians interviewed responded that finding work was their main motivation for emigrating, seven, or about one-sixth, specifically added that helping their family with money problems was a reason for emigration, though the number sending remittances to their family in Ghana approaches 100 percent. One Ghanaian man told me that his job as a furniture upholsterer had not provided "enough pay to live and work in Ghana." Another said he had emigrated "to try to find a life," describing the condition in Ghana as "very troubled, it's in trouble." Yet another described his motivation to emigrate as "so much low pay in Ghana after the devaluation that I had to come to work in Italy." After the expulsions from Nigeria, and following the SAP policies, emigration to other destinations increasingly appeared as a survival strategy not only for the migrant, but for entire families and households remaining in Ghana. At least 20 percent of the Ghanaians interviewed had lived somewhere else before coming to Italy, five in Nigeria. After ten years of structural adjustment, Ghana's foreign debt had risen from $1.6 billion in 1983 to $4.2 billion in 1992, and during that same period no less than two million Ghanaians, almost one-fifth of the entire population, had emigrated to other countries.[32] As we shall see in subsequent chapters, many found their way to Italy, where, after a sojourn in the underground, underdeveloped economies of Palermo, Naples and Bari in the south of Italy, they moved north by word of mouth and arrived at the factories of the Veneto province of Vicenza, site of a major NATO air force base and of one of the world's leading export zones.

Nigeria

Sixteen of the questionnaire-based interviewees, and three of the persons interviewed in a more in-depth fashion, were Nigerians. Only one, born in Kano, was from the northern part of the country. All the rest reported coming from a zone stretching along the southern coast from Oyo about 170 km north of Lagos, west through the region around Benin City, with the largest concentration coming from the Port Harcourt region—center of Nigeria's oil industry. The Nigerian immigration to Italy is related to four specific developments linking Nigeria itself with the outside world. One, the growth of organized crime within Nigeria as part of a worldwide commerce in people and drugs, I will examine in the next chapter. Another is the repressive quality of the Nigerian military government, which has been the target of large-scale protest within the country, but which so far has resisted every attempt to replace it. Several of the Nigerians interviewed specifically mentioned the political situation in their country as a reason for emigrating. One man said that "the political situation" was his motivation for emigrating, while another responded that he left Nigeria to seek greater political freedom. Another said he left to avoid a difficult or dangerous situation. One Nigerian factory worker with whom I conducted an in-depth interview told me, "When the political situation changes in my country, that is when I will consider going back." One man summed up the situation eloquently: "Nigeria is bad, man."

The third factor linked to the Nigerian immigration to Italy is the rise and fall of oil prices and their social impact. Everyone of the Nigerians interviewed had arrived since 1985, the year of the coup d'etat that brought the military government of General Babangida to power just after Babangida's predecessor had rejected the draconian terms of a $2 billion IMF structural adjustment loan (a 50 percent devaluation, a rise in the local price of gasoline and opening up to trade and foreign investment). The first major flow of Nigerians took place between 1987 and 1989, with the majority of interviewees arriving in that period. This followed the oil price collapse of early 1986, which ended the 1970s-era oil boom that had provided the resources for the building of infrastructure, hospitals, schools and universities, while at the same time driving local subsistence agricultural, fishing, and trade activity into crisis. The Mobil Oil refinery on the Atlantic Coast near the junction with the Qua River ruined the local fishing industry and eliminated an important local source of protein. Further, land use patterns have been severely disrupted, not only by oil spills onto crop land, but also by the absolute priority given by law for land use by oil interests, including the right to immediately take possession of land even before allowing for the harvesting of crops in the field.[33] The lowering of oil prices dealt a devastating blow to a region already economically disoriented by the dominance of oil. Many local businesses were dependent indirectly on the oil industry or at least on the circulation of the wealth and social spending generated by oil production and the revenue that came from it. Thus 13 of the 19 (including three in-depth interviews) respondents in this study described themselves as small business people or traders before migrating. More than half had families with a background in agriculture.

The fourth horseman of the Nigerian diaspora is the structural adjustment program that was imposed in early 1986, after the Babangida coup and the oil price drop. The military government, the oil price fall, the SAP as well as the subsequent migration are all different facets of the same process of expropriation. In this sense Nigeria shares the general fate of the oil-exporting countries. In order to fully appreciate how these various forces are linked, it is necessary to reconstruct the political events which at both the local and global levels caused huge shifts in the organization of wealth production and circulation in the mid-1980s and early 1990s. For the following analysis, I rely on the work of the Midnight Notes Collective published in the volume *Midnight Oil: Work, Energy, War 1973–1992*, which I participated in producing.[34]

The 1970s had seen a rise of investment in capital-intensive industries as a response to the profits crisis and the wage demands of industrial workers from the mid-1960s to the mid-'70s, but after the Iranian Revolution and the initial price boom immediately following it, oil prices began to level off in early 1980, falling slightly in 1982. But the price dropped severely in 1985-86 when Saudi Arabia abruptly doubled its oil production during a period of a few months.[35] This action by Saudi Arabia was itself linked to the United States' de facto 50-percent devaluation of the dollar in the same period. Despite the official mythologies of the independence of national banks, the international financial community has shown that it responds to social conflicts, most recently in the bailout of the Mexican peso in 1994 following the Zapatista uprising in Chiapas. The dollar had been held high by Federal Reserve policy, which seems almost certainly to have intended to bring about a recession, which in fact immediately preceded and overlapped the election of Ronald Reagan. The high interest rates had, among other things, dramatically and exponentially increased the amount of foreign debt owed by Third World countries, debt which had to repaid in dollars. By 1981 interest rates had reached 21 percent. Combined with declining prices for the basic commodities, which were their primary sources of income, the interest rates meant that many countries were unable to repay their debts. Between 1982 and 1984, 66 countries were forced to agree to IMF structural adjustment programs. The rescheduling of debt and its multiplication during this period meant that even when interest rates fell back close to earth again following the Mexican debt crisis—indeed precisely in response to this crisis—most Third World countries were hopelessly locked into a cycle of debt repayment and SAP programs.

These programs inevitably led to a series of serious social conflicts in almost every country that imposed them.[36] But it was the mass movement in South Africa against the apartheid state in 1985, and the subsequently announced moratorium on debt payments to foreign banks by the South African government in August 1985, which led promptly to the dollar devaluation. This devaluation, decided upon in New York's Plaza Hotel on September 22, 1985 at the meeting of the finance ministers and central bankers of the then G-5, was meant to prevent the South African regime's collapse, and even more importantly to eliminate the possibility that other nations would follow the South African example and relieve themselves of the impossible burden of endless debt payments by simply stopping the payments altogether. Saudi Arabia began to increase oil production, eventually doubling it within a nine-month period, and offering a $2.50 per barrel discount in September 1985, simultaneous with the devalution of the dollar.[37] The real price of oil fell to below its pre-1973 level, due to the combined 50-percent dollar devaluation (oil is always valued in, and bought and sold, only in dollars), and the 50-percent fall in the price of oil. This oil price fall, as Professor Caffentzis has painstakingly showed, probably saved the U.S. economy, and the second Reagan Administration, from a recession in 1986–1987.[38] The price of oil fell below $10 by the summer of 1986.

The effect of this price fall on the economies of the oil-producing states was devastating. Most were de facto bankrupted:

some like Venezuela, Algeria ,and Nigeria were forced into accepting structural adjustment programs; the period of perestroika in the Soviet Union arose at this time, amounting to an attempt to carry out similar restructuring without falling under the IMF's control—an effort that was subsequently abandoned under Yeltsin; Libya was bombed by the United States and Iran bribed with missiles to prevent these states from attempting to challenge the new oil price conditions within OPEC.[39] In Nigeria, the newly installed dictatorship of Babangida, faced with the IMF's insistence on the conditionalities that the Buhari government had rejected but faced also with popular protest, called for "a national debate on the IMF." The Nigerian people responded with a massive outpouring of opposition to the IMF loan and its conditionalities: demonstrations, publications, academic meetings. As Professor C. George Caffentzis has described it, "From the palm wine bars to the most decorous policy-making institutes, from the yam farms to the factories of Ikeja, there was an almost universal rejection of the 'death pill': the IMF loan and its conditionalities."[40] Babangida, fearing for the survival of his government, publicly rejected the IMF loan in December 1985. In January and February the price of oil fell more rapidly, and imports to Nigeria stopped entirely, based on its rejection of the IMF conditionalities. In April 1986, with an IMF team due in Lagos for a meeting with the government, protests against a feared government betrayal were met with the massacre of at least twenty students and residents at Ahmadu Bello University and a nearby village, carried out by an elite "kill and go" police squad. Subsequently, students rebelled in cities around the country, more were killed by police, though in some cities, police barracks were burnt, prisons opened and their inmates freed, and the Nigeria Labour Congress called a general strike on June 4. Only Babangida's threat to impose martial law calmed the protests.

By the late 1980s, with the migration to Italy already established, the devaluations of the Nigerian naira had in effect tripled the foreign debt in local currency.[41] Privatizations of land, elimination of subsidies on fertilizers and other agricultural inputs, and the encouragement of agribusiness continued the pressure on the local rural economy.[42] The massive pro-democracy movement in Nigeria in the early to mid-1990s, including a three-month long national general strike, failed to remove the increasingly repressive military government. Several interviewees mentioned the execution of Ken Saro-Wiwa in November 1995 as an example of why going home was not yet a possibility. Since, as we have seen, most of the Nigerians in Italy have come from the Niger River Delta region, they would not be unaware of the Ogoni struggle led by Saro-Wiwa, nor of the effects of oil multinationals on the local economy and environment. Saro-Wiwa called Nigeria a "modern slave state" and its rulers "indigenous colonizers."[43] Yet the repression in Nigeria in turn serves a program of privatization and wholesale theft of public wealth, and a deterioration in Nigerian living conditions, which has taken a similar form to that in other countries undergoing structural adjustment. The large-scale resistance in Nigeria has called forth a very serious political repression. The combination, along with the continued imbalance of the local southern Nigerian economy by oil production and dependence, has given way to a new Nigerian diaspora, as many Ibo, Yoruba, and other southern Nigerians become workers of the world.

Senegal

The Senegalese in Italy are almost all Mouride Muslims. The Mourides are a Sufi Muslim brotherhood founded in 1886 by Amadu Bamba, based upon reverence for and service to the marabout teachers and leaders and on a theology that glorifies work.[44] They are the predominant religious affiliation among the Wolof, who constitute the overwhelming majority of the Senegalese immigrants in Europe. Ottavia Schmidt di Friedberg estimates that 90 percent of the Senegalese in Italy are Wolof, and cites social workers' estimates that this group constitutes at least two-thirds of all Senegalese in Italy.[45] One research study found that 75 percent of the Senegalese in Milan were Wolof. Studies of Brescia and Pavia found that the majority of Senegalese migrants came from near Touba, the holy city of the Mouride brotherhood; a 1991 study of Milan found a majority from near Touba.[46] Of the 47 Senegalese interviewed for this study, 35 reported being from the area around the city of Touba. Eight others, including six who claimed the region near Dakar as their home, were from outside this region, while the remaining four were from an area bounded by Thies, Touba, and Louga. Forty of the 47 listed peanut growing as one of their family's main occupations.

The Mourides have long been central to peanut production, the main export crop of Senegal (accounting for over a fourth of the national total, and over two-thirds in the largest producing regions), and it was the brotherhood and its ability to mobilize large-scale labor power which enabled the French colonialists to institute peanut production over a wide zone of the Senegalese interior.[47] The peanut, Jean Suret-Canale, tells us came with the railroad to West Africa. The need for village residents to pay taxes and to purchase clothes and other necessities, which had previously been made by local craftspeople now ruined by French competition, meant that the previous crop rotation was altered to increasingly make room for peanuts for export.[48] By 1909 around 60 percent of all West African peanut exports went to France, of which Senegalese production accounted for nearly three-quarters.[49] But the production of peanuts was plagued by a general shortage of available land and especially labor power, by a very low Senegalese yield—one ton per hectare, compared with double or triple that in other areas—and by the methods of cultivation. Due to the extreme and, according to Suret-Canale, increasing poverty of the Senegalese farmers as they became more fully immersed in peanut production, they relied on a very restricted set of tools and lacked both animal power and fertilizer.[50] The land and labor shortages were due to the continuing importance of communal land holdings and to the rural population's relative self-sufficiency for food production. The latter was gradually undermined by the advent of peanut cultivation: rice imports from French Southeast Asian colonies already amounted to 29,000 tons by 1915.[51] But peanut production did not become a monoculture under French rule. Instead, until independence, it was generally mixed with millet production for home consumption. The low yields were a problem until the post-independence Senegalese government subsidized seeds and fertilizer, though they were in part an inevitable result of the deforestation, which came with peanut export production and which was later exacerbated by Mouride production methods.

The peanut economy, and the French military breaking of the warrior castes which had previously dominated Wolof society, led to a weakening of the extended family, the village community and the reciprocal ties, which had exploited but also protected and sustained the working population. In this crisis of the social fabric at the end of the 19th century, Mouridism presented itself as a new social tie binding the various former classes of Wolof society on a new reciprocal basis through submission to the Marabout (or Serign)—the Sufi master—and through agricultural work, which led to salvation.[52] The acceptance of Amadu Bamba's leadership by Shaykh Ibra Fall, a former warrior, led many of the former ruling class to accept Mouride organization as a replacement for the social fabric which had been ripped apart by French rule and the export economy. For ex-slaves, the expression of the dignity of, and salvation through, agricultural labor, and of the protection and blessing by the Sufi leader, meant that the brotherhood held the attraction of a social bond that was reciprocal and protective, but on a less openly exploitative basis than the previous Wolof system. The French authorities were at first concerned about the potential threat of such a movement, which by 1912 already counted at least 80,000 members,[53] and they exiled Amadu Bamba twice. But after the start of the First World War, they came to see the potential usefulness of the Marabout hierarchy, which could guarantee peanut production and even military recruitment in wartime. The brotherhood was afterward encouraged by the French colonial government.[54] Mouride work groups, called *dara's*, under the leadership of a Marabout, began to colonize the forest areas of the Senegalese interior, cutting down trees (and thereby severely undermining soil fertility and stability). By the late 1950s, the Mourides accounted for about one-eighth of the Senegalese population, and one-fourth of peanut production.[55]

Mouride organization is both hierarchical and reciprocal, with unquestioning submission to the will and teachings of the Sufi master, in exchange for his blessing (*baraka*) and material aid, the basis of both social organization and ideology. One part of the *talibé*'s (member, or student) obligation to the Marabout is a type of corveé labor called Tukket, which involves work, usually on Wednesdays, on the Sufi master's fields.[56] The dara, then, is both the principle historical means of Mouride colonization and settlement, and the main organization of collective labor. It is therefore the main means of Marabout enrichment as well. After Senegalese independence the Sufi leaders had become among the largest landholders and richest individuals in the country.[57]

After independence, the Senegalese ruling "socialist" Party developed an unwritten alliance with the Marabout (the leaders of the brotherhood and the large landowners among the otherwise small farmer Mouride population) based on peanut export. In recent years, however, the relationship has been strained, with the Mouride cultivation practices criticized for soil exhaustion and deforestation as well as for their concentration of holdings of national land and commercial interests. The material basis of this break was a structural adjustment program implemented with extraordinary rapidity in 1984, which cut government subsidies to crucial agricultural inputs such as fertilizers, essential to sustain the peanut monoculture. As international terms of trade for peanuts worsened, the government was willing to listen to the IMF and World Bank. One of the SAP's goals was to increase export production—primarily peanuts—despite the country's excessive dependence on this product and the ecological damage already done. The SAP further encouraged the rise of agribusiness for agricultural export production, exacerbating the already serious food shortages, and therefore driving up imports.[58] But for small farmers, the loss of the fertilizer subsidies for a cash crop that exhausts the soil, was the final blow for many. Abdoulaye Ndiaye writes,

Senegalese farmers were unprepared to do without the agricultural inputs . . . that had been provided by the state. With the government out of the seed distribution business, farmers were left on their own for obtaining key inputs. Given their low income levels, the challenge has been difficult, if not impossible to meet.

For the entire agricultural sector, the use of fertilizer, which averaged 100,000 tons per year before the policy-reform program started, declined to less than 25,000 tons in 1989. Fertilizer subsidies were eliminated, leading to a five-fold price increase. . . . Of the 1,700 collection points established for peanut commercialization identified in 1984, only 750 remained by 1988-89.[59]

This crisis of peanut farming is directly responsible for the collective choice of migration by Mouride members. The principal historian of the brotherhood writes, "Agrarian crisis in northern Senegal has prompted beleaguered Mouride disciples to seek economic salvation in the town."[60] One interviewee explained to me that the capital city of Dakar had grown to become a very large city due to the migration of people fleeing the peanut/agricultural crisis, but that in Dakar there wasn't work enough for everyone. Others said they had migrated from Senegal due to a natural disaster, refering to the lack of rain, "non piove più": it doesn't rain anymore, one told me. But this natural disaster, is in large part a result of long-term deforestation leading to drought. It was greatly worsened by farmers' inability to use fertilizer to revitalize the earth somewhat, and by the changed marketing policies of the government cited above. One said, "Earlier, I worked just fine in Senegal. But things failed in 1982, the politics and economics changed, everything changed." (my translation from Italian). This migration, first to the cities of Senegal and the subsequent growth of Mouride commercial activity, is the background to the international migration, first to France and more recently to Italy. As a result, the Mourides have become an international commercial network stretching from the West Side of Manhattan to Italy to Dakar. At the same time, the brotherhood has become the basis of community for migrant men who spend years in the country of arrival, traveling home for a month or two every couple of years.[61] Whereas the Ghanaians often consist of married couples and even their children (though they usually have large extended families dependent on their remittances), the Senegalese community in Italy is 90 percent male, of whom virtually all have wives and children in Senegal who depend on the remittances sent from men working in the Italian factories.

The Philippines

The Filipina community in Italy, unlike many of the previously discussed migrant groups, consists predominantly of

women, working in almost every case as domestic workers—
cleaning homes, cooking, and caring for old and young in an Italy
whose population is increasingly ageing. This is a migration
organized more actively by the Philippine state and the Catholic
Church. The Philippine government's foreign debt, run up during
the Marcos dictatorship, became an excuse to export female labor
power. The Aquino government increased its encouragement of
migration in order to use hard currency from remittances to cover
the debt problem, and the number of Filipino/a emigrants rose
from 440,500 per year from 1982–1985 under Marcos to 637,300
per year from 1986–1989, mostly under Aquino. In 1988, with
the foreign debt at just under $3 billion, remittances by overseas
Filipino/a workers amounted officially to $856.8 million or 28.7
percent of the debt total and 12 percent of exports.[62]

The experiences of the Filipina interviewees were in keeping
with the findings of most of the literature on Filipina immigration.
All had completed high school, in accord with findings that most
migrants are not from the poorest parts of the country, such as
Mindanao, but rather from well-educated or highly skilled
backgrounds from a wide variety of zones, mostly from Luzon.[63]
Geographic similarity in this case results more from the
organization of migrant women's social networks than from any
particular geographic concentration of the effects of structural
adjustment. Rather, as in the examples we have seen of other
national migrant groups, these effects, while impacting the
majority of the population, have hit certain groups hard in such a
way that they have seen migration as a means to restore the
possibility of their own social reproduction. Female teachers,
nurses, office workers, technicians, engineers, doctors and
scientists have dominated the Filipina migration, seeking wage
levels that would make it possible to remit sufficient money to
keep families and children afloat, or to start a business or buy a
house upon returning home.[64] Of the ten Filipina women
interviewed with questionnaires, and two others interviewed in-
depth, five were trained nurses, two teachers, one a health
technician, one a university graduate chemist, one an office
worker, and the other two unemployed high school graduates. All
worked in Italy as domestic employees.

Their migration reflects conditions in the Philippines both of deteriorating standards of living for well-educated (as well as, obviously, for less well-educated) workers as well as changes in land tenure. With land concentration worsened under the Marcos, a process furthered by World Bank policies, as Walden Ballo and others have shown, many rural families have divided land holdings among sons and encouraged daughters to obtain a higher educational and skill level.[65] As in Africa, therefore, we do not necessarily have a complete gap between a middle class of educated workers and the rest of the working population. Indeed, the need to have at least one child well-educated and able to command a salary sufficient to help meet the needs of even an extended network of families, as well as perhaps contribute to the schooling of other children in the family, is common to many parts of the Third World. The effect of the first IMF-imposed devaluations in the early 1970s under the Marcos dictatorship, drove much of the population into crisis.[66] Emigration from the Philippines, by now a planetary phenomenon, grew substantially in this period. After the Aquino government took power, policy continued to be based on IMF and World Bank prescriptions—not surprisingly, considering that key economic positions, including control of the central bank, went to former IMF employees.[67] James Goodno has, in great eyewitness detail, demonstrated how recent policies have emphasized repayment of the debt, favored export production by multinationals, and ruined the economic interests of farmers, workers, professionals and small business people.[68] The movement around the planet of Filipinas, in response to the needs created by structural adjustment in their home country, has created a diaspora that is circulating a widespread political experience unafraid of challenging exploitative relations on whatever continent it finds them.

Yugoslavia

Thirty-six of the interviewees were from the ex-Yugoslavia. The means by which they identified themselves leaves some confusion about nationality and religious affiliation, since the response "Serbia," "Bosnia," "Yugoslavia," or "Croatia," leaves unsaid which part (I intentionally avoid the inappropriate term "ethnicity" in discussing Yugoslav matters here) of the population the interviewee identifies with. Similarly, the response regarding nationality, "Bosnian" or "Serbian" and so forth, leaves geographic origin uncertain. Nevertheless, interviews revealed data that allow us to understand the origins of the current migration. Not surprisingly, virtually all interviewees from the ex-Yugoslavia responded that they had left because of the civil war. One difference between all the migration communities from Eastern Europe and other groups of migrants was that they returned home less often and expressed less interest in eventually leaving to return to their place of birth. Three Bosnian Serb men whom I interviewed told me they had left when the United States, officially intervening to end the fighting, had bombed their homes—"We don't have anything to return to," they explained. The large majority of ex-Yugoslav migrants came from working class families, with construction trades and factory work being predominant. Indeed, the urban nature of the war, and the extent to which the economic crisis preceding it affected urban workers, define the origins of the ex-Yugoslav migration to Italy.

Ignored by most commentaries, whether of the mass media or of published accounts of the war, was the extent to which the late civil war in Yugoslavia was a foreseeable result of a draconian structural adjustment program, one likely intended to destroy the country's Communist Party government and its "socialist" economy. Michel Chossudovsky has retraced the steps of the IMF effort to restructure Yugoslavia and its violent results:

Macro-economic restructuring applied in Yugoslavia under the neoliberal policy agenda had unequivocally contributed to the destruction of an entire country. Yet since the onset of war in 1991, the central role of macro-economic reform had been carefully overlooked and denied by the global media. The "free market" had been presented as the solution. . . . The social and political impact of economic restructuring in Yugoslavia had been carefully erased from our social consciousness and collective understanding of "what actually happened." Cultural, ethnic and religious divisions were highlighted, presented dogmatically as the sole cause of the crisis when in reality they were the consequences of a much deeper process of economic and political fracturing. . . . The ruin of an economic system, including the take-over of productive assets, the extension of markets and "the scramble for territory" in the Balkans constitute the real cause of the conflict.[69]

Unlike Chossudovsky, however, we can trace the roots of the Yugoslav crisis further back than to the 1980s, for the country's economic exposure to IMF rule had begun in the mid-to-late 1960s, when a series of devaluations and partial marketization were required in exchange for debt rescheduling, along with a political thawing to the West.[70] As we saw in chapter 2, hundreds of thousands of Yugoslavs worked outside their home country already by 1973. With the eventual preference by European receiving states for migrants from Third World countries, this earlier Yugoslav migration reached its numerical limit by the early 1970s. The flow, which began in the early 1990s, mainly toward Germany and Italy, came under the rubric of a refugee flow and developed as one of the effects of the Yugoslav civil war. Yet the categorical difference between economic immigrants and political refugees is an artificial distinction not corresponding to real conditions.[71] In this case, and in the cases of Somalia and Rwanda as well,[72] the war that created refugees stems from the same moving forces which led to the "economic" migrations of Senegalese, Nigerians, Filipinas, and Ghanaians. We should perhaps discuss the political origins of economic migrations, given that today, as in the nineteenth century that Karl Polanyi and Karl Marx wrote about, the free market and its economic consequences are the result of real political choices and policies. These policies are put into place by a limited number of institutions that represent the interests at the global level of a few major nation states and multinational corporations and banks. The four horsemen of the Apocalypse, known in dramatic lore and biblical study as Famine, Plague, War, and Death, today take similar forms throughout the Third World and the former "socialist" countries. The angels who come as their heralds carry briefcases and wear three-piece suits and the seven scrolls have written on them the IMF conditionalities that spell out the arrival of the horsemen to many a debt-ridden country. Their instrument is structural adjustment, and in Yugoslavia, as elsewhere, it has been a pitiless judge of sins.

From 1966 to 1979, Yugoslavia had averaged 7.1 percent industrial growth annually. Following the first round of new economic reform imposed by the IMF in order to satisfy foreign commercial creditors, and to accord with National Security Decision Directive 52 of the United States (at the time secret, since partially declassified) calling for "an expanded effort to promote a 'quiet revolution' to overthrow Communist governments and parties," industrial growth fell to 2.8 percent from 1980-1987.[73] It fell to zero the following year and by 1990 stood at -10.6 percent. The economic reform had wrecked the economy in the course of a few years.[74] By 1989, currency devaluation and price deregulation led to an inflation rate of 2,700 percent. A financial aid package was promised the country by the United States and international financial agencies in exchange for a wage freeze (with inflation at nearly 3,000 percent), the end of social-worker ownership of enterprises and large cuts in government expenditures. The first of these meant deprivation, the second expropriation, and the third that the transfer payments by the federal state to the various regional states would be drastically reduced just as privatization was coming into effect in conditions of austerity. One could hardly think of a better recipe to trigger a scramble for the suddenly scarce resources among different regions under these conditions. Civil war became thinkable precisely after this round of conditionalities.[75]

This economic package went into effect in January 1990, and included the liberalization of interest rates, the rechanneling of transfer payments by the federal republic to the states to be used instead for debt repayment, reductions on import controls and a series of currency devaluations, with the dinar pegged to the deutschmark. As a result, real wages fell 41 percent in the first half of 1990, and inflation that year stood at 70 percent. Following a devaluation in 1991, inflation rose to 140 percent in 1991, 931 percent in 1992 and 1,134 percent in 1993.[76] The cut from the federal budget of over 5 percent of the country's entire GDP, and the use of money's formerly channeled toward the local states by the federal government for foreign debt repayment, meant, as Chossudovsky titles it, "a state of de facto secession." The federal system had in effect been abolished by the IMF conditionalities without replacing it with any other means of redistributing resources. In addition, within two years of the implementation of the IMF conditionalities of 1990, 1,137 firms, formerly employing over 600,000 workers in a total workforce of 2.7 million were closed by new bankruptcy requirements that were part of the structural adjustment program. In 1990, 20 percent of the employed workforce went unpaid as worker-owned firms now exposed to the new regulations tried to stave off bankruptcy.[77]

To be sure, that nationality-based civil war was the horrific denoument to this process of adjustment involves a highly mediated and complex set of factors. In a collection of writings by Yugoslav journalists, many as critical of the Tito regime as of those which followed it and split up the country, the theme of opportunistic fomenting of national hatred by certain politicians and parties as their solution to the crisis in the midst of a free-for-all over dividing up federal resources is unmistakable.[78] Yet this opportunism, playing on potential, but not necessarily active, faultlines within various republics, also played along with policies formulated in the West. In December 1990, the Central Intelligence Agency reported that Yugoslavia would fall apart within 18 months from ethnic conflict.[79] Slobodan Milosevic and Franjo Tudjman, the ultra-nationalist leaders of Serbia and Croatia, respectively, both utilized their parties' local control of the media to demonize opponents and each others' nationals, in a sort of macabre dance that reinforced the power and influence of both by providing each with a demonizable enemy.[80] Yugo-slavism, or the idea of a federated multinational republic, was a popular idea until the confluence of economic hardship, the post-1974 fragmentation of decentralized management resulting from devolution reforms, and the deliberate fostering of national hatred by well-organized political machines anxious to maximize their resources under the conditions of the 1980s and 1990s made a break up thinkable. Mirko Tepavac argues that "only a few years before fighting broke out in 1991, Yugoslavism, or more precisely the principle of a Yugoslav federation, would have won a majority in any honest referendum in all the republics and autonomous provinces, without exception." Blaming the lack of democracy, rather than any endemic national hatred, for making possible the fostering of ultra-nationalism, Tepavac concludes, "But it was not Tito who murdered Yugoslavia. The murderers are among us."[81] From a very different perspective, Slavo Radosevic likewise argues that "A rational observor could have found plenty of evidence to show that a human tragedy on such a scale was unthinkable."[82] Radosevic argues against any monocausal view that accepts as given that ethnic, religious, or national hatreds were the reality behind the war: "The most common monocausal explanation is the one which sees the Yugoslav conflict as a problem of historically embedded hatred. Scheirup calls it the 'pressure cooker' approach: the social explosion is to be explained in terms of totalitarian regimes suppressing historical, culturally grounded conflicts which erupt when the 'lid' is lifted as a result of 'democratisation.'"[83] For Radosevic, this assumption of longstanding, deep-seated national hatred boiling over as soon as the 'lid' was lifted is "fundamentally wrong."[84] Like Tepavac, Radosevic stresses the manipulation of insecurities and fears in the context of the growing crisis of the late '80s and early '90s:

> The question is especially intriguing if we take into account that *"historically rooted hatred" was not the outcome of the everyday experience of millions of inhabitants of Yugoslavia before 1991.* In a matter of months, however, the dynamic of conflict created a situation in which different ethnic identities became sharply polarized, and everything that had been shared was forgotten. *This could not have happened if it had not been for systematic daily attacks on people's perceptions of 'others'. In Bosnia especially,* where ethnic cultures were not geographically segregated, *new identities could be generated only by systematically imposed "forgetting" or by systematic terror.*[85] (Emphasis added.)

Susan L. Woodward, while de-emphasizing the premeditated planning by politicians like Milosevic and Tudjman, does agree with Chossudovsky that the roots of the breakup lay in the attempts by military and political authorities to respond to the economic crisis provoked by the policies of international agencies.[86] She writes:

> By 1979, the Yugoslav foreign debt had reached crisis proportions, at about

$20bn, in part as a result of rising Western protectionism, the decline in foreign demand for Yugoslav labour (cutting the contribution of workers' remittances to the covering of the trade deficit from one-half to one-fourth by 1979), and the deteriorating terms of trade for Yugoslav exports. Commercial banks had initially reacted to the Polish debt crisis by stopping all further lending to countries in the area, including Yugoslavia. By 1982 the IMF was taking a much tougher line on conditions for loans, in response to a global debt crisis which had, indeed, resulted from overlending by multinational banks and IMF policy toward newly industrializing countries during the 1970s. The core of this liberal reform for Yugoslavia—a long-term macroeconomic stabilisation programme aimed at cutting domestic demand, labour costs and inflation—was introduced in 1982, in conjunction with yet another conditionality programme of International Monetary Fund (IMF) credits.[87]

These policies, according to Woodward, "exposed all localities, regions and social groups to declining standards of living and rising unemployment; at the same time they exacerbated social differences and inequalities."[88] IMF officials demanded the restriction of the local decentralized economic management embodied in the 1974 constitution, particularly republican control of foreign exchange. This meant a serious reversal of local control by the central state, making independence increasingly thinkable: "The changes in the pattern of federal-republican relations entailed in the reform programme appeared, moreover, to deprive the republics and provinces of the soveriegnty over economic resources that they had gained between 1968 and 1978."[89] As foreign capital flowed into Slovenia and Croatia, these republics were threatened with the loss of any control over foreign currency. Meanwhile, in poorer republics, the IMF-imposed programs were leading to greater impoverishment and underdevelopment:

The combination of an economic policy aimed at promoting exports to Western markets and declining domestic investment in transport, construction and industries such as mining, timber and heavy industry, were leading to deindustrialisation in the poor interior of Croatia and Bosnia and Hercegovina, areas which also happened to be ethnically mixed. The near collapse of markets in the Middle East as a result of the Iran-Iraq war and in the eastern CMEA bloc was disasterous, particularly for the economies of Macedonia and Bosnia and Hercegovina. Legislation to privatise firms and end the system of workers' self-management and protected employment in order to encourage foreign investment brought the first mass layoffs due to bankruptcy in forty years, beginning in Montenegro. When the largest firms of the republics of

Serbia (Smederevo, steel), Croatia (INA, oil), and Bosnia and Hercegovina (the Agrokomerc food-processing conglomerate) were threatened with bankruptcy, and as the banking system attempted to socialise the debt among its members, a banking crisis began to engulf most firms in all republics, followed by a political crisis for republican politicians. Hard-pressed republican parliaments instigated tax rebellions, refusing to pay their federal obligations. They increasingly opposed any loss of governmental rights *vis-a-vis* the economy in the name of marketisation and, *by October 1987, were coming to reject the explicit political conditionality for IMF and World Bank loans that required radical economic reform, functional integration of the country and effective federal power.*

By 1988, the country was experiencing a social upheaval of revolutionary proportions as a result of the economic hardships occasioned by the debt-repayment stabilisation programme and the resulting ceiling on upward social mobility, the stricter criteria for employment in the public sector and the rising level of internal economic migration. *Growing resentments over competition for jobs, unemployment and declining status and income found expression in anger at people and regions considered, 'less efficient'*, at the country's system of proportional representation to protect national equality, at women and minorities, and at the privileges of party members or holders of foreign currency bank accounts. Young people started to play with right-wing symbols and ideas and, particularly in Slovenia and Croatia, developed links with anti-communist movements in East European countries. Growing activism on the part of the churches also introduced an external influence, since the major religions of the country were international and internationally organised: Roman Catholicism, Eastern Orthodoxy and Islam.[90] (Emphasis added.)

As this crisis grew, foreign governments intervened on the side of one or the other of the national minorities in the increasingly conflictual republics. The United States, European governments and the Vatican and other religious authorities all spoke out on behalf of various groups or republics against others or the central government. In March 1991, the European Parliament resolved that "the constituent republics and autonomous provinces of Yugoslavia must have the right freely to determine their own future in a peaceful and democratic manner and *on the basis of recognized international and internal borders*" (emphasis added).[91] "At least as consequential as the growing support for Slovene and Croatian independence" writes Woodward, "was the declining foreign support for the federal government."[92] Foreign government interpretations of the crisis, international agency-imposed austerity, economic hardship, and the opportunist fomenting of national hatred as part of a strategy to gain advantage in a deteriorating situation characterized by revolt, competition and rending of the social fabric—all played a role in the destruction of Yugoslavia and the onset of war.

Many of the immigrants in the Veneto were opposed to the war and had fled to avoid military service. Since the various republics made it illegal to avoid the draft, many now cannot return. Others had expressed dismay at the ultra-nationalist ideological basis of the war. War refugees in other parts of the world have expressed similar views. "I was raised to judge people for what they are and what they do, as individuals not as members of religious or ethnic groups," wrote one Sarajevan in exile in a recent collection of refugees' comments.[93] Another wrote:

I was born in Sarajevo in 1965. My father was Jewish and my mother is Croatian Catholic. None of this seemed of any importance a few years ago in Bosnia-Herzegovina or anywhere else in the former Yugoslavia. Maybe I was wrong. Unfortunately, now it is very important.

Friends always came to our house. We liked them not because of their religion or nationality, but because they were true friends, or at least good people. That is what my partents taught me, and what I still believe in.[94]

Yet another wrote, "My father was a Serb, my mother a Muslim. For as long as I can remember, they declared themselves to be Yugoslavs. I myself prefer not to be considered a member of any of the world's tribes."[95] Finally, another Sarajevan expresses a sense of the multinationality of Yugoslav culture whose destruction was caused by war, rather than the other way around:

We knew that we belonged to different ethnic and religious groups, *but there were no divisions between us, no hatred among us*. We lived together happily, and never thought that it should be any different. And we were Serbs, Croats, Muslims, Jews and others, particularly the offspring of so-called mixed marriages, like myself. We all shared our youth, our interests, problems, passions, often *without even knowing each other's nationality or religion*.[96]

The civil war was an avoidable disaster that became thinkable and possible under the conditions imposed by structural adjustment. The postwar involvement of the IMF and World Bank in the so-called reconstruction of the economies of the ex-Yugoslavian states has involved the fire sale of large parts of the

Yugoslav economy to foreign investors and a Bosnian constitution in which the first governor of the central bank is appointed by the IMF directly and "shall not be a citizen of Bosnia-Herzogovina or a neighboring state."[97] Small wonder why Yugoslav migrants in Italy express little interest in returning, regardless of their region of origin. Their refusal to participate in a war that did not serve their own or their country's interests but protected those of international elites and of opportunistic nationalist politicians— itself part of the antiwar effort that was present in each and every republic—is testimony to the, for now, wrecked hopes of Yugoslav nationalism and socialism. Those hopes seem dead for the foreseeable future, but, like Yugoslavia itself, they didn't jump to their deaths, they were pushed. Indeed, it was precisely those who had sought to stop the war and to bring down the Milosevic government that bore the brunt of a NATO assault intended to destroy the infrastructure of a people committed to maintaining their industrial and subsistence levels without surrender to Western pressure. As The *New York Times* reported on September 17, 1999:

It is not only milk that is in short supply. Gasoline, whether in state-run gas stations or on the black market, is also hard to find and has doubled in price in the last two weeks. The currency, the Yugoslav dinar, has slipped further in the past weeks, trading on the black market at 13 to the German mark, from 12 just a week ago, more than double the official rate...For many people, tired and worried about the winter, the last thing they want is unrest. Many of them took to the streets every night for three months in the winter of 1996-97 to persuade Mr. Milosevic to install the democratic municipal governments that had won the 1996 elections. Eventually he relented, *and the opposition—while functioning in some cities, notably many of those worst damaged by NATO's bombs this spring—disintegrated.*[98]

It is likely that under such conditions, migration will seem to increasing numbers of Yugoslavs as a means to deal with the hardships of life under such conditions in the post-NATO attack Yugoslavia.

Albania

The Albanian immigration to Italy has arrived in two waves:

in March 1991, when the country opened its borders and its economy to Western-sponsored restructuring; in spring 1997, when a series of pyramid schemes brought about the bankruptcy of nearly every household in the country. A seperate migration from Serbia-controlled but ethnically Albanian Kosova is reshaping the Albanian community in Italy. The first migration was linked to an abrupt collapse of the national currency, real wages, and the social safety net, which international financial agencies have insisted be reduced.[99] Most of the migrants interviewed came from either building trades or factory work, and a serious fall in real wages would be a blow to such people. Most Albanians laid the blame on their previous government. One spoke of having been arrested unjustly by the communist regime; another, when asked the question, "When did you first think of emigrating?" responded, "When I saw that our system was an old system" (my translation from Italian).

The interviewees for this study were all arrivals from the period of 1991 and shortly aftewardr. Several ethnic Albanians, who identified themselves as such, arrived from the Serbian-occupied Kosova region, and were therefore technically Yugoslav citizens. Many of their motives for migrating were specifically political, though their relation to the larger Albanian community in Italy is complex. While there is no doubting the unpopularity of the Communist Party-governed ancien regime in Albania, at least according to the Albanians in Italy, their departure from Albania coincided with an economic crisis, which compounded the problems already present due to the previous planned economy by seriously undermining the one attribute of the "socialist" systems that seems to have maintained the support of the population in these countries—guaranteed employment and the social safety net. Economic stability was seriously undermined in Albania by its exposure to world market competition and prices. Exports fell in 1991 to $50 million from $400 million in 1989.[100] The national debt rose at the same time to over $550 million—more than 40 percent of GDP. Between December 1990 and March 1992, inflation ran at 346 percent, while the price of certain consumer necessities rose even higher. A family budget which required 1,300 *leke* in December 1991 needed 4,500 *leke* by March 1992 to obtain the same goods.[101] Medical care cuts meant that though health care was free, it was now necessary to pay for medicines, which either had prohibitive prices or were simply no longer available.[102]

Italy has a history of colonial intervention in Albania. Italian invasion during the Second World War drew Albania into that conflict, and in the wake of fascist collapse, led to Communist Party rule after the war. Italian neo-colonial influence, however, remains significant, both economically and culturally. Over 400 Italian firms now have production facilities in Albania, and Albanians see Italian television transmitted into their homes every evening.[103] The overnight privatization of the economy under the Barisha government in a country previously isolated from market influences, as in Russia and elsewhere, meant that Albanians were both desperate for a way to obtain money quickly, since it had suddenly come to hold an importance in their lives previously unknown, and gullible enough due to lack of experience to fall en masse for the pyramid schemes. Though legally blocked, the flow of Albanians to Italy has continued by illegal methods.

Albanians who stormed the gates of foreign embassies in the summer of 1990 when the right to leave the country was established, and who later sailed en masse across the Adriatic to Italy, expected to find the hospitality that visiting strangers are entitled to according to Albanian cultural standards. Ismail Kadare, one of the country's best-known writers and human rights activists, explains:

to understand the Albanians—even ever so little—one must consider that the arrogance with which they demanded asylum from the embassies is not unrelated to their ancient Code—which despite socialism's attempt to stamp it out, reveals itself from time to time, usually when one least expects it. According to the Code, the owner of a house is obliged to open the door and grant refuge to anyone who knocks at the door. A refusal to open the door would be severely punished. So the old formula, "Do you welcome friends, O master of the house?," now transformed into, "Do you welcome friends, O foreign embassy?," was as commanding as ever for the Albanians. That is also why, after their arrival in the West, Albanian refugees gave the impression at first of being "refugees of a peculiar kind." They were neither obsequious nor grateful; on the contrary, they were rather arrogant and capricious, as the French press in particular remarked. But that was because it seemed to them that in showing hospitality, France, the GDR and all the other countries were simply fulfilling their moral duty, and like friends who had knocked at a door one dark night, these refugees ought to be the object of great respect; and the Marlboro cigarettes that French journalists reproached them for demanding were the least they might expect!

There's no question that this encounter was just one more misunderstanding, added to other tragic misunderstandings which, from age to age, have confronted the Albanian people.[104]

The Italian expulsion of thousands of Albanians in 1991 surely soured relations between the two countries, and the 1997 refusal to allow entry, by blockading the Adriatic—a move which resulted in one collision and at least 100 lost lives—exacerbated this souring of relations. The comments of Italian businessmen on a national talk show television program hosted by the respected journalist Gad Lerner, in which they discussed the ease with which they used Albanian women's need for jobs to get their female employees into bed, enraged Albanian public opinion. When the revolt against the government-sponsored pyramid schemes exploded, Italian-owned factories were attacked by the hastily organized militias and associations that spontaneously organized the uprising. Organized crime gangs were hired by Italian business owners to defend their property. In the end, only a UN intervention led by the Italian military was able to keep the Albanian government in power and protect Italian overseas investments.

The Kosova migration is treated here rather than with the other Yugoslav migrations. This choice is based upon this study's subject matter, which transcends nation-states and instead examines movement, and on the Kosova immigrants' own self-identification as Albanians when asked. Rising against Serbian rule in 1913 and again in 1981, Kosovans have long sought full republic, rather than merely provincial, status in the Yugoslav federation, though virtually all interested parties see this demand as a first step toward reunification with Albania. Many of the Kosovan immigrants were intellectuals who had fled repression by the Serbian government and were working to provide remittance support to what they described as "our government"— meaning the repressed unofficial shadow government of Albanian Kosovans. Kosova has been kept by Serbian rule in conditions of relative underdevelopment and poverty compared with the rest of

Serbia: In 1990 industrial wages averaged $180 monthly compared with $230 for the rest of Yugoslavia, while 51 percent of the population worked in agriculture compared with 38 percent for Yugoslavia as a whole.[105] That intellectuals are a significant part of the emigration is not surprising given employment conditions in Kosova. Unemployment in 1990 stood at 178,000, or three times the number of waged employees in the province. One writer comments, "Even these are mostly administrative employees, so that employment has the nature of bureaucracy, it is unproductive. And you have this enormous number of students—51,000—but maybe the figure is a little exaggerated. Where is this nascent intellectual proletariat to go? A number of Kosovars are now travelling around trying to find jobs in other states of the Federation, or even going to West Germany and other countries abroad."[106]

When young Kosovars rose in revolt in 1981 they were repressed with tanks and machine gun fire. Repression followed. Between 1981 and 1986 150,000 Kosovars were interrogated by police and 7,000 imprisoned. Of 35 executions in Yugoslavia from 1975-1985, 16 were in Kosova.[107] According to Amnesty International, of 594 political arrests in Yugoslavia in 1982, 64 percent were ethnic Albanians.[108] The emigrant Kosovars in Italy therefore take on characteristics of political exiles. College professors, architects, and skilled workers work in blue-collar jobs in Italy, sending remittances to political organizations seeking Kosova independence and spending their spare time organizing conferences and publications over the issue. While in Italy, they have sought to use their political capacity for association to mobilize the Albanian community in Italy against the scourge of criminal organization that exploits Albanians and provides anti-immigration advocates in Italy with arguments for restricting entry.

Unfortunately, this study was completed before the 1999 NATO attack on Yugoslavia, an action characterized by a cynical use of the Kosovar struggle by U.S. foreign policy, the super-session of a genuine popular movement by the much shadier KLA, and by yet another round of hypocritical policy-making toward Albanian refugees by Western European states, Italy included. The Yugoslav and Albanian presences in Italy became factors in Italy's critical public stance toward the war, and therefore a factor in European and NATO policy making. Perhaps more importantly, the Adriatic Sea was permanently damaged as a result of the NATO bombing campaign, a clear message that the corridor between Yugoslavia, Albania and the Italian coast is off limits for purposes of unrestricted migration. Meanwhile, the war was functional to capitalist plans to reorganize the European division of labor with Germany at its center and areas such as Albania, Serbia, and perhaps Southern Italy and Greece as sources of low-wage, flexible labor power.[109]

Romania

The Romanian migration was a response to the collapse of industrial employment which followed on privatization and market reforms. Employment quickly plummeted after 1989, as the guaranteed job of "socialist" bloc days was eliminated. The Romanian immigrants in the Veneto were people who had been deeply affected by these changes. Writing in 1993, an OECD report stated:

Although frequently underestimated abroad, Romania has undertaken major structural reforms over the past three years. . . . Today the legal infrastructure for a market economy has now been largely established, agriculture has been privatised, a private sector is emerging in other sectors, trade has been liberalised and the framework of an ambitious mass privatization programmed is nearly complete. The macroeconomic performance has, however, been disappointing, offsetting these impressive achievements: the collapse in output is now longer and deeper than in most other countries in transition, inflation remains very high and there is a chronic shortage of foreign currency.[110]

All seven of the Romanians interviewed, men and women, had been industrial workers before migrating. A glance at what happened to Romanian industry in the early part of the 1990s under this highly touted reform and privatization program leaves little doubt about motivations for migration (see Table 17).

This is an industrial picture so uniformly bleak as to dwarf the Great Depression. Combined with price increases associated with the lifting of food, raw materials and energy prices in April

Table 17. Index of Industrial Production in Romania
by Sector (1989=100)

	1990	1991	1992
Total Industry	76.3	58.9	51.5

Source: OECD, *Romania: An Economic Assessment* (Paris, 1993).

1991 and on most consumer goods that same July, industrial decline meant that emigration as a means of survival for families of industial workers became a serious option, if not a necessity.

The events of the Romanian Revolution of 1989-1991 make for some of the most extraordinary reading of the century, from the spontaneous joining hands by ethnic Hungarians and Romanians to protect a Protestant minister who opposed the Ceausescu regime in Timisoara to spark the revolt, to the rapid switching of sides by part of the military and secret service to join the revolution, to the startling, uncertain attempt in September 1991 by coal miners to seize state power from the remnants of the Communist elite who governed under the National Salvation Front umbrella. The elite blocking of the effort at a real democratization of Romanian society and their preferred project of "underdevelopment" as an economic strategy since 1989[111] has meant a continuity with the Ceausescu era's imposition of IMF-sought austerity. Industrial workers have paid especially dearly. Ceausescu's was the only government anywhere to have paid off its foreign debt completely, reaching that goal just months before the dictator's execution following his and his wife's secret trial. To accomplish the goal, a level of deprivation was imposed on the nation that had no parallel elsewhere in Eastern Europe. Romania was the most repressively and worst-governed state in the Soviet Bloc.[112] Industrial workers played a key role in bringing down the regime in December 1989, only to be disappointed afterward by economic strategies that meant job loss, austerity and the movement of Romania toward Third World status. Indeed, factory closings and de-industrialization may well have been part of a necessary and conscious strategy to break the hold of workers' councils that had taken over *de facto* management of many industrial enterprises during the revolution. After describing the phases of the late 1980s in which workers began to suspect that austerity was intended to keep the regime in power as much as to pay off the foreign debt, followed by Ceaucescu's increasing distancing of himself and his policies from the working class as a source of state legitimacy, Pasti writes:

The third stage of the process started when the political bureaucracy had to use its power against the working class in order to get from it more work hours in more difficult conditions and for smaller pay, a drastic cut down of individual consumption, and to suppress any attempted protest or rebellion, as were those of the Jiu Valley miners or Brasov workers in 1987. The fourth and last stage was the revolution, in which the workers rose against that power and against the policy it promoted. It was precisely the workers' uprising that led to the victory of the revolution. It was the workers who, on the morning of 22 December, stirred the Bucharest population and ensured the victory of the demonstrations against Ceausescu that had started the day before and had been suppressed by the militia and the army on the night of 21 to 22 December. And what is important is that they started from factories, as workers and not as "simple citizens."

For a short while the victory of the revolution meant the working class' return to power. But it could be a short-lived reality which was anyway running against the current. None of the elites that were poised to compete for the power was willing to accept the working class' sharing in it. The cultural elite would not take it, because it had no connection whatsoever with the working class and would rather ignore its existence. Its projected future of the country, vague when it was not about the role it would play itself, relied on an idyllic image of the Romanian peasant, farming the land and hosting foreign tourists in order to raise the hard currency necessary for imports, while paying little attention to industry and its people. For the industrial technocracy though, the workers had a well-defined place in the technical organization of the production and that was the place as executants, unconditionally obeying by the industrial discipline. It could not think of any reason why it should yield the political power or at least part of it, to the industrial executants.[113]

The policies of de-industrialization,[114] then, were unopposed by the civil society-minded elite while the technocrats and would-be private capitalists sought such policies to break the danger of working-class seizure of political and economic power. This latter was a real threat, and indeed, up through September 1991, it was becoming reality:

The December revolution was termed as an anti-communist revolution. Eventually, things did take that course, toward the dismantlement of all structures and realities that could be considered as specific to communism. But it is doubtful that in December 1989 and even for many weeks after that the workers really wanted to give up communism. If the name is used to define the political and economic regime of Ceaucescu's last years, then the revolution was definitely an anti-communist one, and the workers too, were anti-communist. But if you mean by communism an economic and social system in which the working class shares in the power because it is a working class and not because the workers too, are citizens like all other citizens, then you cannot take the anti-communist character of the revolution for granted. The workers did not rise against a society where the working class is in power. On the contrary, they rebelled against a regime which, although declaring that it ruled in the name of the working class, had left no trace of power for it, having started instead to govern against it. And the workers equated that regime rather with Ceausescuthan with communism itself. What the working class was after in December 1989 and in the next months was rather a comeback to the principles of the ideal communism . . . much, if not the majority of the population regarded the revolution as a way of eliminating Ceausescu, viewed as the source of all evils, as a way of improving the extant socialism rather than of building capitalism.[115]

In an effort to realize this project, workers attempted, through their unions and in many cases through workers' councils, to manage production and the economic life of the country. But the desperate condition of Romanian society, after the years in which Ceausescu had exported almost all production beyond a subsistence level (meat was all but unknown on Romanian tables for years, for instance), and the lack of raw materials and even energy sources (despite having oil, the country imported most of the petroleum it used), meant that overcoming economic chaos was an uphill battle. With the technocracy determined not to cede power to the workers, and working instead to integrate the country more fully into the capitalist world, even if on the basis of exporting raw materials, the battle was probably doomed from the start: "The industrial technocracy was ready to use the trade unions in order to press harder on the administration for a redistribution of some resources to the enterprises' advantage," writes Pasti, " but it was not willing to let the unions control the use of the resources."[116]

As the economy hurtled downward, and the elite moved toward a policy of austerity and restucturing that stressed agricultural and raw material export, the lives of industrial workers worsened. In the first six months of 1991 inflation reached 100 percent, negating the wage gains made by unions and workers' councils.[117] Average monthly wages by the end of the year sufficed only to buy three pairs of shoes or a winter coat. Unemployment doubled to an official figure of 300,000.[118] In September 1991, the miners, previously manipulated by the National Salvation Front government to attack its opponents, marched in the tens of thousands on Bucharest, publicly made peace with the student opposition whom they had beaten a few months earlier, and tried to redeem themselves in the eyes of the nation by taking over state power, albeit in a hesitant, confused manner without a wider political organization linking them to other workers and opponents of the regime. After seizing the Parliament building they were driven from the Presidents' office by the armed forces and retreated. From that point on the fate of Romania's industrial workers was sealed, at least for the immediate future.

Many Romanians began to migrate at this time. One writer estimates at half a million the numbers of Romanians migrating by the end of 1991.[119] Another places the figure closer to 800,000 by late 1990.[120] The sense of disillusionment, despair, and loss of hope engendered by the aftermath of the revolution and the conditions that followed it are made explicit in virtually all accounts of this period. At the same time, the country again fell into debt ($1.7 billion in unpaid debt in 1990–1991)[121] Though the sample for this study is too small to generalize greatly, the fact that all of the Romanians I met in Italy had been industrial workers suggests they are likely well-represented among migrants. That several of the Romanians interviewed identified themselves as communists—usually without being asked—suggests that Pasti's analysis of the aspirations of the Romanians working class may be accurate. Romanians expressed a startling preference for the guarantees, however realized in the breach, of the Communist Party-era over the recent policies of post-Communist era leaders. (These attitudes stood in stark contrast to the bitterness expressed against the Communist era regime by Albanians interviewed.) One man said, "It was better before. You were guaranteed work and enough to eat. Now we have nothing." A young Romanian woman told me, "It was bad before, but these leaders we have now are worse. I see that here in Italy the government helps you. But there they do not help us." These accord with findings that the Romanian people express ambivalence toward the revolution today.[122] One Romanian writer has referred to the post-revolutionary period as "Purgatory."[123] Another analyst of the current post-revolutionary situation finds the likelihood of a "second revolution."[124]

More recently, the Constantinescu government appealed for an IMF loan of $500 million in order to finance a structural adjustment program to liberalize energy prices and the exchange rate, privatizations, and an austerity budget. This request came despite a recently revived 4.4 percent growth rate and an unemployment rate of only 6.4 percent, well under that of almost every Western European nation. The SAP is expected to lead to zero growth and 12 percent unemployment.[125] The Romanian emigration continues, and the Romanian capital of Bucharest has become one of organized crime's centers for the flow of undocumented persons across Europe.[126]

Predictions of more revolutionary activity proved correct. In 1999 miners made yet another attempt to seize state power, and were suppressed at the gates of the capital by military force. Like Yugoslavia and Albania, Romania may see more of its citizens attempt migration as a solution to problems created by the increasingly repressive and violent "transition to capitalism."

Morocco

The Moroccan migration to Italy at first sight appears more than any other to be merely a continuation of a longstanding and massive migration chain dating from the 1960s. Even upon closer observation, some of the conditions leading to migration as a strategy stem from longstanding factors—inequalities in land ownership in certain regions, high unemployment in the cities, and a culture of migration fueled by the existence of a large-scale network of relatives in Europe, the Middle East, and the United States. Nevertheless, the results of the structural adjustment reforms—imposed in three cycles in 1981, 1984 and 1991 and resulting each time in serious rebellions against the increasingly repressive monarchy—have exacerbated the problems of inequality, subsistence, employment, and the lack of political freedom in a way that seems at the very least to provide continued motivation to consider migration due to conditions at home.

An OECD study recently found a close link between trade liberalization and free market policies in Morocco and the migration and remittance flows.[127] It argued, however, that trade liberalization, by stressing export production—which it assumed to be more labor intensive than import-substitution production—created a net increase in employment and therefore reduced the migration flow.[128] The authors at least attempted to trace a link between structural adjustment and migration, their econometric model-based approach shares most of the faults of economic models of migration. Of the 41 Moroccans interviewed for this study, ten (24 percent) had been unemployed in Morocco; 11, or 27 percent, were students, and in some cases arrived in Italy to continue their university studies; the rest had been employed either in urban trades, industry or commerce, or in agriculture. Similarly, one study of Moroccan immigrants in Rome found that 47.1 percent had been students before leaving Morocco, 35.7 percent employed (of whom 20 percent were employed part time) and 14.3 percent had been unemployed.[129] A study of Moroccans in Livorno province found that 26 percent had been unemployed in Morocco, 66 percent had been working, and the other 8 percent had been students and others.[130] Thus, although unemployment seems to be a factor, underemployment seems to be an equally important theme—judging from the large percentage of previous part-time workers found in the Rome study and the fact that students are well represented. This latter group, consisting of would-be professionals and office, technical, and management employees, is not likely be put off migrating by a growth of manual labor-oriented export jobs.

The occupational diversity of Moroccan immigrants before emigrating is so wide that we cannot easily make generalizations about the roots of migration. Almost every economic category seems to be affected. A regional breakdown of the migrants' origin is a surer guide to arriving at a concrete analysis of the migration. Most Moroccans were from urban areas, with

Casablanca dominant; the remainder, about a quarter of the interviewees who responded that they were from rural zones, came from the villages of the agricultural region of central Morocco near Beni Mallal. This region has been recently troubled by drought, but has for longer been troubled by grossly unequal land ownership patterns. Most of the immigrants coming to Italy from Morocco since the 1980s have come from this region.[131] In the Beni Mellal area, 40 percent of the rural working population has less than one-half acre to cultivate—all told this group has access to only 12 percent of the arable land. Less than two percent of the local population has one-fifth of the land in the region. Italy is the destination for 80 percent of the emigrants from this zone.[132]

Casablanca is heavily represented among the emigrants. This city, according to Dal Lago, "Has been transformed, in the course of just a few years, from the port and industrial center, heart of the country, to a typical metropolis of the Third World, in which degraded peripheries grow incessantly, and bidonvilles inhabited by tens of thousands of people surround the old industrial quarters and the new centers."[133] Unemployment for young people in Morocco (ages 15-34) was 51.1 percent for men, 60.7 percent for women in 1992.[134] Students are heavily represented among the migrants, suggesting that they have little likelihood of employment at a professional or highly skilled level in their home country. Even if they found work, the wage levels available to them at the professional level in an economy that has undergone structural adjustment programs for the whole of the 1980s and 1990s are inadequate to survive on, and inferior to wages available abroad for other types of work: "The fifty-thousand lire (about $30) that a cigarette contraband street vendor (or farm worker, or construction laborer) can make in Italy in one day" writes Dal Lago, "is equivalent to the daily salary of university professor or a middle level functionary in Morocco."[135] (My translation from Italian.) The urban population was hard hit by three waves of structural adjustment which involved the lifting of subsidies on basic necessity consumer goods. Three times—in 1981, 1984, and on the eve of the Gulf War—the result was serious urban insurrection.

Since the Treaty of Fez in 1912, which forced an indebted Morocco into a French protectorate, foreign debt has held significant political meaning in Morocco. By 1987, with prices for phosphate—the country's main source of export income—falling on the world market, the World Bank listed Morocco as having a higher long-term debt-to-GNP ratio than even Mexico and Argentina.[136] Indeed, long-term debt was 118 percent of GDP that year, and 30 percent of export earnings went to debt servicing. Morocco was eighth on the list of most heavily indebted countries. This level of indebtedness followed six years of structural adjustment, beginning in 1981, when subsidies were lifted on agriculture—an IMF conditionality—and prices were subsequently raised on food. The program also included raising the costs of secondary school. As a result, rural workers and farmers clashed with police in land seizures, strikes broke out in factories, students occupied universities, and a June 1981 union protest turned into "true urban *Jacqueries*." Protesters were killed in several cities; 600 died in Casablanca alone.[137] A second round of adjustment, involving more cuts in subsidies and more price increases on basic consumption commodities, led to revolt throughout Morocco, with estimates of 200 killed in the repression.[138] After this revolt, the government began to take tighter control of neighborhood cultural centers, closing some and replacing personnel in others. Controlling the cultural domain both through rigorous censorship and harassment of opponents, and through its own sponsorship of meetings, conferences, and celebrations became its deliberate policy by the mid-1980s When, in 1986, the Moroccan national soccer team performed better than expected in international competition, the government blocked off streets and made sure the military presence in the streets was sufficiently impressive to discourage the celebrations from becoming demonstrations.[139] An OECD study on the political feasiblity of structural adjustment in the Third World referred to the 1981 Moroccan anti-IMF revolt and summarized, "For many years thereafter, Morocco was cited as an example of the high political and economic costs associated with IMF programmes." It then congratulated the Moroccan government and the IMF for moving more slowly in 1984, thereby blunting opposition: "The riots and demonstrations in 1984 were not as serious as those in 1981," it argued, calmly counting the numbers of dead resulting from an economic reform.[140] Apparently this wisdom did not last long, since on the eve of the Gulf War a third round of IMF-imposed reform led to a third round of revolt. A December 1990 general strike demanded doubling of the minimum wage; banks, limousines, and government offices were physically attacked; and a five-star hotel was burnt to the ground after all the television sets had been looted.[141]

The social groups most heavily represented in the migration to Italy—poor rural farmers, urban tradespeople, students and would-be professionals—were all seriously hit by the structural adjustment programs and the repression that followed their revolt against it. The cuts in farm subsidies have hit an already struggling poor rural population hard; the price increases, increased unemployment, and increase in food prices seriously undermined the survival strategies of urban residents; and the combinations of increases in school prices and the 60 percent fall in teachers' wages[142] since 1979 greatly injured the hopes of students for a decent career. The massacre of hundreds of people in Casablanca in 1981 is unlikely to be wholly unrelated to the flow of migrants from there in the years following the revolt.

As Dal Lago has traced, the migrations to Italy and Spain from Morocco in the 1980s, of which he claims to find four distinct flows, are not merely continuations of the migration into France of the 1960s and 1970s.[143] The presence of previous migrants in the village, neighborhood, or family would tend to encourage consideration of migration as a strategy, but since the pre-existing social network chain was in France—which has seen little new Moroccan migration since the 1970s—this is not sufficient to explain what instead appears to be a new flow of predominantly young men and increasingly some women. The Moroccan case appears to be linked to the results of structural adjustment, the revolt against it, and the repression following that revolt—these make up the daily reality that subsequently faces students, farmers and small merchants and artisans in the wake of 15 years of neoliberal policy.

CONCLUSIONS

It would not be hard to give other examples involving other migrants groups: Tunisia where in 1984, 100 people were killed in anti-IMF revolts following price increases, or the role of the IMF in destroying the livestock economy of Somalia, which played a leading role in bringing on the civil war and the refugee flow toward Italy; the role of the World Bank and IMF in destabilizing access to means of subsistence in India, Bangledesh, or Vietnam, or the vast expropriations of land and economic security under privatization that are the background to new migrations from China to every part of the planet, including Italy.[144] My intention in emphasizing the role of structural adjustment in the origins of contemporary migration is not to return to a rigid understanding of so-called "push factors." On the contrary, migration is by no means an automatic response to austerity, hardship, expropriation, or war. Other options exist, ranging from starvation and violent death to the creation of social movements for domestic social change and armed rebellion. Only in certain places and at certain times do people decide to migrate; the point is that migration is a solution to the problems encountered at home. It is collective action; it is a geographic expansion of a social struggle that appears too difficult to win through staying at home.

That the current migrations are closely linked to, and indeed possibly a desired effect of the SAPs seems clear. But they are also collective actions. If migration is not only a desperate exodus but an organized solution to a problem at home, then we must turn to the way in which these networks seek to address problems through migration. Structural adjustment involves a de-stabilization of previous forms of subsistence and social reproduction, and creates a situation of serious disequilibrium in which subsistence become problemmatic as wealth is concentrated and value flows out of the region. Migration seeks to create a new equilibrium system, to organize a new means of obtaining and using wealth which re-creates some form of social reproduction under such conditions of disequilibrium. In chemistry and biology, such a self-organized order is called a dissipative system. We shall examine the role of migrant social networks as dissipative systems in the next chapter, and argue that this metaphor helps us to understand how what is often called the global labor market is the creation of planetary forms of social reproduction that seek to reverse the flow of value caused in the migrants' home regions by SAPs and their results.

Thus the networks of Mourides, of the Ghanaian and Nigerian Pentacostal Church, of Filipina women's family, church and friendship links, are crucial means of enabling new arrivals to find a job or a place to sleep, to save money and to see that it arrives where it's supposed to, and to organize to improve conditions.[145] For the creation of abstract labor power is no guarantee of its further development into concrete labor. Expropriation, in other words, does not guarantee exploitation. Capital, as Karl Marx stated, comes into being through expropriation—an expropriation whose history "is written in the annals of mankind in letters of blood and fire." Yet Marx also showed that vagabondage and political resistance were as likely results of such expropriation as the cheerful acceptance of exploited labor in the market. Various other activities are required to create a labor market, to bring together labor and capital. In the following chapter, we shall examine some of these means, including the crucial role of the transnational migrant communities themselves; these, in reconstituting material life, have made the world labor market possible. But the latter is a means of recuperating this reorganized material life and of channeling its resources and peoples into value-producing activity for capital. Who controls that market, and under what conditions labor and capital are brought together, remains an open question. It is to the struggles which are determining the outcome of that question that we now turn. In doing so, we move, with the migrants themselves, from the various social conflicts in which capital—in the form of the international financial agencies—has used its spatial advantage to impose austerity and expropriation in a variety of locales, to conflicts over space itself, and the control of the movement of people and of money.

Notes

1. Luigi Di Liegro, *Immigrazione: un punto di vista* (Rome: Sensibili alle Foglie, 1997), p. 31.
2. Caritas, *Dossier Statistico Immigrazione 1996* Rome 1997; Veneto, 72,500 stranieri 'regolari', *Il Gazzettino* (Padua), March 20, 1997.
3. Larry Lohmann, "Against the Myths" in Marcus Colchester and Larry Lohmann, eds., *The Struggle for Land and the Fate of the Forests* (London: Zed, 1995), pp. 26-34.
4. Caritas Italiana, Fondazione E. Zancan, *I bisogni dimenticati:rapporto 1996 su emarginazione ed esclusione sociale* (Milan: Feltrinelli, 1997), p. 162.
5. Ibid., p. 174.
6. Donald Martin Carter, in his study of the Senegalese in Turin, *States of Grace: Senegalese in Italy and the New European Immigration* (Minneapolis and London: University of Minnesota Press, 1997), found that the majority of subjects of his study were artisans in Senegal, and concluded that this was true for all of Italy (p. 6). Artisans were considerably less represented in the present research, and do not figure prominently in other studies of Senegalese in Italy. Thus, Ottavia Schmidt di Friedberg, *Islam, solidarietà e lavoro* (Turin: Fondazione Agnelli, 1994), found that the majority of Senegalese immigrants came from agricultural castes, while a significant minority were from aristocratic ones, though she mentions artisans as among the other groups present (p. 68); It is of course possible that the higher percentages of artisans among Turin Mourides are the result of social network activity among craftworkers, leading to a concentration of artisans in the Turin region as opposed to elsewhere in Italy, but not enough is yet known about the specific compositions of Senegalese concentrations to confirm this guess.
7. Kojo Arthur, *Ghana's Food Crisis: Alternative Perspectives*, Africa Research and Publications Project Inc. Working Paper #16 1983, p.3.
8. Eboe Hutchful, ed., The *IMF and Ghana: The Confidential Record* (London: Zed, 1987), pp. 15, 21.
9. Ibid., p. 7.
10. Ibid., p. 20.
11. Kojo Sebastian Amanor, *The New Frontier: Farmers' Response to Land Degradation, A West African Study* (London: Zed Press, 1994), pp. 44-47 and *passim*.
12. Ibid., pp. 46, 90; John Mihevc, *The Market Tells Them So: The World Bank and Economic Fundamentalism in Africa* (London: Zed, 1995), pp. 160-161.
13. Ross Hammond and Lisa McGowan, "Ghana: The World Bank's Sham Showcase" in Kevin Danaher, ed., *50 Years is Enough: The Case against the World Bank and the International Monetary Fund* (Boston: South End Press, 1994), p. 80.
14. Mihevc, *The Market*, p. 159.

15. Ibid., p. 156.
16. Hammond and McGowan, "Ghana," p. 80.
17. Mihevc, *The Market*, pp. 159-60.
18. Ibid., p. 214.
19. Ibid., p. 214.
20. Hammond and McGowan, "Ghana," p. 80.
21. Mihevc, *The Market*, p. 161.
22. Hammond and McGowan, "Ghana," p. 81.
23. Ibid., p. 82.
24. Kojo Sebastian Amanor, *The New Frontier: Farmers' Response to Land Degradation—A West African Study* (London: Zed, 1994), p. 193.
25. Hammond and McGowan, "Ghana," pp. 81-82; Amanor, *New Frontier*, p. 33; Unione Regional delle Camere di Commercio Industria Artiginato e Agricoltura del Veneto,*Fascicolo di aggiornamento alla relazione sulla situazione del Veneto nel 1995 Import/Export 1993-1995* (Venice: Camera di Commercio del Veneto, 1996), p. 236. Ghana exported 8,630 tons of wood to the Veneto in 1995, valued at US$13 million, the entire rest of its exports to the Veneto consisted of about US$500,000 in agricultural and forest products and US$2,000 in machine parts.
26. I have derived these figures from Unione Regionale Delle Camere di Commercio, Industria, Artigianato e Agricoltura del Veneto, *Fascicolo,* pp. 46-47, 236-37; this volume is the Veneto Chamber of Commerce's offical statistical analysis of all Veneto import and export trade.
27. Kwesi Jonah, "The Social Impact of Ghana's Adjustment Program 1983–86" in Bade Onimode, ed., *The IMF, The World Bank, and the African Debt: The Social and Political Impact, Vol.2* (London: Zed Press, 1989), p. 142; Mihevc, *The Market*, p. 156.
28. Silvia Federici, "The Debt Crisis, Africa and the New Enclosures" in Midnight Notes, *Midnight Oil*, pp. 305-06, 315; Committe for Academic Freedom in Africa, *CAFA Newsletter* no. 1-12 (1991-1997).
29. Federici, "Debt Crisis," p. 312.
30. Ibid., p. 305 and various interviews.
31. Hammond and McGowan, "Ghana," p. 81.
32. Mihevc, *The Market*, p. 161; Federici, "Debt Crisis," p. 312.
33. Federici, "Development and Underdevelopment in Nigeria," in Midnight Notes, *Midnight Oil,* pp. 87-89.
34. Midnight Notes, *Midnight Oil.*
35. Midnight Notes Collective, "Oil, Guns and Money," in Midnight Notes, *Midnight Oil*, pp. 7-9.
36. Ibid., pp. 17-21.
37. Ibid., pp. 13, 21: see also, in the same volume of *Midnight Oil*, C. George Caffentzis, "Rambo on the Barbary Shore," pp. 284-86.
38. Caffentzis, "Rambo," p. 284.
39. Ibid., pp. 287-94.
40. Ibid., p. 289.
41. Zuwaqhu A. Bonat and Yahaya A. Abdullahi, "The World Bank, The

IMF and Nigeria's Rural Economy in Onimode," *The IMF, Vol.2*, p. 164.

42. Ibid., p. 166.

43. Ken Saro-Wiwa, *A Month and a Day* (London: Penguin, 1995), p. 7.

44. See, among others, Abdoulaye-Bara Diop, *La Sociètè Wolof* (Paris: Karthala, 1977), which stresses the hierarchy and inequality of Mouride social organization; L. Behrman, *Muslim Brotherhoods and Politics in Senegal* (Cambridge: Harvard Univ. Press, 1970); Ira Lapidus, *A History of Islamic Societies* (New York: Cambridge Univ. Press, 1990), pp. 837-38; Donal B. Cruise O'Brien, *The Mourides of Senegal* (Oxford: Clarendon Press, 1971) and his "Charisma Comes to Town: Mouride Urbanization 1945–1986," as well as Christian Coulon, "Women, Islam and Baraka," both of which appear in Donald B. Cruise O'Brien and Christian Coulon, eds., *Charisma and Brotherhoods in African Islam* (Oxford: Clarendon Press, 1988).

45. Ottavia Schmidt di Friedberg, *Islam, solidarietà e lavoro: i muridi senegalesi in Italia* (Turin: Fondazione Agnelli, 1995), p. 96.

46. Ibid., p. 65.

47. See Lapidus, *History*, O'Brien, *The Mourides of Senegal*, p. 246.

48. Jean Suret-Canale, *French Colonialism in Tropical Africa 1900–1945* (New York: Pica Press, 1971) pp. 16, 46, 34.

49. Ibid., p. 10.

50. Ibid., pp. 46, 220-21.

51. Ibid., p. 47.

52. Lapidus, *History*, p. 834; Suret-Canale, *French Colonialism*, p. 433.

53. Lapidus, *History*, p. 834.

54. Ibid., p. 835: O'Brien *The Mourides of* Senegal, p. 14; Schmidt di Friedberg, *Islam*, pp. xiv-xvi; Surel-Canale, *French Colonialism*, p. 234.

55. O'Brien, *The Mourides*, p. 216.

56. Ibid., ch. 8, "The Dara."

57. Ibid., p. 217.

58. Abdoulaye Ndiaye, "Food for Thought: Senegal's Struggle with Structural Adjustment," in Danaher, *50 Years*, pp. 85-86; Abdoulaye Bathily, "Senegal's Structural Adjustment Programme and its Economic and Social Effects: The Political Economy of Regression," in Onimode, *The IMF*, p. 130.

59. Abdoulaye Ndiaye, "Food for Thought," p. 86.

60. O'Brien, "Charisma Comes to Town: Mouride Urbanization 1945–1986," in O'Brien and Coulon, *Charisma*, p. 135.

61. O'Brien, "Charisma Comes to Town"; Ottavia Schmidt di Friedberg, *Islam*, pp. 113-25.

62. Bridget Anderson, *Britain's Secret Slaves: An Investigation into the Plight of Overseas Domestic Workers in the United Kingdom* (with contributions from Anti-Slavery International, Kalayaan and the Migrant Domestic Workers) (London: Anti-Slavery International, 1993), pp. 32-34.

63. Noeleen Heyzer, Geertje Lychlama à Nijeholt and Nedra Weerakoon, *The*

Trade in Domestic Workers, Vol. 1 (London: Zed, 1992), p. 45; Giovanna Campani, "Le reticoli sociali delle donne immigrate in Italia," in Marcella Delle Donne, Umberto Melotti, and Stefano Petilli, *Immigrazione in Europa: Solidarietà e conflitto* (Rome: Università degli Studi di Roma La Sapienza Dipartimento di Sociologia, 1993), p. 274.

64. Elizabeth Uy Eviota, *The Political Economy of Gender: Women and the Sexual Division of Labour in the Philippines* (London: Zed, 1992), p. 144.

65. Eviota, *Political Economy*, pp. 140-41; Walden Bello, *Develpment Debacle: The World Bank in the Philippines* (Berkeley: Institute for Food and Development Policy, 1982); The International NGO Forum, "World Bank and IMF Adjustment Lending in the Philippines," in Danaher, *50 Years*, pp. 63-65.

66. Bello, *Development Debacle*, passim; James B. Goodno, *The Philippines: Land of Broken Promises* (London: Zed, 1991), p. 59.

67. Goodno, *The Philippines*, p. 114.

68. Ibid., passim.

69. Michel Chossudovsky, *The Globalisation of Poverty: Impacts of IMF and World Bank Reforms* (London: Zed, 1997), pp. 258-29.

70. Cheryl Payer, *The Debt Trap* (New York: Monthly Review Press, 1974), ch. 5.

71. Aristide Zolberg, Astri Suhrke and Sergio Aguayo, *Escape from Violence: Conflict and the Refugee Crisis in the Developing World* (New York: Oxford Univ. Press, 1989), p. 31.

72. See for instance, Chossudovsky, *Globalisation*, ch. 4, 5.

73. Chossudovsky, *Globalisation*, pp. 244-45.

74. Ibid., p. 245.

75. Ibid., p. 245.

76. Ibid., p. 246.

77. Ibid., p. 251.

78. Jasminka Udovicki and James Ridgeway, *Yugoslavia's Ethnic Nightmare* (Westport: Lawrence Hill Books, 1995).

79. Ibid., p. 4.

80. As painstakingly shown in Slavko Curuvija and Ivan Torov, "The March to War (1980–1990)," in Udovicki and Ridgeway, *Ethnic Nightmare*, pp. 73-104; and Milan Milosevic, The Media Wars in the same volume, pp. 105-22.

81. Mirko Tepevac, "Tito's Yugoslavia," in Udovicki and Ridgeway, *Ethnic Nightmare*, pp. 70-71.

82. Slavo Radosevic, "The Collapse of Yugoslavia: Between Chance and Necessity," in D.A. Dyker and I. Vejvoda, eds., *Yugoslavia and After: A Study in Fragmentation, Despair and Rebirth* (London: Longman, 1996), p. 77.

83. Ibid., p. 65.

84. Ibid., p. 65.

85. Ibid., p. 77.

86. Susan L. Woodward, "The West and the International Organizations," in Dyker and Vejvoda eds., *Yugoslavia and After*, pp. 158-59.
87. Ibid., p. 159.
88. Ibid.
89. Ibid., p. 161.
90. Ibid., pp. 161-62.
91. Ibid., p. 163.
92. Ibid., p. 163.
93. I.R., "I Lived Happily," in Zdenko Lesic, *Children of Atlantis: Voices from the Former Yugoslavia* Central (Budapest-London-New York: European University Press , 1995), p. 36.
94. N.M., "I Thought It Was a Bad Joke. I Was Wrong," in Lesic, *Children*, p. 38.
95. S.K., "I Shall Do Anything To Be with Ljiljana," in Lesic, *Children*, p. 40.
96. A.B., "There Was Total Confusion," in Lesic, *Children*, p. 44.
97. Quoted from Chossudovsky, in Lesic, *Children*, p. 256.
98. "Belgrade a City in Need of Milk, and a Little Peace," *New York Times*, Sept. 17, 1998, p. A10.
99. See the excellent first-hand study by Kosta Barjaba, Georges Lapassade and Luigi Perrone, *Naufragi Albanesi* (Rome: Sensibili alle foglie, 1996), p. 67.
100. Ibid., p. 65.
101. Ibid., p. 65.
102. Ibid., p. 65.
103. *Liberazione* (Italy), April 9, 1997, p. 2.
104. Ismail Kadare, *Albanian Spring:The Anatomy of Tyranny* (London: Saqi Books, 1991), p. 75.
105. Arshi Pipa, *Albanian Stalinism: Ideo-Political Aspects* (New York: Columbia University Press, 1990), p. 45.
106. Ibid., p. 45.
107. Ibid., p. 152.
108. Ibid.
109. See International Action Center, *NATO in the Balkans* (New York: International Action Center, 1998).
110. Organization for Economic Cooperation and Development, *Romania: An Economic Assessment* (Paris: OECD, 1993), p. 1.
111. See Vladimir Pasti, *The Challenges of Transition: Romania in Transition* (New York: Columbia University Press, 1997), pp. xviii–xix.
112. On the Romanian regime and the Revolution of 1989, there are now several excellent accounts: Martyn Rady, *Romania in Turmoil* (London and New York: I.B. Tauris & Co., 1992) is particularly good on analysis of the democratic opposition in its various compositions, and helps sort through the many rumors which gripped public opinion in the aftermath of the revolt; Nestor Ratesh, *Romania: The Entangled Revolution* (New York: Praeger, 1991) is relatively unsympathetic to the miners, and

stresses the international implications of Romania's Revolution and subsequent policies; Vladimir Pasti, *The Challenges of Transition: Romania in Transition* (New York: Columbia University Press, 1997) is the best description of class conflict during the pre- and post-Ceaucescu periods and elucidates the role of workers, and of the miners in particular in revolutionary activity and the politics in the post-Communist Party era; the events of 1989–1991 as seen by Western journalists can be found in the collection of New York Times reports in the volume *The Collapse of Communism* by the correspondents of the *New York Times*, Bernard Gwertzman and Michael T. Kaufman, eds. (New York: New York Times Company, 1991).

113. Pasti, *Challenges*, pp. 269-70.
114. Indeed by 1992 the Stolojan government announced "zero economic growth" as its objective, one which was achieved for two successive years. More recently this sort of goal has again become state policy, see below. Pasti, *Challenges*, p. 36.
115. Ibid., p. 270.
116. Ibid., p. 271.
117. Rady, *Romania in Turmoil*, p. 196.
118. Ibid., p. 197.
119. Ibid., p. 196.
120. Ratesh, *Romania*, p. 152.
121. Ibid., p. 152.
122. Pasti, *Challenges*, pp. 61-62.
123. Ratesh, *Challenges*, p. 120.
124. Rady, *Romania in Turmoil*, pp. 194-95.
125. "Romania Seeks Large IMF Loan," *International Herald Tribune*, February 3, 1997.
126. Antonio Nicaso and Lee Lamothe, *Global Mafia: The New World Order of Organized Crime* (Toronto: MacMillan , 1995), pp. 18-20; Rossana Mungiello, "Lavoro coatto a fine secolo in quattro grandi aree economiche," *Altreragioni* 6 (Milano) (1997).
127. Organization for Economic Cooperation and Development, *Development Strategy, Employment and Migration: Insights from Models* (Paris: OECD, 1996).
128. Ibid., pp. 76-78.
129. Francesco Susi, *I bisogni formativi e culturali degli immigrati stranieri* (Milan: FrancoAngeli, 1988), p. 210.
130. Odo Barsotti, ed., *Dal Marocco in Italia* (Milan: FrancoAngeli, 1994), p. 195.
131. Alessandro Dal Lago, "La nuova immigrazione a Milano: Il caso del Marocco," in Giusseppe Barile, Alessandro Dal Lago, Aldo Marchetti and Patrizia Galeazzo, *Tra due rive: La nouva immigrazione a Milano* (Milan: FrancoAngeli, 1994), pp. 174-75.
132. Ibid., p. 175.
133. Ibid., pp. 138-39.

134. Ibid., p. 140.
135. Ibid., p. 183.
136. Kevin Dwyer, *Arab Voices: The Human Rights Debate in the Middle East* (New York: Routledge, 1992), p. 100.
137. Ibid., p. 107; Dal Lago, *Due Rive*, pp. 164-65.
138. Dwyer, *Arab Voices*, p. 107; Dal Lago, *Due Rive*, p. 165.
139. Dwyer, *Arab Voices*, pp. 17, 33.
140. Stephen Haggard, Jean-Dominique Lafay and Christian Morrisson, *The Political Feasibility of Adjustment in Developing Countries* (Paris: OECD, 1995), p. 75.
141. Midnight Notes Collective, "Oil Guns and Money," in Midnight Notes, *Midnight Oil*, p. 20; *New York Times*, December 17-18, 1990.
142. Dwyer, *Arab Voices*, p. 18.
143. Dal Lago, *Due Rive*, p. 173.
144. On Tunisia see Dwyer, *Arab Voices*, pp. 144-200; on Somalia, Bangladesh, India and Vietnam, see Chossudovsky, op.cit., pp. 100-07, 125-68; on China, see Silvia Federici, "Inscrutible China," in Midnight Notes, *The New Enclosures* (Jamaica Plain, Massachusetts, 1990).
145. Thus, for instance, the same Mouride networks, often also kinship based, that are used to arrive in Italy and make one's first contacts will also be used to gain access to goods to sell, communicate other job and housing possibilities and also bring together Mouride employees of various firms for a union meeting.

4

MIGRANT COMMUNITIES, DISSIPATIVE SYSTEMS AND THE OTHER WORLDWIDE WEB

INTRODUCTION

In July 1984, Pap Khouma arrived at the airport in Rome from Dakar. Back in Sengegal he had heard from others who had been to Italy of a city called Riccione, on the coast of Emilia-Romagna. He had an address of a cousin of a Senegalese friend he had met while working as a street vendor to European tourists in Abidjan, in the Ivory Coast. Speaking no Italian upon arrival, he luckily ran into another Senegalese at the airport who helped him get directions to Riccione, over 200 miles from Rome, and bought his train ticket. Finding that the friend's cousin no longer lived at the apartment in Riccione, he was helped by the other Senegalese residents of the apartment who brought him to a second apartment where another group of Senegalese promptly agreed to let him stay; as he put it in his autobiography, "The guys don't ask me about anything."[1] Later, they warned him against going out alone to get to know the city, since street selling is not legal, and they are all without work permits.

The autobiography of Pap Khouma, *Io venditore di elefanti* (I, seller of elephants), is one of the very few pieces of immigrant literature yet to come out of the immigrant experience in Italy. In the story of his arrival in Italy and his initiation into the craft of street vending—and as he emphasizes, in Senegal at least, it's considered a craft—we find many themes that are increasingly characteristic of migrant organization, and of how the world labor market is being made by migrant activity. Virtually every moment of his migration process was lived out within the organizational possibilities of a Mouride/Wolof social network. From the decision to migrate, to the choice of destinations, from work to housing, from how to defend oneself when up against the law, to with whom and how to socialize, from whether to stay abroad to how to bring or send money or gifts to family in Senegal, the loose but active network of contacts, information, and mutual aid laid the basis for his life options and choices. He began to consider emigrating for the first time in November 1979, feeling fed up with conditions in Senegal:

In Senegal there's a lot of people who go all around without doing anything. Walking along the white streets of Dakar is the national pastime. My country, divided by caste, is poor. It's always getting poorer, because after ten years of drought the cultivation of peanuts went into crisis. Other countries produce them and the prices went down. There's a socialist government in Senegal. I never really understood why it's called socialist. . . . To protest is the second national pastime. . . . In the villages corruption is widespread. If money arrives, whoever's on the side of the government pockets it.[2] (My translation from Italian.)

In this context, emigration is widely viewed as both a personal solution to escape such a situation, and as a collective strategy for overcoming conditions:

Africa is poorly governed. Too many profiteers. You can study and work, but it doesn't change, because those in control aren't disposed to concede you a little bit of space. So people have to leave there. Only those who manage to escape, who manage to reach Europe have hope. Only a few have work. Everyone depends on them. Because of this you can't return: if you return you go alone and join the many who live on the work of the few. The job I have, for me there couldn't be anything more. I must remain in Europe.[3] (My translation from Italian.)

Since migration is seen as participation at the center of a collective strategy, the choice of migration is expected to be taken in conjunction with others. The first time Pap emigrates, to the Ivory Coast, he tells his father the day before he plans to leave. The older man replies, "But why didn't you tell me before? I could have given you my blessing. . . . Go anyway son. Behave yourself. Don't ever smoke cigarettes. Don't drink alcohol" (my translation from Italian).[4] After having returned to Senegal for several years, Pap decides to go to work in Europe—to Spain because "the ticket costs less." He first goes to ask his *set-kat*, which he translated as searcher or diviner, for advice. The set-kat, after consulting with cowry shells, Pap's own hand, and traces of sand on the shore, tells him to go to Germany instead of Spain. Since getting into Germany is too difficult directly, he plans to arrive first in Italy.

Without wanting to reduce the set-kat's method of decision-making to a Western rationalist approach, we may nevertheless guess that such advice is given by a community counselor in close touch with information available from others in the region who have emigrated. Informal community leadership in Wolof society, still a largely illiterate population, is linked to social relations of an oral culture. Elders known as *griot*—storytellers who are able to memorize the entire histories of the family lines of entire villages—are still very widely respected, and the oral exchange of life histories and of information and experience remains a vital institution in Senegal: "Every old person who dies is a library that burns," one Wolof man told Valerio Belotti.[5] Choices as to immigrant destination are made in the context of ancient community institutions, but based upon a contemporary diaspora that allows for possible destinations as diverse as the Ivory Coast, Morocco, the United States, Germany, France, Italy, and Saudi Arabia, taking into account their varying conditions. In Abidjan, Paris, and various cities in Italy, Pap Khouma regularly found a group of Senegalese with whom he could stay for at least some period of time, with whom he could eat, and who helped him look for work and housing, obtain the goods—usually on credit—to be sold on the street, even on occasion to take the rap when police arrived so as to protect those whose position was more vulnerable if arrested or deported.

Such experience suggests the creation of worldwide networks

of communication, information, resource distribution, and cultural and religious affiliation. Such networks, in one form or another increasingly common to migrant communities from diverse parts of the world, would seem to be a working class answer to "globalization." That is, given the increasingly global nature of markets, of the exchange of goods and services, raw materials, money, and capital, such networks enable communities that have been impacted by these developments to regain access on a planetary scale to wealth and resources. Further, it enables migrant communities to interact with these forces on the basis of at least partial autonomy, rather than as the atomized individuals who make up the *homo economicus* of neo-classical and neoliberal imagination. These social networks, as Professor Nestor Rodriguez has argued in the case of Mexican migration, constitute transnational migrant communities. Such communities autonomously arrange for employment opportunities, meet other needs such as housing or health care, sustain family and community relations, organize religious and cultural practices, develop political and other associations, and mobilize the transfer of resources across political state boundaries.[6] They are a form of social order improvised from the previously existing social relations in the country of origin, and transformed into a new set of social relations capable of sustaining the lives of the individuals and communities in the country of origin, of which they are both a part and an expansion. We may compare them, therefore, to the concept of dissipative systems in chemistry and biology as developed by scientist Ilya Prigogine.

In searching for the basis of order in states of disequilibrium, Prigogine examined how heat convection takes place. When a thin stratum of water is heated at a uniform temperature from below, a heat flux moves from the bottom layer of water to the top, creating a heat disequilibrium in which the water itself remains at rest. However, when the difference in heat value between bottom and top reaches a certain point, a heat convection takes place, in which the instability of the previous movement of heat is replaced by an order in which hexagonal cells form. Heat rises through the center of the cells, while colder liquid moves downward toward the cell walls.[7] The point is that at a certain intolerable moment in a state of disequilibrium, an order of a different type, able to maintain its internal coherence while remaining open to the externally based flows of energy through its own system, manages to hold together in a state of disequilibrium. Prigogine called these, with an eye to the inherent seeming contradiction "dissipative structures," meaning structures that are internally— that is, structurally—closed while remaining organizationally open. The example of the whirlpool in a bathtub is often used to make this idea clear. Water continuously flows through the whirlpool, but its own coherent structure remains stable.[8] Thus, the dissipative structure remains an open system, able to allow energy to flow through it, while maintaining its structure. This structure in turn is a coherent one precisely because it is open to the flow of resources from outside itself.

Later, Prigogine examined the characteristics of dissipative structures, which by now are recognized as having many of the features of living systems. The first criteria is that dissipative systems' characteristics cannot be derived from their parts; rather, they arise from "supramolecular organization." Second, the further it is from a state of equilibrium, the greater a dissipative structure's nonlinearity and complexity. The further the structure moves from equilibrium, and increases in complexity, the more such systems are very sensitive to initial conditions.[9] The greater its nonlinearity, the greater the number of possible solutions available to the structure. At certain moments of instability, either internal or caused by contact with external forces, a type of bifurcation occurs in which the structure can branch off into another state, all the while maintaining a certain level of structural coherence. As Fritjof Capra puts it, "At the bifurcation points, states of higher order may emerge spontaneously."[10] In other words, dissipative structures can grow and develop, analogously to living entities, both in scale and in complexity. Prigogine describes dissipative structures as islands of order in a sea of disorder, feeding on energy of the disordered environment surrounding them, in order to generate and maintain their own internal coherence, while the general state of entropy or disequilibrium around them grows.

Migrant communities and their social networks may be

compared usefully to dissipative structures. For as we have seen, they represent a response to a state of disorder, instability, or disequilibrium—namely the destabilization of subsistence resulting from the effects of structural adjustment. As C. George Caffentzis has illustrated mathematically, the results of structural adjustment constitute a qualitative leap in the transfer of value produced worldwide from the bottom of wage scale – that is, the Third World—to the areas of highest organic composition of capital.[11] This transfer of value on a planetary scale, making subsistence in diverse locales increasingly problemmatic, may be thought of as similar to the movement of heat molecules in the uniformly heated stratum of water. The organization of migrant networks provides subsistence and maintains the coherence of the community or family in the sea of instability created by the new conditions. The migrant community provides order in a state of disequilibrium. Further, in taking advantage of diverse solutions—at first migration itself, then the organization of employment, and in choosing between diverse destinations—the migrant community shows itself able to change, grow, and increase its own complexity, while maintaining its own coherent structure under changing influences and conditions. Finally, like the vortex of a whirlpool, it is open to energy flows—in this case money in the form of wages, as well as goods—that flow through its structure, and, in the form of remittances, it reverses within its own order the previous flow of value in an analogous way to the heat convection.

No doubt there are limits to such a metaphor. However, it seems to me useful as a means to grasp the innovative nature of contemporary migrants, such as their own self-organization, their relation to structural adjustment, and how they maintain subsistence in the home country, all while using networks with the capacity to grow in scale and complexity and to organize the transfer of resources. While in chapter 2 the relation of migrants to the world market, the state, and employers was described as increasing in autonomy, here we can clarify the extent and limits (so far) of this autonomy. In other words, migration is organized more by migrant networks than by states or employers who directly seek overseas workers. The relational quality of migration in a world economy is more complex than can be fully grasped by the Kantian concept of autonomy. Migrant communities may be relatively more or less independent or autonomous, like any working class organization, but as a social order, even these remain, as the old socialist adage about utopian communities had it, "in a sea of capitalism." Thinking of migrant networks as dissipative structures advances our understanding of migrant activity by placing it in the context of a larger situation that is not under its autonomous control, and which works to influence it from without, but also enables us to understand migrant networks as themselves forms of order with their own rules, internal coherence, capacity for growth. Perhaps most importantly, such a viewpoint treats migrant communities as a means of taking in flows of wealth and resources and reorganizing their use according to their own needs. As such they are both structurally closed—that is, they continue to exist in a form determined largely by their own response to conditions—while remaining organizationally open. Dissipation creates order in disspative systems, and the flow of remittances, goods, and people through the migrant networks—flows that are constantly changing in quantity and velocity—are precisely what maintains the structure of the migrant community, which remains a coherent social form even when new opportunities, obstacles, or events present them- selves. Thus, even while resources distributed by and through the network are based in large part on wages—hence, on a capitalism that limits community autonomy—the organization and use of these is under migrant control. Keeping this useful metaphor in mind, then, we will examine the activity of migrant networks and how they function across the planet in such a way as to result in the arrival of migrants in Italy.

Three aspects of migrant community networks are most important. First, such networks are planetary, withan increasing ability to determine placement of individuals and groups within certain sectors of local labor markets, and an increasing ability to choose between specific destinations based upon conditions. Second, in organizing the transfer of resources in the form of remittances, exchange of goods, and gifts, they are similar to dissipative systems in re-creating an order in a state of disequilibrium. Third, such networks are expanded forms of mutual aid, and as such represent a partial re-embedding of the global economy within social relations of their own making. I will also discuss the relationship of other agencies—states, churches and religious associations, and organized crime networks—to migrant networks; I see these relations as ambiguous, in part attempts to subordinate the autonomous migrant communities to other projects, in part a use by these same communities to take advantage of information, aid, resources, or political power available through such international agencies for migrants' own projects. The international dimension of the planetary labor market is essentially built out of such interaction and its outcome. The local aspect of the same labor market is the subject of a later chapter.

MIGRANT TRANSNATIONAL COMMUNITIES: THE OTHER WORLDWIDE WEB

An astounding percentage of the immigrants interviewed for this study had lived in countries other than Italy and their own country of origin, and an even greater number had relatives in at least one other country. Of the 41 Moroccans, for instance, 27 had relatives in third countries (Germany, France, Belgium, Egypt—one replied "all over Europe"); 11 reported having lived in other countries before Italy (France, Denmark, Libya, Saudi Arabia); and 10 had relatives living in Italy, usually brothers or cousins. Among the Senegalese interviewed, third countries where they had lived included Mauritania, France, Algeria, and the Ivory Coast. Countries where they had relatives living included Central Africa, Spain, Portugal, the United States, and France. All told, just under half, 23 of the 47 interviewed, reported having relatives in third countries, while 20 of the 47 had themselves lived in a country other than Italy and Senegal. Eighteen of the 47 had relatives in Italy. One Senegalese man whom I interviewed in a more in-depth fashion had lived in 14 different countries throughout the Middle East, North and Sub-Saharan Africa and Europe. Five of the 16 interviewees from the Philippines had relatives who worked in the Gulf States of the Middle East, and three had themselves worked either in Saudi Arabia or Kuwait. Other studies confirm this extraordinary mobility and diversity of destinations among migrants. One Senegalese man interviewed by Valerio Belotti said he wanted to migrate to avoid "having to obey the elders no matter what" and to take care of his child. He reported that other experienced migrants advised him to go the United States, but his mother opposed the move, and he thought Saudi Arabia "would be like staying home, with the same problems." In the end he went first to Paris, then returned home to Senegal, and finally ended up in Italy.[12] Another had a brother who had emigrated to France and then to Italy. Yet another had worked in Morocco before arriving in Italy.[13] One Moroccan interviewed by Belotti had lived in France, another had considered going to Spain or Portugal, but ended up choosing Italy. One Ghanaian in the same study of Bassano-area migrants had lived in Mogadishu, Somalia, as well as in Togo and Nigeria. He had brothers who had lived in Kuwait, influencing him to move to Saudi Arabia for a time.[14] One Somalian woman in a study of migrants in Turin had lived and worked in Saudi Arabia for three years.[15] A Lebanese man in the same study described his family's movements across Senegal, Mauritania, the Ivory Coast, Saudi Arabia and Italy.[16] The Senegalese Mouride network engages in both migration and the movement and sale of goods virtually across the entire planet.[17]

The present-day migration represents a vast circulation of experience across many countries of destination. The list of possible destinations, by now including Ireland, Japan, and South Korea, seems ever to expand. In many countries, particularly in Asia, labor-recruiting agencies are employed to find workers who want to migrate. But though the agent has the contacts to heavily influence the decision of where to migrate to, it is not clear that the migrants and their families and communities lose any say in the choice of destination. Indeed, in the Philippines and elsewhere, agencies specialize in certain destinations and industries.[18] Giovanna Campani has found in her study of the women's migrant social network running between San Pablo in the Philippines and Florence, Italy, that "The network of San Pablo is an example of how a family migratory chain can be managed exclusively by women (the men rubber stamp the decision-making process and their opinions don't count)" (my translation from Italian).[10] Loans are organized by barrio women of San Pablo, previously arrived migrants help newly arrived women find work and housing in Florence, and remittances are organized and guaranteed through female networks of contact. In countries like Senegal, Ghana, or Morocco, migration decisions are made within the context of the whole family or of the community relations, which are roughly the same as those whom the remittances of migrants would be expected to help. The more the migration network expands, the more information is available on work and other conditions in each possible destination, and as in the case of the set-kat of Pap Khouma or the mother of the Senegalese man interviewed by Valerio Belotti cited above, such factors may be taken into account to influence the decision of destination. It is a decision often take together with others.

These networks are increasingly able to project themselves on a planetary scale and take advantage of opportunities in different locales. Like dissipative systems, given changing conditions they are able to adapt or change the direction of flows of people and resources based upon both minute and large-scale changes in the world economy. Thus, the closing of borders in France, Germany, Nigeria (for Ghanaians), or the Persian Gulf (as a result of the war) led to the increasing importance of Italy, Spain, and other countries as destinations. We recall that the numbers of legal immigrants in Italy declined slightly overall and for most national groups in 1993-94 before rebounding substantially from 781,000 to 922,000 in 1995.[20] These numbers coincide with an economic downturn in the Italian economy in 1993–1994 and a subsequent growth in 1995. Since the migration to Italy is not organized on the basis of state-to-state agreements, as was, for example the migration to France in the 1960s, the decline cannot be assumed to mechanistically or structurally reflect the needs of Italian industry. It may also involve the human agency of migrant networks, which limited their numbers on the Italian peninsula in the face of dimished opportunities. Likewise, the subsequent increase in migrant numbers cannot be attributed to any particular loosening of the Italian border; since 1990, the Italian border has officially been closed to immigration in accord with the Schengen requirements of the European Community. It was only over the following years, however, that visas were required for certain Mediterranean basin countries considered "emigration risks."[21] Migrant networks show an increasing versatility in their ability to take advantage of available opportunity structures in diverse parts of the world, and to withdraw from situations like the postwar Gulf or a recession-plagued Italian economy when necessary.

There is considerable evidence that migrant social networks, like those of the European migration at the start of the 20th century, are able to largely control employment within firms, workplaces, industries and sectors of the economy. In terms of the individual migrant's opportunities, this appears in the form of aid in finding work. Fourteen of the 47 Senegalese interviewed said they had found work with the help of friends or relatives already employed at the same workplace. Another 29 said they went in person to search for work, a response that I found in at least some cases included going in person to a place where friends or family already worked. The Moroccan social network appears to be even more well organized with regards to employment—21 Moroccans, the majority of all interviewees of that nationality, had found work through friends or family already employed. The Filipino/as were more likely to have found work through a Catholic agency— 10 of the 16 interviewees responded that they had found their current jobs with the help of a religious association, while the other six found work through friends or family. Since Filipinos and Filipinas are often active either as staff or volunteers by church groups, these two responses are not mutually exclusive.

A majority of the Ghanaians, 22 of 41, said they had found their jobs through friends or relatives, while 15 went in person. Employment patterns for Ghanaians reflect this influence of social networks in job finding: 18, or 44 percent of the Ghanaians interviewed using a questionnaire worked in tanneries. The rest of those employed were divided between plastics (4), furniture (4), foundries (4), machine tools (3), soldering (4) and food production (2). Ghanaian social networks and community life in Italy are heavily church oriented. Twenty-one of the questionnaire-based interviews with Ghanaians revealed membership in the evangelical Pentacostal Assembly of God church, which has a predominantly Ghanaian congregation in Vicenza, and a predominantly Nigerian congregation in Padua. Two Ghanaians were Jehovah's Witnesses, and two belonged to the Khalik Catholic association, which helped them find their factory jobs. The Assembly of God minister, the Rev. Simmons Odame, with whom I conducted two interviews, had himself worked in a tannery. All told, ten of the Ghanaians who worked in tanneries, or nearly one-fourth of the total interviewed with questionnaires, reported being members of the Pentacostal Church. Many reported spending their spare time in church activities, reading the Bible at home, attending church services on Sunday, or associating primarily with other church members. The Assembly of God is international in two senses. First, its network extends now across at least North and South America, Europe and Africa. The Rev. Odame travels extensively on church business throughout North America, Europe, and Africa. Second, its congregation in Vicenza is multinational, including Ghanaians, Nigerians, Italians, English, and for a time also Americans (soldiers and their families at the Vicenza NATO air force base). During and after the Gulf War, concerns about possible terrorist attack against American soldiers resulted in base personnel and their families being restricted to church services on the base grounds.[22]

Studies of migration to the United States have revealed similar patterns of migrant placement in jobs: Massey et. al. have shown the extensive networks by which Mexican villages can respond rapidly to employment prospects in Los Angeles, and Bach and Portes found similar network-based employment structures in their study of Cuban and Mexican migration to the United States.[23] Philip Martin has even recently criticized the effects of migrant control of personnel decisions in various industries and cities as expelling U.S.-born workers from employment opportunities.[24] As we shall explore in the following chapters, migrant communities tend to be able to organize employment in industries that local-born workers either have already abandoned or hope to abandon. We find Ghanaians in tanneries, foundries, and soldering work, Senegalese in slaughterhouses or street vending, Filipinas/os in domestic work. In the next chapter we will see how a dialectical interaction between the planetary and local labor markets, and between the transnational migrant communities and the local nation state, structures the labor market in the particular locale.

Obstacles notwithstanding, migrant networks constitute a dense web of information, employment help, and resource allocation across national boundaries. The examples of the Ghanaian Pentacostal, Filipino Catholic, and Senegalese Mouride networks reveal also that religious organization can be extended across borders, leading to an expansion of cultural space available to a community and reenforcing other linkages such as family, friendship, and nationality. Since, in each of these cases, there are other bases for social relations beyond religious ones—family and geographic links, and in the case of the Mourides, the Wolof ethnicity—we should probably see these religious networks as overlapping with and interacting with networks based on family, community, and friendship. The religious organizations can, however, provide some basis for organization and for collective interaction with the Italian community. To be sure, Catholic associations mediate job searches for domestics between Filipina women and potential Italian employers.[25] Senegalese who worship together also attend labor union meetings together; they use religious bonds, and even local religious leadership, to communicate the time and place of a meeting to the community members.[26] But informal communication links are also important. The Filipino community meets in the main municipal piazza in Padua every Thursday and Sunday afternoon on domestic workers' days off. Senegalese men often live several to a house or apartment, largely due to the cost and scarcity of housing in the Veneto. Informal contact at the workplace itself is also very important. Three-quarters of the Ghanaians interviewed worked with other immigrants, and well over one-third were employed at workplaces where at least one fifth (and in some cases half) of the employees are immigrants. This is no small fact in a region where immigrants make up less than 2 percent of the population. The concentration of immigrants in certain industries, itself a result of migrant network job-placement activity, can facilitate informal contact and communications.

The two main responses by immigrant interviewees regarding job finding, namely, going in person to look for work and having help from family or friends, both represent innovations in the Italian labor market. Until the mid-1990s, it was not lawful for employers to simply hire job candidates of their choosing in firms of over 15 employees. They had to use a list at the government-run placement office (no private temporary or other employment agents are legal in Italy to this day), which involved a number of criteria for determining who could be hired for certain jobs. The immigrant practices of going in person to Veneto factories to ask for work and helping friends and family get hired revolutionized the local job market and span the period in which the legal status of job searching was somewhat liberalized. The migrant networks effectively play a major role in the creation of a planetary labor market by also making local labor markets.

The planetary networks of migrant communities can be the bases for more than job placement. They make possible commercial networks and political organization, and provide for the circulation of remittances to the family and community in the country of origin. The Mouride commercial network by now extends throughout much of the planet, reaching to every destination where Mourides travel as migrants. Indeed, developing as a commercial network from its origins in peanut cultivation was the first great transformation of its own internal organization accomplished by this Senegalese Muslim brotherhood. At first, fleeing problems in the peanut production zones, Mourides moved into Senegalese cities, where they took up trade, which had been for many peanut growing families an off-season form of labor.[27] The Mourides moved into import-export commerce as talibé (literally students, the name used for ordinary followers of the religious leaders) emigrated to cities in nearby countries of West Africa—Gambia, the Ivory Coast capital of Abidjan (where Pap Khouma met the contact that led him to his first residence in Italy) and the tourist beaches of the Ivory Coast.[28] The urban and migration experiences also led to the creation of a new Mouride institution, the da'ira, a residence and Koranic school usually under the leadership of a marabout and including mostly or exclusively his talibé. Where the dara had been the form of organizing collective agricultural labor, the da'ira became the means of organizing the community under emigration and urban conditions, and of organizing commercial activity and the sending of remittances.[29] Da'iras have been organized in Paris, New York, Atlantic City, and Japan as well as in various parts of Africa and Europe. In Italy, due to the perennial difficulty of finding housing or access to public space for immigrants, no da'ira exists. Rather it is approximated as the talibé of a particular marabout will often live together, and come together on weekends from diverse parts of the same province for common religious activity. Ottavia Schmidt di Friedberg found that in Italy when there is either a marabout or an elder in the household, domestic chores are often organized on the basis of the *takket* (the labor obligation to religious leaders), as the youngest male usually cooks or cleans and all younger men are expected to run errands or provide household tasks for the elder.[30]

The commercial network is based upon street vending of various goods, usually crafts made in Africa or in some cases in Asia: wooden elephants and other sculpted works, silver bracelets, earrings and necklaces, string bracelets, music cassettes, and cigarette lighters. These goods, and the goods consumed by the Senegalese men overseas, are transported and distributed for sale by a complex organization that combines the features of a multinational corporation, a religious association, a family network, and a face-to-face news agency. "Transporters"—often the Senegalese women who do not show up in the emigration statistics—move back and forth between Dakar, New York, Paris, Naples, Abidjan, Istanbul, Marseilles and Naples, buying goods to be sold on the streets or consumed by Senegalese migrants who seek familiar foods and clothings.[31] Most local distributors in Italy converge on Via Firenze in Naples to buy wares to bring back to the network of vendors in their local Italian city, and these goods are then distributed from a central post, often someone's apartment. A recent study of street vending on the beaches of Emilia-Romagna helped bring this extraordinary network to light, confirming the findings of Schmidt di Friedberg and the autobiographical comments of Pap Khouma. The network is indeed informal, with no global center or fixed hierarchy, and is decisively not based upon either organized crime (Senegalese, Italian or otherwise), nor on debt-based forced labor, contrary to Italian public speculation that seems to reflect local experience with such networks as the cigarette contraband sales by the Naples Camorra.[32] The Mouride network has consistently proven able to extend itself, transform its operations, and grow in complexity like a dissipative system. From peanut cultivation to urban commerce to a planetary network of trade, the brotherhood's overall form has remained stable while the scale and form of the flows of people and resources through its networks have grown and changed dramatically.

Other mercantile networks exist in addition to the Senegalese system. Nigerian businesses in Padua carry out import/export activity with Nigeria and have contacts inside Nigeria which seem to aid emigrants arrive in Italy.[33] An informal but quite regular market is set up every Sunday on the outskirts of Padua by Polish migrants who travel by tourist bus from Poland selling everything from lamps to knives to clothes to Polish money as souvenirs (with pictures of Lenin). There are also substantial networks of drug sales and prostitution—the former involving young Moroccan and Tunisian men, the latter involving Albanians, Romanians and to some extent Yugoslavs—often under conditions where women are either forced or convinced under false conditions to work in Italy. There is also a Nigerian prostitute network that seems unique in not involving pimps in Italy, nor local use of force by men. Instead the women owe their expensive transit fare to the network. The need to pay this transnational debt payment keeps the women working.[34]

Networks may also engage in political activity, as the case of the Philippines networks shows. The Filipina network has demonstrated the capacity of such international networks to link workers in activities that go beyond work and resource circulation. Faced with difficult and dangerous work conditions, as well as physical and political repression in various continents, Filipina communications links have proven capable of mobilizing politically on a breathtaking variety of fronts to defend the work conditions of domestic workers. In Canada and Hong Kong, for instance, Filipina domestic workers have formed unions. This capacity to organize can transcend national boundaries, and women from the Philippines have at times proven to be a politically advanced agent of class conflict on a planetary level in struggles against the contemporary slave trade and forced emigration, sexual violence and workplace harassment, rape, the death penalty and forced labor. After the March 17, 1995 execution of Filipina domestic worker Flor Contemplacion in Singapore, thousands at her funeral service berated Philippines President Ramos for the government's failure to act to save her life. Hundreds of Filipina women occupied their embassy in Kuwait after the Persian Gulf War to protest sexual abuse, rape, and violence by their employers, as well as other harsh conditions. International protests held by Filipina women helped reverse the death sentence against Sarah Balabagan, a 16-year old Filipina convicted of killing her employer after he raped her in Abu Dhabi, UAE. In 1994 in Houston, Texas, two Filipina servants to Saudi Prince Saad demanded the right to quit his service, claiming they were being held against their will and demanding that they be paid the legal U.S. minimum wage. Filipinas have also organized against the forced transportation of women from Asia and the Middle East to England by their employers, and have organized associations such as Kalayaan, the Friends of Filipino Domestic Workers, and the Association of International Domestics for Development.[35]

There are other examples of cross-border political activity in the Veneto. Nigerian grocery stores in Padua sell magazines and newspapers from their home country which are critical of the military regime. A group of Albanian migrants from Kosovo worked in the Vicenza area through the mid-1990s in order to pay "taxes" to their government in exile before the NATO-Yugoslav War. Eritreans, Somalians, and Iranians in the Veneto have been active as part of support efforts for Eritrean independence and postwar reconstruction, for mediation between clans and factions during the civil war, and in protest of human rights violations by the Islamic regime in Iran, respectively. Many of these efforts dovetail into self-organization in the region—union activity, immigrant associations and anti-racist marches.

REMITTANCES AND DISSIPATIVE SYSTEMS

It is perhaps in their ability to organize a flow of remittance payments to family, community, and even religious and political associations in their country of origin that transnational migrant communities most resemble dissipative systems. For just as they mobilize the movement of persons, goods, and political ideas and protests around the world, they mobilize a massive transfer of wealth back to their country of origin in the form of money remittances and, to a substantial extent, gifts for family and friends. The former can be quantified, but only as a measure of the dimension of movement of funds, since migrants have many methods of transporting funds personally that are not counted. The latter is far more difficult to quantify, but many migrants, returning home every two years, bring as many gifts from Italy to Senegal, Morocco, India, and Ghana as they can carry onto the plane. One Romanian man drove a station wagon packed with a refrigerator, shoes for most members of the family (some of whose sizes had grown in the meantime), clothes, music cassettes and cassette players, and the like all the way to his home country from Italy. But it is the remittances of funds to families, friends and communities that is the main objective of the migrants to Italy, and it is a massive presence in the world economy.

The World Bank estimated in 1990 that the flow of remittances by migrants worldwide was $65.6 billion, second only to crude oil as a form of international flows of money. Coffee, the next most important commodity for overall flow of money, was a distant third. By 1992 this total had risen to $71 billion. Estimates for remittances that are not officially counted conclude that the worldwide total comes to between $100 billion and $120 billion. Remittances have become, as Peter Stalker puts it, "a major form of transfer of resources from industrialized countries." By 1988 remittances from highly industrialized countries, not including the oil-producing Gulf States, amounted to $29 billion—equal to half of all the official development aid for the same year.[36] For some countries migrant workers' remittances have become an essential part of the economy. In 1989, remittances to Yugoslavia amounted to $6.3 billion, equal to nearly half the value of the country's exports. Moroccan remittances similarly stood in value at over 40 percent of the country's exports, and at 6.5 percent of the entire GDP. By 1994, Moroccan remittances were estimated by the National Exchange Bank of Morocco to have risen to 20 billion *dirhams*—equal to half of the country's exports, one-third of its imports, 150 percent of the value of Morocco's tourist industry, 250 percent of the value of its leading export product (phosphates), and equal to the entire interest payment on its national foreign debt.[37] Tunisian remittances equaled nearly 5 percent of the country's GDP that year. In 1986, the Philippines Overseas Employment Administration estimated remittances of Filipina migrants at $680.4 million.[38] Again, these estimates do not include money transported personally during visits home, or sent via friends and family members. Thus, a survey of 600 overseas Filipina workers found that only 40 percent of their remittances were sent by official bank transfer, with home visits, money couriers, and in-kind transfers in the form of goods accounting for the greater part of remittances.[39]

The total officially counted remittances by immigrants in Italy to their home countries amounted to 404 billion lire in 1995, or about $260 million.[40] The total remittances sent by Italians living abroad back to their communities, mostly in southern Italy, amounted to 556 billion lire the same year. Italy, despite ceasing to have a net emigration, continues to have a net inflow of remittances. Remittances represent the purpose of migration for most of the interviewees and their communities. The emigration decision is often taken in concert with family and other community members, and reflects the need to devise a strategy for survival in the face of structural adjustment and its impact on the local community. While involving the all-important willingness of individuals to migrate, emigration is a decision that takes into account family and community needs. Many interviewees said they had taken the decision to emigrate together with family or neighbors. Three-fifths of the Ghanaians responding to the question, "How did you decide to emigrate?," answered either "I decided together with my family" or "I decided together with friends or neighbors." Seven of the 35 Ghanaians who responded to this question answered that they decided with friends and neighbors rather than only with their own family. Every interviewee from the Philippines who responded to this question, 14 of the Filipino total 16, said they had made the decision to emigrate together with either family, friends and neighbors, or both. Moroccans seemed to be somewhat less likely to make the decision to emigrate collectively, with only 7 of the respondents stating that the emigration decision was made collectively. In contrast, nine of the 15 Nigerians reported consulting their family in making the decision to emigrate.

Other studies have found considerable collective decision-making by migrants in the choice of emigration. Peter Stalker, in a study for the International Labor Organization, writes that, "When looking at motives for migration, it is important to realize that most migrants are playing their part in a family survival strategy. The person who migrates may have little choice in the matter, since the decision is likely to be made by the head of the family."[41] This family strategy is essentially based upon remittances. The migrant network constitutes a structure for the transfer of wealth back to the family and the region of origin. In many respects, migrant communities act as organizations in developing this structure. One study of the Philippines showed that families tend to send the family members they think will be the most reliable senders of remittances. This often results in sending daughters rather than sons. The criteria used by many transnational communities is *the maximization of remittances sent home, rather than the maximization of wages* to be obtained—men after all might earn higher wages for the types of work available to them as migrants than do women domestic workers.[42] Among Mourides, the religious brotherhood's network, as well as informal communications reaching the Senegalese countryside, organizes and even guarantees the sending and receiving of remittances. There is evidence that some part of remittances also go directly to the marabout, in lieu of a part of peanut cultivation, but this seems as yet unconfirmed in the literature.[43] Yet complex organization in mobilizing migration as a family or community strategy seems common to many migrant networks:

Just as a cautious investor will diversify their portfolio of shares, so the careful head of family can try to build up a diversified portfolio of workers. Some may be allocated work on the family farm, others sent to take a salaried job in a town, others will travel abroad. The head of the family, and the person who travels, effectively make a contract between them—a form of co-"insurance." The head of the family pays for the travel and living expenses while the migrant is looking for work, and may also promise to send money at times of unemployment. The migrant promises to send money home, increasing these remittances on occasion if the family is in particular difficulty from illness, or crop failure.[44]

The overwhelming majority of the migrants interviewed for this study reported sending remittances home. Indeed, for every group of migrants interviewed involving at least nine persons, the percentage of remitters was around 90 percent or higher. This was true even for those respondents who seemed to make it a matter of personal pride to state that they had decided to migrate as an individual choice. By far the most common answer to the question, "If you do send money, what is it used for?" was "to pay for the everyday needs of the family." This answer was the most common for every migrant group interviewed. Every Moroccan who responded to this question answered that remittances were used for everyday expenses; one added that the money also went to cover schooling costs for a family member. Likewise, among Ghanaians, nearly every interviewee responded that the remittances they sent went to pay everyday family expenses. Of 41 Ghanaians interviewed, 37 answered with this response, though six added that some remittance funds went to pay for relatives' school expenses as well. Three did not answer and only one stated that his remittances were going to buy a house instead of for everyday needs.

It is more difficult to quantify amounts remitted by the immigrants in the Veneto. In part this is because questions involving the regularity with which remittances were sent drew fewer responses than more general questions about remittances. Likewise, asking migrants how much they send in remittances without having strong data for frequency still made it difficult to judge how much was sent abroad in a certain period. A further problem is that while some migrants responding to questions concerning remittances stated that they sent remittances every month, many stated that they send remittances two-four times per year; it is also largely impossible to quantify gifts and remittances in kind. Given these problems, we must be satisfied for now with two very different scales of measurement: individual responses in all their variety, and the official total of remittances for all nationalities by immigrants in Italy. Wages for factory work in Italy average about 1.5 million lire net pay, or about $900 a month. Those few immigrants who answered questions about remittance payment amounts stated that two or three times a year they were able to send between 300,000 and 500,000 lire, while others stated that they sent about 200,000 lire every couple of months when possible. These figures amount to about one million lire a year, or about $650. The total annual remittances of immigrants in Italy is, as we have seen, officially about 400 billion lire, sent by about 900,000 legal immigrants, or between 400,000 and 450,000 per immigrant per year, equal to about $300. Including money remittances that are not offically counted as estimated above, estimated by some analysts as more than double these official numbers, we arrive at a figure around one million lire per year per immigrant, again about $650 a year. We can compare this estimate to that for remittances on a worldwide scale: The estimated 100 million immigrants in the world remitted an estimated $71 billion, or about $700 per year per immigrant.[45] Thus, the remittances of immigrants in Italy would appear to be close to, if perhaps a shade smaller, than the average remitted by immigrants worldwide. Obviously, not every immigrant works for wages or sends remittances. It was estimated worldwide that about 30 million of the 80 million immigrants in 1990 were employed foreign workers.[46] In the Veneto, of the 72,000 extracomunitarian immigrants counted officially in 1995, 18,000 were employed. This is a 25 percent employment total, as opposed to about 37 percent worldwide. However, the scale of off-the books work in the Veneto, for immigrants and Italians, is very high as we shall see in chapter 6.[47] Further, in the first six months of 1997, the number of employed immigrants had risen to 26,000, though the figures for total legal immigrants present in the region is not available for this same period. In all likelihood, the percentage of employment of immigrants in the Veneto is equal to, if not higher, than the worldwide average. On the whole, then, we may say that remittances by immigrants in Italy and in the Veneto are within the general range of the worldwide average. The flow of people to various parts of the world through the networks of migrant transnational communities, and the flow of money and other resources back to the region of origin, by these same networks, may be described in terms of a dissipative system. If the results of structural adjustment are to exacerbate inequality, to increase the flow of wealth from certain regions to institutions in the wealthier zones of the planet, thereby de-stabilizing subsistence organization, we may describe the flow of remittances as similar to the heat convection seen in Prigogine's discussion of heated water. A new social form of organization, able to grow in complexity and in scale, and to mobilize both people and resources acts to re-stabilize the situation in a way that allows for the flow of resources through its structure, while maintaining that structure even under changing conditions. It is more difficult to describe the net effect of this flow of resources. To be sure, it in no way equals the flow of wealth out of the same regions. This is true whether measured in money terms or in value terms. Indeed, it is unclear whether migration, taken on its own, necessarily results in a net flow of wealth in value terms back to the region of origin, though in money terms it would seem that it does after a given period of time.

To make this point clearer, we must examine more closely two distinct questions. The first is the cost of emigration for the emigrant and her or his community in money terms; the second is the value relation embodied in migration in terms of the social reproduction of the migrant worker, and of the value produced by her or his labor in the country of destination. The first question entails above all the price of transportation and its organization—an issue discussed in some detail historically in chapter 2. There we found considerable continuity in the existence of private transport of labor power, whether in the African slave trade, the transportation of European or Asian indentured labor, or in the turn-of-the-century European migrations. With the exception of the slave ships, the emigrants in each of these cases either bore the cost of transportation or had this cost covered for them by either employers, creditors in their home country, or the transport firms themselves, in exchange for repayment in money or in a period of indentured labor. In today's migration context we find both the payment of transportation costs by migrants or their families and the payment of these costs by creditors in exchange for repayment with considerable interest or by work directly for the network that covered the price of transportation. In some cases we find both types of transportation payment together. The question of how transportation is arranged and how its cost is covered goes to the heart of the issue of the autonomy of migrant networks and communities, and the very freedom of migrant labor power in the world today. We find at work simultaneously both an extensive autonomy of the migrant communities and their ability to use the rapid and relatively inexpensive methods of contemporary travel to develop their networks more extensively— and the return of some of the most archaic forms of unfree labor and commerce in human cargo which were thought to have been largely eliminated from the world market centuries ago. As in other aspects of the current world economic scene—forms of craft or small-scale production, forms of rebellion based on seemingly pre-capitalist identities, the importance of debt, or the new wave of enclosures of common lands and goods—capitalism seems to be calling on its entire history in the search for appropriate forms of organization of the market for labor power.

The contemporaneous existence of the most advanced forms of planetary transnational networks of communities of working people and of the return of the trade in unfree workers thus appears as a time-space compression, involving the jamming together of centuries' worth of differing social forms. In fact, the contradiction is only apparent. The forms of unfree trade in workers can be understood as itself a part of the enclosures, both an effect and a consituent part of structural adjustment under-stood as a worldwide regime of control over labor power. Further, the private organization of for-profit illegal and semi-legal transport both operate as parasites within the overall context of the extensive and overlapping planetary contacts that are organized in migrant community networks. These networks I call "the other worldwide web," a planetary web of contacts, overlapping networks, and organizational resources created by migrants from dozens of countries. Initially independent of one another, these networks show signs of intersecting and cooperating, and organize a counterflow of resources of epic proportions. The forced migration systems may be understood as means of subordinating the potential for the autonomy of these networks from the grid of capitalist value production, of reducing their capacity for mobility to mere functionality for the world market for labor power. In short, the new commerce in forced workers is a part of the very mechanisms that drove migrant communities toward the strategy of migration in the first place, and an attack on the capacity of these communities to control the planetary migration process and the making of the world labor market. Let us look more closely at the relations between these forces as they interact in the arrival of migrants into Italy. To do so, we should first turn to that sphere of action where the two opposites, the autonomous migrant networks and the commerce in unfree workers, meet, namely in the private transport systems which operate around the world to carry workers to their destinations.

To many of the world's countries of immigrant destination, recruitment agencies organize employment and transportation for often exorbitant fees. The average cost to workers from the Philippines for finding a job in the Middle East is around $900.[48] A worker from India might pay between $1,500 and $2,000 to make a base pay of $175 a month. Some agencies in Asia will charge employers a one-time commission of between $100 and $400.[49] Filipina women who work as domestics in Singapore, 35,000 in all, paid about $850 each for air fare. In Malaysia, agents charge double fees for air fare. Filipina workers in Bahrain reported having to pay air fare fees to agents in both their home country and Bahrain. Filipinas paid around $200-$260 dollars apiece to agents in Bahrain, and women from Sri Lanka paid between $140 and $340.[50] Many of these workers take out loans either from family or friends or local creditors in order to cover the cost; some even put their land or house up as collateral. The practice of paying agents for travel costs, however, seems to be linked to two conditions: (1) work recruitment in areas of the world where state organization of migration is still dominant—such as the Middle East and the Asian Tigers; and (2) illegal entry into industrialized countries. Hence, as in the past, private profiteering from transport is related to the unfree nature of work for certain categories of workers or to their legal status, which approximates unfree conditions.

Entry into Italy essentially takes two forms: arrival by boat or much more commonly air, at first legally with a tourist or religious pilgrim's visa, or illegally, usually by boat or across the mountains and forests of Slovenia by land. In the first group of cases, the cost involved is merely the normal price of a plane ticket from Dakar, Lagos, Casablanca, or Manila, to Rome, Palermo, Naples, or Milan. In the second case, a worldwide network of transporting human cargo has grown up, occasionally making headlines in U.S. or European newspapers, but more often remaining in the shadows. A third system, presumably rarer, and seemingly an amalgamation of the two, is the illegal trade in visas to enter the country. In 1995 two officials of the Italian embassy in Lagos were accused of selling visas, often for thousands of dollars. This practice had been well known to the network of Nigerian immigrants in Italy before the scandal broke.[51]

The first and legal method of entry, of course, is legal only as entry, since technically Italy's borders are closed to new immigration as part of its adherence to the Schengen accords. In practice this relation to other European states has been strained throughout the 1990s, since Italy still allows entry for reasons of tourism, religious pilgrimage and study fairly easily. Since the end of an amnesty program in spring 1996, however, no new work permits are to be given out, at least in theory. This essentially criminalized all those who did not take advantage of the last amnesty and all those who have arrived since then. This includes many who arrived with legal visas and then remained without a resident permit, as did Pap Khouma, for instance. Flights leave twice a week from Dakar to Rome on the main Italian airline, and the cost is around 2 million lire, or $1,250. This can of course be an exorbitant amount for a family in a Third World country, and indeed many immigrants raise this sum either through loans from family or other community members, or by first emigrating to another country—the Ivory Coast or Mauritania in the case of West Africans, the Middle East in the case of some Arab workers—then saving up the cost of plane fare to Europe or the United States. The ability to make use of the most advanced means of transportation is also fundamental to both the mobility of migration networks—to rapidly change residence or take advantage of work opportunities as conditions change—and also to the ability of migrant communities to remain in close contact. Most of the Senegalese workers in the Veneto seem to return home every two years for several months; many Tunisian and Moroccan workers are often able to spend part of every year with family in their hometown. Along with reduced long-distance telephone rates—several businesses run by immigrants in Padua specialize in this—modern means of transportation and communications make possible much more extended and frequent contact among the various geographical parts of the other worldwide web of migrant communities.

At the other end of the spectrum of migration are the various criminal organizations that use previously established "roads" for drug or weapon smuggling to also ship people. This practice has given rise to various methods of illegal transportation of persons across borders. In the United States, recent years have seen scandals involving shiploads of Chinese workers sinking on the way to New York, a syndicate specialized in smuggling deaf Mexicans to sell goods on the subway, and the illegal transport and exploitation of Thai women in garment factories. In Europe, the two main paths are by land through Asia, Russia, and Eastern Europe, and by sea across the Mediterranean via various ports. It is necessary, however, to distinguish between two phenomena which, though they can overlap, are also somewhat distinct. The first is the illegal shipment of willing immigrants who have paid exorbitant fees because of their desperation to find a means of entry into Europe. The second is the either forced transportation of unwilling persons, through kidnapping, debt repayment default, sale of children by their parents for debt or lack of subsistence, false promises of work opportunities, or other coercive methods. The first usually involves payment for the passage into Europe in advance by the migrant, their family, or a third party. The latter usually involves the migrant working under unfree conditions directly for the network that has coerced them into leaving home. The relation of these two distinct forms of illegal transportation to the worldwide web of migrant communities differs Their relationship to migrant communities is one of exploitation, yet the transport of migrants, however illegally and at whatever exorbitant cost to the migrant, has a far more ambiguous relation to migrant networks than the outright theft of labor power. However high the fares demanded by the transporters of human cargo, and however dishonest their promises of conditions may be, they also provide a sort of service to the distinct network of migrants who wish to enter the industrialized countries. That is, both sides use the other, to the profit of the transporter and the success at arriving at the destination—in many cases, at least—of the migrant. It is far from an equal relationship, but given the increasingly tight nature of borders in most countries of migrant destination, it is hard to imagine by what other method migrant communities would be able to arrive in certain places. The unfree transportation of workers is far less ambiguous, though these two types of activities may be engaged in by the same actors.

Italy as a long peninsula, across the Mediterranean from Morocco and Tunisia, and sitting on the ex-Cold War border between East and West Europe at a time of instability in Yugoslavia and Albania, is a site of perhaps daily attempts to enter surreptitiously. One widely used road runs from China and Pakistan through Moscow, where the Russian Mafia manages transport, usually through Bucharest, into the ex-Yugoslavia or Albania, or to Tunisia, or Greece, and then by boat onto southern Italian beaches or ports by night.[52] Passages from Tunisia to Italy by smugglers cost between $500 and $2,000. The Italian Mafia uses big motor cruisers, which are faster than most of the local nation's coast guard ships and fit up to 50 people per voyage. This route became even more widely used when Spain cracked down on the Moroccan state, for its lax patrolling of its coast and liberal allowance to its citizens to leave, by threatening trade sanctions.[53] Belgian police recently uncovered a network that had promised at least 4,000 residents of the Philippines transportation and work in Western Europe, then took them to Italy where they worked as undocumented domestics and manual workers and in many cases were pressed into prostitution.[54]

Italy has frequently been confronted by stories of the illegal transportation of workers into the country. In August 1990, half a dozen Pakistanis walked into the police station of Castel Maggiore on the outskirts of Bologna and told police of how they and 150 of their co-nationals, all men, had been living together in a large farmhouse, working in factories (those few who had permits), construction work, and restaurants. With the annual August vacation time observed in Italy, many found themselves without work for a month and the community was in trouble, leading them to the police.[55] There is reason to think that the clandestine arrival of such workers is very common in Italy. In October 1996, the financial police announced that 4,832 foreigners had been expelled at the borders attempting to enter Puglia or Sicily since the start of the year. The same report claimed that between five and ten vans or minibuses arrived from Albania every night, each carrying between 10 and 20 persons.[56] Sixty-nine people were arrested trying to enter within a few hours at the port of Lampedusa, and 42 arrested in two operations over two days in Sicily and Puglia in the same month. In 1997, one report called the arrival of clandestine immigrants at Lampedusa "daily" and the Italian government sought to involve the Tunisian authorities in helping to stem the tide. Sometimes the unfortunate migrants who have paid a fortune to arrive in Europe never make it: they are cheated by the transporters, caught upon entry by the police, or, more tragically, their ship wrecks on the way, as happened near Sicily to 300 persons from Sri Lanka and Pakistan who lost their lives when their ship went down.[57] This was the worst accident of its type so far, but far from the first: in October 1994, a small boat from Morocco trying to enter Italy went down, 2 of its 26 passengers died. The previous August, 25 Tunisians had leaped from a boat into the water rather than be arrested and repatriated. Over the next two days they were all found in farmhouses along the coast.[58]

The more tightly borders are closed to legal entry, the more migrant networks are forced to rely on illegal transport methods, which involve exploitation through exorbitant fares, the risk of being brought to a different destination and under different conditions of work than those agreed upon, the possibility of arrest, and the danger of shipwreck. The actions of nation states in controlling the extent to which their borders are legally opened is a major factor in determining the conditions under which the world labor market is made. Though entry in quantitative terms is reduced by the legal closing of borders to immigration, by no means is it prevented altogether. Rather, the conditions under which migrants enter, their legal status upon entry and therefore their legal status and degree of power in the labor market and the workplace are greatly impaired. Further, as we have seen, the need to enter surreptitiously means that the autonomy of migrant networks is compromised—they must rely upon transport systems that involve greater degrees of exploitation and danger than under legal conditions. It is with Italy's efforts after 1990 to conform to the requirements of the Schengen Agreements governing movement into and through the European Union that we see a notable increase in reports of clandestine entry, as the Italian border increasingly closed and visas became required for entry even from other Mediterranean basin countries. There's a degree of continuity with the previous history of migrations and labor markets, in which state control has historically acted primarily to limit the possibilities of autonomous action by migrant communities, rather than merely to stop entry. This limitation of autonomously organized entry is what provides the room for private, exploitative efforts to gain partial control of the transport of migrants. A pirate-like network, itself an aspect for centuries of every cycle of primitive accumulation of capital, attempts to replace the web of migration networks organized by the migrant communities themselves. The apparent contradiction between the state's historical encouragement of privateering during the African slave trade and its official closing of borders to privateering in the transportation of contemporary migrants may be less important than the common impact of both activities. In both cases, the state's action led ultimately to a growth of privateering in the transportation of workers across borders.

Comparisons of the current labor market and the slave trade are not solely hyperbole. For along with the growth of privateering in the transport of workers willing, even desperate to enter Europe, comes the rise, or better, the return of practices that resemble the methods by which enslaved Africans, and kidnapped or press-ganged Europeans and shanghaied Asians, were transported in previous migrations. As in the United States in recent years, a disturbingly large number of stories involving the coerced transportation of workers from their homes and their exploitation in unpaid or unfree conditions have come to light in Italy during the 1990s. Such stories involve a variety of national networks. At one time or another, Chinese, Albanian, Romanian, Russian, Yugoslav, Nigerian, and Nigerois networks have been charged with the forced transportation of workers, in most cases women forced to work in Italy as prostitutes, but also including drug sales and even factory work in some cases. In July 1995, Stella, a 21-year-old woman from a village near the Niger capital of Niamey was approached by a young man who told her, "In Italy there's work in the factories or as a domestic. We can advance you 50 million lire ($32,000) for expenses, which you can repay gradually when you start to get paid." She was then brought by plane to Russia, then by train across Europe to Padua. By the time she had been convinced by a Catholic volunteer service worker named Franco to take advantage of an amnesty program, obtain a legal permit, and live with his family and work for his artisan shop, Stella had repaid 35 million of the 50 million lire loan. But the organization, in Padua headed by a matriarch named Kate, threatened to kill Stella or her family in Niger if the rest wasn't repaid, something that was largely impossible on legal wages. Stella had made 4 million lire ($2,500) a month as a prostitute or well over double average factory wages, and nearly five times domestic workers' wages; she had paid Kate 1.5 million lire per month for room and board. This network allegedly met every night in a bar in Padua to take the money earned by the women.[59]

In another case in Padua, Claudia, a 14-year-old Albanian girl, was kidnapped from her family's home by 20 armed men, including a boy who had twice previously approached her in front of her school claiming to be in love with her and asking her to go with him. Beaten "every night" and transported to work "one week in the South, one week in the North" of Italy, she was rescued by a male client who took her to the police station in Padua. Her mother subsequently wrote her, "Don't ever come back here, they'll kill you if you do."[60] Another case involving Albanian traffickers, and entitled ironically by local newspapers in Padua, "Another case of ordinary slavery," involved two Albanian men charged with holding an 18-year-old woman against her will and beating her savagely to force her to prostitute herself. The woman in this case refused to cooperate with police and denied being a prostitute, but stated that she had been carried across the Adriatic in a boat and then brought to Padua.

There are similar cases involving Romanian and Russian women in the Veneto area that have come to light in recent years.[61] In late 1996, authorities in the region charged that Chinese triads acted as slave merchants, bringing workers to Padua where they were were held secretly in an apartment and forced to work in Chinese restaurants. Other cases have even involved factory work by Chinese workers in Veneto villages and farmhouse, producing textiles and leather goods.[62] Such stories of forced labor are not restricted to migrant networks. In the course of this research I interviewed a young Romanian woman who had come to the Veneto as part of a training program for a Veneto-based industrial firm. She was to be paid a small stipend and the family that owned the Italian firm offered to let her stay with them. For fourteen months she was kept virtual prisoner in their house, told not to ever go out alone (because Italy, they told her, was too dangerous for women to ever go out by themselves, even in the daytime), and forced to work without pay—cooking, cleaning and caring for the grandmother who was ill at home. Finally, angry at never being paid her stipend, she argued with the family and was kicked out onto the street where she luckily met one of the nuns who runs Padua's *cucina popolare*—a soup kitchen largely frequented by immigrants—who took her in, and with the legal assistance of a local left-wing labor union's immigrant office, was helped to find legal work. These phenomena must be understood as part of a generalized and planetary return of unfree and forced labor, and of the commerce in such workers.[63] The trade in women, in children and even in human organs[64] are examples of the resurgence of unfree work and migration as forms of primitive accumulation.

These forms of commerce in humans clearly represent a throwback to the types of activity involved in other periods of primitive accumulation of capital, though in some cases these horrors have reached new levels of sadism. These arise as means of subjecting migrant mobility to the needs of capital in such a period. Flexible production has not found the means to guarantee the bringing together of labor and capital on a worldwide scale given such mobility. The neoliberal regime is clearly more interested in blocking access to migrant entry under autonomous conditions than in organizing the bringing together of labor and capital for production. This relation, too often collapsed under the metaphor of the labor market, has always, as we have seen, required organized efforts to find workers, already separated from the means of production and subsistence, who could be geographically located where labor power was needed. Slave traders, privateers, state organization of coolie labor, and even the padrone system and its replacement by direct recruiting of labor by migrant workers have been among the necessary methods used in procuring labor for capital. For it is not enough that the workers exist; they must be physically located where production takes place and they must be convinced or coerced into working for particular capitalists. Today, in Italy and elsewhere, this recruitment is carried out by migrant social networks. But for certain kinds of work, or when labor power is simply unavailable in the desired quantities, the methods of primitive accumulation take over. Given the state's concern to block the migrant use of mobility, privateering takes on a more important role in organizing the labor market, and slavery, or its approximation, becomes increasingly possible.

MIGRANT EMBEDDEDNESS AND SOCIAL REPRODUCTION

The migrants' relation to their community in the country of origin cannot be reduced entirely to the narrowly economic factors involved in the remitting of resources. Rather, migrants from many of the sending countries are embedded in relations of extended family, village, and religious association. Such relations are the basis on which the migrant social network is created and it is to sustain these relations, even if under new circumstances, that the migration project itself is organized. Many migrants, as noted above, indicated that they see themselves as part of large families, especially those from West Africa. Given the West African practice whereby many family members are dependent, at least for the money-based part of their social reproduction costs, on a single wage earner, we see that the migration network in part constitutes a geographic expansion of the social relations in which migrants' lives are embedded to the planetary scale. This reality is well illustrated by the case of the Senegalese Mouride network. The sharing of goods to sell with new arrivals on a no-interest basis, the social importance of trust as social wealth (which guarantees that loans are paid back and hospitality extended for fear that one's family back in Senegal should hear that one acted improperly toward others), the common comment which I and other researchers have heard frequently from West Africans that they think their own culture more hospitable to strangers or more based on the idea that "all our co-nationals are brothers"—all of these aspects indicate that the rules by which the migrant social network governs itself are not those of the market, nor of *homo economicus*. Rather, they are cultural standards evolving under new conditions but based, as with the growth in complexity of any dissipative structures, on the community's own history. Ottavia Schmidt di Friedberg underlines the reciprocity that was the basis of the Mouride community relation, even under conditions of inequality. Further, she argues that the Mouride commercial network also serves other social functions beyond those strictly economic or profit and earnings-maximizing: to maintain contact for the migrant with the family in Senegal; to guarantee that someone trustworthy will transport remittances to where they are intended to go; to provide some aid in case of emergency; to raise funds to send dead immigrants back to their hometowns for burial; to provide cultural activities and familiar consumption products to the migrant and provide company for the long period away from home; even, as in the case of the man who told me he was working in Italy to save money to be able to pay a bride-price for marriage upon his return home—there are, in short, many culturally-based motives for the migration and economic activity itself.[65]

Such practices, as with the finding of jobs for friends and relatives and the sending of remittances to extended families, impose the migrant community's priorities on the heartless and unforgiving nature of the world labor market. For the immigrant, upon arrival in the country of destination and upon entering the labor market in that country, has by no means necessarily exited the social relations in which he or she grew up. Rather, social obligations entered into in the country of origin are to be realized precisely through the migration process, and by keeping faith through the regular sending of remittances. In return, the migrant knows that he or she always has a place to return to later, especially if it has been maintained by means of his or her remittance payments. In this sense, the worldwide web of migrant transnational communities constitutes not only a set of contacts and communications methods different from the grid of capitalist value production and realization, but an alternative means of organizing planetary work, communications and commercial relations, albeit a contradictory alternative. Seeing the dense set of mutual obligations, sharing of resources, and exchange of information and goods in this way enables us to understand the labor market as the meeting point of the two increasingly planetary sets of interactions and inter-relations: the capitalist grid linking all profit-making activity and value production by means of a world market, and the worldwide web of migrant communities with their myriad sets of reciprocal relations.

These relations, being reciprocal, necessarily link the migrant to subsistence and to social reproduction in the country of origin. It has been widely noted that the use of labor power in the First World that has been created and reproduced in the Third World represents a subsidy to the capitalist institutions of the industrialized world; They take advantage of the skill levels of such workers gained through social costs being covered either through public expenditures or through housework and domestic labor carried out in the country of origin. Silvia Federici labels this relation a "global apartheid which has transformed the Third World into an immense labor reserve that functions in relation to the metropolitan economies in a way analogous to that in which, until recently, the homelands of South Africa functioned in relation to the white areas."[66] My image of immigrant networks as dissipative structures is brought into question by an analysis of the flow of value inherent in such migrations, and not in a way limited only to the famous "brain drain" debate. For, following Fortunati and others, if part of the value personified in the worker, which is then transfered by work activity into the product, is the result of the reproductive work largely done by women in the household, the exploitative relation would seem to be magnified in the case of Third World workers whose production of value occurs in the First World, while their reproduction has at least up to migration taken place in the Third World, and in part continues to do so.[67] Seen in value terms, since the reproduction cost of the worker is lower, while value production for the capitalist increases—given higher productivity in the First World—then migration would seem merely to increase the transfer of value from the worker to the capitalist, from the Third World to the first. The image of a dissipative structure acting to create a convection in the flow of value would seem misguided since the disequilibrium is merely increased. The analogy is a limited one, as with any characterization of human activity in terms of the rest of the natural world.

Nevertheless, it seems to me still a useful one. For the value aspect of social reproduction cuts both ways. Immigrant workers are likely to be exploited more intensively because of their immigrant status, including their lack of the legal protections that accompany citizenship; likewise, the non-presence of their family in Italy, which would require social costs to the capitalist or the local state through higher real private or social wages, instead benefits employers. The purpose of the migrant is not maximization of monetary wealth for its own sake, but for the realization of social reproduction of the extended family, community, or social network to which remittances are sent. These communities are in parts of the world where, although for many goods world market prices are gradually being imposed (what has been called the "dollarization" of global prices) the cost of necessities remains lower than in the First World. The same hierarchy of wages that means that one hour of work in Senegal, Morocco or the Philippines has less value in national currency terms than one hour in the United States or Italy also imposes lower costs of reproduction in most sending countries. Hence, the remittance payments of Filipinas have often allowed their families to purchase a better quality house, as has been observed of many areas of emigration throughout the world. The single largest use of remittances is for housing, according to one report; another shows that households with access to remittances are more able to save than non-remittance-receiving households.[68]

That remittances are used for houses and savings, two activities often related to rural values and to a risk-minimizing rather than benefit-maximizing strategy, is one indication that the economic activity of migration, from the viewpoint of the migrant community, is functional to objectives that are not strictly economic, narrowly defined.

Similarly, the paying for schooling of a relative (who will then also be expected to help the family upon starting her or his career), the use of migrant savings to cover culturally expected costs of marriage, or supporting of religious institutions all tend toward treating the wealth obtained through migration as a use-value. That is, the migrant network acts as a dissipative structure in creating a convection in the flow of money to areas where the community can put it to most use for its own objectives, even if the overall transfer of value continues to flow toward the North. To the extent that the migrant community can control the migration process, and those resources made available to it through migration networks, its members may in the long run be able to minimize their dependence for their social reproduction on market participation. This is why the efforts of privateers and kidnappers of workers or the attempt to use debt through exorbitant transportation costs on the part of clandestine profit-based networks should be understood as attempts to subject the logic and practice of the migrant web to the imperatives of the grid of value production. In short, it means the flow of wealth from migrants' wages goes toward building the criminal network's profit-making commercial activities, rather than to funneling resources into the dense web of migrant community social relations in order to maintain its own extra-economic life and activities.

Any perspective that sees over one hundred million migrants and the hundreds of millions of family, friends and community members who make up the other worldwide web as acting on illusions—on such a scale for so long a period of time—rings false. Migration is a collective activity in the decision to migrate, the objectives for which it is taken, the use and organization of resources, and the social struggles involved in the course of this collective experience. It is carried out in the increasingly complex manner to resolve problems of family and community self-reproduction under conditions of destabilization of previous relations and activities. In the organization of migrant networks and communities on an increasingly planetary scale, migration has created an alternative order, that like dissipative structures found in natural processes, is able to sustain a coherent inherent structure, restoring some semblance of order under conditions of disequilibrium. In so doing, it has created a dense and far-flung set of contacts, making up a far more profound and extensive worldwide web than the electronic techniques that are now accessible to only a fraction of the world's population. This web is under attack from nation-states, which fear its ability to dominate mobility in a form autonomous from state priorities, and from capitalist agencies that seek to wrest control of hiring, entry and transportation processes from migrant communities and channel these activities into narrowly profit-based forms of exploitation. Yet as the forms of work and trade that make up flexible production and neoliberalism increasingly dominate economic activity in every part of the world, this web takes on a significant role in competing with state and privateering ventures to carry out a necessary function of the labor market—to bring together workers and capitalists.

The dismantling of previous forms of work and regulation has created a vacuum in the fulfilling of this basic function of capitalism. We have examined the forces that give a human reality to the abstract language of labor markets. We shall now explore how these forces participate in the making of the labor market in concrete terms in a specific country where flexible work was developed earlier than elsewhere. We have seen how the class conflicts examined in chapter 3 in specific places led to an expansion of the terms of these struggles to the worldwide level, as communities in crisis turned to migration to restore conditions of their own reproduction. That expansion has led to a conflict over control of the movement and mobility of persons across borders, and into labor markets and workplaces between the worldwide web of migrant communities and the states and privateers. We now turn from this conflict over space, and how it is being remade in the form of transnational communities and a world labor market, to how these same forces interact with the realities of local markets and conflicts in a specific place. For as the migrant networks expand the sphere of their own struggles, and create a planetary space for themselves, they enter and interact with other class compositions and forms of work in other places, and in so doing bring these places, their markets, workplaces, and workers into the world labor market and into their own worldwide web.

Notes

1. Pap Khouma, *Io, Venditore di elefanti* (Milan: Garzanti, 1990), p. 25.
2. Ibid., p. 17.
3. Ibid., p. 17.
4. Ibid., p. 19.
5. Valerio Belotti, ed., *Voci da lontano: breve viaggio in quattro comunità di immigrati che vivono e lavorano nel bassanese* (Bassano del Grappa: Libreria TEMPOlibro Editrice, 1994), p. 23.
6. Nestor Rodriguez, "Battle for the Border: Autonomous Migration, Trans-national Communities and the State," *Social Justice* 23(3) (Fall 1996).
7. Ilya Prigogine and Isabelle Stengers, *Order Out of Chaos* (New York: Bantam Books, 1984), p. 142.
8. See, for further examples and explanations, Prigogine and Stengers, op.cit.; Fritjof Capra, *The Web of Life* (London: HarperCollins, 1996), p. 8.
9. Prigogine and Stengers, *Order*, p. 140.
10. Capra, *Web*, p. 184.
11. See C. George Caffentzis, "Africa and Self-Reproducing Automata," in Midnight Notes, *The New Enclosures* (Jamaica Plain, Massachusetts: 1990); and "The Work-Energy Crisis and the Apocalypse," in Midnight Notes, *Midnight Oil*.

12. Belotti, *Voci*, pp. 30-31.
13. Ibid., pp. 46-47.
14. Ibid., pp. 130-32.
15. Istituto Ricerche Economiche-Sociale del Piemonte, *Uguali e Diversi: Il mondo culturaliùe, le reti di rapporti, i lavori degli immigrati non europei a Torino* (Turin: Rossenberg & Schiller, 1993), p. 53.
16. Ibid., p. 30.
17. Ottavia Schmidt di Friedberg, *Islam, solidarietà e lavoro: I muridi senegalesi in Italia* (Turin: Fondazione Agnelli, 1994), pp. 113-24.
18. Peter Stalker, *The Work of Strangers: A Survey of International Labour Migration* (Geneva: ILO, 1994), p. 35; see also Noeleen Heyzer, Geertje Lycklama à Nijeholt and Nedra Weerakoon, *The Trade in Domestic Workers: Causes, Mechanisms and Consequences of International Migration* (London: Zed, 1994), pp. 45-64.
19. Giovanna Campani, "Le reticoli sociali delle donne immigrate in Italia," in Marcella Delle Donne, Umberto Melotti and Stefano Petilli, *Immigrazione in Europa: Solidarietà e conflitto* (Rome: Università degli Studi di Roma La Sapienza, Dipartimento di Sociologia/CEDISS, 1993), p. 279.
20. See Luigi DiLiegro, *Immigrazione: Un punto di vista* (Rome: Sensibili alle foglie, 1997), p. 31.
21. Umberto Melotti, "International Migration in Europe: Social Projects and Political Cultures," in Tariq Modood and Pnina Werbner, eds., *The Politics of Multiculturalism in the New Europe* (London: Zed, 1997), p. 90.
22. Interview with Rev. Simmons Odame, January 13, 1997, Vicenza, Italy.
23. Massey, Alarcon, Durand and Gonzales, *Return to Aztlan* (Los Angeles: University of California Press, 1987); Portes and Bach, *Latin Journey* (Berkeley: University of California Press, 1985), pp. 11-20.
24. Philip Martin, "Network Recruitment and Labor Displacement," in David E. Simcox, ed., *U.S. Immigration in the 1980s: Reappraisal and Reform* (Boulder: Westview Press, 1988), p. 71.
25. ACLI, a Catholic service association, with links to the CISL Catholic labor union federation, has a placement center for domestics in Padua, which in turn has links to a Catholic Church with a heavily Filipina congregation. See also Melotti, "International Migration in Europe," pp. 88-89.
26. These comments are based on my participant observer activity in conducting this research, and on numerous conversations with -Silvano Cogo, a CGIL labor union representative to immigrant communities.
27. Donal B. Cruise O'Brien, "Charisma comes to Town: Mouride Urbanization 1945–1986," in Donal Cruise O'Brien and Christian Coulon, eds., *Charisma and Brotherhoods in African Islam* (Oxford: Clarendon Press, 1988), p. 135.
28. Schmidt di Friedberg, *Islam, Solidarieta' e Lavoro*, pp. 20-22, 37.
29. Ibid., pp. 20-22.

30. Ibid., pp. 84-85.
31. Ibid., pp. 119-21; and Valerio Belotti, from research on vending on the beaches of Emilia-Romagna (to be published); Valerio Belotti, *Vendere in spiaggia: l'abusivismo commerciale nella Riviera emiliano-romagnolo* (Vicenza: Istituto Poster, forthcoming).
32. Ibid., pp. 119-23. Again I thank Valerio Belotti for allowing me access to the conclusions of his unpublished research findings, Belotti, *Vendere in spiaggia*.
33. Interview with Paul Ocoye, President, National Union of Nigerian Citizens in Italy, February 17, 1995, Padua.
34. "Sul marciapiedi col diploma," *Il Gazzettino* (Padua), June 27, 1997.
35. "I nuovi eroi del lavoro," *Il Manifesto*, April 13, 1995; "Philippine Maid Hoping for a Pardon," *International Herald Tribune*, September 18, 1995; "Royal Seal: The Case of Saudi Prince, Maids in Texas Tests Issue of U.S. Immunity," *Wall Street Journal*, December 28, 1994; "Ramos Is Assailed at Rites for Maid," *International Herald Tribune*, March 20, 1995; Heyzer, Lycklama à Nijeholt and Weekakoon, op. cit.; Bridget Anderson, *Britian's Secret Slaves: An Investigation into the Plight of Overseas Domestic Workers in the United Kingdom with contributions from Anti-Slavery International, Kalayaan and the Migrant Domestic Workers* (London: Anti-Slavery International, 1993), pp. 32-34.
36. Stalker, *Work of Strangers*, p. 122.
37. Di Liegro, *Immigrazione*, p. 23.
38. Stalker, *Work of Strangers*, p. 123; Heyzer, Lycklama à Nijeholt and Weekakoon, *Domestic Workers*, p. 70.
39. Stalker, *Work of Strangers*, p. 125.
40. Di Liegro, *Immigrazione*, p. 22.
41. Stalker, *Work of Strangers*, p. 33.
42. Ibid., p. 33.
43. Schmidt di Friedberg, *Islam*, p. 121; O'Brien, "Charisma comes to Town."
44. Stalker, *Work of Strangers*, p. 33.
45. Stephen Castles and Mark Miller, *The Age of Migration* (New York: The Guilford Press, 1993), pp. 4-5.
46. Ibid., p. 5.
47. See, for instance, "Economia, nell Alta tiene," *Il Gazzettino* (Padua), December 13, 1996; see also Gian Antonio Stella, *Schei: Il mitico nordest* (Milan: Baldini & Castoldi, 1996), ch. 1.
48. Stalker, *Work of Strangers*, p. 35.
49. Ibid., p. 35.
50. Heyzer, *Domestic Workers*, p. 53.
51. This information was obtained through various interviews; given the nature of the questions involved however, I shall not be more precise than this.
52. Antonio Nicaso and Lee Lamonthe, *Global Mafia: The New World Order of Organized Crime* (Toronto: MacMillan, 1995), pp. 33-34; "Darkness

Hides Migrant Flood into Italian Underworld," *Independent*, January 8, 1995.

53. Ibid.; see also "Aliens Find a European Gateway at Spain's Coast," *New York Times*, October 18, 1992.

54. "Belgians Uncover Asian Labor Scam," *International Herald Tribune*, November 7, 1996. ‑

55. "150 Pakistani invisibili," *Il Manifesto*, August 14, 1990.

56. "L'esercito contro i clandestini," *Il Manifesto*, October 8, 1996.

57. "I fantasmi del Mediterraneo," *Il Manifesto*, January 5, 1997; "La prima lista di naufraghi," *Il Manifesto*, January 10, 1997.

58. "Naufraga la nave degli schiavi," *Il Manifesto*, October 1, 1994.

59. "Io, schiava della 'mafia nera,'" *Il Gazzettino* (Padua), November 15, 1996

60. "Storia di Claudia, lolita per forza," *Il Mattino* (Padua), December 13, 1996.

61. "Schiavi dell'est a Piacenza, Arrestati 5 imprenditori," *Il Manifesto*, October 21, 1994; "Sbattuta sul marciapiede a sedici anni," *Il Gazzettino* (Padua), December 20, 1996.

62. "I cinesi 'mercanti di schiavi,'" *Il Mattino* (Padua), December 28, 1996.

63. See, for instance, Mungiello, op. cit.; "La nuova schiavitù sommersa," *L'Unità*, August 7, 1992, based on the report in *Newsweek* the same week; "Slave Trade in Children Grows in West Africa, Based On Recent Arrests," *International Herald Tribune*, August 12, 1997.

64. See, among others, "A Grisly Market for Organs in India," *International Herald Tribune*, May 5, 1995; "A Market for Human Organs," *International Herald Tribune*, May 6-7, 1995.

65. Schmidt di Friedberg, *Islam*, p. 121.

66. Stalker, *Work of Strangers*, pp. 36-38; Silvia Federici, "Riproduzione e lotta feminista nella nuova divisione internazionale del lavoro," in Mariarosa Dalla Costa and Giovanna Franca Dalla Costa, *Donne, sviluppo e lavoro di riproduzione* (Milan: FrancoAngeli, 1996), pp. 65, 66-73.

67. See Leopoldina Fortunati, *The Arcana of Reproduction* (Brooklyn: Autonomedia, 1996); Federici, "Riproduzione"; see also Michael Burowoy, "The Functions and Reproduction of Migrant Labor: Comparative Material from South Africa and the United States," *American Journal of Sociology* 81(5) (1976): 1056-57, on the separation of the renewal and maintainence of the migrant worker in bracero or apartheid-style regimes; see also Mariarosa Dalla Costa, *The Power of Women and the Subversion of the Community* (London: Falling Wall Press, 1974) on the use of value theory and reproductive work.

68. Stalker, *Work of Strangers*, p. 126.

5

IMMIGRANTS AND THE RE-MAKING OF THE WORKING CLASS IN ITALY

INTRODUCTION

The presence of immigrant workers in Italy represents an anomaly in at least two senses. First, Italy had been until very recently a country with a net annual outflow of immigrants since its unification as a nation-state in 1861. The number of Italian citizens living outside the country still dwarfs even the highest estimates of immigrants inside Italy. Second, the Italian case is one of immigration to a country with relatively high unemployment, and even to regions within Italy where unemployment is particularly high. This chapter will show, however, how these seeming anomalies are in fact evidence of the new model of world migration outlined in the previous chapters. Further, Italy can be seen as a model example of the current migration patterns; against some recent points of view, I will argue that Italy is not in fact necessarily following the path of previous democratic states received migration flows. Instead, I will argue that only a conflict model, understanding the dialectic between migrant community self-activity and the state intervention, particularly regarding immigration law, can comprehend the way in which the migration experience has developed in Italy. Such a model will aid us in understanding the reality behind the seeming anomoly of immigrants in a country of emigration with high unemployment, and also provide us with tools for grasping the role of immigrant workers in Italy in the transformation of the labor market in that country, and in the re-making of the working class in Italy. The migrant communities may be said to have acted as a social subject, as a working class subject, not *after* their entry into various sectors of the labor market in Italy, but rather in order to impose their presence in various sectors of the economy of Italy.

THE ITALIAN ECONOMY—FROM DUALISM TO THE THREE ITALIES

The Italian economy into which the immigrants began arriving in large numbers by the early 1980s has been characterized since at least Italian unification by the theme of dualism. The unification of Italy was largely the work of the Piedmontese state under Count Camillo Cavour, who, utilizing a complicated series of diplomatic alliances and wars, gradually succeeded in bringing most of the northern and central parts of the peninsula under their control by 1860 (Venice and Rome were annexed later), and of Giuseppe Garibaldi, who with his red-shirted band of a thousand men managed in a dramatic series of battles to sweep away the opposition of the Kingdom of Naples within a few months and take control of the whole of the South, promptly handing it over to the Piedmontese king. The nature of this unification cum conquest laid the basis for the treatment of the South as virtually a colonized country. Many commentators have argued persuasively, the South has since played the role of the agricultural colony of the North, which used protective tariffs for industry and the deindustrialization of the post-unification South as a basis for northern industrialization. After 1880, a trade war with France, that wrecked wine exports on which hundreds of thousands of Southern peasants depended, and the import of cheap American wheat convinced the Italian Parliament to favor industry, and in particular northern Industry. This laid the basis for the massive emigration from Southern Italy after 1880.[1]

This dualism in the Italian economy, dividing an under-developed and largely agricultural South from an industrialized North, has led historians, sociologists, and political scientists to question whether Italy is to be properly understood as an advanced industrial capitalist society, as an underdeveloped society, as a semi-peripheral unit in the capitalist world system, or as a state which, by geographical and historical accident, encompasses parts of two or even three different social systems.[2] After the Second World War, Italy saw an extraordinary rapid growth in northern industry, while millions emigrated from the South both to northern cities and to work in the economic boom elsewhere in Europe, as discussed.[3] The exodus from the South into large factories in cities like Turin and Milan recomposed the working class in Italy in a decisive way: The previous basis of working class organization based on craft work and northern workers was replaced by an increased number of semi-skilled southern workers. These, in alliance with the skilled northern workers who remained in certain departments of factories, produced one of the most intensely militant series of struggles over wages and working hours, as well as over control of production, in the entire postwar world.[4] This migration was the Italian version of migrations related to the growth of mass assembly production in Western Europe after the war. Italy, in other words, had already gone through such a period; without relying on a schematic approach, we may nevertheless argue that the current immigration to Italy is in no sense an extension of those which had previously visited other European countries, merely occuring later in Italy due to its more recent arrival in the club of advanced industrial nations. In fact, precisely to arrive at that status, Italy had *already utilized migrant labor power* in mass assembly production from the 1950s through the 1970s, along with the rest of Europe. The subsequent world economic crisis has been explained in different ways, from a saturation of markets for mass production goods to the result of the Arab oil embargo of 1973, and is seen by many authors as resulting from a profits squeeze caused by the cycle of working-class struggles and demands of the preceding years. The crisis hit Italy as sharply as the rest of the industrialized world. The results were similar to those of other countries: a rising inflation and unemployment through the 1970s, an increase in automation in certain sectors such as autos and petrochemicals, a shift in investment and job growth to services, and, after 1979, a weakening of unions and working-class movements.[5]

Compared with other industrialized countries, what was unique about Italy at the end of the 1970s, was the continuing importance of small-scale industry, small firms, and widespread self-employed craft labor.[6] As Michael Blim, Arnaldo Bagnasco, and others have convincingly shown in their various interpretations of small-scale production, the roots of small-scale firms cannot be reduced to a decentralization of production dependent upon the larger firms, though this may have accelerated the changes in the structure of production in Italy.[7] Bagnasco was perhaps the first to emphasize the geographic concentraltion of small-scale enterprise in the center-northeastern parts of the country, what he named "the Third Italy." In 1971, seven Italian regions, all in the center and northeast, had over 60 percent of all industrial manufacturing workers in companies with 250 or fewer employees. All seven had between about one-fifth and one-third in firms with 10 or fewer workers.[8] Although the traditional region of heavy industry, the Northwest, including the industrial regions around Turin, Milan, and Genoa, continued to dominate overall production, there was an unmistakable trend toward this region's greater importance in the country's overall industrial production and especially its export structure. Already in 1971, Tuscany in central Italy accounted for over one-quarter of Italy's exports to the United States, while the central region of Emilia-Romagna and the northeastern region of the Veneto together accounted for over one-fifth of Italy's exports to Germany.[9] From 1961–1971, despite massive state encouragement of investment in the South for heavy industry, the increase in the number of industrial workers was 28.7 percent in the Center-Northeast, as opposed to 20.4 percent in the South. All told, in 1971, the Third Italy accounted for over one-fourth of the country's exports, the South only one-tenth.[10] Meanwhile, Italy-wide, industrial workers declined as a percentage of the population between 1971 and 1983, and the percentage of workers in small firms overtook that in large firms.[11]

While the Third Italy grew in prosperity throughout the 1980s, the South, or Mezzogiorno, saw a contradictory process in which overall consumption standards roughly reached those of the rest of Europe, while employment stagnated or even declined. The use of remittances from migration both abroad and to central and northern Italy, the state investment in infrastructure in the South, the abandonment of agriculture since the 1950s by millions of families, and the industrial investment of the 1960s on under the Cassa per il Mezzogiorno development program had transformed the South from the agricultural, latifundia-dominated region of the pre-Second World War period into a modern and urban sector of the country. Along with certain gains won during the working class insurgency of the 1970s, such as national wage contracts that necessitated that wage levels be equal in every part of Italy, these transformations sharply diminished the flow of migrant labor power from Italy's South. The problem of development of Italy's Mezzogiorno can no longer be seen as a question of underdevelopment, analogous to the problems of Third World countries, and least of all can it be seen as predominantly an agricultural question. Indeed, the South has a higher con- ✓ centraltion of urban residents than the North. Rather, the issue is the structure of employment itself in the Mezzogiorno, itself linked to the clientelist political structure.[12] An unwillingness on the part of northern capital to employ southern workers, who had come to be seen as either politically dangerous or unwilling to work, along with a drying up of investment, private and public, in the South during the 1980s and 1990s and its replacement with transfer payments, all fed forms of clientelist job markets, the underground economy and precarious and irregular employment.[13] Workforce participation rates have dropped in the South in recent years. The collapse of the Christian Democratic Party, whose clientelist network was the primary form of job-finding in many cities, has not done away with clientelism, nor created a free market, but seems merely to have opened the door to a more underground form of clientelist job market as well as providing space for the unprecedented, growth of organized crime in the Italian economy.[14] Thus, in Calabria, one study found that

90 percent of all building and public works contracts, 40 percent of the transport sector, 20 percent of credit and finance and 15 percent of trade in the region were controlled by the 'Ndrangheta, the Calabrian organized crime syndicate. One-third of the school children in Naples had not completed compulsory schooling, three times the national average, and a recent piece of investigative reporting found thousands of children working in off-the-books industries throughout the city and its hinterland.[15]

In the 1980s Italy was the site of a second economic miracle, an export-led boom centered in the Milan area, and the Third Italy that carried Italy to the historic "sorpasso"—the overtaking of Great Britain to become the fifth largest economic power in the world. The rise of small-scale export industry in the Third Italy has brought prosperity to parts of the country that had been peripheral to the nation's previous economic growth and, in some cases, like the Northeast—including the Veneto region—areas that in the 1960s were still largely characterized by sharecropping as the predominant rural employment. The vast majority of the country's population had been integrated into modern networks of roads, schools, communications. Italy had become a rich country. Yet within the context of a modern, industrial and even high-tech and white-collar service economy, there remained pockets of extremely high unemployment (offically over 10 percent nationally for the whole of the 1990s, and in parts of the South in some cases reaching 50 percent), illegal work, organized crime, precarious employment, and clientelist employment structures.

In addition, two forms of strike—a strike on investment in the South and employment of Southerners, and their own refusal to migrate north for work, preferring to remain at home now that consumption could be maintained in a First World manner in their own region—fed the growth of what Bagnasco refers to as three separate labor markets sealed off from one another.[16] Another type of strike, the extraordinary decline of the birth rate in Italy, now the lowest in the world, has led to an aging of the Italian population. This is part of the larger trend in this direction throughout the industrialized world, itself related both to increased standards of living and to the increasing autonomy of women and their own life expectations. In Italy, where reproductive work was made an explicit subject of political activity in the 1970s feminist movement, the declining birth rate, along with the legalization of first divorce and then abortion, should be understood as diffuse representations of a growing refusal by women to remain reproducers of labor power as their primary role in economic life.[17] This aging of the population strangely coexists with massive unemployment of young people, especially in the old industrial centers of the Northwest and in the South, while labor market shortages have developed in the new centers of growth in the Center and North. In short, the development of increasingly un-linked labor markets within the same nation-state has accompanied the growth of flexible, small-scale production. The unemployed and underemployed of the South and the deindustrialized parts of the Northwest have shown no interest in migrating to the new job growth areas. By the 1980s Italy's pension system was showing signs of stress, as the often untaxed growth of the underground and small-scale economy and the growing number of pensioners placed the country's newly won prosperity in question. It was into this strange labor market—with its blockages, clientelism, and organized crime, refusal of migration or dirty and low-paying work by the unemployed, and declining a working age population—that the immigrants began to arrive in large numbers in the early 1980s.

THE IMMIGRANTS IN ITALY
AND THE VARIOUS LABOR MARKETS

By the 1970s there were already several distinct groups of immigrants working or living in Italy. The earliest group, a small Chinese community that established Italy's first Chinatown in Milan, entered between the two world wars. After a period as street vendors, it expanded into leather work and by the 1960s had opened Italy's first Chinese restaurants.[18] By the 1980s, a Chinese community was well-established in the leather trade in Prato, near Florence, which that city has been at the center of for at least five centuries. The level of self-employment by the Chinese community, following the Chinese diaspora model carried to many countries, is almost unique among the immigrant communities in Italy, and the Chinese remain one of the few exceptions as a community that emigrated to Italy as families.[19] By the 1960s domestic workers entered Italy as immigrants in some numbers, many arriving with Italian family members as Italy's trusteeship over Somalia ended in 1960 and Ethiopia annexed Eritrea in 1962. These women later encouraged the migration of other female relatives.[20] By the mid-1970s there was a considerable presence of women immigrants in Italy, virtually all from Catholic countries and all working as domestics. These included women from the Cape Verde Islands, Seychelles, Mauritius, El Salvador, the Dominican Republic, Peru, the Philippines, and the Kerala area of India. It also included the immigration by small numbers of men from Slovenia and Croatia into Lombardy, Piedmont, and especially Friuli-Venezia Giulia to do construction work, in the latter case after an earthquake. The role of Catholic organizations in helping these migrations to Italy was crucial. With the increase in women's labor force participation in Italy, and a refusal of this work by women from regions—including the Veneto—who had previously migrated to work as domestics, the demand for maids was high. Women were 50 percent of the immigrants in Italy by the end of the decade—a percentage that Italy exceptional. Demand for male migrant labor remained very low until the mid-1980s when male migrants entered a labor market that had not necessarily expressed a demand for their labor power.[21]

Also in the 1970s, a Tunisian community developed in Sicily, predominantly engaged in fishing, and to some extent in seasonal agricultural work; in the North, Yugoslavs were recruited to help with the construction work in Friuli after a severe earthquake. Each of these migrations helped lay the basis for later flows under different labor market conditions in the 1980s and 1990s. Italy, including the Veneto with its University of Padua, had long had foreign students. As the 1970s and early 1980s brought either wars or repressive regimes to power in countries such as Eritrea and Ethiopia and Iran, or brought the lure of participation in the social movements in Italy of the 1970s, many decided to stay in Italy and find work or start families. These migrants and their political experience would later become an important link for newly arriving migrant workers with the immigrant networks already in place. This connection would ease the development of political associations and mobilization in the late 1980s and early 1990s. Finally, political refugees arrived from countries like Vietnam, Chile, Argentina, Uruguay, Brazil, Libya, Palestine, Turkey (Kurds), Iran, Ethiopia and Eritrea, Somalia, and Sri Lanka (Tamils).[22] Until 1989 Italy remained one of the few countries that maintained the geographic parameters of the Geneva Convention on Refugees of 1951, essentially barring non-Europeans from political refugee status. Aside from East Europeans, and a few exceptions from Vietnam and Chile, refugees received only a provisional status through the United Nations High Commission for Refugees.[23]

Thus, the pattern which we saw in chapter three, of a greater diversity of nationalities in the Italian immigration case, was already established by the start of the 1980s even with very limited total numbers of immigrants in the country.[24] The early to mid-1980s saw both numbers and diversity of national origin increase dramatically, as Italy experienced migration from North Africa, especially from Morocco and Tunisia; from West Africa, especially from Senegal, Nigeria, and Ghana; and from South and East Asia, especially Filipinas, but also including Sri Lanka and the Indian sub-continent.[25] This migration would eventually reduce the percentage of women among immigrants, though it remains quite high by the standards of other receiving countries. The country's foreign population grew rapidly during the decade, from 186, 400 in 1975 to 298,700 in 1980, to 781,100 by 1990. One year later the total was around 900,000. These of course are only the official count of permesso di soggiorno—of residence permits.[26] Already by 1977, it was estimated that the number of foreigners in Italy was closer to 400,000, or double the official count.[27] Estimates are difficult in Italy, given that the initial flows were underground, and many have remained so despite three amnesty periods during the 1980s and 1990s. This is due to several factors: the fear of losing jobs predicated precisely on the employer's wish to avoid social security payments and taxes; the illegal nature of the migrant's work; the fear of expulsion for periods of unemployment; lack of legal recognition of work like street vending; the continuing flow of illegal entries; the expiration of permits to stay for limited periods and reasons, such as tourism. Nevertheless, the growth of the immigrant population is impressive enough, even if it remains small in absolute terms: The average annual increase in the immigrant population from 1986 to 1990 was 16.7 percent. During the period 1982–1990, only Germany had a higher absolute increase in immigrant population among European nations, and not by much. This difference, attributable to the entry of family of members of already resident immigrants, was of a very different nature, and was dwarfed by the huge increase in the percentage of immigrants in the Italian population, which almost tripled during these eight years. Again, when we remember the high percentage of uncounted and undocumented immigrants in Italy, this growth becomes even more impressive. To what should we attribute it?

First to the blocked entry into other areas of Europe. Italy and Spain remained the main countries that maintained loose entry standards for foreigners after the 1970s, until both entered the Schengen system in 1990. Second, to the mobilization of the networks of those migrants already present within the country before the mid-1980s, from among the various groups of early arrivals mentioned above. The populations of Somalis and Ethiopians (mostly Eritreans), which stood at 1,151 and 4,527 respectively in 1980—mostly based upon refugee entry with some student visas—both rose to 19,553 and 14,050 respectively by 1993, though the number of Ethiopians declined sharply, to fewer than 10,000 two year later, following Eritrean Independence and the fall of the Mengistu government.[28] Likewise, the Filipino population, already numbering 3,676 in 1980, grew more than tenfold to 40,695 in 1991. The number of Brazilians rose from 2,413 to almost 17,000—an increase of over 700 percent, from 1980 to 1991, and continued increasing to over 22,000 in 1995. In 1980, notwithstanding the long-time existence of Milan's Chinatown, the population of citizens of the Chinese People's Republic numbered only 463 in all of Italy. This number had grown to 20,632 by 1991. The Tunisian increase was perhaps the most dramatic—rising from 1,488 in 1980 to 46,393 in 1991.[29]

However, since the migration has continued into Italy

notwithstanding restrictions on entry adopted after 1990, and since much of the new migrations after 1980 were from countries not represented among the earlier immigrant population, these two factors are not sufficient to explain either the rapid growth of Italy's foreign-born population or the continuation of the flow of migrants into the country. As Giovanna Campani argues, the analysis of "push" factors is not sufficient to explain the attraction of Italy as a host country for immigrants. She is right to take Melotti and others to task for overemphasizing them, and to urge instead a closer look at "pull" factors—namely the growth of the Italian economy over the last decade and a half and the worldwide demand for women in the domestic service and sex work industries. But beyond these important examples, "pull" factors are equally inadequate, especially in describing determinants of male migration to Italy; the immigrants only very recently managed to gain access to stable jobs within the industrial sector and are still largely excluded from either white collar work or business ownership. The high unemployment figures in many parts of Italy would have at least diminished the glow of the "pull" factors under such circumstances. Campani is on firmer ground when she calls for understanding how the restructuring of the North and South of the world and the internationalization of the labor market provide the context in which the migrations to Italy takes place.[30] And I agree with Campani when she states, "Immigration into Italy has become a model case because of the power of the informal economy."[31] Further, there is no question that, "This informal economy (which has the virtue of the 'flexibility' so much appreciated by the ultra-liberal economists) needs an unorganized labour force that is prepared to accept any kind of working conditions, and immigrants can provide this type of labour force."[32] Nevertheless, the coincidence of a need and a supply does not explain the presence of the supply. Indeed, just as the coexistence of large unemployment and labor shortages for growing sectors in the same country requires explanation precisely because it does not fit with a structuralist interpretation of the functioning of the reserve army of labor,[33] the presence of immigrant labor power in the same country cannot be completely explained by this same labor demand, nor can the even more complex role of immigrants in the labor market up to the late 1980s, whereby immigrants were in largely marginal service sector or primary sector areas of the economy rather than in the areas of greatest growth. Admittedly, these sectors represent precisely those where work conditions are most flexible, but recruitment by these sectors, with the exception of the sort of forced enlistment of workers into fully illegal forms of work, has not been a factor in the arrival of immigrants. The creation of employment spaces which are self-organized, such as street vending, lends even less credence to the pull factor theory. And even if we agreed fully with Campani, and there is no doubt that her linking of the informal economy with the presence of immigrants and their flexibility in the labor market is an insight of great value and importance, this would leave us to explain the South-North migration begun in the late 1980s and continuing to today in which immigrants are moving into the industrial sectors of the center and northeast, thus rejecting the informal sector. I have dealt to some length with Prof. Campani's perpective because her work on women immigrants in Italy and their social networks, and on the Chinese community in Tuscany, are among the most important studies we have of immigrant communities in Italy. Also, because her emphasis on economic conditions within Italy is an important improvement over much of the "push" factor-based analysis of immigration into Italy. Many studies in the latter camp border on panic over population or income-gap figures, thoroughly abstracting migration from the social conditions in which it is organized. Campani argues against Melotti for encouraging inadvertently the "creation of the image of immigration from the South as a threat" as well as the view of a "demographic bomb" developed by some demographers and by anti-immigrant forces in Italian politics.[34]

Immigrants do personify many of the characteristics sought by employers and celebrated by neoliberal social scientists for "flexibility": A willingness to work long hours; the need to accept lower wages than workers with citizen rights and born in the host country; legal vulnerability and therefore a weaker position with regard to making demands on employers; and a lack of the expectations that might be derived from a historical relationship to the labor movement in the host countries.[35] However, two characteristics limit immigrant flexibility in present-day Italy, and therefore the functionality of immigrant labor power in the Italian economy. The first is the tendency of the immigrant workers to be more interested in money than in jobs. This may sound paradoxical, but only if we forget that while money surely does not grow on trees, wage labor is also not a natural phenomenon for proletarians, but a means to an end. Migrants have developed various methods of gaining income that do not involve wage labor for Italian employers, such as Chinese restaurants, street vending, and drug sales and prostitution. Further, many prioritize returning home to Senegal, Morocco, or Tunisia every year or two for several months rather than holding onto a legal factory job. In short, gaining access to money, at first in the fastest way possible, was the main strategy of many immigrants, rather than having steady work. It was only later that there was a collective movement toward the zones where steady employment and pay could be found. Obviously, such behavior lends itself precisely to employers seeking workers who will not demand regular employment and social security benefits, and many have taken taken advantage of this characteristic of the immigrant workers. But up until the mid to late-1980s, the immigrant presence in the Italian labor market was marginal. Such workers were not necessarily at the disposal of employers because many simply did not have employers. Not that many didn't want them. Indeed, immigrants imposed themselves on the regular labor market, but they did so in part as a political subject as much as abstract labor.

Ultimately, a conflict model is necessary to understand the very presence of immigrants in Italy and in the Veneto, and their role in the labor market. The migrations are a response to the developments within the class conflict in the countries and regions of immigrant origin, themselves brought on by policies of international agencies, and are organized by transnational communities through extensive and increasingly worldwide networks. Italy, with the exception of the Yugoslavs in Frioul and the domestic workers, had in no way recruited immigrants to come and work in its industries, whether in the zones of industrial growth in the Third Italy and the Milanese export giant, nor in the agricultural, service and artisanal informal economy where many immigrants eventually gained their first waged working experience in Italy. The immigrants arrived by the mid-1980s in a country that was in Europe, first and foremost, and therefore one where movement throughout Europe, they hoped, would be easier. Many immigrants interviewed in this and in other studies took advantage of this possibility, living in several European countries during their sojourn. Second, they arrived in a country that had *schei* (Veneto dialect for money). Italy had become a rich country during the 1980s, and immigrants were sometimes aware of this through contact with Italians—first or second hand or even virtual—while outside Italy. One recalls Pap Khoum vending to the Italian tourists in Abidjan, or the Albanians watching Italian television. When asked by a judge why he insisted on robbing banks after having been caught so often, Willy Sutton answered, "because that's where they keep the money." Many immigrants could as easily respond in the same way to why they came to Italy. Vending on the beaches of Emilia-Romagna, as thousands of Senegalese and Moroccans do every summer, can net four to six months' worth of a factory salary in two months of intensive sales work. There are no Italian employers taking advantage of the flexibility of this kind of work. Many, perhaps even most, immigrants found themselves in the mid-1980s labor market performing work off-the-books in a flexible labor market in restaurants, hotels, tomato fields, and small industrial workshops. But it far from clear that their very presence can be explained by the use to which their labor was put.[36] Such a viewpoint would also make it more difficult to explain the subsequent movement geographically north and sectorally into more regular, legal factory work, and out of the limited opportunities of the informal economy.[37]

The presence of immigrant workers in Italy preceded the demand for their labor power. The migrations were carried out through the web of migrant workers, and migrants themselves extended that web to incorporate another economy and local labor market into the world labor market, for the first time as receiver, and not only sender, of labor power. This view is in contrast to the work of Wallerstein, Hopkins, and Arrighi, for instance, for whom incorporation into the capitalist system is seen as: (1) a one-time event, after which the country in question may be said to be wholly "internal" rather than "external" to capital—a view which leaves social relations static and without room for relative dependence or independence in relation to the world market and the money economy; (2) something accomplished by capital and only by capital, a characteristic of the alleged self-expansion of capital, and unrelated to the social relations within a society, and without regard for how their incorporation into the capitalist grid may impact that grid itself; (3) an economic incorporation into the world market, seen in a reified way—as economic relations and not as social relations. Understanding the activity of the migrant web gives us one example, and history furnishes us with others, of how working class subjects can also incorporate the class compositions of certain regions into the circulation of class conflict at the world level. In no way is this critique, or this study, sufficient for developing the new political science to understand what working class incorporation might mean, but hopefully this work will further progress toward such an approach. This perspective would begin by recognizing that working social subjects, as E.P. Thompson and others have demonstrated, are not born the day they begin to work for wages or come under market control.

The presence of immigrant workers and their experiences in Italy provide us in fact with a fine example of just such a previously existing social subject entering the labor market after developing a political character. A dialectic has developed between the self-activity of immigrant communities and the labor market in Italy. This relationship is mediated in part by the state, and so changes in the structure of Italian immigration law can be shown to have consisted of responses to the activity of immigrants within the country. For that reason, the movement of immigrants in the labor market is part of the re-making of the working class in Italy. The immigrants were a politically organized force *before* they entered regular waged work in large numbers. Just as we saw in chapter three how expropriation became, under conditions of structural adjustment, a weapon for reducing a working class to abstract labor power, we shall now see how a working class presence re-formed itself in the process of entering the workplace as concrete labor in the factories and other workplaces of Italy, forcing changes in Italian law along the way. Finally, in entering into the dialectic of the working class in Italy, the immigrants bring the working class in Italy into the dialectic of the worldwide working class, and incorporate the labor market in Italy into the larger world labor market. In other words, by expanding the sphere of their own class conflicts through emigration to Italy, immigrants bring Italian class conflicts out of a parochial and local sphere of action and into the larger arena of class conflict worldwide. Undeniably, the migrant web and the activity of migrants in Italy are not the only forces bringing about this incorporation. Italy's increasing dependence on export for the world market and entry into the European Union inevitably mean incorporation of class conflict in Italy into the mechanisms of class conflict at wider levels as well. But we should not neglect or underestimate the role played by immigrant workers in "globalizing" local economies and classes. This role is well understood, ironically, by the racist right in Europe and elsewhere, which continue to see in immigrants, as much as in the various free trade agreements such as the EU, NAFTA and GATT, the living symbol of the incorporation of their folklorist community into a less controllable and unsentimental world market. Let us examine more closely the dialectical relation between immigrant organization, the job market, and the law in Italy since the 1980s.

IMMIGRANT COMMUNITIES, WORK, AND THE STATE IN ITALY, 1983–1997

Immigrants arrived in Italy in increasing numbers in the 1980s, often landing at the airport in Rome, less often in Milan, and sometimes at the port cities of the South: Naples, Bari, and (by air) Palermo. With the exception of Milan, these cities are all in the economically less well-off part of the country, and all are cities with distorted labor markets. Of the largest southern cities, only Naples can be said to have any industry to speak of, and most of that is part of an underground economy linked to family and clientelist networks, often employing children and young women at substandard wages and conditions. Rome is possibly the largest non-industrial city in the Western world. This geographic situation meant that immigrants with limited verbal skills in Italian, often found themselves in labor markets where their options were very limited and did not include even unskilled or semi-skilled factory work. These are also areas with high jobless rates, sometimes reflecting real unemployment, sometimes underground work. Many of the first job experiences of immigrants in Italy involved contact with the South. These often included seasonal work in agriculture on the outskirts of the urban centers (especially near Naples), vending, some construction work, domestic work for both men and women, and work in the restaurant and hotel industry. A majority of the West Africans of all nationalities interviewed with questionnaires for this study had lived in at least one southern city, and many recited what became a familiar series of previous addresses moving diagonally across the Appenines toward the northeast: Palermo, Rome, Parma, Vicenza; or Bari, Rome, Bologna, Padua; or Naples, Rome, Florence, Montebelluna. Many worked as domestic workers in southern cities, but finding the pay low or tiring of the personal authority relations involved in domestic work, they began to seek out ways of moving north or finding more stable employment. Like many other historical migrations, at first the immigrants gravitated toward Italy's largest cities, some of which, like Rome, Milan, and Turin, quickly took on a cosmopolitan look. Nevertheless, despite optimistic talk of a "multicultural society" or of "solidarity," which was common in the Italian press at the time, and the suddenly arising cottage industry of social science books on migration and multiculturalism during this period, the immigrants in the late 1980s were anything but well-integrated into the general life of Italian society. Thus, of 270,000 immigrants in 1981, only 96,000 had waged jobs, at least officially. By 1987, immigrants in Italy had officially doubled to 572,000, but only about 150,000 officially worked. These numbers of course in no way reflected the reality of how many immigrants worked. After two rounds of amnesties to allow immigrants to be regularized, the number of employed immigrants grew faster than the total immigrant population—to about 350,000 out of just under one million—while the number of immigrants in Italy on student visas fell by 40 percent and those present for religious or family reasons also grew more slowly than work-related declarations of residence motive.[38]

Immigration, especially in its early phases, commonly demonstrates a marked division of labor by both national origin and gender; this pattern has reproduced itself in many different countries. Yet the ethnic segmentation of the labor market in Italy in the late 1980s was especially rigid[39] Further, the gender-based division of labor of immigrant employment is highly marked, and the difference in gender composition of diverse nationalities is extreme. The large majority of the Filipino, Cape Verde, Salvadorean, Mauritian, Somalian, Eritrean, and Sri Lankan communities in Italy are women—70 percent among Filipinos, 80 percent among Cape Verdans. Virtually all of these women are employed as domestic workers or maids.[40] In 1991, one-sixth of all regularized domestic workers in Italy were immigrants, but there was considerable geographic concentraltion of immigrant domestics. Thirty-nine percent of all immigrant domestics worked in the region of Lazio (which includes Rome); 26 percent were in Sicily, 23 percent were in Lombardy and 13 percent in Campania. These last three regions contain the major cities of Palermo, Milan, and Naples, respectively, and immigrant domestics were and continue to be concentralted in the South (except for Milan) and in the country's largest cities. In 1992, the province of Rome held 97.9 percent of all domestics in the region of Lazio, Milan was the workplace of over 80 percent of all those in Lombardy. Two-thirds of all of Sicily's domestic workers were in Palermo, but that city was unique in Italy in that three-fifths of its 4,000 domestics were men.[41] By contrast, the Veneto and Emilia-Romagna, the two major industrial regions of the Third Italy, were each the site of only 4 percent of the domestic workers in Italy, and combined had fewer than two-thirds the number of domestics as Sicily, and less than one-fourth the total for Rome.[42] As we shall see in the next chapter, this level of domestic employment reflects the different labor markets and histories of the urban South, with its large dependence on personal services and wide social inequalities, and the Third Italy, with its history of widely distributed access to small property.[43]

Street vending was a specialty of Senegalese, Moroccans and Tunisians, though the latter two groups have engaged in this work in some regions (like Emilia-Romagna and the South) and not in others (like in the Veneto). Agricultural work by immigrants was concentralted in the South, and largely involved West Africans and some North Africans. Construction work is concentralted in the Northeast, first Friuli Venezia-Giulia and later also in the Veneto, and is performed primarily by Bosnian Serbs and Croatians, or by workers from the Mahgreb countries. More recently, Nigerian and Senegalese workers have also entered construction work in the Veneto. Fishing was a Tunisian specialty in the South. Prostitution has involved largely ex-Yugoslav, Albanian, Nigerian and Central African women. Drug sales have involved young men from Morocco and Tunisia. Hotel, bar, and restaurant work employs Mahgreb-born and Latin American men, while men from the Philippines and Ghana had also done domestic work in the South for a time, before migrating North to find factory work. Chinese community members worked in Chinese restaurants, shops, and in the leather working industry in Tuscany. This community, along with the Ghanaian and to a lesser extent the Filipino, are among the only ones to show a strong representation of couples or families in Italy.[44]

Enrico Pugliese was among the first to study the immigrant presence in the Italian labor market carrying out groundbreaking early studies of immigrant agricultural workers in the South. He argued in 1991 that immigrant self-creation of work—such as cleaning of offices (in cooperatives more or less self-organized), restoration work, and service work like gas station attendents and some auto mechanic work—was more significant than usually recognized as centers of especially male immigrant employment.[45] Likewise, construction work absorbed many early male immigrants in the labor force in the mid-1980s through the early 1990s before the factory doors opened to immigrants on a significant scale. Pugliese stressed the predominance of agricultural work in the South, especially sectors like tomatoes and fishing and the very differing conditions found in this sector. In parts of Sicily, such as near Ragusa, farm workers were among the first immigrants to win monthly fixed salaries (legal workers in Italy are paid by the net monthly wage, and the hourly wage is essentially an aliquot part of the monthly wage based on a certain number of hours), though at salaries lower than those fixed by national contract agreements. But in the tomato industry, the need for labor power is particularly variable by season, and working conditions reflected this and the unorganized nature of the workforce of the late 1980s.[46]

Thousands of male immigrants, mostly North and West Africans, worked in agriculture, such as in the export-oriented tomato fields near Naples.[47] In the town of Villa Literno, outside Naples, about 300 immigrants of various nationalities had created a shanty town to be near the fields. Their conditions, which included low pay, no health or other benefits, and lack of even a hospital within 30 kilometers, as well as long hours at precarious, seasonal and back-breaking work in the hot climate of the Campania, came to light after a South African man, Jerry Essan Masslo, was murdered in August 1989.[48] The murder of Masslo dramatically changed the political situation of immigrants in Italy. Various immigrant communities in many cities protested, a number of anti-racist groups either were formed or energized for the first time, and public opinion for a brief moment was shocked and sympathetic to immigrant conditions and the danger of a growing climate of racism. Masslo's death is often credited with passage of Law 39 (1990), usually called the Martelli Law, which improved the legal conditions of immigrants in the country, and allowed for the legalization of the conditions of many thousands.[49] But the passage of the Martelli Law was due to a more complex interplay of forces than a mere response to public opinion and moral outrage. In fact, legal changes in Italian immigration law have responded to immigration activity and eventually to organized immigrant protest.

Prior to the mid-1980s, Italy had an extraordinarily archaic legal system regarding immigration. The basis of this legal structure was still the 1931 Law of Foreigners, which was instituted by the Mussolini regime. It was primarily designed to bar the entry of anti-fascists. It severely limited entry and movement within the country (still a factor, since immigrants must register with the police station in any new city they move to in order to stay beyond 48 hours), residence, and ownership of property. As late as 1986 it was impossible for foreigners in Italy to own automobiles, for instance, and foreign-owned businesses needed to have an Italian partner.[50] Foreigners under the post-fascist laws of 1948 could be expelled if they could not prove that their financial assets were both legally obtained and sufficient. Even worse, things were hardly moving in the direction of welcoming immigrants. In 1982 the Ministry of Labor instructed local authorities to issue no more work permits to non-European Community citizens, and in 1984 alone, 12,500 aliens were refused entry, another 13,645 expelled, and 26,684 either arrested or placed under police authority.[51] Efforts at reform were blocked in 1980 and also in 1982 after consultation with labor unions, which at that time showed no sympathy for immigrant issues.

The first change in this bizarre structure came in 1986. After a decade of immigrant inflow, and in the face of the undeniably increasing entry of workers from new areas in the mid-1980s, two different motivations combined to pass Italy's first overhaul of its immigration laws. The first was the increasingly obvious need for the state to reassert some control over the presence of foreign workers. With over 400,000 legal immigrants, but estimates that at least half that number remained clandestine, the Socialist coalition government of Prime Minister Craxi sought to improve both controls over ingress and the state's ability to know who was in the country and in what numbers. The second motivation was that of immigrants and their newly won allies in the Catholic and labor union communities. The two largest parties of the time, the Christian Democrats and the Communists, each had activists within their ranks, in Catholic associations and labor unions, who had been active in defending conditions of Italian emigrants abroad. These had begun to mobilize in defense of the needs of immigrants in Italy, and to develop the first links with the loosely organized community groups and networks of the immigrant communities. These interests came together in an umbrella organization called the Comitato per una legge giusta (committee for a just law) which was the initiative of the Catholic labor organization ACLI (Associazione Christiane dei Lavoratori Italiani) and the Catholic charity group Caritas, which had been involved in service work among immigrants for some time. This pro-immigrant lobby carried out a public opinion campaign in various cities and in the media arguing that immigrant were not stealing jobs from Italians, calling for recognition of the goal of a multiethnic society, and gaining allies in Parliament for changing the law.[52]

Law 943 (1986) showed a heavy prediliction for controlling the flows and unseen activities of immigrants, and trying to maneuver immigrants into the waged labor market more securely. Immigrant workers obtained the same legal rights as Italian waged employees under the ILO convention of 1975, but future entries of foreigners were to be tied to labor market needs (a dead letter from the start). Finally, an amnesty enabled undocumented workers to regularize themselves, and those who either hired or transported undocumented workers in Italy were to be penalized. The amnesty led to 105,000 regularizations of foreigners, less than half of the most conservative estimates of clandestine workers. But for those able and interested in becoming legal, it was a victory, the first gain of immigrant efforts in Italy. Many immigrant workers did not apply for legalization, fearing that the legal requirements of equal pay and legal workplace rights would price them out of the job market. They did so either out of a shrewd evaluation of their employers' motive for hiring them or were told this directly by their employers.[53] The law also applied almost exclusively to full-time waged employees, and had no provisions concerning self-employment (street vending was not recognized as legally sanctioned work), students, seasonal workers, or professionals and members of cooperatives. Campani, among others, has been critical of studies of immigration that consider this act "generous"compared with legislation in other European states.[54] This was the legal structure in place in 1989–1990 when immigrants themselves began to stir after the murder of Jerry Masslo.

The 1980s in Italy had been a period of defeat for working-class movements and organizations. The more militant extra-parliamentary movements of the 1970s had been all but destroyed by a wave of mass arrests that sought to link wide sectors of mass workers, students and women's organizations to terrorism. An entire generation of social movements was criminalized more or less to this day, and at one time in the mid-1980s Italy, with 3,000 activists in prison, had more political prisoners than any postwar Western country had ever experienced. The political vanguards of the factory struggles that had sparked the wider working class initiatives of the 1970s were also diffused by technological change, the decentralization of production to small firms and its geographic dispersion to regions without historically strong working class presences. The defeat of a FIAT workers' strike in 1980 broke the back of union militancy. The 1980s in Italy thus saw an economic boom, a cultural turn toward yuppieism, and a conformism unknown in the country for decades.[55] Yet after the Masslo murder, an anti-racist movement grew that rapidly demonstrated its ability to generate new energy and provide perspective to a left that had been sorely divided (between parliamentary and extraparliamentary groupings), which during the 1989 collapse of the socialist bloc was in serious ideological dissaray, and which had not shown much capacity for initiative or political growth for a decade.

Based on existing immigrant community networks, and the organizational abilities of the Catholic, Communist, trade union, Green and autonomist (extraparliamentary) forces, which had been building contacts with immigrant groups, a new anti-racist movement developed in 1989–1990. It would feed into a cycle of immigrant protests that helped break the political silence of the Italian left as the 1980s came to a close. Already in the immediate aftermath of the murder at Villa Literno, there were local protests there and in other cities, both by immigrant groups and autonomist social centers. On October 7, 1989, hundreds of thousands of people marched on Rome against racism and called for a multicultural society, the first demonstration of its kind in Italy. This march brought together forces that are to this day often estranged from one another, which had rarely worked together, and which in some cases had in the 1970s been on opposite sides of bitter and even armed conflict: Communists, autonomists, Greens, Catholics, immigrant organizations, anti-mafia activists, trade unionists, and women's organizations.[56] In the wake of this protest, immigrant associations grew rapidly. Already by the late 1980s immigrant communities had established formal associations (which were legalized by 1986) though in many cases legalization amounted to gaining formal recognition for groups that had existed informally.[57] By the end of 1991 there were over 300 officially registered immigrant organizations, some based on one nationality, some with pan-immigrant membership bases and yet others including Italian members also.[58] About half of these made defending their culture of origin their organization's main objective, 27 percent listed winning social integration into Italian society, 13 percent claimed to be explicitly political in their orientation, and 7 percent sought to change Italian public opinion regarding immigration. Overall membership is hard to determine, but one-quarter of the associations claimed between 100 and 300 members, while 21 claimed more than this. A conservative estimate would place the number of immigrants joining or forming associations in the tens of thousands during the period of a few years.[59]

Other kinds of organizing occured in the wake of the Villa Literno violence as well, as unions began for the first time to try recruiting the immigrant agricultural workers in that area, and helped mobilize a center for habitation and cultural exchange called "solidarity village." Perhaps more important, for the first time all three union federations sent representatives and won a contract with the growers representing the agricultural workers. From this time on, the labor unions began to take more of an interest in general in immigrant affairs, collaborated with immigrant associations in campaigns involving racism, housing, and workplace issues,[60] and began to recruit immigrant staff members for the first time. By December 1991, the left-oriented CGIL federation had 114 immigrant staff members of 27 different nationalities in its offices throughout Italy.[61] To be sure, unions often mediated between immigrant workers or immigrant associations and local authorities or the central government in a way that limited the autonomy of immigrants politically. Unions continue to show reluctance to put resources under the independent control either of immigrant staff or of immigrant associations, and rarely make demands in contracts relating to specific needs of immigrants regarding housing, health care or racism in the workplace.[62] But their generally favorable attitude to immigration and equal rights, their efforts to organize immigrants, and their sponsorship of large national demonstrations has helped to de-marginalize immigrant organizing efforts with respect to the larger working class movement in Italy.

Other kinds of organizing occured independently of the unions, parties, and other national organizations, particularly with respect to the very serious problem of housing. Housing is in perennial shortage in Italy, and the public housing is especially difficult to get into even for Italians. Two-thirds of Italian families own their own home, however, and that fact combined with the extended age at which many young Italians continue to live at their parents' house (itself a function of job unavailability or job precariousness for young Italians), means that the shortage is manageable for most people most of the time thanks to the family-based unofficial safety net.[63] For immigrants, whose family networks are usually overseas, and who lack longstanding homeownership in Italy to use as a housing base, the problem of lodging becomes very severe in many cases. When asked as part of this study to identify the main problems which immigrants face in Italy, all nationalities of immigrants except Yugoslavs and Filipinas listed housing as the most serious problem by pluralities of over 80 percent. Housing has proven to be the one problem that remains largely impervious to permanent solution by the immigrant community networks, although most immigrants find housing with other immigrants of their own nationality or with their help. But since tenants' rights in Italy make eviction of tenants who have a rent contract and who use the rented address as their permanent legal residence virtually impossible, many homeowners and landlords resist renting apartments to working families who may then stay permanently, preferring to rent to students, or to rent without a contract (which is technically illegal) or keep apartments off the market altogether. While this would seem to favor immigrants, who would be unlikely to stay their whole lives at the same address, this context can more often work against them. Given the underground nature of much of the private housing market, landlords have a great deal of discretion regarding to whom to rent apartments. The irregular or off-the-books nature of immigrant workers' wages, the precarious or unofficial nature of their employment conditions, their lack of local references, and both racist fears of foreigners and more legitimate concerns about keeping tenants accountable who may leave town tomorrow have all combined to make housing extremely hard to come by for immigrants. But as serious as it remains today, in 1990, before immigrants' presence in regularized, legal and consistently paying industrial jobs was established, the housing problem was reminiscent of Engels' descriptions of mid-19th century Manchester's Irish districts. Or rather it would have, but the housing conditions made even the family and community relations described in these works impossible to establish for many groups. Even ethnically based ghettos failed to grow outside of exceptional cases like the Tunisian fishing community in Mazara, Sicily, and the Chinatown in Milan, since even that requires some basis of available living space.

It is not surprising then that urban housing conditions led to the most militant and spontaneous eruptions of immigrant protest in 1989-1990. What is surprising is that the protests showed as great a degree of unity and cooperation among many different nationalities as they did. All over Italy, immigrants of different national origins together occupied public housing projects, abandoned buildings, municipal offices, city-owned edifices and train stations, and churches, either directly appropriating these spaces for at least temporary lodging or demanding that housing be made available. By May 1990, at least 200 immigrant men of various nationalities had made the train station in Vicenza, the Veneto's most industrial city, their nightly lodging. Three hundred persons near Naples found lodging in the decrepit Castelvolturno, an aging Baroque palace that came to be managed by the Catholic charity Caritas. In May 1990 it was site of a physical conflict as hundreds of immigrant residents sought to evict six of their co-residents who were involved in drug sales along with the Camorra representatives who sought to establish a base of operations there. In Brescia, an industrial center near Milan, 700-800 immigrants had occupied a series of abandoned houses. In Milan 500 immigrants occupied an unused building complex in the fall of 1989. Housing occupations and protests were particularly hard-fought in Bologna and Padua. In Bologna an occupation lasting over a year involved 800 persons of a wide variety of national origins who occupied unfilled public housing units that were meant to hold fewer than 400. Bologna, long the center of Italy's Communist Party (now the Democratic Party of the Left) carried out negotiations for months, ending in July 1991 in the legalization of about half of the occupants who had legal resident permits and the eviction of the rest from the buildings on Via Stalingrado. In Padua, a grouping of informal networks and formal associations came together to mobilize the occupation of various municipal offices, public structures, housing projects, and the train station, fighting with police against eviction on several occasions. This struggle involved Moroccans, Nigerians, Eritreans, Senegalese, and Tunisians together in an effort to gain access to both housing and respect in a city that had up to that time not recognized in any public way the presence of immigrants.[64]

Housing occupations would continue in subsequent years, and various cities, along with Catholic associations, sought to alleviate the housing emergency, if only to reduce the seriousness of protest. Other protests continued to take place as well. Sometimes these faced a reaction against immigrants that could turn violent. In Rome in mid-May 1991, 400 Somalian refugees who sought to occupy public space at the Campidoglio were attacked by the police and carried off the site. The Somalians responded with a demonstration to protest this treatment, and the provincial government responded by making available 700 million lire ($450,000) for 11 shelters to be at the disposal of the Somalian community. In Rome, in 1994, 258 of the first 1,700 people requesting public housing were immigrants, though the municipal government faced criticism from the far Right for allowing immigrants onto the list. In Bologna, Senegalese street vendors fought police for the right to use public space to make a living throughout 1990 and 1991. In Venice, the mayor announced publicly to street vendors, "Blacks, the police won't stop you," citing "commercial aggression on the part of the West" toward the immigrants' countries of origin. In Brescia in early 1992 immigrants held demonstrations demanding that more legal resident permits be given to those who remained without official documents. In Turin, immigrant workers held a mass meeting with CGIL union officials and complained of special difficulties they faced with pay and working conditions, such as the year-long training period for nurses, who are paid less than $200 per month, a wage level that is livable only when one has access to an Italian family network. They demanded greater access to regularized, steady-paying factory jobs. CGIL officials responded that they favored equality of conditions and a "multiethnic society" but that immigrants "can't ask that Italian workers give up their jobs and homes merely to avoid the charge of racism" and urged immigrants to accept a gradual "immersion" into industrial employment "10-20 people at a time," rather than a simultaneous hiring of hundreds. Occupied immigrant centers were struck by arson, or demolished by officials in several cities. In Villa Literno, Italian residents demonstrated and called for the removal of immigrants, and in Milan 500 bus drivers went on strike to call for the removal of a sleeping quarter for Arab workers near their union cafeteria.[65]

Despite the growth of a racist backlash and despite police and official repression over various sites of struggle, the immigrant movement of 1989–1990 yielded results. Access to at least some housing was gained in many cities, and in others, occupations received de facto legitimation from authorities. Immigrants in some cities had won the right to sell on the street and in general immigrants won for themselves renewed access to be treated in a manner consistent with human dignity. But one of the gains was also a significant change in Italy's legal system of immigration, though it was, as in the past, a mixture of state concessions to immigrant demands and the codification of state objectives quite unrelated to the aspirations of immigrants. Italian immigration law followed a combined pattern of concessions and repression. Nevertheless, the new law 39 (1990), better known as the Martelli Law, although it signaled Italy's compliance with the requirements of the Schengen Accords by officially allowing for

systematic legal border control, by recognizing various rights of
immigrants already within Italy, it represents to this day one of
the more advanced pieces of legislation in the history of the Italian
nation-state.

Following the murder of Jerry Masslo and the protests in its
immediate wake, Vice-Premier Claudio Martelli sought to use the
moment to carry out an overhaul of Italy's legal system
concerning immigration. First passed as a decree law in 1989 (a
law which must be passed into law within 60 days by Parliament
or it expires), it was later amended after a fierce debate especially
with the Republican Party's leader La Malfa who tested the
waters for how xenophobia would play only to lose ground at
election time, and after unions and Catholic groups were
convinced that a more liberal law would produce a Le Pen-style
reaction. The law combined real gains for immigrant status with
an effort at regaining control of the border and restricting entry in
order to comply with Schengen. The law granted the right of
asylum to non-European refugees, loosened residence requirements, and provided for the right of non-European Union citizens
("extracomunitarians") to enter for reasons of tourism, education,
health or work; it surpassed the conditions of Law 943 by
allowing for self-employment; and it made the social and cultural
integration of immigrants into the country's social life and labor
market an official goal for the first time. Perhaps most
importantly in terms of immigrant gains, it provided for a second
amnesty. This one, well publicized in immigrant communities
with literature in several languages, was far more successful than
that of 1986, as 216,000 immigrants were regularized under its
conditions (see Table 18). But the law's primary purpose from the
state's point of view was to restrict entry, at least officially, and
to regain control of the border. It provided for entry visas "where
prescribed"—shortly afterward Italy required visas for all entries
from the Mahgreb countries for the first time—a particularly
insistent demand of Italy's partners in the European Union. The
law also provided for expulsion of aliens, and gave wide
discretion to border police about entry. The Ministry of the
Interior, and in particular border police and the local questuras
(national police stations), maintained most of the administrative

Table 18. Regularization of non-EC Residents in Italy 1986–1990

Regularized under:

	Law 943 (1986)	Law 39 (1990 Martelli)	Resident Dec. 31, 1990
Morocco	19,283	50,538	77,971
Tunisia	8,919	29,918	41,234
Algeria	671	2,132	4,041
Libya	169	176	2,604
Egypt	5,261	7,180	19,814
Ethiopia	2,392	1,512	11,946
Somalia	1,208	4,344	9,443
Senegal	7,531	16,643	25,107
Ghana	3,296	6,600	11,443
Nigeria	1,104	3,776	6,855
Cape Verde	682	530	4,991
Mauritius	1,218	2,799	5,367
Philippines	9,538	13,351	34,328
China	4,498	9,747	18,665
Sri Lanka	9,494	4,527	11,454
India	1,241	2,339	11,282
Pakistan	958	3,137	6,497
Bangladesh	385	3,444	4,883
Brazil	905	2,867	14,293
Argentina	900	2,518	12,893
Colombia	474	960	5,524
Dominican Rep.	530	1,685	4,415
Peru	632	1,976	5,253
Chile	813	787	4,248
Venezuela	216	387	5,046
Yugoslavia	6,386	12,226	29,790
Poland	466	5,539	16,966
Hungary	72	424	4,147
Romania	180	686	7,494
USSR	24	334	6,447
Turkey	774	1,576	4,695
Iran	2,900	2,601	14,630
Lebanon	467	1,592	5,802
Jordan	473	999	5,703
Other Developing Countries	5,807	9,348	62,171
Other Countries	5,445	6,839	117,689
Total	105,312	216,037	635,131

Source: Continuous Reporting System on Migration/SOPEMI, Annual Report 1990 (Paris: OECD, 1991), p 22, taken from Veugelers (1993), p. 40.

control over immigrants.

That the intention of the law was at least in large part to convince both Italy's European neighbors and prospective immigrants that the country was getting tough about closing its border could not be misunderstood when, in the immediate aftermath of the law's going into effect, the collapse of the socialist regimes in Eastern Europe led to a massive crisis involving Albanians seeking refugee status, eventually leading to a mass expulsion that made headline news around the world. In July 1990, 4,000 Albanians landed at the ancient southern Italian port of Brindisi. In March of the next year, 21,300 more landed seeking refugee status, and the administrative system for meeting their needs broke down. By default, the government solved the problem by granting work permits to all of the entrants, even at a time when it was closing the border to newly arrived foreign workers. But when another 15,000 arrived at Bari in August, the government quickly deported them all and began to use the navy to block the coast against more arrivals.[66] This has set the tone at least officially for Italian border policy ever since, including in the spring of 1997 when the collapse of a series of pyramid finance schemes bankrupted the majority of households in Albania. This led to the first full-scale armed revolt against casino capitalism and the arrival of several thousand refugees at Brindisi who were quickly taken into custody, along with a naval presence in the Adriatic, which led to over 100 persons drowning after their boat collided with an Italian naval vessel. Llike elsewhere in Europe this closed border policy has fed a growing polemic against so-called *clandestini*—undocumented immigrants—who are increasingly accused of bringing organized crime, prostitution, drugs, and violence into Italy. Indeed, racist discourses, occasionally put into violent practice, grew noticeably in Italy throughout the mid-1990s, though in response an anti-racist movement continued to be active, organizing enormous national demonstrations in February 1995 and February 1996, the latter also directed against the notorious Dini Decree on immigration.

In the spring of 1990, students, starting in Palermo and followed, city by city, by those further north (exactly the reverse of the circulation of 1960s and 1970s era struggles), occupied university faculties in virtually every Italian city, protesting against the planned privatization of the universities. They succeeded in blocking that plan, and gave birth to the famous student movement of the early 1990s known as the Pantera, after a panther that had escaped from the Rome zoo and was never found, though also a memorial to the Black Panther Party for Self-Defense in the United States during the 1960s (the Italian students used the same image of a panther as was used in the U.S., for instance). This student movement, with its critique of neoliberal capitalism, provided political space for many of the 1970s-era militants among intellectuals who had spent the 1980s in prison or silent for fear of repression. With the outbreak of the Gulf War the following winter, the student networks and what remained of the far left held local actions and planned a national demonstration against the war, autonomous unions held public transport strikes against Italy's intervention, and the Women in Black, a group in solidarity with the women of Palestine, held actions across the country. Within a short two years, the Italian left and working-class movements had rebounded from a politically disastrous decade to find their voices and new priorities. Anti-racism and anti-war stood at the top of the list of issues capable of bringing together a disunited and long-repressed movement, carrying it back into public spaces and national debates. The immigrants in Italy, despite their small numbers had become an integral part of the working class and left movements in Italy, and had contributed through their own actions to the revitalization of the organizational life and unity of purpose of the Italian left.

How was this possible? How do we explain the fact that a numerically very small, politically unrepresented, often penniless and homeless, and extremely diverse group of immigrant communities managed to organize a nationwide movement only a few years after arrival in the country. How was this accomplished under conditions of depoliticization that had resisted the best efforts of what remains the most numerous, institutionally strong, resource-wealthy, and organizationally militant left in all of Europe? And how was this mobilization able to wring concessions, material and legal, from a country whose external obligations constrained it to move precisely in the opposite direction—toward restriction of immigration and denial of its status as a country of immigrations? These extraordinary accomplishments can be explained only if we adopt a perspective that flies in the face of much of conventional wisdom regarding both migration and working-class organization. The occupations and demonstrations of 1989–1990, spontaneous as they seemed, were organized and spread by very real organizational forces, which had not at that time necessarily merged into formal association. The same networks that helped immigrants find a job, obtain the goods to be sold in street vending, or to obtain a bed to sleep in, were used to mobilize politically and to spread news of the actions around the country. As we have already seen, some formal immigrant associations already existed, and more were formed during the insurgencies themselves or in their aftermath.

The degree of unity among such a variety of nationalities would seem more difficult to explain, particularly since the immigrant groups had not even spent more than a few years in the same country, and would therefore have had limited experience in working together. Yet perhaps we should investigate our assumptions that such capabilities and unity should be the exception. For as we have seen in chapter three, today's immigrants are already the heirs, and in many cases the veterans, of a whole generation of social conflicts, liberation movements, and social guarantees won after the Second World War. Such experiences, along with knowledge of both the material possibilities that exist in the advanced economies and therefore worldwide, and of the level of legal rights and guarantees won by the people of the First World, lead to very broad expectations on the part of such workers. These expectations are not restricted either to the limited opportunities existing in the (pre- or post-SAP) countries of origin, or to second-class citizenship and the lowest rung on the job hierarchy as a supposedly inevitable aspect of integration in a new country. Immigrants often express an awareness of the history of the relations between their own countries and the West at meetings and in discussions: many Moroccans and Tunisians see Europe through the eyes of the Gulf War, and Nigerians, Ghanaians, and Senegalese often express pan-African or anti-colonial sentiments. One Somali elder, speaking at a Padua meeting on immigration, told a largely Italian audience, "You don't want me here, but I know why I'm here. It's because your country invaded my country and destabilized it, and left Italians there and gave me the idea to come here." Though a certain Third World solidarity among various groups can best be described as latent, rather than active, under harsh living conditions in Italy, this sentiment seems to have come to the forefront and provided for a certain willingness to work together to face common problems. Further, the existence of a common legal identity, used in public discourse to lump all of the non-European Union citizens together under a single name, "extra-comunitarian"—with its explicit reference to non-membership and participation in the local community—has aided in the formation of a united front based upon that identity. This is similar to the process in the 1960s and 1970s in Great Britain that led to the use of the political category "Black Britain" to unify Asians, Irish, British-born people of African descent, and West Indians as an autonomous part of the working class movement.[67]

Yet this ideological propensity to unity would have remained only the latent sentiments of ragged and underemployed immigrants had the organizational capacity not existed as well. For the networks of the migrant web, making contact with others of differing nationality who are often of the same regional language groups (or West African pidgin for instance), religion (Islam, Catholic or Pentacostal) or who work together is hardly to be considered an impossibility. Immigrants from many different nationalities came to know one another across Italy, eating at the same soup kitchens, vending in the same piazzas, picking tomatoes in the same fields, washing dishes in the same home or restaurant, sleeping at the same public shelter. Various webs crossed each other, linked together, expanded in contacts and complexity, and transformed themselves. During the demonstrations and occupations of 1989–1990, through the formation of immigrant associations and participation in labor unions and in the activities of the autonomist social centers, the networks of immigrant communities, while maintaining their own integrity, were partially transformed into a multinational working class force in Italian cities and workplaces. This process is not dissimilar to that identified by social scientists who have long seen urbanization and the factory as forces for the overcoming of parochialisms and the creation of new, broader-based interests and identities. For ex-peanut or cocoa farmers from rural West Africa or young men from Morocco, urban Italy presented the possibility the city has always offered: a place to develop one's social self in a way not limited to any one mode of production or class composition from the past. But as we have seen, these social subjects, even before migrating, were already anything but isolated peasants lacking knowledge of the world outside. The Mouride network, or the variety of relatives' experience of different host countries that one might hear after a holiday dinner in Morocco, remind us of the wealth of knowledge available to even the remotest potential immigrants. The immigrant experience of the Italian early 1990s should not be reduced to a sort of picaresque adventure in which the country mouse becomes the city mouse thanks to the concentraltion of population and workers, which is ever the tendency of the capitalist market.

Richard Jeffries, among others, has pointed out that the working people of the Third World are not entering capitalism upon entering either newly built factories in their home country or the cities of the First World. Rather, it is as an already formed working class that this new incorporation takes place, and the expectations and knowledge of social struggles that such workers bring with them to new sites reflects this fact. Jeffries writes, "The trade union movement in Ghana and several other African states have in fact developed an organizational and political strength which their counterparts transparently lacked at a comparable stage in the historical evolution of European industrialism."[68] The common experience of the struggles against structural adjustment and widespread knowledge of the near universality of the debt question in the Third World would only enhance the possibilities of working together upon arriving at common destinations. The IMF has sown dragon's teeth, and they have popped up, housing occupations and anti-racist demonstrations, across the Mediterranean.

The immigrants also demanded an even wider unity and

integration. In the early 1990s they sought to enter regular factory employment in the industrial Center-North of Italy.[69] Ultimately, the most important gain made as a result of the struggles of 1989-1990 may be the rapid and increasingly large immigrant insertion into the industrial areas of the Italian economy. Yet this arrival forces us to ponder another riddle: namely, that political mobilization and militancy should lead to the integration of immigrant workers into the more stable and well-paying factories. Nevertheless, it is the case that the migration in large number from the South to the North and entry into factory work on a significant scale by immigrant workers already living in the Center-North coincides with the period of greatest mobilization and its aftermath.

The mass moblization helped increase immigrant awareness of legal conditions in Italy and of the possibilities of the labor market. Further, while immigrants in Italy already believed they had rights, this idea was linked to the system of legal rights in Italy as a result of the mobilizations. More concretely, anger at the various humiliations experienced daily as itinerant workers and vendors boiled over by 1990 into a demand for legal equality, for opportunity, and for access to the Italian system of citizenship rights. The Martelli Law, won as a result of these mobilizations, helped to open the door to immigrants seeking access to legal rights in Italy, above all under conditions of steady work. Indeed, the lessons of street vending, seasonal agricultural work, and so forth was that the income derived was irregular and the legal status was marginal at best. The factories offered the best means of obtaining a legal resident permit, an income sufficient (hopefully) to provide for stable dwellings, and freedom (hopefully) from the unwanted contact with police authorities that street vending and similarly visible activities drew upon its practitioners. Racist demonstrations by local shopkeepers protesting unfair competition from street vendors in Florence can only have reenforced this conclusion. Since large and medium-scale industrial firms would be likely to hire only regularized workers, the possibility of regularizing one's legal status, finding a more stable and well paying job were logically connected.[70] The Martelli Law encouraged that possibility, as Table 18 indicated, by encouraging much larger numbers of immigrants than previously to become legal, fully documented workers, and thereby encouraging employers to consider them as part of the regularly available workforce.[71]

Even so, there is little evidence of recruiting for factory work by employers before the mid-1990s on any significant scale. Immigrants began to move north, hearing of available jobs, or merely of the presence of factories in various cities from relatives or friends. One Senegalese man told Valerio Belotti that he had heard one could find steady work in Vicenza, in the Veneto, and took a train there. Upon exiting the train station he saw a group of U.S. soldiers (there is a large NATO Air Force base in Vicenza) driving around seeming to enjoy themselves and decided he liked the energy of the city and decided to stay and find work. Many immigrants of different nationalities told me they had moved north to find work that would enable them to become or remain regularized and on-the-books, citing this as a means to avoid being ripped off by unscrupulous employers and being harassed by police for having irregular legal status. Upon arriving north, as we have seen, housing was a problem, and many immigrants ended up in the public shelters that had been built after the end of the Second World War to house those who still had no place of their own. (These were later used to house the newly arrived Southerners who moved into the factories of the North during the 1950s.)[72] Others immigrants found shelter at various Catholic charities, and at public soup kitchens like Padua's Cucina Populare, managed by nuns from Caritas. After some early hirings of immigrants in workplaces in the Third Italy, employers seeking immigrants would on occasion contact these public dormitories and eateries to ask about how to hire immigrants.[73] But such examples were rare, and in any case demonstrate the lack of any systematic recruiting by employers of immigrant workers in the early 1990s. In the following chapter we shall explore more closely the mechanisms of hiring of immigrant workers in the labor market of the Third Italy. We may summarize how this came about for the most part: immigrant workers went door to door in the industrial zones of central and northern Italian cities asking to be hired. This represented an innovation in Italian employment practice then and now, but it proved effective at accomplishing something that Italy's labor market was incapable of doing on its own, namely bringing together workers and employers. As we have seen, the areas that have seen growth have separate labor markets from those which have high levels of potentially available workers. It took both the geographic mobility of immigrants—reproducing the historical movement of labor power on the Italian peninsula from South to North—and then the individual mobility of immigrant workers going on foot, bicycle or by bus to the factory doors to ask for work to unblock this faulty labor market mechanism in many regions. These methods, followed by the familial pattern of immigrant social network placement described previously, had by 1995 resulted in nearly 105,000 newly hired immigrant industrial workers on the books; of these, 18,000 had been hired or re-hired that year alone in just the Veneto.[74] Thirty-six percent of those hired nationally, and over 70 percent of those hired in the Veneto, worked in industry. This is in stark contrast to the numbers previously cited for domestic workers in various regions.

As immigrants became full-time, regularized waged workers, the Italian state began to treat them as a potential source of dependent wage labor. Polemics defending at least a limited immigration of workers began to appear in debates on television; and in public meetings local officials were quick to point out that the relative youth of immigrant workers compared with the advanced age of much of the locally born Italian population meant that the former could be useful, as taxpaying workers, to solving the crisis of pensions and the budget deficit facing Italy. Some voices, notably the world-renowned demographer Massimo Livi-Bacci, arguing in the immigrant *annus mirabilis* of 1990 in favor of such a "need for immigrants," sought to counter xenophobia and the seemingly perpetual state of emergency that informed public discourse over the presence of immigrants.[75] But by the mid-1990s, a host of public officials were explicitly trying to convince local citizens of the need for immigrants to pay taxes to cover the pensions of aging Italian citizens. Immigrants were described as being of "child-bearing age," a reference to the low birth rate in Italy, and hence a rich source of future labor power.

This approach implied that immigrant men were admissable only as a taxpaying mechanism to make up for the failings of Italian society, while immigrant women were seen as baby machines precisely because Italian women had rejected this role. These implications troubled few, at least publicly.[76]

Such an approach contained an inherent animosity toward clandestine, and therefore non-taxpaying, immigrants. It further suggested an approach aimed at guaranteeing that immigrants should be maintained as a dependent wage workforce, which implied little encouragement of the formation of immigrant small business (the relation of small business to the payment of taxes in Italy is complex, but we should note that it is generally understood that where small businesses can successfully avoid taxes, waged workers cannot, at least without the complicity of their employers). These concerns—to guarantee employers a waged workforce now that the possibilities of immigrant labor power were recognized, and to force that workforce to remain both dependent on wage labor and regularized and therefore taxpaying (while minimizing its costs, and thereby maximizing its net worth, to the state and to employers)—became a priority of various political forces concerned with immigration. That immigrants showed a capacity to mobilize politically, and make demands on employers, local authorities, and the state no doubt encouraged the interest in reestablishing some social control over such a labor force.

In March 1994, after an unprecedented series of scandals and government crises, culminating in the arrest of a large percentage of parliamentary deputies and two former prime ministers and presidents for participation in the corrupt kickback system that came to be dubbed Tangentopoli (Bribe City), Italy's system of postwar political parties collapsed. The party that had dominated every government since 1948, the Christian Democrats, ceased to exist overnight, fragmenting into several tiny factions, and the Socialist Party likewise disintegrated. The Communist Party, the largest in the Western world, changed its name and program under pressure from the collapse of the socialist bloc, becoming the Democratic Party of the Left (PDS), though parts of the Party which opposed the move created a rump party known as

Rifondazione Comunista (Communist Refoundation). The neo-fascist Italian Social Movement, long held to 5-8 percent of the national vote, also changed its name and program, disavowing dictatorship, and renaming itself the National Alliance. But they were not the only right wing force seeking to gain from the situation. The Northern League, led by Umberto Bossi, a regionalist, anti-Southern Italian and anti-immigrant party that seeks seeking either federal autonomy or independence for the northern half of the country (which it named the Padania) grew as older parties were discredited and disappeared. A new election system, reducing the proportionality that had encouraged small parties and coalitions, was put into place for the elections to be held in March 1994. Spurred by fear of a leftist victory in the vacuum left by the Christian Democratic implosion, billionaire and media monopolist Silvio Berlusconi and his hastily formed network cum party Forza Italia, in alliance with the National Alliance and the Northern League, swept the elections, bringing the right to power in Italy for the first time in the postwar era.

Coming into power in May, the Berlusconi government quickly set about trying to reduce health services and pensions, and again tried to implement the ill-fated privatization of Italy's universities. That autumn was Italy's hottest in nearly 20 years, if not since 1969, as students again occupied universities across the country and battled with police in Naples on several occasions in November. A general strike on October 12 by the labor union federations involved perhaps 20 million people, with as many as 2 million participating in various protests around the country. Another general strike was planned in December. On November 12, over a million and a half people marched on Rome in protest against the government's budget cuts. That same November, 250,000 people, most of them immigrants, demonstrated against racism and demanded equal rights, better access to housing, and the facilitation of obtaining legal resident permits for all immigrants in the country. When the Northern League bolted from the coalition in December, citing reasons which appeared to convince not even their own voters, the Berlusconi government fell, having lost its parliamentary majority after less than six months. Political science versions of the fall of the Berlusconi coalition often underestimate the massive outpouring of opposition and the Italian political classes long-time sensitivity to mass protest (in 1960, workers' violent protests in Genoa toppled a government that depended on rightist votes, and the government instability of the 1960s and 1970s was due in part to sensivitivity to the extent of mass protest). Further, even those accounts that pay due attention to large-scale extraparliamentary expression of opposition to Berlusconi leave out the immigrant element in the protests.[77] Yet its absence would have marked the exclusion of an increasingly important sector of the country's working class and left from the social protest of the moment. Instead, mobilizing on the basis of their own needs, immigrants and their allies moved on a massive scale, alarmed by hostility toward immigrant workers of a regime including both the ex-fascist party and the regionalist and racist Northern League. In doing so, immigrants integrated themselves more fully into the political life of the working class in Italy, and contributed to its understanding of the rightist regime, providing a unifying theme of anti-racism to the left and enhancing the leftist discourse of universal rights which underlay its defense of health care, pensions, and university education in the other protests against the government. An article in the leftist newspaper *Il Manifesto* referred to immigrant communities as "the fifth estate," meaning that they had become an integral part of Italy's political life.[78]

But subsequent years would see an attempt by the state to put into practice means of subordinating immigrant workers to the labor market, and dividing them both within immigrant ranks and from other workers in Italy. The government of Lamberto Dini, a technocrat who had been finance minister under Berlusconi and who had previously spent 14 years with the International Monetary Fund, including time spent on the IMF committee overseeing southern African debt questions, succeeded that of Berlusconi at the start of 1995. The votes of the leftist PDS and the cooperation of Rifondazione Comunista were the bulk of its parliamentary majority. In September, the government began debate on a decree on immigration that would supersede most of the progress made for immigrants by the Martelli Law. Eventually known as the Dini Decree, and issued in November, it was based on a series of proposals by the Northern League that allowed for expulsion of immigrants from Italy permanently for even minor infractions such as drug possession or prostitution. It also allowed for "preventive expulsion" in the case of any immigrant considered by authorities to be a potential menace to the state. Essentially a public order measure, the law made being an undocumented immigrant an offense, and therefore itself cause for deportation, and made possession and maintenance of a residence permit dependent on continual waged employment. While those immigrants already present in Italy who were self-employed, including shop and restaurant owners, could remain at their current positions and renew their residence permits on that basis, no new permits would be given out for self-employment or free-lance work. Street vending was not recognized as valid employment for residence purposes.

The reaction of the left and Catholic forces in the government and civil society was muted. The Dini government depended on the adherence of the Northern League, and the withdrawal of the League's votes and the fall of the government would unquestionably have brought Berlusconi back into power. A further complication was that everyone agreed on the need to schedule new elections, since the previously elected government no longer existed, but no majority concensus existed on when to hold elections and under what set of rules. The immigration decree became the means of assuring the Northern League's acceptance, and Forza Italia's and the National Alliance's acquiescence, of a plan for holding elections and allowing the Dini government to continue as caretaker in the meantime. Immigration policy had thus become not only a force for unity among working-class left forces but also, in a very different way, among the political elite of the parties. Iinstead of opposing what was clearly regression concerning immigrant rights, these forces close to immigrant groups sought compromise, wresting additions that were probably intended to soften the bill, but which may have brought on more hardship than the original version and lent legitimacy to the League's view of immigration.

An amnesty program was added, though it depended on the immigrant's employment in taxpaying waged work, and provided for fines for employers who employed undocumented workers. Employers would also be required to pay six months of social security benefits per year for immigrant employees, putting the total sum in a type of escrow account upon hiring, and family reunion was guaranteed for regularized immigrants provided they had employment and sufficient housing space. This latter requirement made the right a dead letter and blocked one of the paths to immigrant improvement of conditions that might have improved living conditions—the pooling of wages and other family resources. The six-month requirement regarding social security represented a step back from the long tradition of universal equality of the French Revolution and the advances of the Martelli Law, and it provided employers with a new incentive to keep immigrant employees off the books or to fire them altogether. Smaller employers especially balked at the idea of paying several thousand dollars' worth of benefits for a new employee, and an immigrant who as far as the employer was concerned might leave for another town or job the next day, leaving an un-reimbursable payment as a net loss to the employer.[79]

The decree almost immediately created hardship in immigrant communities, as employers fired hundreds of immigrant workers—often hiring them back only if they agreed to now remain undocumented and off the books. Long-time residents in Italy were expelled for not having a job on the books, and hundreds were denied permits either due to unemployment or because they were self-employed. I carried out many of the interviews during this period, spending every day for months in the offices of the CGIL immigrant worker office in Padua or the Vicenza municipal office for Immigrant Welcome. Respondent after responding told me of their difficulties bringing over their family, the ruin of their plans for starting businesses, and their fear of expulsion or anger at the threatenend expulsion of friends or family members. Many were told by employers to quit and come back to work without documents. Others feared being fired for trying to take advantage of the amnesty, since their employers did not want to pay the social security advance. These stories were common throughout the Third Italy's industrial zones.[80]

Expulsions had begun already by mid-November 1995, and the press reported that the immigrant communities had remained indoors for fear of arrest and expulsion.[81] The law and order orientation of the debate as the decree went into effect encouraged a general crackdown on immigrants. The same day that decree was agreed on in Rome, a "Blitz" was carried out involving mass arrests in neighborhoods in Padua that had large numbers of immigrants. People were forced into the pre-dawn streets in their bed-clothes as police searched 280 apartments for fake identifications, drugs, and weapons.[82] The Padua immigrant umbrella organization, Associazione Immigrati Extracomunitari, protested the action, and a demonstration followed in the city's piazzas against both the so-called blitz and the Dini Decree, drawing perhaps 300 people.[83]

Nationally as well, immigrants responded to the climate of repression and to the regressive Dini Decree. Tens of thousands marched in Turin against the decree in November, shortly after it was issued. Local demonstrations were almost continuous in one or another Italian city. In February 1996 perhaps 50,000 marched again in Rome. In Rome on March 31, 1996, hundreds of thousands called for the decree to be withdrawn. A year after the decree went into effect, 60 immigrants occupied a church in Milan, in frank imitation of the more highly publicized occupation in France that protested planned expulsions and sparked massive national protests and a serious debate among French intellectuals over refusing complicity in certain aspects of the state's identification of immigrants and their activities. Thus Italy's immigrants renewed their membership in a worldwide circulation of struggles, as well as deepening their involvement in those of their host country.[84] Deeply hated by Italy's immigrant communities and anti-racist movement, the decree was declared unconstitutional along with all other decrees that had endured beyond 60 days, as Italy's Constitutional Court annulled all decrees that had not been passed by Parliament. With street protests against the decree, and now with a leftist majority as the PDS and its allies of the Center-Left behind liberal Catholic economist Romano Prodi won a majority in national elections, Parliament had no stomach for trying to pass the despised decree as a law against strong opposition from its own electoral base. As the law went out of effect on November 8, 1996, the Martelli Law unexpectedly became, by default, the immigration law of the land once again.

About 250,000 people requested regularization of their legal status under the Dini Decree, leaving an estimated one-third of the undocumented immigrants cut out of the amnesty program, which successive governments have promised would not be extended, nor followed up with another in future legislation. In February 1997, the PDS Minister of the Interior, Giorgio Napolitano proposed new legislation that would answer some of the immigrants' demands for political rights, especially the vote in local and regional elections, and would replace the resident permit system with a multiyear U.S.-style green card system. (In theory resident permits could be granted to workers for up to two years, but they were frequently granted for as little as 3-6 months and therefore needed constant renewing as well as registration in any new city the immigrant went to live in.) The proposed law would guarantee family reunion rights, and recognize the legal status of immigrants who worked as wage workers or self-employed. But it also planned to streamline the system of expulsions, allowing it only for serious offenses, an aspect which blocked its passage due to continuing polemics about undocumented immigrant criminality by the Northern League and the National Alliance. (Italy's system of passing legislation is very consensual, rarely resulting in the passage of legislation over the total opposition of parliamentary minorities.) The left remained concerned with provisions that would allow immigrants awaiting expulsion to be held in internment camps temporarily. The state once again sought the means to concede something to the insistent mobilizations of immigrant communities, while using the opportunity to limit immigrant political autonomy and the independent use of border entry by immigrant networks. This reproduced a pattern that we have seen recur since the trade in indentured servants in the 17th century.[85]

In the end, provisions for the vote in local elections were left out of the new law. Newly arrived and arrested undocumented immigrants began to be held in camps in the Spring of 1998. The results were disastrous: Throughout July and August, immigrants in various camps sought to break out of the camps, rebelled, fought guards, and even armed themselves.[86] Several leaders of rebellions died when crowds of immigrants were fired upon inside the camps. Meanwhile, the Italian press declared a new emergency of illegal arrivals off the various coasts. On the one hand, the brief opening resulting from immigrant self-activity and a new government of the left was closed. On the other, the rebellions in the camps and subsequent controversy put the Italian state on notice that the policy of interment before deportation would not be accepted quietly. The new repressive attitude seems clearly to be a response to the newly built power and influence of immigrants, and a signal by the leftist government about how far it will go to contain social revolt in Italian society in order to enter the European Union as a full member.

After a decade of struggles for rights, for housing, and against racism and police repression, immigrants in Italy had established themselves as an important presence in every part of the country. Officially topping 1.1 million in 1997, with perhaps another 200,000 to 300,000 remaining undocumented, immigrants constituted significant percentages of the population of at least some major cities. In Rome, immigrants officially numbered 230,000 and in Milan another 204,000 by February 1997. In such large cities, immigrants had to some extent managed to create, though with difficulty and to a lesser extent than elsewhere, the familiar features of immigrant communities. An evening stroller in Rome, Milan, or even smaller but cosmopolitan Bologna had no trouble finding Chinese, Arab, Ethiopian, Indian, and West African restaurants. There were over 1,500 Egyptian-owned firms in Milan, mostly pottery and ceramic workshops, and the Tunisian community in Mazara, Sicily and the Chinese neighborhoods in Prato had become mainstays of Italy. But as immigrants moved north into factories, and as they followed northern industry out of its traditional home bases of Turin and Milan, as small factories decentralized production throughout western Lombardy, immigrants often found themselves in regions where, finally, stable and legal industrial jobs were readily available, but housing was not. Perhaps just as serious, the zones of the Third Italy where industry had established itself in small, export-based production zones were often in small, parochial and conservative locales. Local residents not only were unused to the presence of foreigners and regarded it with misgivings and even hostility but often spoke only the local dialect in public, eschewing the national language. The arrival of immigrants to the factories also coincided with the increasing influence and electoral power of the Northern League in many of these areas. Further, while immigrants encountered in areas like the Veneto a local moral economy that had long rejected gross inequalities and fostered a wide diffusion of property based on independent ownership and artisanal work, the arrival of immigrants also coincided with the incorporation of these regions more profoundly into the world market. Flexible production methods enabled the small firms of the Third Italy to reorganize the local economy into a more export-oriented dependence on commercial activity, and in particular on trade with the outside world. This led to a tense contradiction in the local society: The region sought to assert its inward-looking, unwelcoming to strangers, and parochial moral economy under conditions in which its material well-being now increasingly depended on selling products to every corner of the planet. To do so, however, its producers increasingly relied on labor power born in the far corners of the Earth. We have already seen how labor power has been expropriated through structural adjustment; how, in response, social networks laid the basis for transnational communities that organized migration into Italy and elsewhere, establishing the worldwide web of migration across the planet; how these different webs came together to mobilize politically in Italy since 1989 and recompose the working class in Italy; and how this mobilization in turn led in part to a North-South migration of immigrants that is both like and unlike that of southern Italians in the 1950s and 1960s. This mobilization and its aftermath led social subjects from West and North Africa, Asia and Latin America into the factories of regions that have never before experienced migration and which have pioneered new production techniques or revived ancient ones. The immigrants obtain schei—Veneto dialect for money—and but under less than felicitous conditions, and they unexpectedly found themselves in what Umberto Bossi, leader of the Northern League, and his followers call the Padania.

Notes

1. See, particularly on the tariff question and the underdevelopment of the South, Denis Mack Smith, *Italy* (Ann Arbor: University of Michigan Press, 1969), pp. 49, 59, 150-62; Luciano Cafagna, *Dualismo e svilupppo nella storia d'Italia* (Milan: Einaudi, 1989); see also the discussion of unification in Antonio Gramsci, *Selections from the Prison Notebooks* (New York: International Publishers, 1989); Russell King, *The Industrial Geography of Italy* (London: Croom & Helm, 1985); see also Christopher Duggan, *A Concise History of Italy* (Cambridge: Cambridge University Press, 1994), pp. 156-60 on the growing sectional basis of political power in Italy after 1880.

2. See the debate in Giovanni Arrighi, ed., *Semiperipheral Development: The Politics of Southern Europe in the Twentieth Century* (Beverly Hills: Sage, 1985); Ray Hudson and Jim Lewis, eds., *Uneven Development in Southern Europe: Studies of Accumulation, Class, Migration and the State* (New York: Metheun, 1985); Robert Putnam, *Making Democracy Work* (Princeton: Princeton University Press, 1993) sees Italy has having two diverse social formations based upon vastly differing histories; Arnaldo Bagnasco, *Tre Italie* (Bologna: Il Mulino, 1977) sees Italy has instead made up of three diverse social formations.

3. See, among others, Paul Ginsborg, *A History of Contemporary Italy* (London: Penguin, 1990), pp. 210-53; Joanne Barkan, *Visions of Emancipation: The Italian Workers' Movement Since 1945* (New York: Praeger, 1984), pp. 36-56.

4. Ginsborg, *Contemporary Italy*, pp. 298-405; Barkan, op.cit., passim; Steven Colatrella, "We Want Everything: The Rise and Decline of the Autonomous Left in Italy," unpublished M.A. thesis (New York: New School for Social Research, 1989); Sidney Tarrow, *Democracy and Disorder: Protest and Politics in Italy 1965-1975* (Princeton: Princeton University Press, 1981); Alessandro Pizzorno, "Political Exchange and Collective Identity in Industrial Conflict," in Crouch, Colin and Pizzorno, eds., *The Resurgence of Class Conflict in Western Europe Since 1968* (London: MacMillan, 1978); Robert Lumley, *States of Emergency: Social Movements in Italy 1968-1978* (London: Verso, 1991).

5. On the crisis and subsequent shift away from using labor power in mass assembly production and the rise of other forms of work, see Piore and Sabel, *The Second Industrial Divide* (New York: Basic Books, 1984); Midnight Notes, *Midnight Oil* (1992); Ash Amin, ed., *Post-Fordism: A Reader*, Saskia Sassen, *The Mobility of Capital and Labor*, Richard Locke, *Remaking the Italian Economy* (Ithaca: Cornell University Press, 1995).

6. Bagnasco, *Tre Italie*, p. 154.

7. Michael Blim, "Economic Development and Decline in the Emerging Global Factory: Some Italian Lessons," *Politics and Society* (1990): 147; Bagnasco, *Tre Italie*, pp. 114-19 and passim; Anna Bull and Paul Corner, *From Peasant to Entrepreneur: The Survival of the Family Economy in Italy* (Oxford: Berg, 1993), passim.

8. Bagnasco, *Tre Italie*, p. 154.

9. Ibid., p. 165.

10. Ibid., p. 164.

11. Ginsborg, *Contemporary Italy*, p. 411.

12. Massimo Paci, *Mercato del lavoro e classi sociali in Italia* (Bologna: Il Mulino, 1973); Salvatore Lupo, "The Changing Mezzogiorno: Between Representations and Reality," in Stephen Gundle and Simon Parker, *The New Italian Republic* (New York: Routledge, 1996,) pp. 248-49; Judith Chubb, *Patronage, Power and Poverty in Southern Italy* (Cambridge: Cambridge University Press, 1982), pp. 132-34, 168-69.

13. Lupo, Changing Mezzogiorno, pp. 252-56; Charles Richards, *The New Italians* (London: Penguin, 1997), pp. 101-04.

14. Ginsborg, *Contemporary Italy*, p. 410; Lupo, "Changing Mezzogiorno," p. 254; Richards, *New Italians*, pp. 101, 191-232; see also, on the extent of clientelist control of the economy and the growth of economic power of the Mafia, Camorra and 'Ndrangheta, Donatella della Porta, "The System of Corrupt Exchange in Local Government"; and Percia Allum and Felia Allum, "The Resistable Rise of the New Neapolitan Camorra," both in Gundle and Parker, *New Italian Republic*.

15. Richards, *New Italians*, pp. 102-03.

16. Bagnasco, *Tre Italie*, pp. 114-21.

17. The unwaged status of housework was a central issue for the Italian feminist movement in the 1970s; see Mariarosa Dalla Costa, *The Power of Women*; Lucia Chiavola Birnbaum, *Liberazione della donna: Feminism in Italy* (Middletown: Wesleyan Univ. Press, 1986) is an excellent overview of the movement.

18. Umberto Melotti, "International Migration in Europe: Social Projects and Political Cultures," in Tariq Modood and Pnina Werbner, *The Politics of Multiculturalism in the New Europe* (London: Zed, 1997), p. 88.

19. Giovanna Campani, "Immigration and Racism in Southern Europe: The Italian Case," *Ethnic and Racial Studies* 16 (July 1993): 516.

20. Melotti, "International Migration in Europe," p. 88.

21. Campani, "Immigration and Racism," p. 515; Melotti, "International Migration in Europe," pp. 88-89.

22. Melotti, *International Migration*, p. 89; Campani, "Immigration and Racism," pp. 512-13.

23. John W.P. Veugelers, "Recent Immigration Politics in Italy: A Short Story," *West European Politics* 17(2) (April 1994).

24. Melotti, *International Migration*, p. 89.

25. Ibid., p. 89.

26. Veugelers, "Immigration Politics in Italy," p. 35.

27. Ibid., p. 34.
28. Fondazione Cariplo per le Iniziative e lo Studio sulla Multienicità (ISMU), *Secondo rapporto sulle migrazioni 1996* (Milan: FrancoAngeli, 1997), p. 20.
29. These figures, again, may be contested as being too small, given the large number of undocumented immigrants in Italy, or too high, as ISTAT, the official statistical bureau of the Italian state does, finding discrepancies in the Ministry of the Interior's method of counting resident permits, and reason to doubt the low mortality rates of some immigrant communities.
30. Campani, "Immigration and Racism," p. 509.
31. Ibid., p. 509.
32. Ibid.
33. Again, see Bagnasco on this anomoly with respect to the Italian economy, *Tre Italie*, pp. 114-20.
34. Campani, "Immigration and Racism," p. 510.
35. Manuel Castells, "Immigrant Workers," had already identified these characteristics as reasons why capital wanted immigrant workers in the pre-1973 period; Giovanni Mottura and Pietro Pinto, *Immigrazione e cambiamento sociale:strategie sindicali e lavoro straniero in Italia* (Rome: Ediesse, 1996) make a similar argument in the contemporary context of immigrant workers and the labor movement in Emilia-Romagna. However, their work is a fine study of the efforts at unionization by immigrants and of the labor movement to attract immigrant workers, indicating that their understanding of the dynamic is more complex than the structural approach of Castells, p. 23 and *passim*.
36. Regarding this issue, this study agrees with the findings of Pugliese and Macioti, who found that the demand for labor in not sufficient to explain what is happening and warn of the need to avoid confusing the need for labor power for the system with whatever type of personal requirement. Maria Immacolata Macioti and Enrico Pugliese, *Gli immigrati in Italia* (Bari: Editori Laterza, 1991), p. 51 (my translation from the Italian).
37. Ibid., p. 53, makes the same point, arguing against the assumption of much of the literature on immigrants in the labor market that they will inevitably end up as waged workers, despite the persistence of street vending, self-employment and illegal forms of work; in this regard see also C. Dell'Aringa and F. Neri, "Illegal Immigrants and the Informal Economy in Italy," *Labour* no. 2 (1987).
38. "Braccio di ferro sugli immigrati," *La Repubblica*, February 16, 1997.
39. Melotti, op.cit., p. 88; Campani, "Immigration and Racism," p. 515; Richards, *New Italians*, p. 237.
40. Campani, "Immigration and Racism," p. 515; Melotti, *International Migration*, p. 89.
41. ISMU, *Primo Rapport sulle Migrazioni 1995* (Milan: FrancoAngeli, 1996), p. 156; Emilio Reyneri, *Sociologia del Mercato del Lavoro* (Bologna: Il Mulino, 1996), pp. 328-29.
42. ISMU, *Primo Rapporto*, p. 156; Reyneri, *Sociologia*, p. 329.

43. This point, of course, is the main thesis of Bagnasco, *Tre Italie*; see also the discussion on Southern cities in Gramsci, *The Prison Notebooks*.
44. Campani, "Immigration and Racism," pp. 515-16; Melotti, *International Migration*, pp. 88-90; Richards, *New Italians*, pp. 237-43; information and impressions garnered from interviews with questionnaires and other field research.
45. Macioti and Pugliese, *Gli Immigrati*, p. 64.
46. Ibid., p. 63.
47. See also Macioti and Pugliese, *Gli Immigrati*, p. 52, which finds that immigrant placement in the labor market is largely geographically determined, emphasizing agriculture in the South; industry in the North, which in 1991 at the time of their publication was a growing form of immigrant employment, though in 1991 perhaps exaggerated in weight by these authors; domestic workers more particularly in the large cities of the South than those of the North; and street vending more or less everywhere, though predominant in the South.
48. See, among others, Veugelers, "Recent Immigration Politics," p. 41; "Sindaco senza memoria," *Il Manifesto*, August 24, 1990.
49. Ibid., p. 41; see also Melotti, "International Migration."
50. Interview with Paul Ocoye, February 17, 1995; Veugelers, "Recent Immigration," p. 35.
51. Veugelers, "Recent Immigration," p. 36.
52. My description is based on Veugelers, "Recent Immigration," pp. 36-39, and interviews with Silvano Cogo, March 10, 1995, Padua; Grazia Bellini, February 22, 1997, Padua; and Marco Paggi, February 15, 1997, Padua.
53. I have heard many stories, from immigrants, immigrant lawyers, church activists, immigrant association activists and union representatives concerning employers directly declaring their intention to fire any immigrant who sought to take advantage of their legal rights during my years of research. While names of employers and workers cannot be used, it seems to be a common enough practice.
54. Campani, "Immigration and Racism," p. 522; Maria Immacolata Macioti and Enrico Pugliese, *Gli immigrati in Italia*, p. 43. These same authors, notwithstanding other fine aspects of their empirical study, see the previous period of an unofficially open border as reflecting the benevolence of Italian authorities, p. 42.
55. See, among others, Lumley, op. cit.; Committee Against Repression in Italy, *CARI Bulletin* (New York: 1979–1985); my unpublished M.A. thesis, Colatrella, "We Want Everything"; and Ginsborg, "Contemporary Italy," pp. 348-424.
56. Campani, "Immigration and Racism," p. 521.
57. "Immigrati: 300 associazioni in tutta Italia. Un primo identikit," *Il Manifesto*, January 30, 1992.
58. Ibid.
59. Ibid.

60. Ibid.; "Sindaco senza memoria," *Il Manifesto*, August 24, 1990; Mottura and Pinto, *Cambiamento Sociale*, p. 67.

61. Ibid., p. 67.

62. Veugelers, "Recent Immigration Politics," p. 46.

63. See, for instance, Richards, *New Italians*, p. 140.

64. Interview with Paul Ocoye, February 1995, Padua; interview with Michele Fassina of Associazione Immigrati Extracomunitari of Padua, February 1995; interview with Mortesà, December 1995, Vicenza; "Milano, immigrati al rogo," *Il Manifesto*, May 11, 1990; "Vicenza offre lavoro, ma si dorme alla stazione," *Il Manifesto*, May 11, 1990; "Un tranquillo week-end di paura: A Castelvolturno fra 300 negri assediati," *L'Unità*, April 30, 1990; "Brescia: La spina nel fianco della Lega January 1, 1992; Padova: Per un pugno di letti," *Il Manifesto*, August 23, 1990; "Il comune di Bologna sgombera 300 immigrati," *Il Manifesto*, July 21, 1991; "Bologna: La giunta alla prova immigrati," *L'Unità*, September 11, 1990; "Drama casa immigrati: Moruzzi apre il dialogo," *L'Unità* (Bologna supplement), September 13, 1990; "Cacciati dai loro connazionali 6 immigrati sospettati di spaccio," *L'Unità*, May 1, 1990; "I neri all'assolto delle case," *La Repubblica* (Bologna edition), September 11, 1990. As many of the dates of these newpaper articles indicate, some of these occupations were reported on only after eventual eviction by police months after they had begun. I am indebted to Silvia Federici, Ferruccio Gambino and Mariarosa Dalla Costa for providing me access to materials and newspaper clippings regarding the immigrant protests of 1989–1991.

65. "Milano: Demolito il terzo centro per immigrati," *Il Manifesto*, September 15, 1994; "Brescia: La spina nel fianco della Lega," *Il Manifesto*, January 15, 1992; "La griffe del vu' cumprà per firma un cammello," *L'Unità*, May 28, 1990; "Immigrati a Firenze sciopero della fame," and "Nero, la polizia non ti fermerà by Massimo Cacciari," both in *L'Unità*, March 12, 1990; "Gli immigrati alla Cgil: 'non siamo straccioni,'" *Il Sole-24 Ore*, March 30, 1990; "Immigrati: In piazza a Brescia per i permessi di soggiorno," *Il Manifesto*, January 18, 1992; "I tappetini nella 'T': revocati 40 permessi," *L'Unità*, September 4, 1990; "Un metro quadro a Casablanca," *Il Manifesto*, January 18, 1992; "Villa Literno: Arriva la Croce rossa," *Il Manifesto*, August 18, 1990; "Alloggi agli immigrati, è guerra," *Corriere della Sera*, February 2, 1994; "La Pantanella dei somali," *Il Manifesto*, May 16, 1991; "In corteo per i diritti," *Il Manifesto*, May 17, 1991; "Milano, immigrati al rogo," *Il Manifesto*, May 11, 1990; "Via i neri, causa dei nostri mali," *Corriere della Sera*, September 25, 1994; "Sciopero bianco," *Il Manifesto*, May 10, 1991.

66. See Veugelers, "Recent Immigration Politics," pp. 44-45.

67. See A. Sivanandan, *A Different Hunger* (London: Verso, 1992); the music of Linton Kwesi Johnson, and the journal *Race Today* are crucial

to understanding the development of this political identity throughout the 1970s and early 1980s.

68. Richard Jeffries, *Class, Ideology, and Power in Africa: The Railwaymen of Sekondi* (Cambridge: Cambridge University Press, 1978), p. 288.
69. See the discussion of this phenomenon in Emilio Reyneri, *Sociologia*, pp. 334-39.
70. In 1989 official estimates showed, among 963,000 extracomunitarian immigrants in Italy, only 85,000 regularized workers, while 580,000 were estimated to work off-the-books. Presidenza del Consiglio dei Ministri, *Atti della Conferenza Nazionale dell'Immigrazione Rome June 4-6, 1990* (Rome:Consiglio Nazionale dell'Economia e del Lavoro, 1991), p. 93.
71. In contrast to the situation described in the previous footnote, in 1995 newly hired regularized immigrant workers in Italy numbered 111,248 that year alone, of which 48,956 were working in industry, nearly one-fourth—over 11,000—in the Veneto. ISMU, *Secondo Rapporto sulle Migrazioni* 1996 (Milan: FrancoAngeli, 1997), p. 111.
72. Interview with Gianpaolo Feriani, ex-manager of Asilo Notturno of Padua, February 16, 1995.
73. Interview with Suor Lia of Cucina Popolare, January 22, 1996, Padua.
74. Bruno Anastasia and Giancarlo Corò, *Evoluzione di un'economia regionale: Il Nordest dopo il successo* (Venice: Nuova Dimensione, 1996), p. 77.
75. "Bisogno d'immigrati," *L'Unità*, March 22, 1990.
76. This was the approach of public officials of various cities as well as the government. Minister Turco at the conference on the immigrant family organized by ISPES and held in Rome April 17-18, 1997. In Padua, the Assessor Santone, the municipal official in charge of social services and whose office by default handles immigration, has harped on this theme for years, pointing out the increasing age and falling birth rate to be found in the city of Padua, in contrast to the youth and virility of immigrant communities. Interview with Assessor Santone, April 15, 1997, Padua; and public meeting on behalf of United Nations Week of Anti-Racism, March 1997, Padua. Likewise, such sentiments were expressed by several local Veneto officials on Gad Lerner's nationally televised program on immigration filmed in Vicenza in May 1997.
77. See the accounts of Patrick McCarthy, *The Crisis of the Italian State: From the Origins of the Cold War to the Fall of Berlusconi and Beyond* (New York: St. Martin's Press, 1997), pp. 170-90; and Stephen Gundle and Simon Parker, "Introduction: The New Italian Republic," in Gundle and Parker, *The New Italian Republic*, pp. 11-15.
78. "Il quinto stato," *Il Manifesto*, February 26, 1995.
79. The text of the Dini Decree was published in *Il Sole-24 Ore*, November 19, 1995; see also "Spaghetti Apartheid," *Il Manifesto*, September 15, 1995; "Immigrati, c'è l'accordo," *La Repubblica*, November 15, 1995.

80. Interview with Mortesà, Office of Immigrant Welcome, March 8, 1996, Vicenza; "Decreto immigrati, è il caos," *La Repubblica*, November 25, 1995; "Arrivano le prime espulsioni," *La Repubblica*, November 21, 1995.
81. "Arrivano le prime espulsioni," *La Repubblica*, November 21, 1995.
82. "Via Anelli, blitz all'alba," *Il Mattino* (Padua), November 15, 1995.
83. "Muscoli in vista rassicuranti e spettacolari." *Il Mattino* (Padua). November 15, 1995.
84. "19 Novembre: A Torino contro il decreto," *Il Manifesto*, November 15, 1995; "A Roma 15 mila contro il decreto," *La Repubblica*, February 4, 1996; "Una larga intesa," *Il Manifesto*, February 4, 1996.
85. On the proposed new law, see "Immigrati, si volta pagina," *La Repubblica*, February 15, 1997.
86. "Clandestini: rivolte e un morto," *Corriere Della Sera*, August 2, 1998; "Immigrati, ora e' assedio," *Corriere Della Sera*, August 9, 1998; "Sicilia: nuovi sbarchi di immigrati, i centri scoppiano," *Corriere Della Sera*, August 3, 1998.

6

SCHEI: IMMIGRANT WORKERS AND FLEXIBLE WORK IN THE THIRD ITALY

INTRODUCTION[1]

W hile structural adjustment was transforming the countries of origin of the migrants, Italy itself, like most OECD countries, experienced restructuring that either consciously on the part of individual firms and policy makers or as a consequence of attempts to increase profitability, eliminated or weakened the industrial centers of working class power. As in the Third World, these restructurings were resisted and conflictual. While in Asia, Africa, Latin America, or the Middle East, governments either reluctantly or with relief responded to the demands of the IMF and World Bank, in the First World firms moved independently to change investment patterns to increase their profit rates. They were responding not to state or international agency pressure, but acting on the basis of pressures stemming from wage gains and worker mobilizations that spread across the industrialized world in the 1970s.[2] Automation, the use of immigrant workers or the closing of borders to immigrants, sub-contracting and decentralization of production ("the diffuse firm"), and direct investment abroad were all tactics used to overcome a profits crisis rooted in this wave of worker militancy.

In Italy, the wave of rebellion of the late 1960s and 1970s was spearheaded by an alliance between skilled northern Italian workers and southerners new to mass industry, and by the women's liberation movement with its emphasis on the unwaged nature of work in the house and family.

It led capital to counter-attack. Large workplaces were closed or automated, and production was shifted to a huge, diffuse network of sub-contractors in zones where labor organization was weak, class composition was diverse and individualized, and firms were smaller. One of these places was the Veneto. The Veneto is a region (the official political subdivision in Italy) in the northeast of Italy, part of the tri-Veneto, and also of the Third Italy, a designation that includes the northeast and the central part of Italy. It largest cities are Venice, Padua, Verona, Treviso, and Vicenza, all with populations of a few hundred thousand, indicating its artisanal base and relative lack of large-scale industry. Of the roughly 1.5 million immigrants in Italy, about 72,000 are now in the Veneto region. The Veneto features an economy famous for self-employment, a combination of high-tech and ancient craft production methods, export power, and a local society that glorifies independent work. Throughout much of this century the region's political structure has relied on a Catholic "moral economy," in E.P. Thompson's sense, to avoid the worst scourges of capitalism—large-scale poverty, extreme inequality and exploitation rates, and the destruction of community.[3] Lacking both very large cities and centers of industry, it has been a center of emigration both at the turn of the century and after the Second World War, but has not truly been a site of large-scale immigration for centuries. Daily speaking dialect instead of Italian more than the residents of any other Italian region, and long characterized by class relations that have linked a share-cropping and artisan workforce to paternalistic aristocracies, it is therefore a closed society with an open economy. It wants to export its goods to every corner of the planet, but not have too much contact with the outside world beyond work. Recently, it is often argued that the Veneto faces an identity crisis, in which *schei* is replacing the Catholic sense of community, which until merely two decades ago characterized a region of predominantly sharecroppers and artisans.

The Veneto is part of the so-called tri-Veneto region, which includes Friuli-Venezia Giulia (where Trieste is located) and Trentino-Alto Adige. These regions have historically been subject to conflicting border claims between Italy, Austria, and Yugoslavia. The Veneto borders what used to be the "socialist" bloc. It has inherited the legacies of medieval city republics: Padua, Vicenza, and Verona were all independent until conquered by Venice between 1404 and 1406.[4] Its trade ruined by the subsequent post-1492 rise of Atlantic-based capitalism, the region survived the 17th-century world economic decline through a retreat to local-based production and consumption, and increasingly became an agricultural region. Sharecropping (*mezzadria*) dominated the landscape by as early as the 15th century, but the particular structure of worker-padrone relations led, with the rise of industry, to almost unique production relations. While by the late 18th century rent had for centuries been paid almost wholly in grain, sharecropping families were encouraged to grow silkworms throughout western Lombardy, Veneto, and Friuli. This was an inconvenient form of production, since it required farm families to sleep outdoors at harvest time when the worms stayed in the warmth of the family's home, but it also provided access to cash income for the sharecropping working class as well as large-scale capital for the commercial landlords of northern Italy. By the late 19th century, silk production, in small workshops and factories dotting the north of Italy and often owned by the same landowners to whom the grain rent was paid, involved most of the women of sharecropping families, while the men concerned themselves with the grain rent production.[5] With the production needs of the First World War, this structure provided the means for many families to move into small-scale independent firm creation. Farming families were able to engage in small-scale manufacturing of materials needed for war, and so gain access to money income, thereby reducing their dependence on subsistence production of their share of the rent crop. This microsocial transformation laid the basis for an extraordinarily diffuse self-employment in small-scale industry, which was encouraged after the Second World War by the

Christian Democrats who saw widespread, small-scale private property as a counterweight to Communism.

Italy's twenty regions are divided administratively into provinces, which are in turn organized around major local cities, which act as provincial capitals. In the Veneto in particular, these provinces are often roughly coincident with the areas controlled by the medieval independent city-states—a historical experience that continues to have great resonance in the regional and local culture.[6] The Veneto's provinces are Padua, Venice, Vicenza, Verona, Treviso, Belluno, and Rovigo. In recent years, industrial zones have become diffused into the countryside of virtually all the provinces of the Veneto (Rovigo is the only exception), yet the cities also remain economic centers. The Veneto is known for a pattern consisting of a multiplicity of small to medium urban centers, which may be linked to its success as a center of flexible industrial production. The polycentric small to medium urban model appears to facilitate the specialization in particular products by certain towns or local industrial zones. Local entrepreneurs share information concerning technology, remain in contact with merchants based in the provincial cities who provide access to and knowledge of market changes and conditions, and local government provides land for industrial zones and, along with Catholic-linked banks, access to credit.[7]

The sites where the research for this study was carried out, the provinces of Padua, Vicenza, and Treviso, have certain common characteristics as well as local particularities. Each consists of a province where food is still grown to meet local markets, an urban center of a few hundred thousand, and a few smaller cities. In the entire region, only Venice, at about 600,000 people, is an exception to the medium-scale, polycentric mode. But in and of itself, Venice's role in the regional economy has become relatively negligible, catering mostly to tourism. It is nearby Mestre, its sister city and home of the enormous Porto Marghera (once the world's largest petrochemical complex), which is now the basis of the Venetian provincial economy, though the petrochemical complex is due to be shut down in the next few years. Venice is hardly a dominant urban center in the Veneto region, despite its imperial history.

Each province, and the region as a whole, is characterized by an economy based increasingly on small industrial firms, featuring industrial zones both in the urban centers and in the countryside. These are often located within sight of the nearest farm, an expression of the tensions between the recent past and the very recent rapid development of the region. These industrial zones are marked by a concentration of small, and often tiny, manufacturing concerns. Provincial economies consist of an extremely heterogeneous mix of small factories with a tendency toward export, along with small farms, artisanal workplaces, small shops, and local open markets.[8] This economic pattern is similar to that of other regions that also specialize in flexible production methods, such as Emilia-Romagna. Finally, each province is part of a regional culture that is heavily Catholic, and which, despite the historical and recent tendency toward export, can be said to be provincial, if not downright insular, including the widespread use of the Veneto dialect rather than the national Italian language, not only at home but also at work.

On the other hand, each province has some particular characteristics. Vicenza is easily the most industrial part of the Veneto, and according to some standards, the second most industrialized province in Italy after Milan. It includes both the city of Vicenza, site not only of a large industrial zone, but also of an important NATO and U.S. air force base, and the smaller city of Bassano del Grappa, which is increasingly the site of the more dynamic sectors of the provincial industrial economy and of the immigrant worker presence. Vicenza was long the center of Christian Democratic politics in Italy, and for years the province gave the CD its highest percentage of the vote in elections. Padua, a medieval military and political rival of Vicenza until both were conquered by the Venetian Empire in the 14th century, is the educational center of the northeast and the economic and administrative center of the Veneto in practice, though formally Venice itself remains the political capital of the region. The second oldest university on the European continent, the University of Padua is located in the city's center, a fact which has had an impact on the political and economic opportunities available to immigrants—ranging from studying there, to posing as foreign students instead of "immigrants" when seeking housing, to service sector work in the university economy.[9] Considerable financial servicing, marketing, and transportation work for the export economy is organized in Padua for the region as a whole, and the industrial zones of both the city and its provincial area are growing rapidly. This is particulary true of the area north of Padua around Cittadella, an old walled city that is today a site of small factories and immigrant workers. Where Vicenza is particularly Catholic politically, with a historically less influential left, the Padua area has had a significant minority linked to the extreme or extraparliamentary left for several decades, a presence that is arguably hegemonic among the university students and the city's young people, providing cultural and political possibilities for immigrant politics that are less available elsewhere. Treviso, the home of clothing giants Benetton and Stefanel, is the province most closely associated with the politics of the Northern League, which was the provincial and municipal government for Treviso and Montebelluna at the time this study was carried out. Though the regional economy includes a large, extremely diffuse range of production sites for the two clothing multinationals, its export production is as varied as that of the other Veneto provinces, and Treviso ranks second only to Vicenza for overall export production. Each of these provinces, and the region as a whole, have long had in common a widespread family-based small business practice and ethic. Both Benetton and Stefanel, in true Veneto fashion, started as small family businesses, and Belluno's Luxottica was likewise started by a skilled artisan before becoming a multinational power. Each province also fostered a political culture based upon Christian Democracy and a local moral economy that saw a broad diffusion of small property ownership as the best guarantee against both Communism and the ravages of the unrestrained market. Only in Rovigo, at the southern extreme of the region bordering on left-wing Emilia-Romagna, were the majority of farm workers landless, and only in that province has there existed a left-wing political culture and a greater tendency to form cooperatives in opposition to capitalism.

Aside from its recent Christian Democratic heritage and role in the world economy, the Veneto has undergone a series of particular historical experiences that have left a widespread and profoundly rooted regional sense of identity. These include the rise of independent self-governing medieval city states,[10] the Venetian empire, the decline of the trade-oriented economy and the turn toward a provincial economy after the beginning of European colonialism in the New World,[11] a long Austrian occupation and a series of independence struggles,[12] and, after the Second World War, the experience of being a border state in the Cold War. The tri-Veneto region borders on once-Communist Yugoslavia as well as on leftist Emilia-Romagna. This geo-political reality may help explain the resonance of anti-communism which is to this day quite strong in the local electorate, or may explain the importance that the Catholic Church in the Veneto placed on winning hearts and minds and the United States placed on having a military presence.

This history is important because the working population of the Veneto is in part open to policies that are market-oriented, or productivist, reflecting local consciousness of how hard and long was the road to today's prosperity. The result has been a working class that views self-employment—either agricultural, artisanal, commercial, or in tiny factories—as its strategy to avoid exploitation by capital. A sort of self-and family-exploitation, long hours of work by all members of the family, is needed to actualize a local and micro-accumulation of capital. This social basis has been protected by a Catholic political culture that made the Veneto the original so-called "white area." The Church has until recently set limits to the growth of capitalist relations using a variety of means. Among these are a general condemnation of Sunday and night work, so as to defend the family's time together; local-based Catholic-run banks, like the Banca Antoniana—run by the brothers who also manage the Basilica of Saint Anthony of Padua—which have provided easy credit to small businesses and homeowners; Catholic labor unions like the CISL as well as other activist Catholic groups like Caritas; local government encouragement of small business; cooperation among small neighboring firms to share technological innovations and market information with each other so as to avoid local competition ("Gigi, Beppe and Toni against the rest of the world" is a local slogan); and the availability of land for creating industrial zones in nearly every village of the Veneto. This latter, in an area with very high land prices, encouraged clusters of small business monocultures that can collaborate on technology and markets. On the basis of a huge number of small firms and artisanal shops, and export strength, the Veneto is also the site of a demand for regional autonomy from the central state in Rome (seen, quite realistically, as a bureaucratic monstrosity), and even for independence in the form of the Northern League's demand for an independent republic of the Padania, which would include Veneto along with most of northern Italy. Veneto gave the League about one-third of its vote in the last national election, in April 1996, making it the largest single party in the region.

THE ECONOMY OF THE VENETO

The Northeast of Italy is by some measures the most productive industrial economy in the world, and it is, among the OECD countries, possibly the most successful. This region, which has brought the world Benetton, Stefanel and Luxottica (owner of, among others, Lens Crafter in the United States), is, along with Emilia-Romagna, one of the originators of so-called "flexible specialization"[13]—production of small-batch, often high-tech, numerically controlled production for export markets. The development of numerical control technology, which enables design to be changed rapidly, enables small firms to produce small quantities of specialized products, overcoming the traditional economies of scale that gave market advantages to large firms and mass production. Along with a very particular local social composition with a considerable historical basis, it also makes possible a high level of self-employment (*lavoro autonomo*) on an artisanal basis. This latter in turn has led to labor power shortages in the region which are increasingly filled by immigrants from all over the world. The small firms, with the aid of local governments, Catholic-run banks, but most of all through the organization of production by merchants based in the provincial cities like Treviso and Padua, share market information and technology, essentially creating an external economies of scale. Ash Amin explains the crucial role of the merchants in keeping small firms abreast of the latest market developments and the scale of demand for specialized products:

The distinctive feature of the industrial districts which have developed around the provincial towns of central and northeastern Italy is that each one specializes in the production of a particular commodity. The real strength of the areas, however, derives from the way in which production is organized within and between the small firms. Clusters of small firms are productively integrated with each other on a subcontracting basis. Strategic entrepreneurs, usually merchants or small businessmen from the provincial cities, purchase the finished goods on a contractual basis from a number of small firms which in turn subcontract to several smaller family firms and domestic out-workers. . . .

The producers in the countryside have limited marketing outlets of their own, and this is where the towns have played a crucial role. The "strategic" entrepreneurs of the city are not just the merchants who buy the goods from the direct producer, but like the middlemen of pre-capitalist economies, they constitute the main bridge between town and country, between production and distribution. These individuals coordinate production in the small units by supplying them with information on market trends and also orders from the larger merchandising houses.[14]

Such merchants also market the provincial products at trade fairs, both overseas and at local centers such as the *fiera* in Padua, a recently constructed, postmodern structure that regularly brings together producers, companies, and marketers in order to facilitate the penetration of the Veneto's export goods into the world market. Helped by a national currency that has fallen from 900 to the dollar in 1991 to more than 2,000 to one U.S. dollar in summer 2000, this regional and provincial-based export machine has sought to win markets against competitors from the United States, Japan, its European Union neighbors, and the Asian Tigers. To do so, it has emphasized the high quality of the quasi-artisanal local products, unit costs based on the use of the latest technology rather than mere low labor costs, and an ability to adjust to and even influence changing fashions in the global marketplace.

The results are sometimes shockingly successful. The export income *per capita* of the Veneto in 1995 was over 11,000,000 lire—about $7,500—or nearly double the national average. The city of Vicenza alone exported $9 billion worth of commodities, equal to the entire export product of Greece. Vicenza and Treviso, the home of Benetton, one of the few family businesses to become a large-scale corporation, together exported more than Argentina. The village of Rossano Veneto has arguably more firms per capita than anywhere else in the world—one for every two households.[15] With the help of the recently low lira, these mostly small businesses have conquered markets all over the world, despite cheaper hourly wages elsewhere. In a few tiny towns with names like Manzano, San Giovanni al Natisone and Corno di Rossazzo, 80 percent of all the chairs produced in Europe are made, and then sold all over the world, from India to the U.S. The production takes place in 800 firms with a total of 15,000 workers—a little less than 20 workers per company. About 80 percent of all the bicycles made outside of China are produced here, and nearly 90 percent of all the eyeglasses made in the world are produced by Veneto businesses. Conditions are often high-tech at the larger firms, such as Lovato brothers with 130 employees (the world's largest chair producer), and where even varnishing is robotized. Two hundred and seventy other workers produce in artisanal or subcontracted firms for Lovato brothers, and in these the production conditions may be considerably less advanced. Over 69 percent of Veneto firms are founded by ex-workers. This makes a part of the class composition fluid and complicated to define.

This wealth is principally produced through a huge number of small firms and a high degree of self-employment. Already in the early 1980s, the Veneto had seen a significant increase in small business activity compared with a decade before, and this trend has continued into the 1990s. Table 19 lists the number of employees by plant size for selected manufacturing sectors in two regions of the Third Italy—the Veneto and Emilia-Romagna—from the early 1970s to the early 1980s.

The growth of firms during the 1970s in both regions was substantial, but that of small firms particularly so. In Emilia-Romagna, firms with fewer than 10 employees grew by over one-third, and those with between 10 and 49 employees increased by 40 percent. In the Veneto these numbers were even more impressive, as firms with 1-9 employees grew by more than half,

Table 19: The Veneto and Emilia-Romagna: Number of Employees by Plant Size in Selected Manufacturing Sectors

	1-9	10-49	50-499	500+	Total
Veneto:					
1971	105,745	126,173	184,054	81,852	497,824
1981	159,489	200,151	210,881	70,950	641,471
Emilia-Romagna:					
1971	127,566	115,449	167,486	51,491	461,992
1981	170,139	161,854	190,935	60,556	583,484

Source: Marco Bellandi (1989), p. 57.

while those with 10-49 (of which there is reason to assume that the majority had fewer than 15 employees) grew by an astounding 63 percent. This growth continued in the 1980s, but more slowly. Over a 40-year period from 1951 to 1991, the number of Veneto firms of all sizes rose considerably with the exception of the 500+ employees category. Of 79,434 manufacturing firms in the Veneto in 1991, 54,429 had between 1 and 5 employees, an increase of well over 50 percent. But the increase in manufacturing firms with between 6 and 9 workers grew from 1,808 to 9,181 over a 40-year period to 1991, an even more impressive gain of over 500 percent. The increase in firms with between 10 and 49 employees was no less impressive, more than doubling from 1971 to 1991, an overall gain of 800 percent since 1951. By comparison, the number of firms with 500 or more employees, after rising slightly from 67 to 70 from 1961 to 1971 and again to 75 over the next 10 years, fell sharply by 1991 to 49. The number of workers employed by such large manufacturing firms also declined from a high of 81,852 in 1971, to 45,733 in 1991, a 44 percent reduction. Growth in each of these categories of manufacturing firm and employment were, by comparison, slower in Italy as a whole. Indeed, nationally, the number of firms with 1-5 employees remained almost exactly static over the entire 40-year period up to 1991, remaining at 571,970, a gain of only 700 for the entire country in four decades. Over 11,000 very small firms nationwide were lost once the Veneto is excluded, though employment in such firms rose by 190,000, of which the increase in the Veneto consisted of nearly a quarter. Companies with 6-9 employees nationwide, however, grew by almost two-thirds to 71,550 from 1961 to 1991, suggesting that many of the smaller firms may have simply grown to this still quite tiny scale. Firms with between 10 and 49 employees across Italy quadrupled in number over these 40 years, while employment in them more than tripled. The number of very large manufacturing firms fell substantially, as both firms with 100-499 and those with over 500 employees dropped from all time highs in 1981 of 6,407 and 899, respectively, to 5,273 and 590 in 1991. Employment in the former category declined from 1.3 million in 1981 to just over one million in 1991, while employment in very large firms—500 workers plus—fell dramatically from 1,149,615 to only 682,053 in only 10 years.[16]

The figures for employment and firm size for Italy and its regions also reveal another development of significant importance for this study—the relative and in some cases absolute decline of the offically recorded active labor force. In the Veneto, this decline is relative, but striking: Despite an increase of 30,000 firms from 1971 to 1991, employment in manufacturing rose only 181,000 over these twenty years to 678,649. This represents about a 36 percent increase in employment against a 60 percent growth in firms. Meanwhile, in Italy as a whole, the numbers of active manufacturing workers and firms have fallen since 1981, from 6.1 million to 5.5 million workers and by 25,000 firms to 747,692. Further, despite an overall increase of 120,000 firms nationwide from 1971 to 1991, employment in manufacturing rose only by 19,000 net during these twenty years. Although we may at first seek to explain the low rate of manufacturing employment growth, or even decline, in the transformation toward a service economy, which Italy has in common with other First World countries, this flies in the face of the visible increase in industrial activity, indicated by the rise in number of firms, even if manufacturing is relatively smaller in terms of its weight in the economy as a whole. Second, this solution leaves us to explain how it is that 120,000 more firms employ only 19,000 more people. The importance of Italy's underground economy is undoubtedly part of the answer, as some part of the workforce of many firms remains off the books. That some of these firms, especially in the North, use high-tech production and require relatively fewer workers should not be discounted either, but the artisanal nature of much manufacturing means that this can hardly resolve the issue. Rather, even the relatively slower official growth in the Veneto since 1981 with respect to previous periods can be attributed to the increased weight of off-the-books work, especially in small workshops and self-employment, since the 1980s. However, the labor market structure is also a plausible partial explanation. Italy is characterized by three and perhaps more labor markets, which are somewhat closed off from each other. In the South, work is likely to be off the books and precarious, while emigration to other regions is no longer seen as a desirable solution, a view augmented by the unwillingness of many northern employers to hire southern Italian workers after past experiences. The Veneto's relatively slow employment and firm growth, despite rises in exports, instead appears to reflect labor shortages. Ironically this is in part due to the ease with which workers may become self-employed or start a very small manufacturing concern. Self-employment is particularly likely to be easily hidden from official records. The underground economy is both cause and effect here: Its existence reflects, at least at first, employers' efforts to avoid regulation and workers' organization, but its expansion makes possible a labor shortage due to the ease of self-employment in part due to the possibility of avoiding discovery, hence easing tax and social security burdens for self-employed individuals or tiny firms. Despite a period that has been a boom era for the region, the late 1980s and 1990s seems to indicate a general slowing of activity, despite the economic good times. Until recently, workers were simply not available and, lacking a growing labor force, the regional economy was slowed in its development. This interpretation is consistent with a phenomenon that is otherwise confusing, namely, why the number of industrial workers more recently has declined slightly while the region's employers have begun to employ immigrants in industrial work in increasing numbers. The overall decline appears to reflect merely the ease with which very small, artisanal, or self-employment activities are kept off the official records, while this same growth of such activity deprives the labor-short larger employers of access to workers. Immigrants increasingly fill the vacuum in the Veneto's industrial firms.

Correlating overall employment figures with the hiring of immigrants is not a simple task, since the increase in off-the-books work is reflected in an overall decline in total employment as well as in nearly every sector of industry in the Veneto's official statistics during the 1990s. However, we may note that with the end of an industrial recession which depressed figures in 1993, the net growth of newly assumed workers against those leaving employment was 43,999 overall in the region in 1994. This figure includes all economic sectors, and not just industry. However, 48.1 percent of all hirings in the official Veneto economy were in industry that year, allowing us to estimate about 21,000 as a rough figure for net annual hirings for 1994. The number of immigrants hired in the Veneto in 1994 was officially 13,722, of which about two-thirds, or around 9,000, were in industrial jobs. This gives us an estimate of 43 percent, or a ratio of 3/7, of immigrants hired compared with net hirings in Veneto industrial jobs.[17] When immigrants in the Veneto number at most 2 percent of the population, this is an extraordinary statement about the reliance of Veneto employers on immigrant labor power at least as a source of available workers to aid expansion in a situation of overall labor shortage. We will examine the role of immigrant workers in this labor market more closely, but first let's look at the geographic structure of Veneto production.

Much of this production takes place outside of urban centers. The Veneto's longstanding polycentric small and medium city model of provincial economy is now complemented by an increasingly industrialized countryside that resembles nothing so much as the flow of industry to the countryside to escape guild organization during the putting-out system phase of indus-trialization in England and elsewhere in the 17th and 18th century. Virtually every village in the Veneto now has an industrial zone, and these are often adjacent to corn fields on which the regional dish polenta is based. As I write this chapter, I am looking out my window onto a foundry adjacent to a ploughed field. A mixed economy of agricultural and industrial work, both on a small private scale, continues to dominate the Veneto. Edward Goodman provides us with a view of the predominance of such diffuse small industry, artisanal production, and export activity along the narrow stone streets of formerly walled towns and villages in the high plains of the northern Veneto:

> If an image is required it is of the converted makeshift workshops abutting on to narrow streets with hardly room for a van to turn, cheek by jowl with residential accomodation; or the new, small cramped trading estate built onto dirt roads, and the family-based group of six or seven talkative workers grouped round one of the older craftsmen, whilst the quick-thinking entrepreneur listens at a desk of his own, making notes and determined to get on.[18]

Goodman is right to stress the continuity between artisanal production and the new small, energetic export firm. However, we should not fall prey to the temptation to revert to ideal types in describing such firms. While some artisanal firms, employing only father and son, for instance, in industries such as ceramics essentially constitute no sharp break with the handicraft traditions of the past, others just as readily innovate by installing numerical-controlled machinery. Likewise, many high-tech machine-tool export firms remain thoroughly family concerns, or seek to keep costs down by the use of off-the-books overtime or immigrant labor. We cannot easily distinguish the Veneto firms either by technology or by social organization. Instead, we find continuity along a spectrum in which the familial basis of the firm, its embeddedness in local cultural relations, and its instrumental attitude to technological innovation characterizes the economy of the region more than any obvious distinctions between large and small firms, high-tech versus low-tech production, or export as opposed to local market-based demand. A variety of authors have stressed the historical roots of the "modello Veneto" in modes of production and "social capital" going back centuries. For Bull and Corner as for Holmes, the mixed sharecropping-arti-sanal/small manufacturing economy of western Lombardy, the Veneto and Friuli evolved into the small firm of today, with its basis in a peasant-worker and family-based organization of production. Bagnasco and Blum emphasize the role of sharecropping as an experience that led to neither the vast disparities in wealth and widespread propertylessness of the southern Italian latifundia nor the large-scale industry of the Northwest with its industrial proletariat, but rather to the infrastructural basis of small industry in the Third Italy. Brusco stresses the artisanal or skilled-worker founding of most small firms in the Third Italy, while Goodman argues that the local social and cultural organization, with its model of small-scale urbanization and history of independent republicanism based on an independent craft-based economy, constitutes the decisive continuity.[19]

But important as continuity is in understanding the social and historical basis of the small firm in northeast Italy, it cannot explain the very recent transformation of regions that were until 20 years ago ranked with the South in terms of income and quality of life and which today are among the wealthiest in Europe. Goodman's description of the busy-ness of the crowded stone roads of Veneto villages churning out export products produced in tiny workshops or small but ultramodern offices is perhaps not so far from what one might have observed along the streets of the artisanal quarters of a small medieval town, but it is dramatically different from the daily childhood experience of Veneto residents born as recently as the 1950s or early '60s, and bears no resemblance to ethnographical studies of the region in the recent past. Robert Evans, in his study of Arquà Petrarcha, in the Euganean Hills south of Padua (which he called Santa Maria), predicted only a gradual though inevitable shift of young working people from farms to factories in the region, a process which he stressed had only begun by the late 1960s.[20] Other writers have also seen discontinuity in the recent transformation of life in the Veneto as more important than continuity.[21] They often stress the contradiction between the new-found material well-being in the region and the loss of cultural surety and local identity. These pressures, according to writers such as Gian Antonio Stella, a nationally known journalist, have led to a condition in which all previously important cultural values—Catholicism, family, local sense of identity—have been all but dissolved into the worship of "Dio Denaro" (the God Money) and a concern only with obtaining more *schei*. This desire for accumulation is unabated by the achievement of well-being and sufficient savings (according to Stella, the average Veneto household has about $20,000 in savings), and leads to the sacrifice of all time not devoted to work. This in turn means cultural vacuity—Padua, a university city, sells fewer books annually than Reggio Calabria, the poorest large city in all of Italy, at the very tip of the peninsular boot— and neglect of family, community, and the sense of social solidarity embodied in the region's historical Catholicism. Charles Richards argues that the recent murder by a teenager of his parents to gain access to his inheritance (His father, a road repair laborer who still owned the family farm, had an estimated one million U.S. dollars in net worth—and continued to work two jobs. Such stories are not uncommon.), was a predictable result of the family neglect, lack of social values, and cultural emptiness of the Veneto countryside under the pressure of newly accumulated wealth and export-based affluence. Likewise, Stella sees the concern for making more money to the detriment of all other values as reflected in the lack of concern for the conditions of newly arrived immigrants among a people that a mere 20 years ago went abroad in large numbers in search of bettering their conditions. When I interviewed the officer in charge of the Padua Chamber of Commerce foreign commerce department, he told me, "Many of these Veneto businessmen can only think of exporting more and more, every minute of the day. I predict that there will be a lot of work for psychiatrists to do in this area in ten years."[22] The pressures of newly found wealth and dependence on the world market for its exports, have, in the eyes of such observers, led to the widespread support in the region for the Northern League's politics of resentment, racism, and call for secession from Italy. This political transformation of the region was possible when the market pressures were combined with the political changes following the tangentopoli scandal which led to the disappearance of the Christian Democratic Party and its social policies. These policies had helped sustain the region's small-scale businesses while maintaining the local moral economy and thus providing for a sense of community solidarity and local identity. In the wake of the collapse of these policies, the local electorate was ripe for the Northern League's regionalist appeal.

Export-based production seems almost a mania throughout the Veneto, even in the most seemingly remote hillside villages. By 1994 the Veneto had achieved almost 14 percent of the entire export product of Italy, equalling and at times surpassing the level of Piedmont, home of FIAT.[23] That same year, the Veneto had the highest percentage of its value-added product exported of any region in Italy, at 31 percent—meaning that almost a third of all commercial production was exported. And exports continue to rise dramatically. From 1991 to 1994, total exports from the Veneto rose from 25.7 billion lire (about $26 million in constant 1991 lire) to 42.3 billion lire (about $42 million dollars in 1991 lire). From 1992 to 1994 export earnings rose between 50 percent and 60 percent in the provinces of Vicenza, Padua, Treviso, Venice, and Belluno. Verona saw a 42 percent rise in exports during this period, and more rural Rovigo, whose export earnings are miniscule compared the other provinces, nevertheless saw earnings rise 460 million lire to 802 million lire ($800,000 in constant 1991 lire) in three years. Much of this increase was due to the 70 percent devaluation of the lira since 1991, but the devalued lira has helped, not created, the thousands of tiny factories and workshops on the plains, the Euganean Hills, and the foothills of the Alps that dot the Veneto and crank out export commodities, often on a 24-hour basis. And that devaluation could have as easily created a crisis of imports, leading to higher prices. Instead, Veneto businesses have taken advantage of the moment, when a trade surplus with foreign countries has grown from 4 billion lire in 1991 to over 12 billion in 1994, amounting to a 30 percent total net surplus in import/export activity.[24]

In examining the structure of exports, we find that nearly two-thirds go to Western Europe, that is, to Italy's partners in the EU. Ten percent goes to Eastern Europe, and 8.5 percent in 1994 went to North America. Thus, the bulk of exports go to highly advanced economies. With 27 percent of exports destined for Germany, 10 percent to France, 8.5 percent to the United States, and a little over 5 percent to the United Kingdom, just over half of the region's exports go to these four countries.[25] Nor are these largely products that have a low value-added composition. Fully 36.8 percent of exports consist of industrial machinery, making up about a third of the exports to wealthy countries. Some of the so-called "traditional industries"—clothing and textiles, leather jackets and bags, and furniture—are also well represented in the export structure, making up 17 percent, 4 percent and 7.5 percent respectively of total exports. But chemical products are also a significant export at 5.3 percent. The Veneto's exports are varied in capital-intensity, destination, and mode of production.[26] This export-led economy has led to an increase in the Veneto standard of living compared with other regions of Italy. With 5.6 percent unemployment in 1995, half the national average, the Veneto ranked behind only the remote and sparsely populated Trentino Alto-Adige Alpine region in having the lowest rate of official joblessness. At 81.2 percent, the Veneto's percentage of non-food consumption in the household budget was third highest after only Lombardy and Emilia-Romagna (81.7 percent and 81.3 percent). These compare with 72.4 percent for Campania, the southern region where Naples is located, for example. And with an average family income per month of 4,059,000 lire (about $2,500 in 1998), the region again ranked only slightly behind Lombardy and Emilia-Romagna as the wealthiest region in 1995. Since by law, salaried employees in Italy receive a 13th month of pay, this is equivalent to 52,780,000 lire annually, at least for waged employees which comes to about $30,000 per year. Again, given the unknown rate of hidden income, these numbers provide us only with a sense of the living standard. This standard of well-being has been accomplished with a mixed economy of industry and services, in which 35.3 percent of the active population works in industry (third in Italy after Piedmont and Lombardy) and 61 percent in services. It has based itself on export production, small firms, and self-employment.

Yet for all the glamour of such tales of hardworking small-business people, there are more ambiguous aspects to the Veneto economy, which become apparent upon a closer look. The extent to which the social composition consists of self-employment (*lavoro autonomo*) and small business (*piccola impresa*) is overstated by various analyses as well as by political forces ranging from the Northern League to some of the autonomist left. The former see self-employment and small business from a point of view stressing the market and northern initiative, while the latter glorify the combination of computerized production and self-employment as evidence of the end of the law of value and the newly conquered control over the means of production by the working class.

In reality, as such theories of right and left suggest, the extent of small business and lavoro autonomo reflect a serious division within the ranks of the Veneto working class, based upon the legal status of one's work (the form of value of labor power), the subsequent degree of legal and organizational protection, and on one's degree of access to the methods of high-tech production. According to one report,[27] of just under 900,000 waged workers in the Veneto in 1993, 530,000 worked for firms with under 50 employees, and 150,000 were employed in firms with from one to five employees. Yet of the latter number, one third were involved in commerce (that is they worked for small retail shops), 10 percent provided services to firms (largely computer services) and another 10 percent worked in services to persons, including domestic work. All told, 180,000 workers are in these four groups working for firms with less than fifty employees, or over a third of the total cited above. Further, the workers who work in larger firms are concentrated in certain sectors. According to the Istituto della ricerca economica e sociale (IRES), in 1991 nearly 2.5 million employees of firms in Veneto in 1991—the number includes all self-employed, management, and so on, rather than only waged workers—worked for over 529,000 firms, less than five employees per firm. But in the chemicals, synthetics, and artificial fibers sector, 24,000 workers were employed at only 834 firms, or over thirty per firm.[28] In tanneries and leather work (jackets), the proportion is about thirteen per firm, but as we shall see, there is considerable concentration within that industry. Overall, the percentage of workers in very small firms is high by any standard, but that there is considerable variation within sectors.

There is also considerable variation in working conditions based upon size and industry. Most importantly, firms with fewer than fifteen waged employees are exempt from most labor laws and social benefit requirements, leading to an extraordinary number of firms with fourteen employees (plus up to five trainees who are paid less), and then a lot of sub-contracting to other firms with an equal number.[29] Even more important, the category of self-employment often hides the fact that the person works within the factory or office of the company while missing out on social benefits and other rights, or that the self-employed worker does work that is sub-contracted from a larger firm, or supplies services to a few firms and therefore represents merely a means for firms to externalize costs. In addition, different methods of working off the books (*lavoro nero*) have developed to the point of being art forms. These can include paying the workers for the eight hours on the books and then tax free for the three to four additional hours, or off-the-book Sunday work, or keeping some workers on and some off. It can also include a variation of U.S. capital's use of temporary employees as regular permanent employees, but without any of the pay and benefits of regular employees. As Padua-based leftist labor and immigration lawyer Marco Paggi explained to me, "In Italian law renting labor power is strictly prohibited."[30] Only the state is allowed to run employment agencies. The Italian version has taken the form of "cooperatives," whereby alleged members of cooperatives—who at most may have a contract with a firm for loading and unloading or for cleaning the premises—perform regular production work, often the hottest or dirtiest work such as soldering, varnishing, and foundry work. This is useful to the employer since such workers are not covered by any union contract or laws protecting waged employees. The cooperative is a cooperative in name only, since the coop calls the workers when there's work to do for a firm, precisely on a temp basis. Paggi calls the "members" (soci) of the cooperative "orphan workers" since technically but not in reality lacking a boss, they do the same work without any benefits due to other workers. Silvano Ferrazzo, a local leader of the Catholic-affiliated union federation CISL, identified the opening of factories in the countries of Eastern Europe, the "scientific planning of how to make money not paying certain benefits," and the rise of increasingly universal overtime work as three aspects of the problem facing workers in the Veneto.[31] Recently, the practice of hiring immigrant workers has been added. It has also provided a solution to one of the local capitalists' main problems, the lack of available labor power. With about 5.6 percent unemployment, and with self-employment a possibility for at least a considerable percentage of Veneto workers, local capitalists, especially the larger ones, face a perennial labor shortage. A large percentage of the net increase of newly hired workers in the Veneto in recent years have been immigrants, as they have flowed northward in search of jobs that are steady, legal, well-paying, and would allow immigrant workers to obtain a legal residence permit.

IMMIGRANT WORKERS IN THE VENETO LABOR MARKET

Unlike other parts of Italy, the immigrants in the Veneto work primarily in factories, though many also work in construction, domestic work, and restaurants and hotels. There were officially 72,489 legal immigrants in the Veneto at the end of 1995, and an educated guess might be about a third more undocumented immigrants(in all of Italy there are around 1.5 million legal immigrants). By 1996 there were 18,438 waged workers employed in the Veneto, and this number rose to over 26,000 in early 1997. Clearly a large number of working immigrants have legal residence but work off the books, while another perhaps 20-25,000 are altogether without legal documents, though how many of these are working, whether as waged employees or in other fields, is uncertain.[32] Though far behind Lombardy (mainly Milan) and Lazio (almost exclusively Rome) in absolute numbers of immigrants—each had over 200,000 in 1996 officially—the Veneto had by 1995 reached third place in the number of total immigrants. This is remarkable both because the Veneto had relatively little immigration from southern Italy during the postwar era, since it lacked large industries, and because, also lacking the large cities that historically attract immigrants, it had few immigrants until the mid-1990s. As late as 1990, the Veneto had only 19,369 legal immigrants, 8,479 of them women, who worked in industry in very small numbers. This placed the Veneto behind Tuscany, Emilia-Romagna, Piedmont, Sicily, as well as

Lombardy and Lazio, in immigrant presence in the region. The rate of increase in legal immigration in the Veneto from 1990 to 1994 was 59 percent, ranking only behind Lombardy and the sparsely populated Friuli Venezia-Giulia.[33] In comparison, several Italian regions have seen declines in the official numbers of immigrants: in Umbria the legal immigrant population fell sharply from over 50,000 to under 20,000 during this same period; Tuscany and Lazio both also saw declines of around 3-4 percent. In newly hired immigrant workers, the Veneto with over 18,000 in 1995 was second only to the much larger Lombardy with about 20,000. Over 11,000 of these 18,000 worked in industry, and the percentage of industrial workers among employed immigrants in the Veneto has only risen in more recent years.[34] The number of newly hired immigrants is nearly the same as the total number of working immigrants in the region, whereas the Lombardy total of newly hired immigrants is less than 10 percent of the total immigrant population. This indicates that most legally working waged immigrants in the Veneto receive one-year contracts (*tempo determinato*) that need to be renewed annually. The attempt to make immigrant labor power functional to the needs of the flexible production firms of the region is reflected in the structure of contracts. To be sure, many immigrants who seek to return home annually for periods of up to two to three months also prefer annual contracts, confident that there will be industrial work for them somewhere else when they return. It is not wholly at the behest of management, though it is almost surely largely so, that contracts of immigrants seem to be for a limited period in the region.

The percentage of industrial workers among immigrants in the Veneto ialso must be emphasized. No other region in 1995 had such a large number of immigrants hired to work in industry, not even Lombardy. On the other hand, there are relatively few domestic workers in the Veneto. In 1992, the Veneto had only 1,672 domestics, less than one-eighth the number for Rome. These percentages reflect the differences in social structure between the various regions. Rome, with its largely service economy and large number of state and institutional employees, as well as wide variations in wealth, has a large demand for domestic work. The Veneto, with its widespread industry as well as considerable possibility for self-employment for local workers and therefore a labor shortage for many employers, is instead the site of the highest percentage of industrial work among employed immigrants of any region, and of less than 4 percent of all domestic workers in Italy.[35] The relatively egalitarian social structure of the Veneto, with its widespread small-property holdings, tightknit family enterprises, and work ethic, make for a poor demand for domestic workers. Further, ideologically the moral economy in the Veneto considers hiring domestic workers by any except professionals or the truly wealthy to be putting on airs. The parochial nature of the local outlook tends to denigrate not the hard-won accumulation of wealth but the ostentatious display of what Veblen called conspicuous consumption. Savings, not luxury, are highly valued, as is property ownership.

Immigrants increasingly fill vacuums in the local labor market for industry, services, illegal work, and some agriculture. As throughout the rest of Italy, immigrant presence in the labor market is highly segmented geographically and by national origin. The Ghanaians are heavily represented in the factories of the Veneto. Ghanaians interviewed for this study worked in tanneries (44 percent), plastics, furniture, soldering, and foundries (each about 10 percent) as well as producing machine tools and processing food. As a community they are concentrated in the Vicenza-Bassano region. Many Nigerians also work in factories, but especially in Padua, where they are concentrated as a community, some, particularly Nigerian women, have opened Nigerian-owned and operated businesses. Many Nigerian women work as domestics in the Padua area, while Nigerian prostitutes are also a significant presence there. The local press and police are suspicious of the community's alleged role in drug trafficking. A recent scandal revealed that the Italian embassy in Nigeria was selling visas at high prices and there is some evidence that the global and Italian-based Mafias play a larger role in the Nigerian migratory flow than in the other West African presences.[36] Senegalese have established a several-years-old presence in every Italian city as street vendors of African cultural objects as well as such mundane items as cigarette lighters, though their presence on the street is giving way to other groups (Zairans, Malians, Salvadorans) as the Senegalese move increasingly into factories in the small industrial zones on the periphery of Padua. The main concentration of Senegalese in the province is in Camposanpiero, to the north of Padua, and Senegalese workers, though employed in many types of industrial work, are significantly represented in slaugherhouse work.

The Filipinas are nearly all engaged in domestic work, and there is a significant population in Padua, that seems to be closely linked with the Catholic Church. The Yugoslavs tend to work in construction, particularly in the eastern part of the region closer to Venice and in the Vicenza region. The Moroccans seem to be present in all three provinces studied here in significant numbers and work in services (restaurants and hotels), as well as in industry, where they are less specialized than the Ghanaian and Senegalese workers. The large Pavo poultry factory in Montebelluna in Treviso province, however, employs a large number of Moroccans, though I was unable to obtain a sure count (about 250 of around 500 employees are immigrants there). Some young Moroccan men are visibly engaged in illegal trade in drugs in the piazzas of Padua. Albanian men work in industry and in construction work, bringing with them skills learned in their own country. Romanian men work in factories and women as domestics in the Vicenza region. These groups, in short, while hardly comprehensive of the immigrant experience, reflect diverse work experiences touch on nearly every aspect of the Veneto economy. However, they are under-represented in agriculture, which is largely a self-employed sector in Veneto based on small private holdings and employs only 3-4 percent of the local population.[37]

Many of these jobs involve either heavy lifting (construction), high temperatures (foundries or soldering), work with dead animals (slaughterhouses and tanneries), work with human bodies (some domestic work and prostitution) and personal services (drug sales, street vending, baby sitting and domestic work). At least in industrialized countries they are associated with manual labor more than with mental labor, with the use of hands, muscles and genitals more than brains, in word that is often seen as dirty or unpleasant. Semiotically the work with meat and animal skins, the human body, and cleaning work would appear to parallel many of the tasks reserved for either so-called untouchables or for other low orders in a caste system. However, the local labor market is hardly a caste system. The jobs disproportionately performed by immigrants are largely tasks that Italian workers prefer not to do anymore if they have another option. Given the relative ease of opening up a shop and doing subcontracted industrial or artisanal work in the Veneto, this option is available to significant numbers of locally born workers. Foundry, slaughterhouse, and tannery work is unpleasant and often dangerous; it is quite probable that the latter two are defined as dirty in part because of contact with animal bodies. The basis for defining work as dirty is more difficult to determine in an industrialized society based on wage labor than in a caste community, and brings up many questions that are beyond the scope of this study. Nevertheless, it is of some importance in the determination of the opportunity structure open to immigrant workers, at least at first. The immigrants in turn seem to have taken to heart Martin Luther King Jr.'s admonition that there are no dirty jobs, only dirty wages. This said, many Ghanaians, for instance, expressed disdain for the domestic work they carried out in southern Italy before migrating north to work in tanneries and foundries. Even physically demanding industrial work or industrial work involving some health risk and contact with either high temperatures or animal skins and chemicals was preferable to the personal authority relations, and even servility, often associated with domestic work. Dirty work is therefore not only a description of the physicality of the work itself, but also of the social relations involved.

The gradual assumption of many of these positions in the Veneto economy by immigrants has occured in very different ways and to varying degrees. Fully half of the workers are Italians even in the largest enterprises employing immigrants that I have found in the Veneto—the rabbit slaughterhouse near Camposanpiero with about 250 workers, half of them immigrants and most of these Senegalese; the Pavo plant in Montebelluna; and the large tanneries near Vicenza, which often employ over

100 immigrants out of over 200 employees. The social network placement system has clearly made significant inroads into such establishments, but so far there is no sign of Italians being fully excluded from such work, though the media often refers to these jobs as work that Italians don't want to do anymore. Construction work continues to be dominated by Italians, but a dual labor market has developed whose dimensions are difficult to fully analyze. Some firms work only off the books and increasingly employ immigrants of various nationalities—Yugoslavs, Moroccans, Albanians, Nigerians, Tunisians. But most immigrants in construction find work with employers who are registered and on the books. These categories overlap in the Veneto, as firms that usually do legally sanctioned work may work Sundays, or take on extra work during the holiday breaks without informing authorities and thereby avoid taxes for that part of their income.[38] Domestic service has become an increasingly immigrant occupation as parts of Italy, including the Veneto, have become sufficiently wealthy that this type of work in other areas has ceased to be an attractive option; here we may say that there was truly demand for other labor power to carry out the work. Italian prostitutes, in cities like Padua, when faced with the newly arrived competition of women from Eastern Europe and Africa, protested to the new arrivals that by working for a lower price they were cutting the Italian women out of the market. In Padua Italian prostitutes even tried providing services for free on certain nights to keep customers, but all of this effort was in vain, and today the vast majority of Padua prostitutes are from countries like Nigeria, Zaire, Albania, and Yugoslavia. With regard to drug sales, a form of work visibly conducted in the Veneto by young men from North Africa, it is more difficult to know how much of the drug market now takes place through personal contacts and in private homes. But I am told that up until the mid-1980s, sales in the public piazzas were done by young Italian people who were themselves *drogati* (drug users), but this group was hit hard by the AIDS epidemic and came to be replaced by the young men from the Mahgreb. Thus, the replacement of Italian workers with immigrants has taken a different form in different economic sectors. It remains true that many of the forms of work involving

immigrants are first and foremost either physically demanding, illegal, or involve contact with animal and human bodies.

As important as the segmentation of the labor market, is the dual nature of the labor market for immigrants which is defined by neither the physical characteristics of the work nor by the nationality of the immigrants but by the legal status of the person. As we saw in the last chapter, immigrant communities mobilized politically to demand legalization of their members' status and simultaneously sought access to jobs, especially in industry that would enable them to maintain a less precarious legal existence. Many interviewees told me that finding a job "*in regola*" (with legal status)—which enabled them to be legal and on the books all year round—was the main reason they emigrated from other parts of Italy into the Veneto region. Those who remain in an undocumented condition have fewer job options, and this in part explains their availability to do illegal work such as drug sales, or semi-illegal, such as prostitution. The primary division in industrial and manufacturing work is by firm size. Smaller firms and artisanal shops, facing a narrower profit margin, seek to escape paying social security benefits for workers, which in Italy remain a higher percentage of labor costs than in many other industrialized countries. Immigrants who are not *in regola* are more likely to work in small factories and workshops than those whose documents are fully recognized. This division, which then involves pay, working conditions, hours, and the precariousness of employment, is reflected in this study, which involved mainly documented workers since the research sites were all places where such workers go to renew their residence permits. As a result, a high proportion of immigrants were found to work in large firms compared with the statistical variation in the Veneto described in some detail above. This is not surprising, since it fits with many of the priorities of immigrant social network employment policies and the search for steady and stable employment. However, workers in small firms seem to be underrepresented based on the testimony of most well-informed observers in the region, both immigrant and Italian. A recent study found that many of the industries that employ large numbers of immigrants have relatively low rates of hidden or off-the-books work. Tanneries in the province of Vicenza were found to have only 5 percent hidden work, and the chair industry in Udine in the far northeast of Italy had only 2 percent hidden work. Construction, on the other hand, nationwide was determined to have about a 40 percent rate of hidden work, while for industry as a whole this rate was about 20 percent. The same study found that around 7 percent of all workers in the underground economy were immigrants, proportionally greater than their 2 percent of the population in Italy.[39] The legal workers who were interviewed for this study were heavily concentrated in part in sectors with low rates of hidden work (except for construction), while the undocumented workers were not systematically studied for lack of information and research sites. The latter were not wholly ignored for there were other methods for making contact with them, but such study often required participant observer and qualitative rather than survey, formal interview, and quantitative methods of research, and thus much of the information available is of an impressionistic sort.

The size of firms in which immigrant workers find themselves working in the Veneto varies widely. Among Nigerians in both Vicenza and Padua provinces employed in machine tool shops, the number of employees at their place of work was reported to range from six to "around 27 or 28" to 60. Nigerians employed by "cooperatives" either did not know how many people worked for the same concern, or reported the number as over 100. Similarly, Moroccans working in shoe factories in Montebelluna in Treviso Province reported numbers of employees at their workplaces at five, 26 and over 50, while their co-nationals employed by phony cooperatives consistently stated that over 100 persons worked for the firm. These cooperative employee numbers, of course, can be confusing. In some cases they refer to the numbers employed as a whole by what is essentially a temp agency that sends only a certain number of workers to a job site at any one time. In others they may refer to the total number of people working at a single firm in which some employees are technically considered members (*soci*) of a cooperative, but who in fact work every day in production, cleaning, packing, or loading and unloading at the same industrial site, separated from the other workers there only by their legal status as cooperative members. As one Moroccan man told me, "It's difficult to know how many members of the cooperative there are." Among Ghanaians, none reported fewer than 10 other workers employed at their workplace. The majority worked at what are by Veneto standards large firms. Six worked at firms with between 10 and 20 employees, and another six at firms with between 20 and 50. Twenty-three were employed at firms with more than 50 employees, of whom 14 worked at firms with more than 100 workers; nine of these were employed at workplaces with more than 200 employees. Recalling the overall statistics cited previously on firm size in the Veneto, immigrants who have legal industrial employment work disproportionately in larger workplaces. Nor is this simply a function of the concentration of immigrants in a few capital-intensive industries: The Ghanaians working at sites employing more than 50 workers reported being employed at such diverse types of jobs as plastics, making car seats, making plastic furniture, tanning, salami making, and machine tool production. Ghanaians employed at tanneries reported working at firms whose sizes fit each of the employee number categories mentioned here. In short, the concentration within a few types of jobs co-exists with a parallel tendency to employment in larger firms, at least for documented workers. This suggests that employers in larger firms and those whose companies' production involves dirty work have both had difficulty finding workers in recent years until the arrival of immigrants. The level of employment in the region, the actual decline in population, and the easy availability of self-employment (ignoring the chances for survival for small firms and self-employment after starting out) all seem to have limited the possible sources of labor power for employers of larger industrial firms and of firms involving production processes that involve contact with heat, animal products, and so forth.

This study has not revealed any direct wage discrimination between Italians and immigrants performing the same officially designated job category—that is, Italians and immigrants seem to be paid the same wage for the same job description, as Italian law requires. Discrimination rather takes the form of a generalized placement of immigrant workers in the lowest job categories. Hence, while Italian workers are more likely to move into the jobs at a firm that are defined as more highly skilled, immigrants are almost always left in the first level job category, the lowest paid. Sometimes workers performing the same job are placed in different official job categories thereby receiving different pay scales on the basis of nationality. But I did not find any cases of immigrant industrial workers paid less than the legal monthly wage for the job description that they officially performed. Discrimination is thus literally categorical. Payment in Italian industry is based on nationally agreed-upon contracts that set pay scales for each skill category and each level of work responsibility; these contracts go into exacting detail in defining exactly what constitutes one job and differentiates it from another. Immigrants who were in legal jobs were paid the national union pay scale. Wages for most industrial jobs were between 1.3 and 1.7 million lire a month—or from $750 to $1,000. Wages were at the higher end of this range for workers in machine tool and other "newer" export industries, at the lower end in furniture, textiles, indoor horticulture, shoes, and other "traditional" export industries. Somewhat heavier or hotter work, such as slaughterhouses, tanneries and foundries paid around the middle part of the wage range. These are roughly average wages for industrial semi-skilled wage workers in Italy, and so it is not in the wage by category that we find discrimination or any particular advantage to the employer in using immigrant workers. Nor did this study find any significant difference in pay scales or work conditions available to immigrants among the three different provinces studied. Other than a slightly higher availability of industrial as opposed to service work in Vicenza, which is not surprising given its high level of industrialization, the differences between opportunity structures for immigrants were surprisingly few, suggesting that the overall structure of the Veneto economy, and its export orientation, are diffuse enough across the various regional locales that we find similar conditions. One surprise was in fact the almost complete absence of immigrants in the garment firms linked by subcontracting with the network of Benetton's clothing export empire. This was confirmed by months of investigation involving interviews with immigrant workers, immigrant associations, local labor union activists, and two Moroccan workers who were the only exceptions I found to this general situation and who also confirmed that immigrants in that industry are few and far between, such work usually being done by locally born women workers. The characteristics of immigrant workplace conditions of the greatest significance were the contradictory concentration in certain industries and the contemporaneous diffusion of immigrants across most types of industrial work in at least some numbers, along with the almost complete concentration of immigrants in job categories that are at the lowest levels of the pay and skill scale established nationally. This latter feature defines the advantage to employers of utilizing the availability of immigrant labor power.

Concentrated though they are in relative terms in certain industries or larger-scale firms, however, immigrant workers are found in at least some numbers in all sizes and types of manufacturing sites. Several Nigerians, Senegalese, Moroccans, and one man from Togo reported working with numerical-controlled machinery in precision production at machine tool, furniture and shoe factories. Nor are other types of work in tanneries and slaughterhouses to be considered strictly unskilled: Senegalese workers reported doing the highly skilled electric knifework of dismembering the carcass of beef or the more dexterous work of de-ossifying a rabbit. At one meeting of 35 Senegalese workers in a small town outside Padua, many workers complained to me that they performed work requiring a higher skill level or of greater quality than the Italians with whom they worked, but were always kept in the lowest level category for pay and job definition purposes. Indeed, nearly all of the immigrants working in manufacturing that I interviewed, met, or heard of through third parties were stuck at the first category of skill level for official purposes. This was often in contradiction with the actual requirements of the work performed by immigrants even when Italians slotted in higher categories carried out the exact same job. The CGIL union representatives in the region have confirmed that this is almost universally the case. In this way, local Italian workers move up the ladder of officially defined skill level and obtain somewhat higher pay as the lower category jobs are filled by immigrants.

Such practices may be an effort by employers to keep Italian workers from seeking employment elsewhere or setting up shop as artisans (*mettersi in proprio*), or it may be the result of the sort of parochial class alliance implied by the growth of *leghismo*—the politics of the Northern League with its glorification of the small businesses and artisans of northern Italy. The League's calls for "autonomy" from Rome seem to fit nicely with an outlook that sees *lavoro autonomo*, literally autonomous work—that is, self-employment—as a value in itself. The Northern League's anti-tax, anti-bureaucracy message of political secession from the Italian Republic has successfully recuperated many former Christian Democratic voters in the wake of that party's disintegration in the tangentopoli scandal of the early 1990s transforming a long-held value of the Catholic moral economy into a slogan stressing small business, export production, and the opportunities to be found in the free market. Yet for small businesses to grow, and medium and large businesses to remain healthy, both require sources of labor power. The widespread local access to artisanal production meant that the more capital intensive industries and those businesses that were growing most quickly both needed workers from some outside source. As one employer told Daniele Marini, "It's hard to find semi-skilled workers, even if they're signed up at the placement office, because the majority of those who register at the placement office aren't looking for work, but a job, and then they refuse every direction." Another said, "Currently the only Italian manpower one finds are do-nothings and drug addicts."[40] Such comments are ironic, since these characteristics are precisely those attributed to immigrants by the main party for which Veneto small-enterprise owners vote, the Northern League. Thus, Veneto employers' collective consciousness is in contradiction with their individual consciousness—where the former sees immigrants as collectively a burden and a criminal threat, the latter sees immigrants as individually hardworking and attributes these negative characteristics collectively to Italians instead.

The immigrant workers, once they had broken through to the

regular industrial labor market, shattering the invisible walls that separate Italy's labor markets geographically, have provided that source of labor power. In so doing, they have provided locally born workers with one more means of advancement, inasmuch as the latter can move more freely to the higher-paid and higher-skilled positions within firms, as well as moving out of them into artisanal production. This segmentation within the work process and the labor market has called forth a latent racist response that, under the encouragement of *leghista* political perspectives, seems to be on the rise in the Veneto in recent years. As Daniele Marini found, locally born workers had a variety of ways of expressing their interest in maintaining a qualitative separation between their own conditions and those of newly arrived immigrants. Some employers claimed that their Italian workers, while not openly refusing to work with African workers, had one by one left the company to work at jobs where there were "only whites."[41] Locally born workers often insist that any benefit granted to immigrant workers, even if only to bring them up to parity with the other workers, be recompensed by the granting of another to only Italians: "If you do something for the one groups (immigrants), you have to do something also for the others (Italians)," claimed one employer. Another said that beyond helping immigrant workers find housing—the main obstacle to their availability in the Veneto labor market—employers couldn't do anything else for them for fear of provoking a hostile response by Veneto-born workers: "Nothing more than that so as to not create malcontent among the local workers who ask in reply to any facilitation for immigrants a corresponding facilitation for themselves."[42] At one firm, "The key problem that blew up was the cafeteria. The Italians couldn't stay at the same cafeteria. To avoid problems we thought of dividing the cafeteria because the whites didn't want to eat with the blacks. It was a very stupid thing and I still regret it bitterly."[43] Recently immigrants have complained to the CGIL office that at many workplaces the locally born workers have taken to speaking to them only in dialect, or in speaking about them to other Italians only in dialect. This linguistic effort at isolation of immigrants in the workplace takes place in the context of the Northern League's valorization of the local traditions of the Padania, traditions which are often invented in Hobsbawm and Ranger's sense, but which nonetheless provide a source of strength for the effort to essentialize the cultural differences between northern and southern Italians, and between the former and immigrants. For locally born workers these would all seem to be methods by which they can maintain the segmentation by industry and by job category, which benefits them through enabling greater social mobility and pay levels. This is accomplished at the expense of immigrant workers who remain at the bottom of the skill categories, and equally at the expense of any class-wide projects and internationalist perspective. These latter may prove to be more than mere abstractions under conditions of universal competition among workers in the world market and under the unification of European economies inherent in the European Union and its common currency. In short, in order to defend privileges based upon making possible self-employment and a segmentation by skill levels, job categories, and industry between immigrant and locally born workers, the longer-range interests of both locally born Veneto workers and their co-workers born in other countries are being sacrificed.

Yet this convenient segmentation of the labor process, or rather of job categories within the labor process, is more contradictory than it at first appears. Just as it proved ultimately impossible to wholly exclude immigrants from legal industrial work after they had arrived in Italy, segmenting them into only agricultural and unwanted service jobs, it has proven difficult to isolate them in only a few types of workplaces involving tasks unwanted by Italian workers, or in the strictly unskilled jobs at individual workplaces. Immigrant workers, though disproportionately found in work like soldering, foundry work, and tanning, are nevertheless already also found in such jobs as machine tool production working alongside Italians. Such workers handle numerical-controlled production, which is at the heart of Piore and Sabel's definition of the revival of craft work, while others maintain skilled construction jobs as masons and carpenters rather than only as laborers. Similarly, immigrant workers, though disproportionately employed in larger firms, are also found in small factories and artisanal shops across the Veneto and in diverse industries. This immigrant presence across the spectrum of industrial job skills and types of firms, though relatively undeveloped and numerically small, stems from an inexorable feature of abstract labor.

As we saw in the case of the previous immigrations to postwar Europe, immigrants were characterized in the labor market by two contradictory tendencies. On the one hand they seemed to be functional to capitalist production as an industrial reserve army that could be sent home when demand was slack or employed quickly during boom times. On the other hand, they seemed over time to invade sectors of the economy where they became indispensible as a permanent labor supply. In Germany, though immigrants were disproportionately concentrated in certain categories of work, they were nevertheless represented across virtually the entire spectrum of employment in Germany with the exception of the civil service. The very idea of a Gastarbeiter program, even in its softer French version, presupposes that it will be possible to be rid of such workers when they are not needed. However, the continuing presence, and even growth, of ethnic minorities in these countries indicates that many immigrant workers have long ceased to occupy merely industrial reserve-army positions in the economy, but have established themselves as part of the general national workforce. The uses of immigrant labor did at first, and in many cases, continues, to provide locally born workers with opportunities for social mobility as immigrants occupy lower rungs of the workplace or labor market hierarchies based on pay, skill level, education, or other factors. But this process of segmentation and differentiation, by its very nature in creating a potential labor aristocracy of skilled or otherwise privileged locally born workers, undermines itself by enhancing employers' attraction to using immigrant labor more widely. Ultimately, it was capitalism itself that proved the analyses of such insightful scholars as Castles and Kosack, Castells and Piore. If the purpose to capital of finding sources of politically weaker and economically less-costly labor power is to undermine the bargaining position of local labor, it hardly follows that keeping that newly found labor power out of competition with local workers will serve any capitalist purpose in the long run, though in the medium run it serves to politically divide the working class. For locally born workers, if provided with the additional weapon of a monopoly on the skilled and higher-paying positions, are sure to take advantage of such an artificially created labor shortage to pressure for a greater share of wealth and power from capital. Sooner or later the capitalist tendency to use universal competition among workers is virtually sure to show itself, even if not all at once. In the Veneto this process of imposing the rigors of abstract labor power has begun, though it is hardly in full swing. But having a source of flexible labor power only to fill in the gaps left by a local working class is unlikely to remain satisfactory to local employers even in the Veneto, especially as the common European Single Currency imposes the discipline of market values and competition more thoroughly on the local export economy. Yet these tendencies of capital are only that, tendencies. The walls seperating Italy's labor markets are themselves the result of different outcomes of class conflicts and are in large part the creation of the acts and refusals of dfferent sectors of Italian workers. The Porta Pia[44] of labor market separation was the result of the immigrant social network and individual effort. It is now capital's need to turn these outcomes to its advantage and transform them into new engines of profit. But the tendency to create full-scale universal competition among workers, rather than accepting the naturalization of privileged sectors by skill level, nationality or region, is likely to be dominant under the international neo-liberal regime that is currently predominant in world economic affairs. Whether such a project will succeed in using immigrants to undermine the conditions of Italian workers is of course not a given, but is contingent upon capital's effectiveness in transforming immigrant labor power into the types of concrete labor and under the types of conditions that will serve these purposes. It will be up to the struggles of the near future to determine the actual historical result.

One study has found that immigrant workers in Emilia-Romagna's factories were employed because they personified those characteristics considered by employers as defining flexibility: willingness to work long hours and on days that are

nominally free; willingness to move geographically for purposes
of employment (notably lacking in European workers in general
and among Italians in particular); lack of strong commitment to
the historically defined social wage (pensions, unemployment
insurance and so forth); willingness to work at almost any
particular job and to be shifted from one job or one time shift to
another.[45] Yet these are all demands sought in national
negotiations to reform the labor market by employers, and
therefore constitute a wish list with regard to all workers, and not
merely limited to immigrants. As Mottura and Pinto argue:

> If we consider, as we have already stressed, the growing importance given to
> the requisite characteristics of flexibility, adaptability, mobility, it does not
> seem at all absurd to ask ourselves if the characteristics of new migratory
> flows, present also in the countries of Southern Europe in the last fifteen
> years, don't embody the preferred skills of a supply which is increasingly
> more appropriate than that available locally to the new needs of the market.
>
> In this light, the often-stated argument that "in Europe jobs for foreigners
> don't exist" could—in an apparent paradox—mean that in this phase the job
> placement of immigrants, as an active subject, in some segments of the labor
> market which are not quantitatively marginal, appears particularly significant
> in prefiguring the general tendency in action at that level and the new features
> to which it seems to lead.[46] (My translation.)

For immigrant workers to be useful in the long run, they must
enable employers not only to work around the obstacles presented
by work and labor market rules that apply to Italian workers, but
must eventually prove useful also as a weapon for battering down
the Chinese wall of social guarantees and limits to exploitation
won by previous cycles of working-class initiative. As part of the
general push toward increasing and making more flexible the
work week in the Veneto, immigrant workers in construction and
in some shift work in factories were already by the mid-1990s to
be found working Sundays, something previously unheard of, and
many of the interviewees reported working night shifts. When a
photo development firm in Padua announced in 1995 that all of its
60 workers would soon have to work only nights, there was an
outcry from the Church, unions, and local newspapers. But these
needn't have been surprised, for the exigencies of the world
market, the boomerang effect of basing an economy increasingly

on export production, necessarily undermine local moral economies and practices limiting work time and conditions. But for these changes to be effective it helps to have a potentially ready source of workers available as a Trojan Horse in the battle to restore flexibility in work rules, working time, labor conditions, and perhaps also wages. In the study carried out by Daniele Marini for the Fondazione Corrazin in Venice on Veneto employers' attitudes to Italian and immigrant employees, 50 percent of employers who had hired immigrant workers declared themselves satisfied, saying that they had a "first-rate impression" of immigrant workers. Though at first immigrants help to fill the gaps in unskilled work left by Italian workers moving up into more highly skilled positions, many Veneto employers have gradually come to the conclusion that workers are interchangeable and can be placed in certain positions on the basis of "merit"— that is, willingness to work according to the needs of the business. This conclusion is borne out by comments made to Marini by local employers:

In my factory there aren't any specialized personnel. It's enough to be willing to work. The Italians are doing too well, they expect too much. They work only if they get paid a lot, they don't want to work on Saturday, or whenever it's necessary. *The extracomunitarian is the Italian of years ago*: he adapts a little more.

We use the same criteria (e.g. with immigrants) that we use with our own locally born workers: we try to make them understand that one is worthy if he works hard, if he's a correct person in his human relations and at work.[47] (Italics mine.)

But the immigrants are only potentially ideal flexible workers. Without the structural adjustment programs they wouldn't be in Italy, without the legal and other constraints they face they wouldn't be as available at the conditions they currently face. Other mechanisms of exploitation and work organization are needed to exploit this potential. These include the fake cooperatives within industrial firms whereby immigrants and even some Italians work without the legal benefits that employees of the firm would have; the menace to fire immigrant workers, which under the Dini Decree meant possible expulsion, and which forced them to accept illegal status; the usefulness to employers of the near impossibility immigrants face finding houses or apartments, because of both a general housing shortage and racism, obstacles which have left many dependent upon their employers for a place to sleep, often on company grounds. Each of these methods of social control involves foreign workers in disproportionate ways. But the point is that capital always has two contradictory tendencies. One is to segment the labor market to divide the working class and the other is to homogenize abstract labor so as to reduce costs. The conditions in which immigrants find themselves at work are the Trojan Horse for the dissolution of the Veneto moral economy and the subjection of the working class in Italy to the dictatorship of world market conditions.

Such methods are not necessarily decisive however. The presence of immigrants in the Veneto stems from their own capacity for mobilization and their insistent demand to not be segregated into the least stable, most difficult, and worst-paying work. Many immigrant workers have defended themselves through collective action and organization. Increasingly immigrants have joined labor unions to defend their workplace concerns against employers' efforts to take advantage of their labor market position. Workers may join any of a number of available union federation affiliates within the same workplace, so union membership involves an active joining and is never automatic upon being hired as in a union shop. Twenty of the 41 Moroccans interviewed with the questionnaire in this study reported being union members, of whom 17 were members of the left wing CGIL, two were in the CISL affiliate (a Catholic union), and one had turned in his union card. Three of the nine Tunisians surveyed were also CGIL members. Nigerians seemed less likely to join unions, as four of the 15 interviewed with the questionnaire, plus one of the in-depth interviewees, were union members. I would have perhaps attributed even such high percentages of union membership (even the Nigerian percentage is double the percentage of union membership in the United States) to the fact that two of the provincial sites where I conducted questionnaire-based research were offices of the CGIL union federation, but the case of Ghanaians suggests that these figures may not be far from reality, at least for legalized workers.

Fourteen of the 41 Ghanaians interviewed reported being union members, or just over one-third. Since all of the Ghanaians were surveyed in Vicenza, where the research site was a municipal immigration office rather than a union affiliated office, such a percentage suggests that union membership among immigrant workers in legal industrial jobs in the Veneto is surprisingly high. All but three of the Ghanaian union members, however, were members of the CISL federation, which has long been the main power in the Vicenza union movement reflecting the heavily Catholic political culture. It may suggest that Catholic labor activists are making a concerted effort to include immigrants in the sustenance of the Catholic moral economy by encouraging union enrollment. More astounding is the high percentage of union members among the Senegalese interviewed. Thirty-one of the 47 Senegalese involved in this study or two-thirds, were union members, all but two enrolled in the CGIL. This is higher than the slightly over 50 percent unionization rate among Italian workers. This Senegalese rate is undoubtedly inflated both by the CGIL affiliation at two of the research sites as well as the interviews conducted in cooperation with a CGIL organizer. However, since I conducted 27 interviews with Senegalese workers, netting 17 union members, the interviews conducted by my union organizer friend did not yield an outcome remarkably different than that which I found on my own. Further, since four of the seven Senegalese interviewed at the Vicenza site were union members, two of whom were CGIL members, the overall percentage may be exaggerated, if at all, only slightly. I have no doubt that overall union membership among immigrants is somewhat lower than the totals which I found given the circumstances in this study but these findings clearly indicate that there is significant interest in union membership among the legal immigrant industrial workers in the region.

Given the different social backgrounds among these groups it is difficult to find a factor that can account for this interest in the countries from which the immigrants come. Ghanaians and Nigerians both come from countries where unions, though not representing a majority of the workforce, are nevertheless well organized and militant. But the majority of immigrants in the

Veneto from these countries came, from cocoa farming or small commercial backgrounds. And there is little in the Wolof Mouride culture to suggest industrial militance, though Moroccans from Casablanca will likely have seen union activity in recent years even if not employed themselves. Instead, the political culture of labor organization that the immigrants have found in Italy, combined with the experience of industrial work itself—for most a first time experience—have encouraged an openness to union organization. Unions in Italy are powerful, visible, and a central part of the political culture of the country as a whole as well as of most legal above-ground workplaces. Nevertheless, it is unlikely that immigrants would join unions in such numbers if they perceived them as hostile institutions that represented the sort of segregationist attitudes expressed in the demands of Veneto-born workers noted above. This suggests either that the unions are perceived as rising above the parochial and even racist viewpoints of many of their members, or that the stories of cooperation and acceptance as fellow workers of immigrants by other Italian workers are less well known. Certainly this possibility exists: In Tuscany in 1996 Italian workers struck to demand that a Tunisian co-worker be rehired after the company had fired him for returning late from a vacation at home to his place of work of seven years. On September 20, 1997, in response to increasingly insistent demands for secession for the North of Italy by Umberto Bossi, head of the Northern League, 800,000 people went to two demonstrations against secession and racism in Milan and Venice organized by the union federations, and the week before 20,000 militants of Rifondazione Comunista and the network of Autonomia and the social centers marched on Venice with more or less the same program. Though we have no way of knowing how many of these people were Veneti, it is clear that large numbers of Italian workers, and at least a minority of local Veneto workers, oppose the racist politics of the League.

But union membership has not been the only response by immigrant workers to the experience of industrial work, exploitation by manufacturing employers, and racism by both employers and fellow workers. More often their responses have taken the form of participation in associations or community activities among their own co-nationals, or informal collective action taken on their own based upon their own assumptions about the treatment they deserve. Such attitudes and assumptions are in part due to the diffusion of ideas concerning universal rights to treatment and human living standards and human rights, ideologies such as pan-Africanism, pan-Arabism, socialism, communism and anti-colonialism, and at least in some cases to previous experience in political struggles in their own countries of origin. But they are also at times due to expectations derived from participation in class compositions that preceded their experience as wage workers. Like industrial workers of past centuries, today's immigrants are often painfully aware that many of the cultural expectations and statuses that went along with their condition before becoming wage workers are not respected by employers or by the market now that they work for others.

Since often immigrants came from family backgrounds that involved independent trading or commercial activity or land ownership, and policies after independence to foster education, many arrive both highly skilled and conscious of having lost independence and of proletarianization in Italy. "We are a commercial people," Paul Okoye, president of the Union of Nigerian Citizens in Italy, told me, and many Senegalese workers have told me similarly of ambitions to open a business or activity of their own.[48] Nearly all of the Ghanaians I have spoken with have completed at least high school, and among Filipina/os it is not at all unusual to come across a domestic worker with a university degree. Only the Yugoslavs (usually construction workers), Albanians and Romanians (usually factory workers) were predominantly waged workers before arriving in Italy. Various mechanisms hold these immigrants locked into dependent work in the Veneto. For one thing, many of the arrival points in Italy—Palermo, Bari, Naples—are in the South, in areas with high levels of official unemployment and even greater black markets for labor. Their first work experience upon arrival was often precarious or seasonal—tomato picking, street vending, and domestic work. This precariousness of wages, combined with the lack of official documents, made stability, savings, and self-organization difficult, and has hampered the formation of residential immigrant communities and "chinatown"-type markets and locales in Italy.

Such a sense of loss of community, independence, craft, small business status, or educational and skill level often leads to anger at the conditions that immigrant workers encounter in the Veneto. Romanian, Filipina, Croatian and Russian women all complained to me of the directive issued in 1995 by the Labor Ministry that foriegn born nurses and other medically trained persons were not to be allowed to practice their profession anymore in Italy, a policy that forced most of them into domestic work to survive. Nigerians, Ghanaians, and Senegalese at one time or another expressed frustration at the lack of respect for their abilities, skills, and communities that made self-employment so difficult for immigrants in a region where it is so common among locally born citizens. Senegalese, Albananians, and Moroccans showed anger at being held in the unskilled categories at work even though they believed that their skill levels were superior to those of their Italian co-workers. Along with such viewpoints regarding status go cultural assumptions about how people should be treated. While Scnegalese workers seem to be relatively un-militant about wage issues, they highly value being treated with respect by other workers and by employers. This attitude seems to be common to other groups of workers. When the businessman quoted above suggested segregating the cafeteria at his factory all the Senegalese workers quit rather than tolerate such insulting racist behavior on the part of their co-workers and employer. A group of 25 Senegalese Mourides, usually somewhat patient with wage and hours conditions, all resigned at once because of what they saw as racist and disrespectful treatment by their boss at a rabbit slaughterhouse near Padua. The employer hired another 25 Senegalese to replace them.

Nor are immigrant workers' collective actions directed only at employers and Italian workers. Although most immigrants expressed generally positive attitudes to unions and immigrant workers in the Veneto have joined unions in large numbers, immigrants often find that unions do not represent their particular needs, either out of ignorance of the latter or out of fear of alienating Italian members. Further, many union organizers, representatives, and bureaucrats lack experience in relating to people of other nationalities and so make no effort. Silvano Cogo, a tireless union organizer whose principal responsibility is immigrant workers in the CGIL in the province of Padua told me, "I've told other organizers a thousand times to speak slowly in Italian, use simple words, make sure they understand and not to ever speak dialect instead of Italian when talking with immigrants, but they nod their head yes and the next time they go back to speaking dialect rapidly. The immigrants get fed up with this and some ask me what to do. I told one group, just to get their attention, send in your union cards and when they did the organizers asked me, 'Why are they upset?' and I tell them I told you already."[49] Twenty-five workers had sent in their cards to temporarily resign from the union as a protest. But such a critique by action occurs in the absence of advice from well-intentioned union activists: Some immigrants mentioned having been former union members, while others on occasion had changed unions. Cogo told me in spring 1997 that he hoped in the next contract in at least some industries to insert issues of particular relevance to immigrants such as the right to return home to their country of origin for two months a year (every worker in Italy has one month of vacation by law) and some help in supplying housing. Such concerns have yet not become priorities for unions as a whole, though their sponsorship of anti-racist marches is of some importance in interesting immigrant workers.

Immigrant workers also participate in collective actions as union members along with their organizations. Hundreds marched along with Italian workers in 1997 in a demonstration in Rome as part of the metal mechanics' (that is, machine tool, automobile, and other metal industries) contact negotiations. At times immigrants bring to such struggles their own class knowledge of how to conduct collective action and can provide criticisms of the limits of class unity manifested by even the Italian workers, who are so well known among western industrial workers for their militance. Indeed, one Nigerian metal mechanic, criticizing his Italian co-workers' behaviour during a recent national metal mechanics' strike, told me:

What we had, like the experience I had in my factory, the Italian situation is not like the strikes I know in Nigeria, where the union decides to stay out of the job for one week and it is a general, everybody accepts the general. Like the experience I had in my factory, sometimes I believe the workers have divided might. The unity is not there. Some might decide to work . . . at strike time. Some decide to prolong their job more than the hour of the strike if there is a machine that is broken down. So they are a little diverse from the unity they should have if they want to get what they want. That is what I could comment.[50]

In this case, the speaker has experience of the militant union conflicts in Nigeria. Other political cultures, such as the Senegalese workers' background in the Touba-based Mouride network, eschew collective action and stress deference to authority. As we have seen however, Senegalese workers in the Veneto seem almost especially willing once they find themselves in legal industrial work to join unions. A remarkable transformation of the cultural possibilities of Mouride Islam seems to take place. At CGIL union meetings, a union representative speaks on union rules, on immigrant workers' legal rights such as to have their pension, health care costs, and other social security benefits covered by their employer; the Senegalese workers, after listening attentively, begin a question and answer session on the details of what was said, what is written in the contract or what the law says, which in all but the content seems to reproduce the form by which the Koranic schools in Touba teach Islam. Within the shell of the religious meeting's form, these workers are gathered to increase their understanding of a universal conception of rights and to find the means to better implement them. The experience of how to organize together and the very network of organization used is derived from the Mouride Brotherhood's training in cooperation and community solidarity. Yet the experience of industrial work, waged work, cooperative labor, and class conflict has altered the substance of their collective efforts and provided access to new forms of organization which are for the first time organizationally independent from the Mouride Brotherhood. The presence of some Senegalese in left-wing union federations in Italy may represent a slight lessening of the hold of the Sufi hierarchy on the now industrial workers. But it also means that the continued interest in their religious community does not preclude working-class organization.

CONCLUSION

The current structure of the Veneto labor market places limits on the activity of employers, locally born workers, and immigrant workers. Employers, under the pressure of world market competition, into which they are every day immersed more completely by their own export production, need access to a reliable and flexible source of labor power, which the immigrants personify. Yet this very source of potentially exploitable workers also brings with it new problems. The immigrants were already mobilized politically before entering the Veneto's factories, and the constraints that remain as a result of the unavailability of locally born workers means that employers are increasingly committed to the use of such workers despite the political risks. Thus, the manager of the rabbit slaughterhouse noted above was forced to turn to another group of Senegalese workers to replace those who had quit to protest racist treatment. Likewise, immigrant networks' capacity to dominate job placement in at least certain sectors, while bringing with it the risk to the immigrant workers of segmention in the labor market, also limits somewhat the options of both employers and Italian workers. As we saw above, there are already cases of Italian workers who, seeking a racially homogeneous workplace, are unable to expel immigrant workers but must themselves leave to search for employment elsewhere. For the immigrant workers themselves, the requirements of flexible production under world market pressures impose exploitative conditions at work, while both legal restraints and racist behaviour on the part of employers, police, local authorities, landlords, and co-workers limit their own options and space for political and cultural activity.

Finally, the entry of Italy into the European Union and the single currency mean structural pressures for all three of these local actors by the start of 1999. Employers will be under even greater competitive strain; immigrants will face the added risk of rising xenophobia brought about by both the anxieties created by

European union and by the limits of universalism inherent in a unification of only European peoples; Italian workers, thrown into competition at least theoretically with the other workers in Europe for jobs and wages, will, like their other European counterparts, face the demands of capital for a less "rigid," more "flexible" labor market. In this new labor market, workers will be more willing to move geographically where jobs are available (a longstanding source of complaint by European employers), more willing to work with fewer social guarantees, and more willing to accept conditions such as longer working hours that are currently resisted hotly both in Italy and across Europe. That immigrants represent potentially such a flexible workforce, already willing to move geographically, potentially vulnerable enough to be thrust into worsening work conditions in exchange for fewer guarantees, means that the conditions that immigrants today face in flexible production sites and in labor markets like that in the Veneto could be those that are expected tomorrow not only of workers in Italy but all over the Continent.

Is the Veneto Europe writ small? It may be, since the Veneto and Emilia-Romagna first pioneered the use of production methods, some archaic, some brand new, under contemporary conditions of export for the world market. Their model of production, while being altered for local conditions and even for the needs of large capital, has been exported to every corner of the world as the preferred method of late twentieth century capitalist production. It is therefore hardly out of the question that the flexible use of immigrant labor may be the key to open the door to the more intensive and varied exploitation of workers in an economically unified Europe. Yet if the Veneto is Europe, or even the world economy writ small, the Veneto's workplaces are not only nodes in a labor market but also the meeting point for workers of many countries, some of whom, immigrants, are showing their capacity for self-organization and association. They may, in the course of transforming their own experiences as they enter the flexible waged workplaces of the industrialized world, also play an important role in the struggles that will determine just what sort of world the latter will become. What kind of community the European Community becomes may in large part depend on what kinds of community are available to, and created by immigrant workers.

Notes

1. The following two chapters include use of many local studies which were made graciously made available to me, ranging from Laurea Theses of students in the Sociology Department and Political Science Faculty at the University of Padua, to studies, published and unpublished, conducted under the auspices of local foundations, research groups and banks. These include the work of Fondazione Corrazin, including V. Belotti, *Osservatorio sui lavoratori dipendenti nel Veneto* (Venice: Fondazione Corrazin, 1993); Daniele Marini, *Vali più la pratica o la grammatica? una indagine sui bisogni formativo-professionali degli immigrati extra-comunitari: l'opinioni dei datori di lavoro* (Venice: Fondazione Corrazin, 1993); Banco Ambrosiano Veneto and Federazione dell'Industria del Veneto, *Struttura e dinamica dell'industria nel Veneto 1989-1992* (Milan: FrancoAngeli, 1993); Bisogno, Gatto and Nero, op. cit.; Mauri and Brevaglia, op. cit. Terenzio Favo and Ferruccio Gambino have graciously made their files on the press and immigration accessible; Associazione Immigrati Extracomunitari in Padua conducted a survey of migrants who came to their office in 1991 which included 63 people; more elaborate statistical surveys include Comune di Vicenza, op. cit. The local news media I have relied on includes both *Il Gazzettino*, which tends more toward the political Right, and *Il Mattino* which tends toward the Left, while *Il Manifesto*, a national newspaper of the Left, carries extensive coverage of the national news involving immigrants as well as occasionally excellent investigative reporting, though it needs to be supplemented with other more centrist dailies such as *La Repubblica*, *Corriere della Sera* and *La Stampa*. Among the few published journal articles on the region and immigration is Chiara Volpato, "Gli immigrati extracomunitari in Provincia di Vicenza and Levi Bettin," and Chiara Volpato, "L'attegiamento degli studenti Vicentini nei confronti degli immigrati," both in Ubaldo Alifuoco, ed., *Verso una società multietnica Quaderni della Fondazione Istituto Gramsci Veneto*, no. 13. Among Laurea Theses, I am grateful to have access to the material in Manuela Bazzana, "Carcere e detenzione in Veneto e in Italia: Un analysi comparativa," Facoltà di Scienze Politiche Università di Padova, 1994-1995; Ilaria Gasparini, "Le condizioni dei lavoratori stranieri immigrati in Povincia di Treviso," Facoltà di Scienze Politiche Università di Padova, 1992-1993. I am also grateful for the use of the material in the paper, Irene Rui, "L'Operaio in una media industria del Veneto orientale," for Prof. Ferruccio Gambino's seminar on the sociology of labor at the University of Padua, 1995-1996.

2. See the collection of essays in Crouch, Colin and Pizzorno, eds., *The Resurgence of Class Conflict in Western Europe since 1968* (London:

MacMillan, 1978); see also Peter Linebaugh and Bruno Ramirez, "Crisis in the Auto Sector," which first appeared in *Zerowork* 1 (1975) and was reprinted in Midnight Notes, *Midnight Oil.*

3.   In this chapter, and the following one, the term "moral economy" plays a central role in understanding Veneto residents' responses to growing integration in the world market and to immigrants and their activity. E.P. Thompson first presented the term, with regard to crowds and food riots in eighteenth-century England, in "The Moral Economy of the English Crowd in the Eighteenth Century," *Past and Present* no. 50 (1971); the article was republished in his volume, *Customs in Common: Studies in Traditional Popular Culture* (New York: The New Press, 1991). In the same volume, Thompson re-examined the term, and discussed its usage by subsequent studies in regard to cultures, regions and subjects often quite different from those studied in The Moral Economy of the English Crowd. In the article he evinced some preference for those uses of the term which were closest to the questions involving paternalistic and traditionalistic agrarian societies, such as that which Thompson had himself been concerned with. I admit I am not at all convinced he would like my use here in discussing an industrial region (I write "would" and not "would have"—I still find it hard to believe he's left us to fend for ourselves). I base its usage under the circumstances on the transitional nature of Veneto society—any elderly resident recalls sharecropping, and social relations between country and city, between farmer and the formally-educated, retain a note of hierarchy in modes of speech and comportment in the region. Yet at the same time, the Veneto was sight of an active Resistance movement during the Second World War, and has seen former sharecroppers leap at the chance for independence as soon as the market opportunities presented themselves. I don't know that these arguments would convince Thompson himself, but luckily for me, he disavowed control over the use of the term, writing, In any case, if I did father the term moral economy upon current academic discourse, the term has long forgotten its paternity. I will not disown it, but it has come of age and I am no longer answerable for its actions. It will be interesting to see how it goes on. "The Moral Economy Reviewed," in *Customs in Common,* p. 351. Phew! Thompson hardly ever, at least in my opinion, came out second best in debates or polemics, and his usual method of dealing with those who had misinterpreted his work was an ironic aside or footnote with devastating effect. I would hate to be on the receiving side of one myself, though I'd like to think he'd have approved of its use here in any case.

4.   See Frederick Lane's opus, *Venice: A Maritime Republic* (Baltimore: Johns Hopkins University Press, 1973), pp. 226-28 for part of the story behind Venetian expansion on the *terra firma.* See also Giovanni Tabacco, *The Struggle for Power in Medieval Italy* (New York: Cambridge University Press, 1989), p. 315. For an analysis of the post-renaissance history of the region after the rise of trans-Atlantic capitalism, see Peter Musgrave, *Land and Economy in Baroque Italy*

Valpolicella, 1630–1797 (London: Leicester University Press, 1993), p. 17.

5. For an excellent study of the peasant-worker family's historical transformation, its role in the growth of small-scale industry, and the changing family relations based on female wage labor and male subsistence-rent production, see Anna Bull and Paul Corner's study of Western Lombardy, *From Peasant to Entrepreneur:The Survival of the Family Economy in Italy* (Oxford: Berg, 1993); for a study of the worker-peasant moral economy in the Northeast, see Douglas R. Holmes, *Cultural Disenchantments: Worker Peasantries in Northeast Italy* (Princeton: Princeton University Press, 1989). Such works are an outgrowth of interest in the so-called Third Italy, meant to include the Northeast and Central regions of Italy, which were characterized by sharecropping and small-scale entrepreneurship, rather than by large-scale industry and a mass proletariat like the Northwest, or by Latifundia as in the South. This analysis, by now very diffuse in both sociology and political party rhetoric in Italy, derives from Arnaldo Bagnasco, *Tre Italie: La problematica territoriale dello svilluppo italiano* (Bologna: Il Mulino, 1977).

6. See, among others, Juergen Schultz, "Urbanism in Medieval Venice," and Giorgio Chittolini, "The Italian City-State and its Territory," both in Anthony Molho, ed., *City-States in Classical Antiquity and Medieval Italy* (Ann Arbor: University of Michigan Press, 1991).

7. Emilio Franzina, "Veneto: una società dinamica al bivio tra globalizzazione e leghismo," in Paul Ginsborg, ed., *Stato dell'Italia* (Milan: Il Saggiatore, 1994); Fondazione Corrazin, *La Società Veneto 1992* (Venice: CEDAM, 1993); A. Castegnaro, *Il sistema veneto e le migrazioni internazionali: politica e promozione dei diritti civili*, Università di Padova, Dec. 3-4, 1992 (Padua: Cleup, 1993); Ash Amin, "A Model of the Small Firm in Italy," in Edward Goodman, Julia Bamford, Peter Saynor, eds., *Small Firms and Industrial Districts in Italy* (New York: Routledge, 1989), p. 116.

8. On the social structure and regional characteristics of the Veneto, see Emilio Franzina, "Veneto: una società dinamica al bivio tra globalizzazione e leghismo," in Paul Ginsborg, ed., *Stato dell'Italia*; likewise oriented toward the contradiction between globalization and localism in the tri-Veneto region are Raimando Strassoldo, "Globalism and Localism: Theoretical Reflections and Some Evidence," in Zdradvko Mlinar, ed., *Globalization and Territorial Identities* (Brookfield, Vermont: Avebury, 1992); Salvatore La Mendola, "I rapporti di parentela in Veneto," and Ilvo Diamanti, "La mia patria è il Veneto: i valori e la proposta politica delle leghe," both in *Polis* 1 (April 1991); Robert Evans, *Life and Politics in a Venetian Community* (Indiana: Notre Dame University Press, 1976).

9. Ferruccio Gambino, "The Imaginery Acceptance of Immigrants in an Italian City," photocopy of unpublished version in author's possession.

10. See Schultz, "Urbanism"; and Chittolini, "Italian City State."
11. Peter Musgrave, *Land and Baroque and Economy in Baroque Italy: Valpolicelli, 1630–1797* (London: Leicester University Press, 1992); see also Vera Zamagni, *The Economic History of Italy 1860-1990* (Oxford: Clarendon Press, 1993).
12. Piero Brunello, *Ribelli, questanti e banditti: proteste contadine in Veneto e in Friuli 1814-66* (Venice: Marsilio Editori, 1981) is an excellent account of the struggles between rural people in the Veneto and the Austrian authorities.
13. Michael Piore and Charles Sabel, *The Second Industrial Divide*; see also David Harvey, *The Condition of Postmodernity* (Cambridge: Blackwell, 1989); for a study of flexible based production in several Third World countries, see Poul Ove Pederson, Arni Sverrisson and Meine Pieter Van Dijk, *Flexible Production: The Dynamics of small-scale industries in the South* (London: IT Publications, 1994); the debate on this concept has produced an enormous and varied literature. See below for some citations on this debate.
14. Ash Amin, "A Model of the Small Firm in Italy," pp. 116-19.
15. Gian Antonio Stella, *Schei*, p. 15.
16. The preceding statistics are all taken from Anastasia and Corò, *Un EconomiaRegionale*, p. 105.
17. Bruno Anastasia, "I lavoratori extracomunitari," in Ministro del Lavoro Regione Veneto, *Il mercato del lavoro nel Veneto, 1995 Report* (Milan: FrancoAngeli, 1996), pp. 292-93.
18. Edward Goodman, "Introduction: The Political Economy of the Small Firm in Italy," in Edward Goodman, Julia Bamford, Peter Saynor, eds., *Small Firms and Industrial Districts in Italy* (New York: Routledge, 1989), p. 2.
19. Bull and Corner, *From Peasant to Entrepreneur*; Holmes, *Cultural Disenchantments*; Bagnasco, *Tre Italie*; Blim, *Made in Italy*; Sebastian Brusco, "The Emilian Model: Productive Decentralization and Social Integration," *Cambridge Journal of Economics* 6 (1982); Goodman, "Introduction: The Political Economy of the Small Firm in Italy," pp. 11-20.
20. Robert Evans, *A Venetian Community*, pp. 77-101.
21. For instance Stella, *Schei*; Emilio Franzina, "Veneto: una società dinamica al bivio tra globalizzazione e leghismo," in Paul Ginsborg, ed., *Stato dell'Italia*; and Strassoldo, "Globalism and Localism: Theoretical Reflections and Some Evidence," in Zdradvko Mlinar, ed., *Globalization and Territorial Identities*.
22. Interview with Ragioniera Scatolin Camera di Commerio di Padova, Sportello di Commercio Estero, November 2, 1996, Padua.
23. Anastasia and Corò, *Un Economia Regionale*, p. 86.
24. Ibid., p. 90.
25. Ibid., p. 92.
26. Ibid.

27. Ministero del Lavoro Regione Veneto, *Il mercato del lavoro nel veneto Rapporto 1995* (Milan: FrancoAngeli, 1995), p. 117. Official statistics in Italy are notorious for being both inaccurate and contradictory, and the Veneto is right up there with the best of them. Thus different governmental bodies will often come up with completely different numbers.

28. Bruno Anastasia and Giancarlo Corò, *Un Economia regionale*, p. 55.

29. For two excellent reports on working conditions in the small firms in the garment and ski boot export industries in the northeast of Italy, see Devi Sacchetto, "Nodi di autonomia controllata: il tessile e abbigliamento nel Veneto," and Mauro Moretto, "Una zona di exportazione di rango alto e precario," both in *Altreragioni* no. 5 (Milan: 1996).

30. Interview with Marco Paggi, February 24, 1997, at the office of CGIL Labor Federation in Padua.

31. "Economia, nell'Alta tiene," *Il Gazzettino*, December 13, 1996.

32. Anastasia and Corò, "Un Economia Regionale," p. 30.

33. ISMU, *Rapporto 1995*, p. 44.

34. ISMU, *Rapporto 1996*, p. 111.

35. ISMU, *Rapporto 1995*, p. 156.

36. On links between the Russian-, Italian- and Nigerian-based mafias, see Antonio Nicaso and Lee Lamothe, *Global Mafia*, pp. 33-34; for an account of the Nigerian Mafia and immigration links, see David Simcox, "The Nigerian Crime Network: Feasting on America's Innocence and Slipshod ID System," in John Tanton, Denis McCormack and Joseph Wayne Smith, eds., *Immigration and the Social Contract: The Implosion of Western Societies* (Brookfield, Vermont: Avebury, 1996), pp. 109-14. As these titles indicate, this latter article, though informative to some extent, takes a hysterical tone, and bases itself on racist assumptions, such as that the Nigerian overachiever turned criminal springs from a culture that is notorious for corruption; it is part of a volume which in turn consists almost wholly of similarly alarmist readings, including excerpts from a Swiss novel in which western society has been destroyed by overpopulation and violence due to volume of Third World immigration. One can only assume that the first-rate and widely respected immigration scholar Douglass Massey included his short piece to such a collection unaware of the nature of the other selections. This is not to say that the Nigerian network of organized crime doesn't constitute a part of the immigration scene from that nation, merely that its importance must be placed in context and that my own findings both confirm its presence in Italy and strongly contradict Simcox's estimates that 90 percent of Nigerian immigrants in the United States have engaged in criminal activity. The reader is therefore referred to his contribution, and duly warned.

37. For this summary, I have relied on several sources, including Comune di Vicenza, *La Presenza dei Cittadini Stranieri nella Provincia di Vicenza, Rapporto 1995*; Comune di Padova, *Informazione Demografica sulla Populazione, Rapporto 1995*; E. Bisogno, F. Nero, C. Gatto et. al.,

L'Immigrazione Straniera in Veneto e Friuli Venezia-Giulia (Milan: Cedam, 1993); L. Mauri and L. Breveglieri, *Da lontano per lavoro: Indagine sull'inserimento lavorativo degli immigrati nel territorio padovano* (Milan: FrancoAngeli, 1993);

38. Conversations and interviews with Silvano Cogo of CGIL from 1994 to 1997.

39. Centro Studi Investimenti Sociali CENSIS, *Italy Today: Social Pictures and Trends 1996* (MilanL FrancoAngeli, 1997), pp. 36-38.

40. Daniele Marini, *Vale più la practica o la grammatica?: Una indagine sui bisogni formativi-professionali degli immigrati extracomunitari: l'opinione dei datori di lavoro* (Venice: Fondazione Corrazine, 1991), p. 37.

41. Ibid., p. 51.

42. Ibid., p. 52.

43. Ibid., p. 50.

44. On September 20, 1870, Italian troops blasted a hole in the Leonine walls of Rome at Porta Pia and marched into the city, thus completing Italian unification and restricting the Papacy to the Vatican city-state.

45. Giovanni Mottura and Pietro Pinto, *Immigrazione e cambiamento sociale*, pp. 22-24.

46. Ibid., p. 23.

47. Marini, *Vale Piu' La Prattica or La Grammatica?*, p. 54.

48. See Pap Khouma, *Io venditore di elefanti.* This autobiography of a Senegalese street seller of African handicrafts, one of the first pieces of immigrant literature in Italy, makes clear the sense of craft as a vendor which still shapes the initial attraction to this type of work for many Senegalese when they first arrive, but also the difficulty arising from the lack of documents linked to this precarious form of work and the problems with constant police harassment and lodging problems.

49. Interview with Silvano Cogo, April 4, 1997, Padua.

50. Interview with F., December 27, 1996, Padua.

7

THE PADANIA: ASSOCIATIONALISM, IMMIGRANTS AND RACISM IN THE VENETO MORAL ECONOMY

INTRODUCTION

Both migrant communities and clusters of flexible production sites are often described, as we saw in chapter 1, in terms of networks. Despite this similarity, and notwithstanding useful studies of immigrant networks as business networks,[1] the question of how migrant communities relate to the larger social forms concurrent with flexible production remains an open one. Furthermore, the literature on flexible forms of accumulation is divided between scholars who see flexible forms of work as consistent with types of associational democracy,[2] and those who see such forms of production as weakening working class organization and undermining democratic institutions.[3] Neither side in this debate has dealt specifically with migrant associationd or associationism as such, though some writers outside of the Italian context have been concerned specifically with the conditions of immigrant workers under flexible work regimes.[4] Obviously, the relationship between immigrant community formation and associationism to the larger host society is highly dependent on local conditions and therefore, varies. The observations here make no pretense at being universal in their implications. Questions of place—specific compositions and institutional relations, rather than those of world market and spatial conditions—will predominate. The focus here is on the experience of migrants and migrant communities and associations in the specific context of the Veneto. Nevertheless, given that this region is historically important in the development of small-scale flexible work, the issue of the larger relation between flexible work and associational democracy beyond the Italian context is also important to address. The debate surrounding flexible work and associationalism is enlarged by looking at the immigrant experience in the Veneto.

ASSOCIATIONISM AND MORAL COMMUNITY IN THE VENETO

Robert Putnam's *Making Democracy Work* uses a regionally differentiated study of Italian government to derive a series of conclusions concerning democratic polities.[5] Putnam argues that democratic participation is based upon the prior existence of and reinforcement of civic cultures as a sort of social capital, which has led to wide disparities in democratic possibilities and government performance in different regions. The argument has implications that transcend the Italian example. It has been challenged regarding its implications for Italian public life, particularly for its interpretation of Southern Italian history.[6] Here however, Putnam's ideas about the nature of public life and civic culture in Northern Italy are of greater significance.

Putnam reinterpreted centuries of Italian history from the point of view of the extent of popular participation in civic associations and its relation to democratic or republican institutions. He found these institutions sorely lacking in southern Italy, but almost continually vibrant in Italy's north. Civic associations in northern Italy have sustained a tradition since medieval times that has encouraged a sense of civic belonging and pride and knit people and government into a much closer bond than in other regions. According to Putnam, "One key indicator of civic sociability must be the vibrancy of associational life."[7] Such "civic-ness" according to Putnam, is characterized by "social trust," "political participation," "more political sophistication" on the part of the local polity, and "subjective civic competence."[8] These civic relations constitute " a dense network of secondary associations" that provides the type of civil society that, according to Putnam, (citing de Tocqueville and Rousseau) is most likely to sustain republican institutions, democratic decision-making, and good government backed by broad participation in public life.[9] Using Italian census figures, and excluding unions (which he considers a special case), Putnam concludes that such associations are most prevalent in Northern Italy.[10]

The Veneto clearly falls, both geographically and conceptually, within the bounds of Putnam's categorization of Northern Italy. Though rarely near the top of the list of regions that have the characteristic features of civic community, Putnam groups the Veneto, on issues such as administrative efficiency, and voting in referenda (seen as a sign of civic mindedness), with other northern regions.[11] Putnam finds certain anomalies, but does not comment on the Veneto's occasional status as a "border state" in civic terms. As for "particularized contacting" of public officials by constituents seeking jobs or aid in a personal sense, as opposed to contacts regarding a piece of legislation or more general public concern, the Veneto clearly landed in between the northern and southern regions.[12] Similarly, when political leaders in the region were asked several questions meant to determine their commitment to political equality, their responses placed the Veneto roughly equal with Lazio—the region of Rome—closer to the southern regions than the North.[13] Finally, and not surprisingly for the region that for decades voted the most heavily Christian Democratic,Putnam places the Veneto, in terms of the religiosity and attachment to clericalism, in the same field as the most southern regions.[14] Seen as a manifestation not of Putnam's North/South and Civic/Clientelist dichotomies but rather of the persistence of a Catholic-influenced moral economy based on widespread small property ownership, these results are still less surprising. The relative superficiality of Putnam's attention to sociological factors, such as the social composition of the regions rather than merely their broadly painted political history may limit the usefulness of his findings in understanding political results in

Italy. Further, his disregard of ideological questions—despite the persistence of left-wing Emilia-Romagna at the top of most of his measures of civic-ness and the ambiguity of the position of Catholic-oriented Veneto—as well as the total absence of class as an issue in relation to civic culture weaken substantially the Putnam's conclusions. Indeed, the Veneto, as an example of associational democracy and of flexible production, presents social scientists with a series of problems. Most studies of both phenomena have been developed using Emilia-Romagna as a prototype. This is true of Putnam, Piore and Sabel in the *Second Industrial Divide* and most of their critics. Analysts have been intrigued by the existence of a long-time Communist Party-led region that is characterized by high levels of economic growth, relative social equality, and institutional efficiency. The relative neglect of other parts of the Third Italy however, has led to an oversimplification of the relation between flexible work and civic-minded democratic polities, and small-scale production and leftist political orientation. This becomes clearer when the way in which these institutions shape possibilities for immigrant opportunity and social integration is taken into consideration.

In the Veneto the difference in outcomes is not due to a lack of associationalist activism. On the contrary, associational life is quite strong in the Veneto and has had, if anything, a greater impact on the region's political direction than in the rest of northern Italy. Though including leftist unions and other groupings, the main associational presence in the Veneto has long been a Catholic one. Catholic Action, the Church-affiliated political and community organization, was stronger in the Veneto, especially in the Vicenza area, than in any other Italian region. Even in the last phase of Christian Democratic Party history, as the up until then perennial governing party was sliding toward the corruption crisis that finally wiped it out, the Veneto branch of Catholic Action was able to develop competent leaders such as Rosy Bindi, whose leadership of the Veneto CD later helped the Popular Party of Romano Prodi survive the collapse of Christian Democracy to become the titular governing force (the PDS had by far the most votes in the coalition) in the Center-Left coalition, which won the April 1996 elections. Bindi herself became minister of health in the Prodi government.[15] Other associations that are related to the Church, which remains very active in the region, include the Catholic charity organization, Caritas; the Italian Association of Christian Workers (ACLI), a community group which sponsors clubs and cooperative housing among other activities; and the CISL labor union federation. The latter remains the most important union federation in the Vicenza region, and, as we have seen, is the union most favored by immigrant workers in that province.

These Catholic associations and unions had as a goal limiting the development of wide class inequalities and class conflict. As a result the level of open class conflict was less in recent decades in the Veneto than in other northern regions. Sociologist Carlo Trigilia reported in an article from the early 1990s, that hours of strikes per 100,000 employees in the Veneto was substantially lower than in Emilia-Romagna, Piedmont, Tuscany and even the northeastern white zone of Friuli during the major strike years of 1969–1973. From 1974–1978, hours of strikes per 100,000 workers in the Veneto fell much more substantially than in these other regions, reaching only half of the total for Emilia-Romagna, and two-thirds that of Tuscany. By 1979–1982, strike levels in the Veneto were less than half those of Friuli, Emilia-Romagna, and Tuscany, and only slightly over half of those for Piedmont.[16] In Veneto strike hours per capita was substantially lower than the national average, despite a much higher than average rate of industrialization. Further, during this last period, the number of strikers per strike was well under half of that for Emilia-Romagna, despite the similar average size of firms between the two regions, and well under the national average. In short, levels of industrial conflict were notably lower in the Veneto than in other industrialized areas of Italy. Given the roughly similar sizes of firms and numbers of employees throughout the Third Italy, the consistently lower levels of conflict in the Veneto compared with the red areas of Tuscany and Emilia-Romagna are likely traceable to the influence of Catholic organization and ideology, which is paternalistic, but relatively egalitarian, and anti-conflictual. In a comparative study of Bassano del Grappa in the Veneto province of Vicenza and the Tuscan red belt city of Valdelsa, Trigilia found that union membership levels in 1982 in the latter city were much higher, reaching 80 percent compared with 49 percent for Bassano.[17] Wages in the furniture industry were as much as 20 percent higher in the red zone city as in Bassano, and levels of formalization of conflict and negotiation were considerably higher in the red zone city.[18] Though Trigilia stresses that overall conditions of working hours and worker job mobility are not explainable by reference to the political subculture of the region, the regional differences regarding the formalization of organization, such as unionization, of the levels of open strike conflict, and of the formalization of negotiations over conditions are of great importance and do seem influenced by the political culture of the different regions. These differences are important because the level of formalized negotiation over conditions, as opposed to personalized negotiation of worker-employer relations, may be seen as an indication of levels of civic consciousness and of a conception of rights as against paternalistic, corporatistic, or clientelistic relations in the workplace and job market. Putnam's study is most wanting in its lack of any discussion of class relations. For immigrants such issues can be of great importance, as they involve knowledge of workers' rights and their availability in an environment in which work relations are overly personalized. For example, at a union meeting of 35 Senegalese workers in the countryside outside Padua in the Spring of 1995, several who had worked in Emilia-Romagna reported being informed by their employers there of their legal rights to health and pension benefits and social security benefits for their spouses outside the country, while none had been so informed by their employers in the Veneto. In the often familial atmosphere of Veneto small business with its stress on personal and family networks, newcomers can be placed at a great disadvantage. Given the recent prosperity of the export-based economy and regional businesses, this foundation of personal, family, and Church-oriented networks strengthen the hand of the self-employed, business owners, and the locally born against workers and competitors who are not originally from the region. Immigrants, being not only newcomers but also workers who lack citizenship and at times even legal resident documents, can therefore suffer most from a local political and work culture that is not based on formalized rule-setting, negotiations, and a sense of legal and political rights. Veneto-born workers, especially skilled workers, may themselves become self-employed artisans or small business owners further isolating non-Veneto-born workers, particularly immigrants.

Such a class composition combined with a longstanding Catholic moral economy has led to work relations that are paternalistic or corporatist. Thus many issues of hours and wages, as Trigilia found, are settled by individualized agreement between worker and employer, often as a means for both to avoid taxes. This arrangement also allows for widespread working of a second job, often in self-employment or off the books. Putnam's concern with trust as a value in fostering civic consciousness here seems to be present in a distorted form in which trust is used as a basis to defend mutual interests against outsiders—the central government in Rome or immigrants and southerners. The Catholic moral economy has sought to cushion the impact of market forces on the weakest members of local society and provide them with the chance to own property, but it has excluded outsiders. The relative lack of open conflict between worker and employer fed a localism that is corporatist in class and work relations, and antagonistic toward those outside the region. The civic minded-ness of the local culture sees administrative efficiency as an attribute of local character, and it is therefore not incompatible with parochialism. The Veneto thus represents a third type of social organization somewhere between the northern civic-ness that Putnam associates with associational democracy and the amoral familialism and inefficiency attributed to southern Italy. Undeniably associationalist, it derives its moral economy from a class composition providing for either a continuum between skilled workers and small owners or corporatist relations between the two, as well as a localism which is at best parochial and at worst intolerant and even racist toward other regions and peoples. This combination of factors provided fertile ground for the most dramatic political phenomenon of recent years in the region—the separatist Northern League whose anti-Rome, anti-southerner, anti-immigrant politics are an ironic, but logical, result of the political vacuum left by the dissolution of Christian Democracy, the localist interpretation of the moral economy, and the export-based economic prosperity of recent years. Its rise has created a new and difficult climate for immigrant communities in the Veneto.

THE NORTHERN LEAGUE: "LA MIA PATRIA È IL VENETO"

The Northern League is a political party found throughout Northern Italy, but with its origin in the Veneto and neighboring Lombardy. By the mid-1990s it had become a major political force in these two regions. In the elections of April 1996, the Northern League received 30 percent of the vote, making it the largest single party in the Veneto, although it didn't win control of the regional government due to the successful alliance of several Center-Left and Rightist coalitions. Growing out of the *Liga Veneta*, founded in the Veneto region in the late 1970s, and the *Lega Lombarda* of Umberto Bossi founded in the early 1980s, the Northern League grew by 1990 to take over a quarter of the vote in Lombardy, to become the second largest party in the Veneto and Piedmont, and to be Italy's fourth largest party with 9 percent of the national vote (though it in practice is active only in the northern half of the country). Calling for independence for the north of Italy in a "Republic of the Padania" (the name derived from the name of the plains of western Lombardy and the Veneto in the triangle between the Alps, the Appennines and the Adriatic), the League charges the central government in Rome with corruption and inefficiency, with exploiting a hard-working and efficient North through overtaxation while providing southerners with income as civil-service bureaucrats or through transfer payments. It further charges the South with colonizing the North through the Roman bureaucracy; with Mafia-style criminality; and with a culture of indolence and authoritarianism that is in sharp contrast to the Northern tradition of hard work, independence, and liberty. Its defence of an allegedly different culture in the North leads to intolerance of southerners and immigrants.[19] By the Fall of 1997, the League was campaigning openly for a referendum on Independence for the Padania, arguing that the North was already able to meet the Maastricht guidelines for the European Community's common currency and should not be kept out of the EC by the dead weight of the South and the government in Rome. The League also intensified its anti-immigrant rhetoric; indeed racist appeals became the main message in an ultimately unsuccessful re-election campaign for the mayor and city council in Milan in 1997. The anti-immigrant aspect of the League's platform seemed to have more impact in the Veneto, where a series of marches and town council decisions were directed against the alleged criminality and illegal status of immigrant groups. Though the League's call for local decision-making appears to be a democratic approach, its law-and-order attitude to immigration, its intolerance of regional and national differences, and its call to solve the country's problems by separating the wealthier north from the poorer south can hardly be called an example of associational democracy or civic-ness.

Yet the Northern League in the Veneto seems to have grown directly out of the experience of associationalism in the region, and it shows a tendency toward broader political participation among its members than any other Italian party. That this tendency toward widespread participation by Veneto residents from ordinary backgrounds and toward selecting candidates with experience in civic associations is joined with an authoritarian and even racist program challenges Putnam's broad conclusions about democracy being founded on associational participation without regard to the ideological content of that participation or to its class composition. Respect for the democratic rights of minorities and residents born outside the immediate locale would seem as an important an indicator of the successful functioning of democratic institutions as Putnam's criteria of the institutional efficiency of government and the civic consciousness of the population. Indeed, in the Veneto, these two criteria seem to be increasingly in contradiction, as can be seen in the immigrant experience in the region.

There is no doubt that the Northern League has a more popular base with broader participation by various social groups than does any other party in the Veneto. Thus, in one 1992 study in the Veneto region comparing League-elected municipal officials with those of the other parties, the percentages of elected officials from the Northern League who were workers and artisans or shopkeepers and farmers was considerably higher than for the other parties, which had a higher percentage of bourgeois or middle class elected officials Even the Communist Party had a smaller percentage of elected officials who were ordinary workers than did the League. Seen in terms of educational level, the difference is even more striking. Forty-six percent of the League's elected candidates in municipalities in the Veneto had completed only the legally required middle school level (14 years old). Among other parties' elected officials, 35 percent had completed a university degree, 39 percent a high school diploma, and only 26 percent had gone no further than middle school.[20] The Northern League's elected officials were also much younger than those of virtually every other party, including the Christian Democrats and Communists. 31 percent were under 30 years of age, while another 28 percent were under 40. Only the Greens, with 21 percent under 30 and 48 percent between 31 and 40, approached the Northern League.[21] The Northern League opened possibilities for political participation by parts of the Veneto community who had not commonly held elected local office.

The Northern League's activists also show the influence of Veneto associationism. Most League activists in the Veneto gained their political experience in civic associations. In a study of 38 leaders of local branches of the League in the Veneto region, Ilvo Diamanti, perhaps the leading sociological analyst of the Northern League phenomenon, found that only four had not participated as members of associations prior to joining the League, while over one third had been members of at least three associations previously.[22] Only six had previously been members of political parties, leading Diamanti to describe the backgrounds and political outlook of League members as "inside the volunteer associations, far away from the parties." Half of those inter- viewed had belonged to a recreation-oriented association (Put- nam's bowling leagues perhaps?), while over one-third had been in "solidarity associations" that, through charity or volunteerism help less fortunate members of the community. This membership, combined with the nine interviewees in Diamanti's study who had been in religious associations, suggests that the Northern League's leaders arose out of the Veneto moral community and its associational efforts to limit inequality and extremes of poverty. Indeed, an outlook combining work and religious belief, according to Diamanti, characterizes Northern League activists: "Work and religion, first of all, receive an extremely positive evaluation. They are considered, that is, central dimensions for individual life and for social organization. . . . They are not . . . recognized as bases of division and conflicts of interest and identity."[23] Diamanti further describes the use of work as an ideology binding together the diverse interests of the Veneto and at the same time differentiating its residents from those of other parts of Italy and the world:

Work, in particular, is defined as "a central activity of existence and as an aspect peculiar to the Veneto's people, who are held to be—rightly—hard working, even if meek" (from a Vicenza leader of the Liga Veneta). But it is an activity which must not constitute the basis for conflict. The model according to which the League leaders see things, regarding work relations is, in fact, of a substantially collaborative type. There mustn't be, and there cannot be unhealthy contrasts between the different sides. Agreement, recognizing whatever group—workers, entrepreneurs, artisans—and its own perogatives, its own space, is always possible. Contrasts, fractures, instead, are made with the state or with other areas—the South first of all—to which the Veneto's people must send too large a part of their own resources, of the fruit of their labor to "maintain them," to compensate for their lack of ability. . . . Instead of giving birth to a fracture according to class, or at least to the interests of diverse groups, work, in the League point of view, prefigures a territorial fracture, a contraposition against the center.[24]

Since such a point of view portrays hard work as an attribute of the Veneto's residents in contrast to outsiders, its egalitarian aspect is effective only within the Veneto born community, where ironically, it ideologically reinforces the real inequality in power, even if relatively small, between workers and employers. With regard to those born outside the region but who work within its borders, such an exclusion not only from the community, but from membership in the society of the deserving, hard working, and meek, has become the basis for inequality to an extent that was previously rare in the Veneto. This is ironic inasmuch as this ideology stems precisely from the ingrained sense of moral economy of a former sharecropping community, now active in small and artisanal industry, which sought to prevent vast extremes of poverty, propertylessness, and social inequality. The religious sensibility, a sort of Catholic "protestant ethic," has long sought to protect the members of the community from such extremes. Yet what are the current manifestations of this religious sensibility in a Veneto that is prosperous from export trade but wary of outsiders? Diamanti comments that religion is today seen as a personal, rather than social guide. This is a move toward seeing politics as the sphere for the realization of individual economic interests rather than the harmonious agreement among groups so as to prevent inequality and strengthen family and community. He states:

Religion too is recognized as having a central role, or better: the central role among the dimensions of life. But here, even more than for work, there is a tendency to distance oneself from the conception which until now has prevaled in the relationship between politics and society. This was a conception which constituted, in postwar Veneto, the principal source of consensus and, at the same time, of antithesis, in the social-political field, guaranteeing to the Christian Democrats a solid hegemony. Almost all of the League leaders interviewed, in fact, stress the necessary distinction between the individual and social spheres, on the one hand, and the political sphere on the other. Religion, the Catholic faith, the Church itself are important for orienting and sustaining individual and social choice, but they must remain distant from politics, and they must not condition events and choices.[25]

Such a separation between the personal and social or political spheres reminds one inevitably of the historical experience of the role of religion in the rise of capitalism according to various authors. Indeed, since Max Weber's seminal 1905 work, *The Protestant Ethic and the Spirit of Capitalism*, the relation between religious belief and practice and modern economies has remained one of the principal areas of sociological and historical sociological study. Weber found theological innovations in Calvinism that, he argued, paved the way for a type of asceticism that stressed work as a calling and was hostile to ostentatious consumption. This led to the development of the type of individual capable of fostering capitalist productive growth. The ethic of

Puritanism allowed the businessman to engage in competitive economic activity so long as he acted formally within the bounds of religious correctness publicly outside of the economic realm.[26] This "bourgeois economic ethic" in religious form "legalized the exploitation of this particular willingness to work" by making business itself into a calling.[27] The work of a business man thus largely satisfied his obligations to God and society so long as in his other activities he did not go beyond a certain point in offending sensibilities. Furthermore, this ethic separated the religious and political spheres from the economic one, or more precisely relieved religious authority of the obligation to intervene politically in the organization of economic life. Such a viewpoint fit well into the worldview of small entrepreneurs, since it gave them an ideological weapon to use against state, religious and monopolistic regulation of the market economy.[28]

Opposition to state regulation of business activity, of monopolistic practises from the point of view of small business, and of church interference with economic activity rather than concentration solely on the strictly personal side of life were combined into a worldview conducive to the activity of small-scale capitalists in the 17th and 18th centuries. More recently, medieval historian Jacques Le Goff found antecedents to the religious tolerance of economic activity of a capitalist sort by a Catholic Church which gradually allowed for personal salvation notwithstanding the practise of forms of business technically censured by Christian doctrine such as usury. Specifically, the invention of Purgatory allowed for the eventual salvation and entry into Heaven of businessmen who were otherwise contrite or observant of Church-oriented behaviors.[29]

Another scholar of the relationship between religion and capitalism, R.H. Tawney, saw the period between the Reformation and the Industrial Revolution as characterized by "the abdication of the Christian Churches from departments of economic conduct and social theory long claimed as their province."[30]

In short, the kind of separation between personal and political spheres and economic activity that the Northern League activists advocate has historically been linked to the lessening of regulation, both political and religious, of small-scale business activity. This may explain, in part, the increasingly hostile tone of official League statements concerning the role of the Vatican in Italian politics, as well as linking it to the overall Northern League and Veneto business and artisan criticism of state regulation, the alleged lack of a work ethic in the south of Italy, their tax revolt, and their advocacy of anti-trust legislation as well as independence from the Italian Republic. Further, it suggests that the League advocacy of a separation of religious affairs from business life and politics, and the restriction of the latter to the private sphere is related to a desire for both an unrestricted right to accumulate wealth and an unregulated exploitation of labor. For with the eviction from the economic sphere of Catholic religious authority, the personal behaviour of the local business person outside of economic life becomes the sole criteria for judging his or her fulfillment of the responsibilities to the larger community. Veneto-born residents are embedded in a cultural context of family, church, and social network no less than are the immigrants recently arrived there. But the family in the Veneto has for much of the twentieth century been predominantly a nuclear family, appropriate for a certain kind of small-scale accumulation. Much of Italy's south, by contrast, continues to sustain large extended family networks which remain the basis for survival and economic strategy. The Veneto social networks have been based on church and small-business commercial contacts, even though family, not friendship, is the basis of social contact and commitment. Thus, with the loosening of Church regulation, the way is clear for an accumulation-dominated approach to business and to social relations. Certainly many Veneti still live in a cultural world in which Sunday remains a day to go to church and then to have dinner with family., But these are, as for many in the United States, increasingly isolated islands of non-accumulative behaviour in a sea of work. Indeed, for many other Veneto residents, Sundays is a day for the shopping center and consumption; religious activity is limited to major holidays and significant events like baptisms and confirmation, which have become the only excuse for seeing extended family. An attitude conducive to economic incentives grows in influence a little every year, especially as those incentives dwarf the frustrated possibilities of past decades. For immigrants, this attitude structures the treatment they receive as workers in the Veneto, as well as the ways in which their presence in the Veneto comes to be seen politically and culturally. Exploitation at work, discrimination in housing, racism in political and journalistic discourse as well as in individual public behaviour, the lack of willingness on the part of local public officials and civic associations to incorporate immigrant associations in the network of associationalism itself or to take measures to resolve the various social problems faced most severely by immigrant communities, all find justification in this worldview.

That there is a widespread view among locally born Veneto residents that, like the Anglo-Saxon Puritans, they are distinguished by their hard work and piety, helps in this case to reinforce attitudes of superiority or hostility to those perceived as outsiders. Like the 17th century New Englander, today's Veneto small-business person can view recently obtained wealth as a sign of favor or justice, an outward indication of his or her inner worthiness. That others lack this material well-being only confirms the worthiness of the Veneti, for it is precisely through inequality that the worthiness of one group is indicated in the lack of worth of others—in this case southern Italians and immigrants. Southern Italians are increasingly viewed, both as a result of and a source of Northern League propaganda, as lazy and selfish, often living on phony disability pensions or civil-service salaries, which are undeserved, guaranteed incomes. They are also seen as more reactionary culturally and less democratic politically. The League's rhetoric linking southerners to the central state in Rome helps to reinforce the self-justifying nature of this worldview, for in this outlook Veneti are not only more worthy, but are exploited as the working part of the population. This is a sort of regionalist labor theory of value that sees taxes disappearing into a black hole in Rome, which redistributes this money to the unworthy part of the nation.

Until recently it was difficult to place immigrants among the less deserving sectors. One hears frequently in local conversations objections to immigration based on the idea that Veneti have obtained what they have by hard work and that others should do the same in their own country, rather than come to the Veneto to ask for help. But other responses have been more nuanced. The immigrant is easily seen as him or herself a hard worker, and as we have already discussed, the Mourides, to name just one group, hold to a theological view which corresponds closely to the view of work found in the Veneto. Hence, some employers, as seen previously, prefer immigrant workers over local ones (seen as having expectations that are inflated because of the labor shortage) or southern Italians (seen as lacking motivation), seeing them as hard workers, whose motivations are understandable. Some labor union activists have an internationalist perspective, which sees immigrants as fellow workers. But the most common response to the arrival of immigrants, until very recently was a Christian one, founded on the idea of helping those less fortunate. Because of a lack of housing available to immigrants in the region, immigrants often sought to rent habitations outside the major cities, and found many Veneto farmers willing to rent old farm houses, often in badly dilapidated condition, for low montly rents. In part, Veneto farmers perceived immigrants as being less fortunate than themselves, in a condition similar to the poverty they still recalled from only a few decades ago. Often the house rented to immigrants was the original family house, left standing for sentimental reasons, on the land now owned by the Veneto family, but where once they were sharecroppers. In this way, the farmer acts according to Christian charity and also acts in accord with the moral economy that seeks to prevent wide disparities of income and sees the community as the embodiment of and sphere of action of Christian values. Such acts, though materially benefitting the immigrant and admirable in intention, like organized charity work defines the limits of contact between the well-off world of Veneto culture and immigrant social networks. The two virtually never meet on equal terms, as for instance, business partners, or commercial contacts. Rarely do they meet at all as neighbors, and more rarely as friends. With the exception of some of the union or *centro sociale* activity already discussed, it is only on the basis of charity or as political adversaries that immigrant and Veneto networks meet; this is especially true of networks of skilled workers and small business people.

Within the cities, Caritas and other groups have mobilized to aid immigrants. The Cucina Populare, a soup kitchen run by Suor Lia, a local nun, provides two meals a day to up to 300 persons, the majority of whom are immigrants, while the Scalabrini brothers in Bassano del Grappa near Vicenza have set up a housing cooperative to provide living space to several immigrant families. Churches in both Padua and Vicenza have been made available for services in the immigrant communities' first languages, especially French and Tagalog. Thus, the Veneto moral economy was to some extent widened in its practise to include the newcomers to the community. The local Catholic associationism has thus proven able to take a form that protects immigrants, and not only the form that has produced the Northern League's hostility to immigrants. However, this form of Catholic solidarity has limitations, both in the degree to which it is capable of resolving the new problems faced by the Veneto community under conditions of increasing integration into the world market, and in the extent to which its point of view can counter the racism of the Northern League. For by basing their approach to immigrants on the concept of the immigrant as someone in need of help, those motivated by Christian principles inadvertently feed the local racist view that immigrants are in the Veneto seeking help unlinked to a previous worthiness based on work. The view that Veneti have worked hard to get what they have, and are therefore especially deserving—a viewpoint reinforced by the recent memory of poverty and of having obtained affluence by hard and independent work—leads to asking why others don't merely do the same for themselves. In this way, the immigrant becomes defined even through the well-meaning efforts of Catholic activists and ordinary do-gooders, as someone who is less capable or less motivated than local-born residents. After the debate over the Dini Decree, which, it will be recalled, started life as a Northern League proposal to expel illegal immigrants, the League re-emphasized the anti-immigrant aspect of their program and re-defined immigration as a problem of law and order. This turned the public debate over immigration in the Veneto into one of public order, rather than integration. The Catholic view of the immigrant as the "povero Christo" in need of help—unable or unwilling to help him or herself—was tranformed into the immigrant as the potential criminal who, rather than staying at home and working hard like the Veneti had done, came to the Veneto to break the law and take unrightfully what local-born residents had worked hard to obtain.

Associationism in the Veneto has had several different outcomes with regard to immigrants: a Catholic charitable attitude that seeks to integrate newcomers into the previous moral economy; a leftist solidarity on the basis of class or anti-racist principles; or a Northern League-type of hostility which sees outsiders as a criminal threat to the prosperity of the law-abiding and hardworking local community. The response to immigrants by local political forces is arguably a result of political content and ideology rather than associational democracy per se. Indeed, associationism appears in at least one instance in the Veneto context to be consistent with an undemocratic racist and exclusionist response.

That the League finds ready listeners to its anti-immigrant rhetoric is not surprising, as other institutions in the Veneto have demonstrated a limited tolerance for the immigrant presence. Local newspapers, especially in Padua, have in recent years kept up a steady stream of articles portraying immigrants as bringing organized crime,[31] slavery,[32] prostitution,[33] and child molestation,[34] as well as drugs and violence, to the local area. Headlines such as "The Chinese Mafia is Now Close By," "Nigerian Molests Three Little Girls," "I, the True Slave of the Black Mafia," "The Story of Claudia, Forced to Play Lolita" and "The Chinese Slave Merchants" have become common since 1995 in the local press and encourage a sense of alarm concerning the presence of immigrants in the region, notwithstanding both the small absolute numbers of immigrants in the Veneto and the fact that the vast majority are legal residents and employed. Even when articles concerning immigrants are not openly hostile, or concern activities of immigrant-owned businesses or communities, headlines often refer to "the Casbah," the media's name for a tiny portion of the Stanga neighborhood in Padua, or to "Africa," meaning a small cluster of immigrant shops near the Padua train station. Such constant portrayal of immigrants as at best exotic and at worst downright dangerous has helped create a local climate in which immigrant issues are treated by public opinion, local officials and law enforcement officers as a sort of continuing emergency.

The police have treated immigration as a question of public order in practice, suggesting that the Northern League's views are widespread beyond their own party or that their public statements on the issue correspond to an already existing police activity. Immigration is under the administration of the *Questura*, the headquarters of the carabinieri or national police force. The resident permits that immigrants must carry at all times—the *permesso di soggiorno*—must be renewed periodically by going to the windows opened at the *Questuras* for this purpose. Indeed, though immigration law in Italy provides for a *permesso di soggiorno* for up to two years at a time for legally employed immigrants, immigrants in the Padua, Vicenza, and Montebelluna research sites often reported being given permits for six months or less, despite having lived and worked for several years in the region. The immigrant worker often had to take a morning off from work to go to the *Questura* to renew the permit. One grey-bearded Bangladeshi man, who had lived in Italy for 12 years and worked for several years at the same workplace, was given a three-month permit in Vicenza and immediately went from the *Questura* to the immigrant welcoming office where one makes appointments to go to the *Questura*, since it takes three months to get an appointment to renew the permit.

Vicenza has developed a system to help immigrants' deal with the *Questura*. An office of quite competent and dedicated staff, including at least one immigrant, has helped immigrants put their documents in order for renewal, or for a request for family reunion, advising immigrants of their rights and obligations and then making an appointment for them at the *Questura*. Padua and Montebelluna have no such systems, and immigrants go to the *Questura* when their immigrant office is open and wait in very long lines, often with little success. The Padua *Questura*'s immigrant office is open only from 8-10 a.m. on weekdays, excluding Wednesdays, a total of eight hours weekly to serve an immigrant community of 4,000 people. The line for permit renewals there begins to form at about 4 in the morning, as people go early to avoid having to miss more than one day of work. The windows are outside, so waiting in line at the *Questura* means waiting outside in the rain or cold. Certainly it is hard to find evidence of Putnam's institutional efficiency of local government at the immigrant windows of the Veneto region *Questuras*. Nearly every immigrant with whom I have spoken told me that they were regularly sent away because some document was missing from their file, even if they had brought exactly the documents that they were officially notified they would need. My own experience in renewing my permit was the same, as I was often sent back three or four times, having brought the document I was told to produce the previous time, only to be told that yet another document was missing. Also, despite the *Questura*'s status as headquarters to a specifically national, rather than local or regional police force, officers at the immigration window often speak in Veneto dialect to immigrants. This, of course, makes communication more difficult for immigrants applying for renewal of permits, as well as being quite illegal, since Italian is the official national language to be used in all official functions. Immigrants are separated from the officer at the window by a thick piece of bullet-proof plastic, and the combination of the plastic and the Veneto dialect indeed make it difficult to explain any complex specifics which may be important. These are extremely common experiences for among immigrants at the Questura windows.

The police, local and national, treat immigration as a problem of law and order and social control in other ways besides merely engaging in insulting behaviour at the immigration windows. The local criminal justice systems in the Veneto have arrested immigrants in wildly disproportionate numbers in recent years. Local prisons are filling up with Moroccans, Nigerians, Albanians, Tunisians, and Romanians, contributing to the perception that immigrants constitute a criminal element in the region. Virtually two-thirds of all the arrests made in the province of Padua (which includes the countryside outside of the city) in 1996 were of immigrants. Yet immigrants make up only about 2 percent of the entire population.[35] This is about six to seven times more disproportionate than the percentage of African-Americans in the U.S. prison population. It might prove difficult to find another city in the world where one-fiftieth of the population made up two-thirds of all those arrested. The local numbers in Padua province are more than double the totals for arrests of immigrants in Italy as a whole.[36] The combination of a material reality in which immigrants increasingly constitute the vast majority of those arrested for criminal activity and the inevitable local press reports of these arrests which always mention the arrested person's nationality, usually in the headline of the article or television news report, helps to reinforce a view that immigrants are different from Veneto-born residents, and constitute an unwelcome invasion that threatens the community''s precarious and hard-won well-being.

The Northern League has taken it upon itself to mobilize against this perceived invasion, and on several occasions in 1996-97 organized marches to search out and at times attack immigrants believed to be engaged in prostitution, drug dealing, or other illegal behaviour (it is unclear to what extent this perception is accurate in each case). In one small town in the province of Treviso, a march sought out Albanians—this in the wake of the Albanian refugee flow stemming from the revolt in Albania of that winter—to drive them out of town for bringing "organized crime" to the town. In Fall 1997, the Northern League mayor of another Treviso town offered a reward to anyone who turned in an undocumented immigrant to the local police. Public squares in the region's towns were plastered that Fall with posters calling for the expulsion of all *clandestini*—undocumented immigrants. In Milan in nearby Lombardy, the mayor, a League member, lost a re-election bid while running almost wholly on an anti-immigrant platform: "every vote for us means one less Albanian in Milan" was one of the campaign's main slogans. Yet there has been no sign that in the Veneto the League has let up on anti-immigrant campaigning. Anti-immigrant activity has been particularly sharp in Treviso province, where the League has won control of the municipal government in many cities and towns, including Treviso itself and Montebelluna, one of the cities in which this study was conducted.

It is difficult to find a strictly functional explanation of hostility to immigrants by the Northern League, the local police, or the press. Indeed, when we consider that the Northern League, despite the quite varied social base described above, represents explicitly the interests of small business and artisans who are often employers of immigrants, we may question whether this political stance does not harm the interests of at least some of the League's own followers. Furthermore, culturally the contradiction is also striking. The increased openness to the world market through export production in in conflict with an increased insularity in local politics and self-identification. One explanation is that since immigrants work disproportionately at larger firms, the League's opposition to immigration is based on a suspicion of large business with its potential to dominate the regional economy through the use of cheap labor thereby devaluing local labor power. That there is fear of devalorization of labor power, is clear even when the League calls for independence for the Padania so as not to be trapped with the inefficient South in the European Union. Nevertheless, many immigrants do work for small firms, and the large firms in the Veneto tend to be in industries such as poultry and meat, foundries and tanneries, which are not in strong competition with either small-scale artisanal nor high tech small business production. In addition, many of those working in smaller shops are undocumented, meaning that their expulsion would actually deprive their often League-voting employers of a source of labor power. What is more probable is that small employers are betting that in an independent Padania, immigrant labor power would be made available to them as needed, but under conditions where expulsion or other legal repression would keep the workers acquiescent and "flexible." This however, is only a guess, since clearly the Northern League platform, and the more widespread and diffuse "*leghismo*"—the everyday expressions of public opinion in the Veneto region which echo many League themes on Rome, the South, criminality, and immigrants, even among non-League voters—are complex ideas arising in a community in rapid transformation and facing unprecedented contact with outside influences. They are not easily reduced to simple expressions of the small business or artisanal class as such, but reflect the change that class is undergoing in moving from a moral economy that both favors and limits capitalism, to one that is moving increasingly toward the latter.

THE IMMIGRANT COMMUNITY, ASSOCIATIONISM AND POLITICAL REPRESENTATION IN THE VENETO

The immigrant response to the recent rise of anti-immigrant rhetoric and activity has been muted for several reasons. While, as we have seen, the immigrant networks that transcend international borders make political mobilization possible, the housing and work structure of the Veneto has created obstacles to forming permanent organizations and immigrant neighborhoods based on geographic proximity. Those scholars who argue that flexible work has a de-mobilizing effect on workers have a point here in their critique of Putnam, Piore, and Sabel's more sanguine view of the link between small diffuse business activity and associational democracy. Indeed, the mere geographic diffusion of business activity throughout the countryside of the region means that in order to be within commuting distance of work, immigrant employees must themselves be spread around the region. This alone makes the formation of genuine immigrant neighborhoods with the characteristic business enclaves so common to other countries, quite difficult to establish. The condition of the housing market in the Veneto exacerbates this tendency. Finding decent housing nearby workplaces is a major problem for many immigrant workers. Finding sufficient space to meet the legal requirements for realizing family reunion rights is simply impossible for the majority of immigrants in the Veneto. These factors, combined with housing discrimination, which is often overt and is fully legal, make the formation of immigrant neighborhoods, businesses and permanent associations more difficult. This difficulty means that while the networks of communication are capable of mobilizing immigrant direct action even across national lines, and while the immigrant presence in industrial workplaces means that union activity is less difficult, maintaining permanent organizations capable of representing immigrant interests at the local level has been difficult. Many immigrants work outside the city they live in and vice versa. Often a national community will be residentially based outside the larger town where its members work or outside the political, economic, and cultural center of an area. The Senegalese in the province of Padua, for instance, are residentially diffuse throughout the province, but are more or less concentrated near Camposanpiero, about 30 kilometers north of the city of Padua, the provincial seat. This makes it difficult to mobilize the community on behalf of larger immigrant interests in the province, since many of the other groups as well as the provincial government are based in Padua. It becomes very difficult, to get to meetings that are likely to held in the nearest large city. In short, a variety of obstacles particular to the local region's economic and residential structure make organizationally stable relations difficult to establish. To these factors we must also add the likelihood that for many immigrants permanent residence in Italy is not a goal of their migration process.

Let's look more closely at the specifics. Rental housing in the Veneto is difficult to find, and expensive, in part due to the high rate of private home ownership—about 70 percent in the region. The region has not previously seen a large influx of newcomers in need of rental living space. A one-bedroom apartment in a city such as Padua runs about 700,000 lire per month—about $450— and a two bedroom easily costs 900,000 lire—or about $550— and the average monthly industrial wage is 1.5 million lire ($950). Individuals who rent require housemates or another family income particularly if they are trying to save money to send home to their families. Since rental laws in Italy make evictions very difficult, many landlords are reluctant to rent to groups of immigrants under conditions where it might be difficult to force them to move in the future. Racist attitudes connect with market judgements to make housing a serious problem for immigrants in the Veneto, and indeed, nearly all immigrants, with the exception of Yugoslavs, who seem to have an easier time of it, listed housing at the top of the list of problems facing immigrants. Many spend years at *centri di accoglienza*—the welcoming centers, essentially public dormitories for recent arrivals run by Catholic or municipal services and after years still lack an apartment of their own. More live with several housemates, often unofficially, to pay the high rents. Still others rent in small farm towns well outside town where often dilapidated houses are available at cheap rent, at the cost of a long commute into town to work. Of the 16,700 immigrants residing in the province of Vicenza, or nearly one-fourth of the regional total, 9,700 were outside the province's main city.[37]

For immigrants without a car or at least a motor scooter, these commutes can be time-consuming. If one works and lives in small towns, and given the geographic dispersement of firms in the region this is not uncommon, commuting often involves arriving by bicycle to the train station to take a train to the provincial capital city, in order to change for another train to the smaller town where one is employed. Several immigrants described daily commutes of well over an hour in each direction. One Yugoslav woman, who paid 450,000 lire in rent out of a monthly wage of between 1 million and 1.2 million (that is, well over a third of her salary in rent), commuted 25 kilometers from the town she lived in to a slaughterhouse on the outskirts of Vicenza to work. She listed housing as the most important problem she faced, with wages second. An Albanian man who worked as a skilled bricklayer regularly commuted 30 kilometers to work. One man from India told me, "There's a problem with housing. Here you don't find it. In Rome and Calabria you can find it, but here, no. They help us down there [that is, in the the south] but here [the Veneto] they don't help anybody."

Though migrant networks can facilitate finding someone to stay with upon arrival in a new town, and provide a ready list of possible housemates, they are unable to restructure the housing market in the region under these conditions. Thus, small groups of immigrants of one nationality may occupy one or two houses in a town or a neighborhood, but are unable to find enough available housing nearby to develop the critical mass needed to create an immigrant housing market structured in some relation to their own community's needs. Even the exceptions in the region prove the rule. In the tiny village of San Nazario, in the province of Vicenza, immigrants, nearly all from Ghana, make up 114 of the town's 1,800 residents, or about 7 percent. This is a rare example of an immigrant residential enclave in the Veneto. But this is hardly San Francisco's Chinatown in terms of numbers and concentration. The Ghanaians mostly work at two tanneries in Bassano del Grappa about 10 kilometers away, and though they stay in contact with the Ghanaian community in Vicenza and Bassano, and often attend the Assembly of God church services in Vicenza, maintaining contact with the rest of the Ghanaian community in the province takes some work.[38] Maintaining a presence at immigrant-wide association meetings in the city is virtually impossible. Thus the diffusion of production sites and the vagaries of the housing market combine with immigrant networks to create an enclave that is in a very rural setting. For networks accustomed to maintaining links with remote areas of other continents, communications is hardly a problem, but the physical presence and the organizational stability that go with it can be difficult to achieve. Similarly, a clustering of Nigerian shops—two grocery stores, a members-only club and restaurant, and a hairdresser—near the Padua train station does not reflect Nigerian housing conditions in the region. Nigerians face the same problems as other immigrant groups and many must travel to Padua to go to these businesses. Even the small concentration of Nigerian families in three houses on the outskirts of Padua, in the neighborhood of Mortise where I lived while writing this study, is the result of the city's making the houses available to a Nigerian association to provide some response to the previous cycle of housing struggles in 1990-91.[39] Discrimination plays an often overt role, as newspaper ads for available housing frequently include the proviso, "*niente extracomunitari*"—no immigrants. There is no housing anti-discrimination law governing private housing in Italy.[40]

In order to address the, at times, emergency-like housing situation, the volunteer associations in the Veneto have often organized to provide housing, including housing cooperatives. These have led to mixed results. The Scalibrini brothers, a religious order in Bassano del Grappa in Vicenza province, have established both a *centro di accoglienza* for homeless immigrants and a housing cooperative. Immigrants cooperatively own, repair, and manage run down housing.[41] However, after six years, the project has succeeded in housing only 19 families in apartments. The *centro di accoglienza* houses 75 people, but I have heard from some immigrants in the region that they have been pressured by the religious order, their landlord, and local officials to leave their current overcrowded apartments and transfer to the Scalabrini center. The cooperative idea is a popular one with volunteer organizations, and the group Nuovo Villaggio in Padua, run by the Catholic Unica Terra, has also attempted to organize cooperative housing, though the project has barely gotten off the ground after several years of fund-raising. The group has had somewhat more success in its informal efforts to give good recommendations to Filipina domestics to help them obtain apartments, and by Spring 1997 there were 102 Filipina-occupied housing units in Padua.[42] Immigrant association activists often complain that volunteer association projects become a means of raising large sums for the Catholic volunteer groups, which act in paternalistic ways toward immigrant communities, and that in practice very few immigrants are eventually housed. Their view is that such efforts ultimately undermine the independence of immigrant demands that sufficient public and private housing be constructed or placed on the market promptly, and indeed, given the literally tens of thousands of immigrants in the region for whom housing is a problem, the numbers of those aided by such volunteer projects is pathetically small, even if indicative of goodwill on the part of the Catholic associations.

The housing situation adversely affects the ability of immigrant families to united as Veneto residents. Italian immigration law requires the sponsor of family members, who wishes to activate the right of family reunion, to have both an income sufficient to support dependents and sufficient housing space for the family to live together. Immigrant men are often cramped together with five, six or even ten others in three- or four-bedroom apartments. This makes impossible the exercise of the right to family reunion. Since in many cases the arrival of a spouse or even of older children capable of contributing financially by obtaining work would ease the cost of housing, immigrants can find themselves caught in a cruel Catch-22. One Albanian man when asked what he would suggest to ameliorate the situation of immigrants in the region, replied, "housing, to stabilize families"; a Ghanaian man said, "You need housing so you can bring your family here." This problem, combined with other uncertainties of immigrant life, has made it hard to assess how many immigrants see establishing their families in Italy as a long-term goal. Conditions in their areas of origin—the disruption of economic and social life related to war, repression, drought and structural adjustment programs—were so uncertain that immigrants were unsure if they could return. Thus many Bosnians shrugged their shoulders saying that they didn't know if they planned to stay, but would probably like to establish their families in Italy. Among other groups, the majority gave me no answer at all, or said they didn't know. Nigerians often linked returning to their country of origin to the continuance in power of the military regime. But the local conditions in the Veneto seemed to present as great a factor in immigrant ambiguity regarding remaining in Italy and establishing their family there on a long-term basis. For most the question simply remained abstract, since they continued to make remittance payments to a family in their country of origin and they had been unable to realize the conditions needed to bring immediate family to Italy. One recent researcher found that, "Even more than work, it is housing that is the more burning problem for immigrants in the Veneto. The cost of housing is too high with respect to wages for these workers who cannot count on a family structure that can help them in some way...The excessive cost of housing renders family reunion difficult, even if these are rising somewhat."[43]

Thus the numbers of immigrant requests for family reunion remain quite low. Indeed, in all of Italy, in 1995 there were only 16,227 requests for family reunion in a population of 1.5 million immigrants.[44] Of the 65, 004 legal immigrants in the Veneto in 1994, only 10,920 had resident permits for family reunion purposes, and many of these were temporary visas for visiting purposes. In 1994 there were 1,390 family members admitted to the region of Veneto for family reunion purposes.[45] For Padua, by July 27, 1996, 129 family reunions had taken place that year, of which arrivals 56 were children, 59 wives, 9 husbands, and 4 mothers of the immigrant sponsor.[46] There have been a surprisingly high number of "mixed" marriages between Italians and immigrants. In 1994 there were 911, of which the majority were between Italian men and Brazilian or Thailandian women.[47] Italian men have therefore found it easier to establish families with immigrant women in the region than have immigrant men.

There is a growing presence of immigrant children in the school systems of the region, however, and given the very low birthrates in this part of Italy, immigrant children can sometimes constitute a substantial percentage of overall enrollment. Enrollment in elementary schools in the Veneto of immigrant children with non-EC citizenship grew from 466 in 1991 to 1,660 in 1994—more than tripling in three years. That same year there were already 306 children enrolled in the region's middle schools. Thus questions of the nature of the school curriculum appropriate to a multicultural classroom situation have arisen for the first time in the Veneto's school districts.[48] Though we cannot precisely determine the number of immigrant families in the region by the number of school children, these figures do give some idea of the growing dimension of family life among immigrants in the Veneto. Since many rural communities are too small to have their own school district, and since the historical importance of the provincial centers in regional life continues to be strong, and Italian education remains quite centralized as an institution (all textbooks and courses are determined by Rome), immigrant children are heavily enrolled in the larger cities, rather than scattered like their families across the countryside and small urban centers of the region. Parent participation in school district affairs, is fairly low even among Italians since the degree of centralization rules out any PTA-type organization, and it seems to be still lower among immigrants. The presence of immigrant children in schools has therefore not provided any basis for long-term organization. Ironically, while the Northern League has promised to boot out all of the "colonialist teachers from our schools" (meaning southern Italians who teach in the Northeast) the League has remained silent about immigrant school children. Perhaps this stems from the realization that Italians have a very strong attachment to and idealization of children—despite low birth rates—and any political comments on the subject might seem like an attack on innocents and backfire. In any case, immigrant families and family-based communities are on the rise in the Veneto, though, as we see from the family reunion figures, more slowly than the overall increase in immigrants in the region or the rapid growth of the presence of immigrant school children. This would seem to indicate that while some families have been able to stabilize their conditions, for the majority even spousal reunion remains either too difficult or undesired. As a result, localized immigrant community formation remains relatively underdeveloped compared with the remarkable international networks that the same communities are able to maintain. Lacking neighborhood and family-based geographically concentrated immigrant communities, the process of ethnic minority formation and of ethnic business enclaves seems to move very slowly. The geographic diffusion of community members and the small numbers of families make such institutions difficult to maintain.

One institution that has been successfully maintained however, and which at times seems to largely overlap the sphere of community networks is religion. Religious activity often provides the glue that holds together communities that are geographically dispersed. Ghanaians in the Vicenza area and Nigerians in the Padua area may join Assembly of God Pentacostal congregations, which hold services in English in both cities. The Rev. Simmons Odame, the Ghanaian pastor of the Vicenza church, and an official in the international Assembly of God church, told me that the Vicenza congregation, though with a majority of Ghanaians, includes Italians, U.K. citizens, Nigerians, and even U.S. soldiers from the NATO base in Vicenza (until the Gulf War led the U.S. military to ban attending services off the base due to fears of attacks on American military personnel).[49] Similarly, the mosque in Padua, though attended predominantly by Moroccans and Tunisians, is also attended by some Senegalese and even a few Nigerians and Malians. Thus, in some cases, religious organization helps integrate not only individual national communities, but also an international community based on common religious belief. In keeping with its efforts to maintain, in a new form, the previous moral economy of the Veneto, based upon community solidarity with the needs of its weakest members, the Catholic church has provided space for immigrant community use. Thus Filipinas worship and interact at a local church in Padua near the train station set aside for their use; there are masses held in Tagalog and English. The Carbonari brothers, who run the Catholic service group Unica Terra, which also provides aid to immigrants, hold a mass in French for worshippers from Mali, Senegal, and the Ivory Coast. In Vicenza, a Catholic church sets aside one Sunday a month for Eastern Orthodox services for Bosnian Serbs, who often must travel for well over an hour to attend. Other community groups respond to immigrant religious and community needs in similar ways, for reasons of ideological solidarity. Thus the Casa per i Diritti Sociali (the house of social rights), a social center owned by the city of Padua and run by a cooperative of community groups, most of them leftist, is the site of a Sunday morning mass for another Pentacostal service by Nigerians. Though the Rev. Odame has strong words for the conditions of his parishiners in the Veneto, these congregations qua religious communities are not particularly outspoken on social or political issues and do not seem to form the basis for political mobilization.

Immigrant businesses are few and far between in the Veneto's cities and all but non-existent in the smaller towns, and the rate of immigrant self-employment is quite low. But those few businesses that do operate in the region act as magnets for the far-flung immigrants seeking centers of sociality. They therefore tend to be public places, rather than manufacturers or wholesale suppliers, providing a space where customers meet: Restaurants, bars, clubs, grocery stores, telephone discount services, and hairdressers constitute the large majority of businesses run by immigrants in the areas studied. Even the Chinese restaurants and grocery stores in Padua and Vicenza are supplied through Milan's Chinatown, since locally they lack a sufficient market and large enough labor force to provide their own supplies or organize import/export with Asian suppliers. The closest thing to a sufficiently large market in the area is the Nigerian community in Padua, which supports two groceries, a club/restaurant and a hairdresser, all in the area near the city's train station. A long-standing Nigerian import/export firm in the same vicinity makes it possible to obtain Nigerian products—millet, cassava, kola nuts, Nigerian beer and newspapers—and so these make up the city's only real concentration of immigrant business. There are several Chinese restaurants in each of the main cities of the provinces studied, though nothing that would constitute a Chinatown on the model known in other parts of the world. The young people working in the family businesses—all restaurants and grocers—speak fluent Italian, at times interpreting for their parents when mediation with local authorities is needed. There is a Muslim-kosher butcher shop in the Arcella section of Padua north of the train station, with a mixed clientele of North Africans and some Italians. The shop owners, three Moroccan friends, have had serious difficulty finding apartments to live in, at times staying with friends or at local social centers, despite their credentials as business owners. The only other immigrant-run business in Padua is a restaurant/bar owned by a Somalian family that has become the most important space for contact between people of different nationalities in the province.

Both the political left and the Catholic associations sponsor networks of clubs that charge an annual membership fee for a card that allows for entry into any of the establishments run by the network. Private businesses have a more or less established clientele and are defined by political culture, though admittedly in a vague way. One of these networks, ArciNova, had established a bar called Biko's, named for the murdered South African activist, outside the Padua city limits. A dance place that attracted local young Italians as well as Africans and some North Africans, Biko's oftened reminded one of some of Malcolm X's insightful sociological commentary on the Harlem dance scene of the 1950s. Italian women frequented Biko's both because of its ambience as a sophisticated dance place and often as a site for meeting Senegalese men, whose tall, handsome features and soft-spoken manners have made a good impression. But Biko's closed in the winter of 1995-96, and has not really been replaced as a site of multinational cultural exchange. However, the Jubba Club, a Somalian restaurant and bar opened in early 1997, linked to a Catholic network of clubs, has taken up some of its place. Located in the Portello, an old part of Padua where several science and math faculties of the University of Padua are located, and a neighborhood with a relatively large number of immigrant residents, the club, which is named after the largest river of Somalia, manages to unite a clientele of different nationalities and generations.

It is likely that only Somalians could have accomplished this under the conditions of growing geographical diffusion of immigrants and growing hostility to immigrant presence on the part of much of the local community. There are several reasons for this. While politically immigrants have already proven capable of mobilizing in Italy and in the Veneto under the umbrella identity of extracomunitari, as communities they have tended to interact primarily at the political level. The main immigrant associations in Padua and Vicenza bring together activist members of various nationalities who have made it a priority to participate. There is some interaction, as we have seen, at churches and mosques, though on a limited basis, with even these universalist religious spaces largely taking on something of a national or ethnic character in their modes of expression and worship. Senegalese Mourides worship together at each others' houses or the house of a local Marabout, but only occasionally at the mosques predominantly frequented by North Africans from Morocco and Tunisia. Nigerians have complained to me in the Vicenza area that the only Pentacostal church is mostly made up of Ghanaians and that they miss having a church of their own nearby. Thus, beyond a remarkable political unity when various community members believe that the interests of immigrants as a whole are in trouble, the main forms of association bringing together immigrants of various nationalities have been music and dance in the case of Biko's, and food, drink, company, and music in the case of Jubba club. The Chinese groceries, though they do carry specifically African consumer items, remain places of contact between different cultures, but only at a fairly minimal level of contact between customer and staff. The Nigerian shops and businesses tend to have a strictly ethnic character. One does not frequently see immigrants of other nationalities at these businesses, though occasionally Italians stop to buy groceries. The club/restaurant, also a part of a membership network, seems to have an almost exclusively Nigerian clientele except for the occasional Italian (or American) who wanders in for a bowl of pepper soup and a plate of cassava. The Jubba Club, however, has transcended these ethnic limitations in its clientele and staff. This is in large part due to the prestige of Somalian elders among the network of immigrant communities in Padua. With their community rent by many of the clan-based political divisions that characterized Somalian politics during the recent civil war, the elders of the area's Somalian community organized a general council of elders in 1994 to govern the affairs of the community. This made a positive impression among many immigrant communities, and added prestige to projects of the community and its elders. Since Jubba Club found funding from the community's association as a whole, and since it was managed by a well-known and respected elderly gentlemen and his daughters, the club had a good head start in terms of clientele and community relations. Adding on staff from other nationalities—a Senegalese and a Moroccan man—the club has made clear its openness to every nationality of clientele. Even many of the immigrant communities' members who have integrated the least into local society find a comfortable space there to meet friends. Many young Italian people go to Jubba Club on weekend nights, and during the early evening the club is predominantly a restaurant frequented by Italians and immigrants of all ages. While the size, resources, diversity and geographic diffusion of immigrant communities in the region has made it difficult to establish true ethnic niches of business ownership, it seems possible under some circumstances to establish pan-immigrant spaces that are also open to Italians. An Italian and Senegalese music and political discussion center in Mestre, outside Venice, called Teranga also shows the possibilities for a limited number of such spaces. That the main immigrant businesses are nearly all public places, either retail businesses or meeting places like bars or the Nigerian hairdressers' shop, indicates that the market for any wholesale or manufacturing business in the Veneto for ethnic-based consumption remains too small and that the types of businesses that do exist provide a needed outlet for socialization. As meeting places, such businesses are equaled only by the various religious congregations and by the immigrant associations themselves.

According to one study, there are 55 immigrant associations in the Veneto region, though this number included strictly religious groups such as a Ghanaian Jehovah's Witnesses organization and the Centro Islamico mosque. Most of the nationalities have an association dedicated mostly to sociality and to maintainence of cultural traditions, though some explicitly see defending or extending the political rights of immigrants as a goal while many can be mobilized to take on political causes at certain moments. Albanians have not organized an association, though there is a network of Albanians from Kosovo who organize public meetings on the conditions facing their community. Though some of the associations meet fairly regularly, such as the Somalians and Filipinas, and others informally gather often for religious reasons, such as the Mourides, many remain largely paper memberships at least most of the time. Each officially recognized immigrant association by law must hold an annual assembly to elect leaders and discuss a budget and goals for the year, meaning in practice that some structure is maintained year round, but that often a few activists take on the work of the association most of the time. This is largely the case also with the three large umbrella organizations of immigrant associations in the regions studied: the Associazione Immigrati Extracomunitari of Padua, the Associazione Immigrati, and the Coordinamento Immigrati of Vicenza. The Montebelluna area lacks an active immigrant organization, though there are several in Treviso, the provincial scat. Nevertheless, immigrant associations are less active and less independent in Treviso, the province where the Northern League is strongest, as even the umbrella organization has its offices at the CGIL union federation, as do the Senegalese and Ghanaian organizations. In Padua, five people take on the regular activities of the umbrella association: the Eritrean president, a Senegalese, two Moroccans and a Somalian. While certain events are well attended, especially cultural events, the membership is very mobile, and keeping track of address changes or new arrivals and departures is often difficult. Likewise in Vicenza, the Coordinamento Immigrati, the more active and politically oriented of the two associations, rests on a somewhat larger base of activists, perhaps eight or ten in all, with an Iranian, an Albanian, and several Nigerians, Ghanaians, and Senegalese as the main participants at weekly meetings. These groups are easily kept abreast of what is happening in the various member communities through personal contacts, overlapping membership, and leadership networks. But mobilizing the base of the membership on a regular basis is not practical under normal conditions, as work and family responsibilities, geographic distance, and at times apathy minimize the time available for political and associational activity. Nevertheless, such associations provide a certain continuity between periods of widespread protest, and under conditions perceived as emergencies, can mobilize fairly large demonstrations. The Dini Decree was met with protests of several hundred in Padua and Vicenza, largely organized by the associations in cooperation with the far-left social centers.

The relations between the immigrant and other associations in the region is not particularly warm, though there is cooperation at times. Catholic volunteer groups, the strongest types of associations in the Veneto, are often perceived as paternalistic, using immigrant problems without really addressing them, build careers and obtain access to resources, as in the case of small-scale housing projects. Nuovo Villaggio, a Catholic housing group made up of Italians and some immigrants and affiliated with the Carbonori brothers association Unica Terra in Padua, presented a plan to have their associations sponsor immigrants as tenants and guarantee to landlords the payment of rent on a regular basis by having immigrant tenants first pay them. Many immigrant associations were incensed, seeing this as reaffirming, rather than confronting, racist prejudices against immigrants. The volunteer associations often hold conferences, workshops, and public meetings involving immigrant problems, virtually always providing local politicians and their own association leadership with most of the speaking time, leaving immigrants, often affiliated with their own group, as a token presence at an hour of talks on "personal experiences." Immigrant association leaders are rarely invited to participate, never invited to plan such events, and they often express anger during the brief time alloted for public questions and remarks. The Associazione Immigrati

Extracomunitari of Padua has for years demanded a more permanent public office, something generally granted to associations for low rent from city-owned space, and activists express resentment that Catholic associations involved in immigrant activities are regularly granted available spaces. Relations with unions are often somewhat warmer, especially with the leftist CGIL, but in this case, too, immigrant associations are concerned about maintaining their autonomy. Unions do confront political questions involving immigrants and often co-sponsor demonstrations against racism. But unions command considerable resources in Italy, and immigrant groups do not always see their needs listed as high priorities, or see immigrants moving into any positions within the union bureaucracy other than in part-time staffed immigrant offices. When city councils granted to immigrants a right to vote for (non-voting) municipal representatives, the immigrant associations sought to further political goals and political participation by immigrants in the region, while the CGIL opposed participation as backtracking on equal voting rights. While many leaders and activists of the immigrant associations agreed with this in the abstract, they argued that the union was concerned about the growth of immigrant self-representation, which would diminish the union's ability to speak for immigrants in public affairs.

Relations with associations of the political right and the Northern League are generally hostile or non existent. The other exceptions are the social centers that are part of the network of *autonomia*, (the far left) which has rebuilt itself from the repressive period of the 1980s. In Padua, Mestre, and elsewhere, the social centers have made anti-racism an explicit priority, have organized demonstrations together with immigrant associations, and have made their own settings available for immigrant-oriented events on occasion, such as the African Cup soccer matches on satellite television. But here, too, immigrant associations often have the sense that their own issues are at times used to further other political goals, though the sincerity of autonomist anti-racism is not to be doubted. The social centers have a record of engaging in militant activity over issues such as squatting, police brutality and organized crime, and then dropping them after a few months and picking up another issue. As with the CGIL, there is ongoing cooperation between the social centers and immigrant associations, but also a certain distance.

Immigrant organizations remain a presence in the region, though in uneven ways. In the event of a more severe crisis of anti-immigrant activity, these associations may find their membership ready to mobilize as in 1990-91, overcoming geographic dispersion and the other obstacles. However, an organized and sustained response to the Northern League's anti-immigrant campaign has been hampered by several factors. The main area of Northern League demonstrations has been in Treviso Province where the League has its highest voting percentage and controls the mayoral office and city council in several major towns. This is also the province where immigrant association has proven weakest and most poorly organized, relying heavily on CGIL offices for sustaining its daily activities. Padua and Vicenza have come under municipal governments of the center-left coalition in recent years, but Treviso has seen a steady move toward the Northern League. The political atmosphere and political culture of the province may facilitate sustained immigrant activism. Fewer resources are made available to immigrant associations by municipal authorities in the Treviso area, where they lack even the small offices of immigrant groups in Padua and Vicenza. While Padua has students and a far left presence, which makes mobilization somewhat practical and alliances easier to create, Treviso lacks a strong left. Vicenza, though also lacking a strong left, has a strong Catholic labor union tradition, which may help to legitimize immigrant activity. Further, although the diffuse *leghismo*—the growing public view that sees immigration as a problem, a question of law and order, cultural invasion and criminality—is widespread throughout the region, it is particularly strong in Treviso Province. The strength of the Northern League adds legitimacy and public power to this point of view. Individually and collectively, immigrants may conclude that minimizing their visibility is the best approach under the circumstances. If this is the case, it may not be a sensible long-term strategy. The Northern League, though strong in Padua and especially Vicenza, has so far abstained from the sorts of public demonstrations against alleged prostitutes, drug dealers, and undocumented immigrants that it has held in the Treviso area. This may be due to the perception that immigrant resistance in these provinces would be stronger and better organized and that leftist and Catholic opposition would also be more formidable.[50] Immigrants are able to mobilize against the League when they believe they have sufficient allies: In September 1997, thousands of immigrants participated in the anti-racist protest against the League in Venice by the social centers and Rifondazione Comunista and again in the enormous demonstrations in both Venice and Milan against the League's plan for secession.

The combination of immigrant-association strength and the local political culture brought about a watershed in the history of immigrant political participation in Italy. In Padua and Vicenza, in the spring of 1997, immigrants elected a council of representatives that would advise the city council on immigrant affairs and elect a representative to take a non-voting seat on the city council. These adjunct seats were a concession by city councils that were unable to grant the local right to vote in municipal elections without a change in Italian national law, though such a change was pending in the Italian parliament. In the meantime, these adjunct seats, though consultative only, were taken up as the first step toward political participation by immigrants in Italy, and the two Veneto cities were among the first cities in all of Italy to grant such voting rights. It is hard not to conclude that the presence of left-of-center municipal government coalitions in both cities was not a crucial factor in developing this innovative policy, though many leftist forces such as the unions and social centers were opposed, seeing it as tokenism. Immigrant communities, aware of the limitations and even of the element of cooptation involved, sought to circumvent these limitations. First, perceiving that the fragmentation of immigrant votes into ethnic and religious blocks was a danger, several groups ran multinational slates of candidates with public co-signers of the lists (required under Italian election rules) of many nationalities. Further, where there were associations that were viewed as too close to municipal authorities, other lists of candidates of the same nationality were organized. These multinational and independent candidate lists ran in alliance with each other. In Padua there were two Nigerian lists and two Moroccan lists, as well as a multinational list of candidates of the Foreign Students of Padua, all in a loose alliance with the Associazione Immigrati Extracomunitari. Finally, a sustained and intensive campaign sought to drum up enthusiasm and get out the vote among the various communities. In Vicenza, candidates were nominated at a citywide two-day assembly of all national groups, thus avoiding ethnic-based lists altogether.

The results were successful beyond the estimates of optimistic participants. In early March 1997, 227 immigrants attended a two-day assembly and elected representatives of several nationalities, with a Nigerian, an Iranian, a Moroccan, and a Ghanaian winning the top numbers of votes. In Padua on May 25, in an election held at the Office of Social Intervention, on a narrow street in the town's medieval historic center, over 800 immigrants of dozens of nationalities showed up for an election ironically held on the same day as a Northern League voluntary referendum, on secession for the so-called Padania. The street in front of the municipal services office showed a multicultural side to the city that belied the League's claims of a narrow regional culture, as a long line of voters waited, trading comments on the election with those who had already voted but stayed outside basking in the idea that for one day the street belonged to immigrants exercising political rights. Top vote getters again transcended narrow national lines, as a Filipina woman, a Moroccan man, a Senegalese man, and man from the Ivory Coast won the most votes. At the first assembly of immigrant representative, held two weeks later, a Senegalese man was overwhelmingly voted the council's president and representative to city council meetings. Thus, despite the obstacles to ethnic community enclave formation and to permanent organization, immigrants in significant numbers have again proven that they can transcend national, ethnic, and religious divisions and have developed methods of representation for immigrant communities as a whole, perhaps as a first step to full representation at the municipal and regoinal level. Such a change in their legal and political rights would also perhaps confront the Northern League with a crisis, as tens of thousands of new voters in the region would have good reason to oppose their programs: Political representation for immigrants might also give rise to more consistent voices raised against the anti-immigrant rhetoric and activity of League, press, and police. For all that, municipal representation can also be quite limited, as the Padua and Vicenza votes showed. Because many immigrants in both provinces live beyond the main city boundaries, they were not eligible to vote in a municipal, as opposed to provincial, election. Further, full electoral rights might see potential immigrant power defused by the geographic diffusion of immigrants across hundreds of small towns in the Veneto. In Rome, Milan, or Turin immigrant numbers could well constitute a major voting block, and in smaller cities like Padua or Vicenza an important presence, but a handful of immigrant voters in small towns might bring about no substantial change in public perception and political policy toward immigrants.

CONCLUSION

We are in a sense returned to Putnam's admonition that the strength of local community networks and associations will be the surest guarantee of democratic pratice. We find evidence for this thesis in the Veneto, as it also the strength of Catholic, union, leftist, and immigrant associations that provides some safeguard for immigrant rights and needs under local conditions. But we have seen also that an associationism linked closely to a localism, which seems to be implicit in much of Putnam's view of associationism and social capital as local and regional tradition, can also breed an insular and even xenophobic outlook and practice that can threaten democratic rights and practices. At least this is true if we define democracy more broadly to include the rights of minorities rather than narrowly as material well-being and institutional efficiency, as Putnam at times seems to do. Some associations continue to defend the local social capital qua traditional moral economy—that is, Catholic unions and associations; some fight to extend this social capital to include broader definitions of rights and wider sectors of the local populations, such as leftist unions, parties, and municipal governments; and some can even seek to apply these rights to previously excluded minorities on their own behalf, such as immigrant associations and autonomist social centers. Thus, we may conclude that Putnam should not be so quick to ignore the ideological perspective and objectives of associations rather than their mere existence as important factors in democratic polities. When we notice a difference between the center-left municipal and national governments' openings to immigrant political participation, and the political right and the Northern League's call to oppose voting rights for immigrants and to expel undocumented immigrants, we find evidence that the ideological and practical concern of associations, parties, and governments for minority rights and participation is of fundamental importance for making democracy work. If the worldwide labor market shaped by the meeting of structural and political transformations of the world economy and immigrant social networks is to become more than just a labor market, democratic societies will have to find forms of democratic practice that can facilitate the development of communities and of political participation among the world's 120 million immigrants. In doing so, they may find that such democratic forms are in contradiction with the social fragmentation and geographic dispersion of working people, with the erosion of their bargaining position and conditions of work, and with their organizational strength which the current flexible economies often entail. They may also need to confront as well those political forces that seek through xenophobic and other divisive forms of mobilization, to limit democratic polities and workers' political power for their own class or political interests. In seeking to transcend these contradictions, democratic communities could do worse than to look to some of the innovations in the Veneto that seek to enlarge rather than exclude the political participation of immigrants. They would also do well to see how, in their political mobilizations, associations, and participation in unions in the Veneto, immigrants too are seeking to make democracy work.

Notes

1. Among which, see the justly famous, Edna Bonacich, "A Theory of Middleman Minorities," *American Sociological Review* 37(5) (1973); Peter Kwong, *The New Chinatown* (New York: Hill and Wang, 1992); Lucy Cheng and Edna Bonacich, *Labor Migration Under Capitalism* (Berkeley: University of California Press, 1984), pp. 33, 42; Linda Basch, Nina Glick Schiller and Cristina Szanton Blanc, *Nations Unbound: Transnational Projects, Postcolonial Predicaments, and Deterritorialized Nation-States* (Amsterdam: Gordon and Breach, 1994), pp. 49-94.

2. Richard M. Locke, "The Resurgence of the Local Union: Industrial Restructuring and Industrial Relations in Italy," *Politics and Society* 18(3) (September 1990); Robert Putnam, *Making Democracy Work: Civic Traditions in Modern Italy* (Princeton: Princeton University Press, 1993).

3. Mark Lazerson, "Organizational Growth of Small Firms," *American Sociological Review* 53 (June 1988); Fergus Murray, "Flexible Specialization in the Third Italy," *Capital and Class* 33 (Winter 1987); Anna Pollert, "Dismantling Flexibility," *Capital and Class* (Winter 1989).

4. Saskia Sassen, *The Mobility of Labor and Capital* (New York: Cambridge University Press, 1988); Saskia Sassen, "The New Labor Demand in Global Cities," in M.P. Smith, ed., *Cities in Transformation* (Beverly Hills: Sage, 1984).

5. Putnam, *Making Democracy Work.*

6. See Filippo Sabetti, "Path Dependency and Civic Culture: Some Lessons From Italy About Interpreting Social Experiments," *Politics and Society* 24(1) (March 1996).

7. Putnam, *Making Democracy Work*, p. 91.

8. Ibid., p. 90.

9. Ibid.

10. Though not of immediate concern for the purposes of this study, it deserves mention that virtually three quarters of all associations (not including unions which derive a wholly inadequate treatment from Putnam given their central role in much of Italian political life) found in Putnam's research were sports clubs. Associated in the minds of many Italians with physical violence (the Ultras), sometimes linked to extremist political groups or to organized crime, sports clubs were also used by media monopolist Silvio Berlusconi, owner himself of a soccer team, to provide the structure of his party Forza Italia. Though this would seem in part to confirm Putnam's argument of the link between sports associations and political life which in general shows a democratic sensibility, in the Italian case, the Berlusconi phenomenon suggests that sports clubs may be manipulated in the interests of party and leader whose opponents and many foreign critics saw as embodying a new form of media-based plebiscitory politics with ominous implications for democracy.

11. Putnam, *Making Democracy Work*, pp. 95, 98, 104-05.
12. Ibid., p. 100.
13. Ibid., p. 103.
14. Ibid., p. 108.
15. Paul Furlong, "Political Catholicism and the Strange Death of the Christian Democrats," in Stephen Gundle and Simon Parker, *The New Italian Republic: From the Fall of the Berlin Wall to Berlusconi* (New York: Routledge, 1996), pp. 66-69.
16. These numbers are taken from Carlo Trigilia, "Small-Firm Development and Political Subcultures in Italy," in Edward Goodman, Julia Bamford and Peter Saynor, eds., *Small Firms and Industrial Districts in Italy* (London and New York: Routledge, 1991), p. 183.
17. Ibid., p. 182.
18. Ibid., p. 185.
19. Paolo Segatti, "L'offerta politica e i candidati della Lega alle elezioni amministrative del 1990," *Polis* 6(2) (August 1992): 268-69; Ilvo Diamanti, "La mia patria è il Veneto. I valori e la proposta politica delle Leghe," *Polis* 6(2) (August 1992): 241, 246-47.
20. Segatti, "L'offerta politica," pp. 286-87.
21. Ibid., p. 287.
22. Diamanti, "La mia patria è il Veneto," p. 230.
23. Ibid., p. 238.
24. Ibid., p. 239.
25. Ibid.
26. Max Weber, *The Protestant Ethic and the Spirit of Capitalism* (London: Unwin University Books, 1968), pp. 176-67.
27. Ibid., p. 178.
28. Ibid., p. 179.
29. Jacques Le Goff, *Your Money or Your Life: Economy and Religion in the Middle Ages* (New York: Zone Books, 1988), p. 92.
30. R.H. Tawney, *Religion and the Rise of Capitalism: A Historical Study* (London: Penguin, 1969), p. 271.
31. "Rapina su commissione: Banda di slavi in Italia da una settimana," *Il Mattino* (Padua), December 28, 1996; "Io, vera schiava della 'mafia' nera," *Il Gazzettino* (Padua), November 15, 1996, "La mafia cinese ora è vicino," *Il Mattino*, December 7, 1996.
32. "Un'altra storia di ordinaria schiavatù," *Il Gazzettino*, December 13, 1996; "I cinese mercanti di schiavi," *Il Gazzettino*, December 20, 1996.
33. "Storia di Claudia: Lolita per forza," *Il Mattino*, December 13, 1996; "Sbattuta sul marciapiede a sedici anni," *Il Gazzettino*, December 20, 1996.
34. "Nigeriano molesta tre bimbe," *Il Mattino*, November 20, 1996.
35. "Due arresti su tre sono immigrati," *Il Mattino*, January 3, 1997.
36. ISMU, *Secondo rapporto sulle migrazioni 1996* (Milan: FrancoAngeli, 1997), p. 168.

37. Rashad Al Amir, "Servizio Immigrati e Nomadi, City of Venice, Gli immigrati in Veneto," paper presented as part of ISPES-sponsored conference, "Il sostegno alle famiglie nell'autoorganizzazione delle comunità immigrate," October 27-28, 1995, Rome, p. 42.

38. Steven Colatrella, "L'interazione tra famiglie immigrate e famiglie locali: la situazione nel Veneto," paper presented April 18, 1997, at the conference organized by the research institute ISPES, "L'interazione tra famiglie immigrate e famiglie locali," April 17-18, 1997, Rome.

39. Colatrella, "L'interazione tra famiglie immigrate e famiglie locali."

40. The director of the Vicenza Office of Immigrant Welcome, for instance, argues that both the housing shortage and racism are to blame, and told me that one hears the same arguments against renting to immigrants—that they are dirty, they'll wreck the house, and so forth—that one previously heard against renting to the U.S. personnel from the Vicenza Air Base. Interview with Gabrielle Brunetti, March 12, 1997, Vicenza.

41. Interview with Giorgio Maschio of Scalibrini centro di accoglienza Bassanot del Grappa, March 15, 1997.

42. Interview with Signora Pase of Unica Terra, March 14, 1997, Padua.

43. Rashad Al Amir, "Servizio Immigrati," p. 43.

44. ISMU, *Secondo rapporto sulle migrazioni 1996*, p. 24.

45. Rashad Al Amir, "Servizio Immigrati," p. 43.

46. Data provided by Professor Oblek of the Social Interventions Office of the City of Padua, interview, March 11, 1997, Padua.

47. Rashad Al Amir, "Servizio Immigrati," p. 43.

48. Interview with Professor Oblek, March 11, 1997, Padua. This office's efforts with regard to immigrant school children, though well-meaning, have until now largely been limited to producing a video with fairy tales from various countries to be shown in the schools.

49. Interview with Rev. Simmons Odame, January 13, 1997, Vicenza.

50. In July 2000, visits to the Veneto by Austria's racist political leader Heider, sponsored by the Northern League's elected officials, were greeted with large militant protests by unions and social center activists.

8

CONCLUSION: THE MAKING OF THE PLANETARY WORKING CLASS

Contemporary migrations reflect both continuities and innovations with regard to previous migrations. By tracing previous moments in the world labor market, I have attempted to show these continuities: The roles of states in regulating and of private interests in transporting labor power, the structured inequalities and lack of citizenship and workers' rights that migrants, free and unfree, have often faced. But this study has mainly seen contemporary migrations as innovative, not fully fitting with other historical typologies of migrations. In particular, I have stressed their difference with regard to the migrations that immediately preceded them, or which, in the case of the Middle East oil workers, are their contemporaries. In place of states as the primary recruiters and organizers of labor power on a worldwide scale, a world labor market is being formed out of the conflicts across state boundaries between communities of working people organized in networks, international agencies, nation-state authorities, and employers. I have tried to show how much of what seems spontaneous about both migrations and the labor market for flexible production is linked and organized by the worldwide web of immigrant networks. These networks have organized migrations as a response to the structural trans-formations, global in content but very local in form, of local economies and communities in the ex-Second and Third Worlds. I have then shown some of ways in which transnational actors have imposed, in the specific context of Italy and in particular the Veneto region, immigrant workers, though not under conditions of their choosing, in the local economy and political environment. These transnational networks link political activity in Italy with struggles in other parts of the world, and that at times the various networks come together in specific places like Italian cities and factories to form a common web, able to mobilize for common interests across national and religious identities. Finally, I have argued that, although at times the planetary moment—migrant networks, universal working class and world market—seem to override local influences, at other moments, local institutions, such as the Veneto's moral economy, Italian immigration law, the rise of anti-immigrant activity, or the local housing and labor market, can strongly influence the results of migration processes and experiences. In so doing, these local influences, particularly as they provide information about conditions that circulate through the migrant web of communications, can impact the very nature of the world labor market. A dialectical process of development thus poses immigrant communities against capitalist agencies, states, employers and political parties at the same time as local markets and conditions confront the pressures of integration in the world market and the influence of transnational migrant networks. The conflict between immigrant workers and the Northern League in the Veneto therefore appears also as a conflict between the Veneto moral economy and the world market-oriented export economy that has helped make the region prosperous.

I have used the words "planetary" and "world" purposefully in this study rather than the often-used "global." "Global" has become a slogan in recent years more than an adjective. While "planetary" is still largely neutral, meaning essentially processes and institutions that exist geographically across the planet, "global" is often used today in the way "modernization" or "progress" were used in the past. "World" is not the same as "planetary," though I have used the two words interchangeably to avoid repetition; "world" I take to mean the place in which human activity as a whole occurs, and today that seems to me to largely overlap the planet. "International" would not have done at all, since I have sought to portray the actors described herein, especially migrant communities, as existing across state and national borders, rather than merely bringing together geographically distinct entities. These actors move both within specific locales and interact with specific class compositions and divisions of labor. In so doing, the move across both space— understood as the flow of money, goods, and information—and across specific places, creating and transforming communities and cultures. The immigrants thereby change the class compositions which make up various places, while also bringing these into new relations with one another. The world labor market should be understood, therefore, as a series of social relations in interaction as a complex system of mutual causalities, rather than as an abstract grid that is homogeneous across the planet irregardless of local customs, needs, or social compositions. At the same time, this local content shapes the conditions immigrants find upon arrival; local conditions thereby shape the choices available on a planetary scale at which migrant networks operate, and therefore affect outcomes at a level larger than their own immediate sphere.

This study is not unique in seeing migrant networks as planetary actors. Linda Basch, Nina Glick Schiller, and Cristina Szanton Blanc have recently published a series of studies of Caribbean and Filipino networks that see migrant communities as transnational actors shaping and altering the economic, political, and cultural lives of their countries of origin as well as of their country of arrival to such an extent that immigrants may today be said to live in both countries simultaneously.[1] Like the groundbreaking work of Nestor Rodriguez[2] and the authors of *Nations Unbound*, I have sought to transcend the language of migration as involving "origins" and "host countries," and to describe a new reality in which communities are themselves transnational—one can go to the other side of the planet without leaving one's own community. This new reality, according to all three of these studies, has pushed migration to its limits as a concept, if not transcended it. Such a phenomenon suggests that we must re-examine more fully the whole conceptual apparatus of migration studies to see if it needs some new parts, as Basch, Schiller and Blanc argue.[3]

Yet there are some significant differences in our approaches. As their title suggests, Basch, Schiller, and Blanc see migrant networks and communities as "deterritorialized nation states" and see them "engaged in the nation building processes of two or more nation-states."[4] It is true, for example, that Haitian immigrants in New York play a role in the internal politics of Haiti as a nation-state but I find the view that "nation building" is what immigrant networks are up to is a strange and largely unsupported one. The authors assume that we know what they mean by nation building—a phrase that would seem to harken more closely to the political experiences of the immediate post-independence phase of many Third World countries. But Haiti has been independent for two full centuries, and how immigants are "nation building" in the First World countries where they arrive as newcomers at least deserves explaining.

For Nestor Rodriguez, in whose work I find more commonality with my own, transnational migrant communities carry out "autonomous migration" organized independently of state policies and control.[5] Like this study, Rodriguez argues that autonomous migration "means that working-class communities in peripheral countries have developed their own policies of international employment independent of interstate planning. . . . Through autonomous migration undocumented workers themselves have created a guestworker program, which many U.S. employers have supported."[6] Although I have also emphasized the independent nature of migrant networks, I have also stressed that the networks exist in relation to, and indeed in conflictual relation to, the political actors, national and international, that have imposed policies that have disrupted these communities' previous means of subsistence and self-reproduction. Seen in that light, and in the context of the counter-flow of remittances, which seeks to partially reverse the flow of value from peripheral to core economies, migrant communities look independent organizationally but perhaps a bit less "autonomous," as I indicated in chapter four. Finally, once in the country where they are newly arrived, migrant communities

remain organizationally independent and capable of action leading
to changes in the institutions which they find there, as we saw in
chapter five. But they are also subject to the legal, police and
other institutional influences of the internal political and economic
life of these locales; as chapters six and seven indicated, both in
the positive case of the influence of the Italian labor movement
and the negative case of Veneto police activity and Northern
League hostility, these local influences can greatly shape the
experience and opportunities available to immigrants and their
communities.

In describing migrant communities and social networks so
differently, as "deterritorialized nation-states" or as "proletarian
transnational communities," these studies raise the increasingly
important question of how best to describe the content of migrant
social networks. In this study migrant networks appear in chapter
three as particular communities of working people geographically
located, in chapter four as a worldwide web of communications
and resource transfer, and family, religious, and political linkages.
In chapter five they appear as a multinational working class. By
chapter six they are back to being labor power in the factories of
the Veneto, and later appear as union members. In chapter six,
they are nascent ethnic minorities and struggling immigrant
communities, businesses, and associations in certain cities.
Throughout, they are also referred to, at times explicitly, at times
somewhat ambiguously, as part of an emerging working class.
These different ways of describing immigrant networks leads to
the sense that the social networks analysis of migration may have
reached its limits, both conceptually, as requiring further
definition, and as a description of reality, as community, class,
and nation are presented as alternative or compatible ways of
explaining what is happening today.

Perhaps we should try a type of conceptual long division,
taking phrases like "migrant network," "religious network,"
"business network," "working class network," "ethnic network,"
"family network" and "national network," and factor out the word
"network." This leaves us with migrants, religion, business, the
working class, ethnicity, family, and nation. The usual suspects,
in other words, of sociological analysis. Network analysis helped

us learn something about what each of these actors and institutions do, but there are differences between religious and family networks, between business networks of immigrants and those linking workers in common struggle and in the common search for livelihood. And yet, in a world in which each of these types of social relation finds itself under pressure from world market forces, uprooted from its familiar geographic and cultural terrain, all of these vastly different types of network flow into a common web of market relations and proletarianization:

The bourgoisie, wherever it has got the upper hand, has put an end to all feudal, patriarchal, idyllic relations. It has pitilessly torn asunder the motley feudal ties that bound man to his "natural superiorers," and has left remaining no other nexus between man and man than naked self-interest, than callous "cash payment." . . . It has resolved personal worth into exchange value, and in place of the numberless indefeasible chartered freedoms, has set up that single, unconscionable freedom—Free Trade. In one word, for exploitation, veiled by religious and political illusions, it has substituted naked, shameless, direct, brutal exploitation. . . .

The bourgeoisie has torn away from the family its sentimental veil, and has reduced the family relation to a mere money relation. . . .

The former lower strata of the middle estate—the small tradespeople, shopkeepers, and rentiers, the handicraftsmen and peasants—all these sink gradually into the proletariat, partly because their diminutive capital does not suffice for the scale on which Modern Industry is carried on, and is swamped in the competition with the large capitalists, partly because their specialized skill is rendered worthless by new methods of production. Thus the proletariat is recruited from all classes of the population.[7]

Surely something like the process described above has been suggested in this study, but so have the limits to such a process. Indeed, in chapter three I have argued that structural adjustment programs constitute a form of proletarianization. But in chapter four I tried to show that the response of the communities in question is to attempt to integrate the market relations they have encountered into a new system that stabilizes their previous community relations at a disequilibrated state. I have described this effort using the metaphor of dissipative structures. If this is a correct characterization, does it mean that immigrants are not proletarians? There are two ways in which we may describe immigrants and their communities as working class. First, most immigrants are seeking wages, either as their sole means of livelihood, or as a necessity for making remittances that can avoid a further proletarianization. In their forms of needed income, given some diversity of goals, and in the work that they find in Italy and elsewhere, it seems to me accurate to define immigrants and their communities as working class. Second, these communities are in continuous conflict with capital—multinational corporations, transnational financial agencies and governments and employers in the country of arrival. If we see class as conflict with capitalist relations, and take both the formal and real subsumption of labor to capital into account—thereby including the struggles of Ghanaians, for instance, both as cocoa farmers in Ghana and as tannery workers in Italy—then we again find ourselves studying working class subjects. Cautious and heuristic use of the term is advisable, for whatever is happening politically and economically around the planet, it is new enough that humility is in order. Besides contributing to the making of the world labor market, this issue of whether migrant communities are contributing to the making of the planerary working class is a controversial one. That they are playing a role in re-making the working class in Italy (rather than "the Italian working class"), seemed to me, given the evidence I presented in chapter five, easily described and defined. How to describe and define such a process at the world level, however, is more complex and requires further study. We may however, discuss some of the ways in which we might contribute to studying this question, though hopefully we have accomplished a first step toward such an approach.

Seeing immigrant networks as working-class subjects raises the question of the extent to which the working class is characterized by a strictly national existence or exists at the international level as well. The most forceful argument in defense of emphasizing the national differences in working-class formation has been made by Katznelson and Zolberg and the contributors to their collection of essays on European working classes. Along with Gareth Stedman-Jones, Katznelson takes E.P. Thompson to task for studying a case, the English working class, where the language of class predominates—thus implying that, despite Thompson's anti-structuralist arguments to the contrary, there is some automatic process of developing class consciousness that is assumed in Thompson's work.[8] Aside from the obvious fact that Thompson precisely emphasized the specificity of the English case, this argument seems to miss the point.

In such a conception of class as Katznelson's, ironically, there is no room for contingency, despite the stress on local contingency in the studies presented in their work. For the defeat of a class movement naturally implies a decline of class language and symbolism, while growth in working class power and organization results in the opposite. More importantly, the selection of materials in the Katznelson and Zolberg study is equally problematic in that, like Thompson, the study largely ignores the international dimension in the development of the working class in various countries. Katznelson and Zolberg, no less than Thompson, choose a study that will emphasize the differences between certain aspects of working class organization and political behaviour, rather than the commonalities, and moments of interaction between the different national experiences. Thus, two studies of the German working class in their volume fail to use the words "Jewish" or "Polish."[9] A study of the U.S. working class after the Civil War stresses only the lack of solidarity fostered by ethnic difference, while seeming blind even to moments of international solidarity, which it insists on categorizing as "ethnic based." During a strike by East European workers (at that time East European hardly constituted an ethnic identity), the strikers held a support meeting in which solidarity was expressed by "a Ukranian priest," "the editors of local Lithuanian and Ukranian newspapers," a "Slovak merchant" and "a Polish shoemaker."[10] None of the important questions are asked here: was this expression of solidarity among several nationalities a result of common work experiences, of an ideology of religious or socialist solidarity brought separately from each country of origin, or the result of a common struggle against the Russian Empire transformed into workplace solidarity? Instead of asking such potentially fruitful questions, which would subvert the entire point of the collection of essays, namely demonstrating the singularity of every national working class experience, the author uses it as an example of working class ethnic insularity.

Further, there is no study of working class experience in Africa, Asia, or Latin America, where, particularly with regard to anti-colonial movements and the Pan-African movement, some interaction and commonalities would seem apparent.[11] The state plays, in every local area, an important role in the development of working class demands and organizations, but the reverse is likewise the case, and the latter does not necessarily exist or move only within the confines of that same state's geographical jurisdiction.

Similarly, much of the literature that assumes away the working class as a social subject or a structural entity in capitalist society takes a strictly Eurocentric perspective. This is true of the "new social movements" approach, "the end of the working class" approach, and the "postmodern fragmentation" approach, which interprets the changes in the mode of production as the end of both capitalism as a grand narrative and of the working class.[12]

In contrast to such works, writers associated with the world-systems approach have looked at the working class as an international, or rather global entity, and in terms of common activity. For Immanual Wallerstein the working class and capital are both global actors, but the working class seems to exist for him only as wage rates, which then determine where in the world system capital investment flows. However, Wallerstein's tripartite categorization of the world system into core, semi-periphery, and periphery has helped to bring to light certain regional similarities that transcend local national differences.[13] Beverly J. Silver has recently demonstrated statistically that an extraordinary commonality of forms of struggle and cycles of struggle have occured in the 20th century.[14] This research, which remains strictly at the statistical level, begs all the questions: Why do workers in certain regions, or sectors of the world economy act in certain ways? How do struggles, demands and strike waves circulate ? Are the ideas and demands similar during global strike waves?

We are thus left with two groups of literature: one stresses important subjective and national specificities, but seems to see working-class activity only as a compilation of national experiences that are hermetically sealed off from one another;

another sees the working class at the global level, but only as a structural component of capital and indeed as an aspect of capital in that no subjectivity is described. The world systems theorists' foray into social movements literature was not a particular improvement, covering the period from the French Revolution to today in a handful of pages, and reducing all the complexities of ideas and ideologies to a few generalities.[15] There would seem to be an impasse in which we lack the proper tools for an internationally-based study of working class activity and formation. Fortunately, several recent and some older works do provide some tools for such a study.

One aspect common to both the world systems approach and that of the more national state-centered school is the emphasis on state or economic structures to the detriment of the circulation of human experience, cultural expression, and organizational form. This is in part because for both groups of thinkers, the view from the forest appears different from the view from the trees. This is surely a useful insight in one sense, but only if we remember that the forest consists of trees and is therefore shaped by the outcome of their growth both individually and in relation to one another. Unfortunately, the trees look small and insignificant, and most importantly, fragmented in their experiences in relation to the state and the world economy, which seem by comparison large, obviously influential and whole, at least from structuralist or state-centered points of view.[16] Hence, Tilly and Katznelson's call for understanding how "concrete 'huge comparisons' help us to understand how such basic large-scale processes as proletarianization and class formation are generally followed."[17]

Such research projects are precisely what I have not attempted in this study, though not because I don't seek to understand large-scale phenomenon. Let's examine Katznelson's phrase above more carefully. The relation between things may be more important than their existence independent of one other, as world systems theorists have often pointed out. Comparison should not be assumed to be automatically relevant as a methodology, let alone "huge comparisons." Second, although proletarianization happens to many people, and flows from large-scale sources, it is not necessarily a large-scale process.

Proletarianization happens to huge numbers of people, but in very precise *and even small ways*—the arrival of troops in the village, the loss of a farm or shop for debt, the arrival of a slave catcher, the sale of a child by his or her parents, the migration of a son or daughter. The proletarianization of Senegalese peanut farmers, Nigerian artisans, Filipina women, and Mexican tribal peoples *all occur through different experiences* with different cultural and local meanings. All these events take different forms but *the content remains the same for each*: producing available labor power. But the links between Touba, Senegal, Santa Rosa ad Alamino in the Philippines, Ibo Land in Nigeria and Tunis and Casablanca with factories and homes in the Veneto cannot be fully grasped by "huge comparisons" of "large processes" but rather *by examining the relations between places and experiences* linked by human activity, mobility, work, and struggle. Thus, unlike Katznelson, in this study I have been interested not so much in how proletarianization is "generally followed" but how it is specifically experienced and made.

Where the state-centered national comparative approach reminds us to be attentive to the role of the state, even if we don't need to adopt this view of how it operates, the world systems analysis at least reminds us to understand the links between all of these particulars that shape each of the trees in the forest. Unfortunately, it stops there. Examining the role of workers and migrants in shaping the institutions at the global level and their own interactions with one another has never been a priority for this school. Another alternative, which surely approaches the working class as an entitity at the global level, are the recent studies by the World Bank.[18] The Bank's 1995 *World Development Report*, dedicated in its entirety to the world labor market, addresses wage levels, capital flight, the Gulf War,[19] unpaid labor versus paid labor, world migrations, and government policies and labor unions. The World Bank authors demonstrate a conception of a world system, of large-scale processes, huge comparisons, state policy and working-class organizations (the effect of unions and welfare policies on the world labor market). The World Bank, not surprisingly, shows a more imaginative capacity for synthesis of the various aspects of the problem than do many critical scholars. Nor can it be claimed that their view of causal relations is completely one-sided or mechanical, since certain policies and unions are shown to effect wage rates, material well-being and therefore the labor market at the world level (indeed the labor market is assumed to be at the world level throughout). But overall, the interest in working-class experience and aspirations is a small part of the study, and workers exist for the most part either anecdotally or as wage rates (variable capital, in Marxist terms).

Fortunately, we have some other guides. The Pan-African experience and its historians—C.L.R. James, Walter Rodney, Tony Martin, Cedric Robinson, W.E.B. DuBois, Horace Campbell,[20] and others—have always understood that both capital and labor operate as subjects, and at levels which transcend national boundaries. What was the slavery system—which circulated sugar, rum, slaves, and Bibles, but also ideas, African cultural practices and cosmologies, and revolt—if not a lesson in how capital and labor are global subjects, even as one tried to make the other into an object. Indeed, one can object that Katznelson and Zolberg, despite making the same charge against Thompson, chose an example, a comparative study of Western European and North American countries, that would over-emphasize the national character of the working-class experience, while excluding the Atlantic and African experiences in which the circulation of persons, struggles, and ideas is impossible to ignore.[21]

Also within the field of history, two recent offerings—Donna Gabaccia's *Migrants and Militants* on Sicilian workers and her article on the role of Italian migrant workers as a social subject in the international working class before the First World War, and Peter Linebaugh's study of the London working class in its worldwide origins and his study of the Atlantic working class of the 18th century—have illustrated how examination of the circulation of specific persons, groups, struggles, organizations, and demands can greatly expand the field of working class studies.[22] Indeed, viewing the working class from the global point of view, but in terms of particular self-activity and influences, expands as well our understanding of capital and the state. For what will appear as "overseas investment" or as "foreign policy" from a national point of view, will appear as a part of a class conflict that is not contained within any single state border, but in which state borders are themselves merely an instrument.[23] Regarding recent working class experiences, the journal *Midnight Notes* has, with its use of the concept of primitive accumulation, its analysis of the Gulf War, and the revolts against structural adjustment programs, developed a view of a working class subject that both has forms of organization and struggle in common and which circulates geographically, interacting with one another.[24] Harry Cleaver has shown how Marx's own categories require reference to class conflict on a world scale, and to the circulation of struggles among different sectors and regions.[25]

Several other writers, though not conceptualizing a working class at the global level per se, have sought to trace the physiognomy of the workforce in the new international division of labor, the global assembly line or the global factory, or in post-Fordist or flexible production sites by certain subjective charac-teristics—mostly female, often immigrant, low paid and un-unionized, in precarious jobs, lacking democratic rights and welfare state guarantees. The writings of A. Sivanandan, which are similar in kind, stressing the immigrant workforce in England, does conceive of a planetary working class subject and a worldwide class conflict in ways somewhat similar to *Midnight Notes*, seeing the silicon chip-based production in the wealthier regions as linked to the conditions in the Third World and subsequent migrations.[26] Finally, a circle of writers in the Wages for Housework tradition have always seen a global female working class as central to an international working class whose struggles included those over reproduction as well as expropriation and production. Their recent work on women and debt has made important contributions in helping us to understand the transformation of social reproduction and its relation to migration and class conflict.[27]

Are the immigrants in Italy part of the planetary working class, then? A yes answer, while admitting the need for more work to understand the physiognomy of such a class, seems to me justified. This study argues that the world labor market itself is contested terrain even in its origins and by no means a fait accompli. Whether the struggles against such a labor market, and within it, will give rise to a new, more cohesive working-class movement able to act beyond national borders on a more consistent and decisive basis remains to be seen, but my own research indicates that it is not to be ruled out. On the other hand, if such a class does not find avenues for exercizing its own interests, the combination of a labor market segmented by nationality and a workforce geographically dispersed and working under conditions of flexibility does not suggest that the future of democratic politics is necessarily a bright one. If the world reflects the Veneto experience writ large, the dangers of racism, exploitation, forced labor, social fragmentation, and growing inequality may confront the workers of all nations as they move through the worldwide web of their own making to construct the world labor market. But the Veneto experience is also one of class unity transcending the boundaries of citizen and immigrant, of national differences and religious orientations. These different possible outcomes will be the result of processes, both local and worldwide, in which migrant communities seem sure to play an important role. It remains to be seen whether their role will be to link the various sectors of the world working class, but based on the experience in Italy, it cannot be ruled out. Should the making of the planetary working class from the transformations of structural adjustment, flexible work, and migrant communities lead to a more coherent movement in their own interests, and to expansion of their networks of material life at the expense of the mechanisms of value production, our conceptual apparatus for sociological study will require even more retooling than is suggested here. For we recall that the project of the workers of the world, as prophesied so long ago, was to be the abolition of their own condition as workers and to inherit the world.

Notes

1.   Linda Basch, Nina Glick Schiller and Cristina Szanton Blanc, *Nations Unbound: Transnational Projects, Postcolonial Predicaments, and Deterritorialized Nation-States* (Langhorne, Pennsylvania, Yverdon, Switzerland, and other cities: Gordon and Breach, 1994), pp. 7, 21-22.

2. Nestor Rodriguez, "Battle for the Border: Notes on Autonomous Migration, Transnational Communities and the State," *Social Justice* 23(3) (Fall 1996).

3. Basch, Schiller and Blanc, *Nations Unbound*, pp. 21-22.

4. Ibid., p. 22.

5. Rodriguez, "Autonomous Migration," p. 23.

6. Ibid.

7. Karl Marx and Frederich Engels, *The Communist Manifesto* (Oxford and New York: Oxford University Press, 1992), pp. 5-11.

8. E.P. Thompson, *The Making of the English Working Class* (New York: Vintage, 1963); Ira Katznelson, "Working Class Formation: Constructing Cases and Comparisons," in Katznelson and Zolberg, eds., *Working Class Formation* (Princeton: Princeton University Press, 1986), p. 11; Gareth Stedman-Jones, *Languages of Class: Studies in English Working Class History 1832–1982* (New York: Cambridge University Press, 1983), p. 2.

9. Jurgen Kocka, "Problems of Working-Class Formation in Germany: The Early Years, 1800–1875," and Mary Nolan, "Economic Crisis, State Policy, and Working Class Formation in Germany, 1870–1900," both in Katznelson and Zolberg, *Working Class Formation*.

10. Martin Shefter, "Trade Unions and Political Machines: The Organization and Disorganization of the American Working Class in the Late Nineteenth Century," in Katznelson and Zolberg, *Working Class Formation*, p. 239.

11. Some useful recent studies which have found some common aspects of workers' movements in the Third World include, Roger Southall, ed., *Labour and Unions in Asia and Africa: Contemporary Issues* (New York: St. Martin's Press, 1988), see especially Roger Southall, "Introduction," p. 5 and *passim*; Ronaldo Munck, *The New International Labour Studies: An Introduction* (London: Zed 1988), p. 3; Robin Cohen, *Contested Domains: Debates in International Labour Studies* (London: Zed, 1991).

12. See as representatives and analyses of these three viewpoints, Ernesto Laclau, *New Reflections on the Revolution of Our Time* (London: Verso, 1990); and Klaus Eder, *The New Politics of Class: Social Movements and Cultural Dynamics in Advanced Societies* (London: Sage 1993); Andre Gorz, *Farewell to the Working Class* (Boston: South End Press 1983); and my response, "The Working Class Waves Bye-Bye: A Proletarian Response to Andre Gorz," in Midnight Notes, *Lemming Notes* (Jamaica Plain, Massachusetts: 1984); David Harvey, *The Condition of Postmodernity*; see also the critique of such viewpoints in Ellen Meiksens Wood, *The Retreat from Class* (London: Verso, 1986).

13. Wallerstein, *Modern World System*, pp. 1-2.

14. See Beverly J. Silver, "World Scale Patterns of Labor-Capital Conflict" in *Review* 18(1) (Winter 1995).

15. See Immanual Wallerstein, Giovanni Arrighi et al., *Anti-Systemic*

Movements (New York: Verso, 1990).

16. See, for instance, Charles Tilly, *Big Structures, Large Processes, Huge Comparisons* (New York: Russell Sage Foundation, 1985); the phrase about the forest and the trees comes from a lecture in Spring 1992 in Professor Giovanni Arrighi's seminar on "Urban and Industrial Issues" at Binghamton University. In fact, the trees in a forest are linked to one another by a network of underground fungus, and the conceptual distinction between forests and trees, at least in botany and forestry, is a non-existent one. See Stephen Jay Gould, "A Humongous Fungus Among Us," in Stephen Jay Gould, *Dinosaur in A Haystack: Reflections in Natural History* (London: Penguin, 1997), pp. 336-37; see also Aristide Zolberg, "How Many Exceptionalisms?," in Katznelson and Zolberg, *Working Class Formation*, p. 430, where we learn "what is to be explained, the contributions of economic and political structures to working-class formation will now be explored by considering them as independent variables." The problem is not that this influence is not important, but rather that on the one hand the influence is nowhere seen in this study to be reciprocal, or to use a seemingly out-of-date term, dialectical, and on the other hand that the state and economic structures precisely cannot be independent variables both because they are themselves inter-related and because they "contain" human subjects, indeed that very working class which they influence. The view of the state as an "independent variable" rather than as a social relation linked to class interests and conflicts, has recently been revived by the work of Theda Skocpol. See her *States and Social Revolutions* (Cambridge: Harvard University Press, 1983); see also Peter Evans, Dietrich Reushemeyer and Theda Scokpol, eds., *Bringing the State Back In* (New York: Cambridge University Press 1985); for a view which sees state forms as being contingent and even dependent variables resulting from the outcome of class conflicts during industrialization, especially the outcomes of rural class conflicts, see the classic Barrington Moore, *Social Origins of Dictatorship and Democracy* (London: Penguin, 1966); for a marxist analysis heavily influenced by structuralist methodologies which is ironically less attentive to the differences in historical periods, see Perry Anderson, *Lineages of the Absolutist State* (London: New Left Books, 1974).

17. Tilly, *Big Structures*, op. cit., Katznelson, "Constructing Cases and Comparisons," p. 13.

18. World Bank, *World Development Report 1995* (Washington: World Bank, 1995); French version: Banque Mondiale, *Le Monde du Travail dans un Economie sans Frontieres: Rapport sur le développement dans le monde 1995* (Paris: Banque Mondiale, 1995).

19. Ibid. p. 77 (French version). The Bank, perhaps ironically, in stressing the impact of the Gulf War on the recomposition of the migrant working class in the Gulf, echoes, though of course from a very different point of

view, the analysis of Midnight Notes, *Midnight Oil*, which in 1992 stressed this recomposition as a central global working class experience.

20. See, among others, C.L.R. James, *The Black Jacobins*; Cedric Robinson, *Black Marxism: The Making of the Black Radical Tradition* (London: Zed Press, 1983); Tony Martin, *Race First: The Ideological and Organizational Struggles of Marcus Garvey and the Universal Negro Improvement Association* (Westport: Greenwood Press, 1976); W.E.B. DuBois, *Black Reconstruction in America: An Essay Toward a History of the Part Which Black Folk Played in the Attempt to Reconstruct Democracy in America 1860–1880* (New York: Harcourt, Brace, 1935); Horace Campbell, *Rasta and Resistance: From Marcus Garvey to Walter Rodney* (Trenton: Africa World Press, 1987); Robin D.G. Kelley, *Race Rebels: Culture, Politics and the Black Working Class* (New York: The Free Press, 1994).

21. Even a study which takes cases country by country, such as the essays in Richard Sandbrook and Robin Cohen, *The Development of an African Working Class* (London: Longman, 1975), takes for granted that the subject under examination is singular as in the title, and seeks both local specificities and the overall tendency of a class seen to be a continental, if not inter-continental subject.

22. Donna Gabaccia, *Migrants and Militants:Rural Sicilians Become American Workers* (New Brunswick: Rutgers University Press, 1988); Peter Linebaugh, *The London Hanged:Crime and Civil Society in the Eighteenth Century* (New York: Cambridge University Press, 1993); Peter Linebaugh, "All the Atlantic Mountains Shook"; Peter Linebaugh, "Jubilitating: How the Atlantic Working Class Used the Biblical Jubilee with Some Success," in Midnight Notes, *The New Enclosures* (Jamaica Plain: 1990).

23. One social analyst who demystifies the current assumption that greater mobility of capital and labor means greater freedom of movement, and who sees a general state tendency toward the use of borders as social control on a world scale is Alan Dowty, *Closed Borders: The Contemporary Assault on Freedom of Movement* (Binghamton: Twentieth Century Fund, 1987), despite its limitation to liberal categories, this remains a useful study of state activity in relation to migrants, nomadic and stateless peoples and refugees at the global level.

24. Midnight Notes, *The New Enclosures*; Midnight Notes, *Midnight Oil*.

25. In Harry Cleaver, *Reading Capital Politically* (Austin: University of Texas Press, 1980).

26. See, for instance, June Nash and M.P. Fernandez-Kelly, eds, *Women, Men and the International Division of Labor*; Ehrenreich and Fuentes, *Women and the Global Factory*; Kathryn Ward, ed., *Women and the Global Restructuring*; A. Sivanandan, *A Different Hunger* (London: Pluto, 1983); A. Sivanandan, *Communities of Resistance* (New York: Verso, 1990); David Harvey, *The Condition of Postmodernity*; A.

Rothstein and M. Blim, eds., *Anthropology and the Global Factory* (New York: Cambridge University Press, 1992).

27. See Mariarosa Dalla Costa, "Power of Women and the Subversion of the Community"; Giovanna Franca Dalla Costa, *Un lavoro d'amore: La violenza fisica componente essenziale del "trattamento" maschile nei confronti delle donne* (Rome: Edizioni delle Donne, 1978); Mariarosa Dalla Costa and Giovanna Franca Dalla Costa, eds., *Paying the Price: Women and the Politics of International Economic Strategy*, Silvia Federici and Leopoldina Fortunati, *Il Grande Calibano: Storia del corpo sociale ribelle nella prima fase del capitale* (Milan: FrancoAngeli, 1984).

BIBLIOGRAPHY

BOOKS, PAPERS AND PUBLICATIONS

Adler, Stephen. 1977. *International Migration and Dependence*. Hampshire: Saxon House.

Aglietta, Michel. 1979. *A Theory of Capitalist Regulation: The U.S. Experience*. New York: Verso.

Allum, Percia and Felia Allum. 1996. "The Resistable Rise of the New Neapolitan Camorra," in Stephen Gundle and Simon Parker eds., *The New Italian Republic*. London: Routledge.

Amin, Ash. 1989. "A Model of the Small Firm in Italy," in Edward Goodman, Julia Bamford, and Peter Saynor, eds., *Small Firms and Industrial Districts in Italy*. New York: Routledge.

————. 1994. "Post-Fordism: Models, Fantasies and Phantoms of Transition," in Ash Amin, ed., *Post-Fordism: A Reader*. Cambridge: Blackwell.

Amir, Rashad Al. 1995. "Gli immigrati in Veneto." Paper presented as part of ISPES sponsored conference, Il sostegno alle famiglie nell'auto-organizzazione delle comunità immigrate, Oct. 27-28, Rome.

Amjad, Rashid. 1989. "An Overview," in Rashid Amjad, ed., *To the Gulf and Back: Studies on the Economic Impact of Asian Labour Migration*. New Delhi: International Labour Organization.

Anastasia, Bruno 1996. "I lavoratori extracomunitari," in Ministero del Lavoro Regione Veneto. *Il mercato del lavor nel Veneto 1995 Report*. Milan: FrancoAngeli.

Anastasia, Bruno and Giancarlo Corò. 1996. *Evoluzione di un'economia regionale: Il Nordest dopo il successo*. Venice: Nuova Dimensione.

Anderson, Bridget. 1993. *Britain's Secret Slaves: An Investigation into the Plight of Overseas Domestic Workers in the United Kingdom*, with contributions from Anti-Slavery International and Kalayaan and the Migrant Domestic Workers. London: Anti-Slavery International.

Anderson, Grace. 1974. *Networks of Contact: The Portugese and Toronto*. Waterloo, Ontario: Wilfred Laurier University Press.

Anderson, Perry. 1974. *Lineages of the Absolutist State*. London: New Left Books.

Arrighi, Giovanni, ed. 1985. *Semiperipheral Development: The Politics of Southern Europe in the Twentieth Century*. Beverly Hills: Sage.

Bagnasco, Arnaldo. 1977. *Tre Italie*. Bologna: Il Mulino.

Bagnasco, A., and C. Trigilia, eds. 1984. *Società e politica nelle aree di piccola imprese: Il caso di Bassano*. Venice: Arsenale Editrice.

Banco Ambrosiano Veneto and Federazione dell'Industria del Veneto. 1993. *Struttura e dinamica dell'industria nel Veneto 1989-1992*. Milan: FrancoAngeli.

Banque Mondiale, (World Bank). 1995. *Le Monde du Travail dans un Economie sans Frontieres: Rapport sur le dèveloppement dans le monde 1995*. Washington: World Bank.

Barile, Giuseppe, Alessandro Dal Lago, Aldo Marchetti and Patrizia Galeazzo. 1994. *Tra due rive: la nuova immigrazione a Milano*. Milan: FrancoAngeli.

Barjaba, Kosta, Georges Lapassade and Luigi Perrone. 1996. *Naufragi Albanesi*. Rome: Sensibili alle foglie.

Barkan, Joanne. 1984. *Visions of Emancipation: The Italian Workers' Movement Since 1945*. New York: Praeger.

Barsotti, Odo, ed. 1994. *Dal Marocco in Italia: Prospettive di un'indagine incrociata*. Milan:FrancoAngeli.

Basch, Linda, Nina Glick Schiller, and Cristina Szanton Blanc. 1994. *Nations Unbound: Transnational Projects, Postcolonial Predicaments and Detteritorialized Nation-States*. Amsterdam: Gordon and Breach.

Bathily, Abdoulaye. "Senegal's Structural Adjustment Programme and its Economic and Social Effects: The Political Economy of Regression," in Bade Onimode, ed., *The IMF, the World Bank and the African Debt*. London: Zed.

Behrman, L. 1970. *Muslim Brotherhoods and Politics in Senegal*. Cambridge: Harvard University Press.

Bellandi, Marco. 1989. "The Role of Small Fims in the Development of Italian Manufacturing Districts," in Goodman and Bamford, eds., *Small Firms and Industrial Districts in Italy*. New York: Routledge.

Bello, Walden. *Development Debacle: The World Bank in the Philippines*. Berkeley: Institute for Food and Development Policy.

Belotti, Valerio. 1993. *Osservatorio sui lavoratori dipendenti nel Veneto*. Venice: Fondazione Corazzin.

———, ed. 1994. *Voci da lontano: breve viaggio in quattro comunità di immigrati che vivono e lavorano nel bassanese*. Bassano del Grappa: Libreria TEMPOlibero Editrice.

———. Forthcoming. *Vendere in spiaggia: l'abusivismo commerciale nella Riviera emiliano-romagnolo*. Vicenza: Istituto Poster.

Beneria, Lourdes, and Marta Roldan. 1987. *The Crossroads of Class and Gender*. Chicago: University of Chicago Press.

Berninghaus, Siegried, and Hans Gunther Seiger-Vogt. 1991. *International Migration under Incomplete Information: A Micro-Economic Approach.* New York: Springer-Verlag.

Bettin, Levi, and Chiara Volpato. 1993. "L'attegiamento degli studenti Vicentini nei confronti degli immigrati," in Ubaldo Alifuoco, ed. *Verso una società multietnica,* Bologna: Quaderni della Fondazione Istituto Gramsci Veneto n. 13.

Bisogno, E., F. Nero, C. Gatto. 1994. *Gli immigrati extracomunitari nel Veneto.* Venice: CEDAM.

Blim, Michael. 1990. *Made in Italy: Small-Scale Industrialization and its Consequences.* New York: Praeger.

Bohning, W. R. 1981. "Elements of a Theory of International Economic Migration to Industrial Nation States," in M. Kritz, C. Keely, and S. Tomasi, eds., *Global Trends in Migration: Theory and Research on International Population Movements.* Staten Island: Center for Migration Studies.

Bonat, Zuwuqhu A., and Yahaya A. Abdullahi. 1989. "The World Bank, the IMF and Nigeria's Rural Economy," in Bade Onimode, ed., *The IMF, the World Bank and the African Debt.* London: Zed.

Bonefield, Werner, and John Holloway. 1991. *Post-Fordism and Social Form: A Marxist Debate on the Post-Fordist State.* London: MacMillan.

Borneman, John. 1991. *After the Wall: East Meets West in the New Berlin.* New York: Basic Books.

Braverman, Harry. 1974. *Labor and Monopoly Capital.* New York: Monthly Review Press.

Brown, Dee. 1971. *Bury My Heart at Wounded Knee.* New York: H. Holt & Co.

Brunello, Piero. 1981. *Ribelli, questanti e banditti: proteste contadine in Veneto e in Friuli 1814-66.* Venice: Marsilio Editori.

Bruni, Michele, ed. 1994. *Attratti, Sospinti, Respinti: I lavoratori immigrati nelle aziende bolognesi.* Milan: FrancoAngeli.

Brydon, L., and W.T.S. Gould. 1984. *International Migration of Skilled Labour within Africa.* Liverpool: University of Liverpool Press.

Bull, Anna, and Paul Corner. 1993. *From Peasant to Entrepreneur: The Survival of the Family Economy in Italy.* Oxford: Berg.

Cafagna, Luciano. 1989. *Dualismo e sviluppo nella storia d'Italia.* Milan: Einaudi.

Caffentzis, C. George. 1990. "Africa and Self-Reproducing Automata," in Midnight Notes, *The New Enclosures.* Jamaica Plain, Massachusetts.

———. 1992. "The Work-Energy Crisis and the Apocalypse," in Midnight Notes, *Midnight Oil: Work, Energy, War 1973-1992.* Brooklyn: Autonomedia.

———. 1992. "Rambo on the Barbary Shore," in Midnight Notes, *Midnight Oil: Work, Energy, War 1973-1992.* Brooklyn: Autonomedia.

———. 1995. "The Fundamental Implications of the Debt Crisis for Social Reproduction in Africa," in Mariarosa Dalla Costa and Giovanna Franca

Dalla Costa, eds., *Paying the Price: Women and the Politics of International Economic Strategy*. Atlantic Highlands and London: Zed.

———. 1995. "On the Scottish Origins of Civilization," in Silvia Federici, ed., *Enduring Western Civilization: The Construction of the Concept of Western Civilization and its Others*. Westport: Praeger.

Campani, Giovanna. 1993. "Le reticoli sociali delle donne immigrate in Italia," in Marcella Delle Donne, Umberto Melotti, and Stefano Petilli, *Immigrazione in Europa: Solidarietà e conflitto*. Rome: Università degli Studi di Roma CEDISS.

Campbell, Horace. 1987. *Rasta and Resistance: From Marcus Garvey to Walter Rodney*. Trenton: Africa World Press.

Canack, W. L., and D. Levi. 1989. "Social Costs of Adjustment in Latin America," in J. F. Weeks, ed., *Debt Disaster? Banks, Governments and Multinationals Confront the Crisis*. New York: New York University Press.

Capra, Fritjof. 1996. *The Web of Life*. New York and London: HarperCollins.

Carello, Adrian Nicola. 1989. *The Northern Question: Italy's Participation in the European Community and the Mezzogiorno's Underdevelopment*. Newark, Delaware: University of Delaware Press.

Caritas. 1997. *Dossier Statistico Immigrazione 1996*. Rome: Caritas.

Caritas diocesana di Roma and Siares. 1989. *Stranieri a Roma*. Rome: Siares

Caritas Italiana and Fondazione E. Zancan. 1997. *I bisogni dimenticati: rapporto 1996 su emarginazione ed esclusione sociale*. Milan: Feltrinelli.

Castegnaro, A. 1993. *Il sistema veneto e le migrazioni internazionali: politica e promozione dei diritti civili*. Padua: Cleup.

Castells, Manuel. 1979. "Immigrant Workers and Class Struggles in Advanced Capitalism: The Western European Experience," in R. Cohen, P. Gutkind, and P. Brazier, eds., *Peasants and Proletarians*. New York: Monthly Review Press.

———. 1994. *The Information City*. Berkeley: University of California Press.

Castles, Stephen, and G. Kosack. 1973. *Immigrant Workers and Class Structure in Western Europe*. London: Oxford University Press.

Castles, Stephen. 1984. *Here for Good: Western Europe's New Ethnic Minorities*. London: Pluto Press.

———. 1989. *Migrant Workers and the Transformation of Western Societies*. Ithaca: Cornell University Press.

Castles, Stephen, and Mark J. Miller. 1993. *The Age of Migration: International Population Movements in the Modern World*. New York: Guilford Press.

CENSIS. 1997. *Italy Today: Social Pictures and Trends 1996*. Milan: FrancoAngeli.

Chandler, Alfred. 1977. *The Visible Hand: The Managerial Revolution in American Business*. Cambridge: Harvard University Press.

Cheng, Lucy, and Edna Bonacich, eds. 1984. *Labor Migration under Capitalism*. Berkeley: University of California Press.

Cheru, Fantu. 1989. *The Silent Revolution in Africa*. Atlantic Highlands and London: Zed.

Chittolini, Giorgio. 1991. "The Italian City-State and its Territory," in Anthony Molho, ed., *City-States in Classical Antiquity and Medieval Italy*. Ann Arbor: University of Michigan Press.

Chossudovsky, Michel. 1997. *The Globalization of Poverty: Impacts of IMF and World Bank Reforms*. Atlantic Highlands and London: Zed.

Chubb, Judith. 1982. *Patronage, Power and Poverty in Southern Italy: A Tale of Two Cities*. New York: Cambridge University Press.

Cleaver, Harry. 1980. *Reading Capital Politically*. Austin: University of Texas Press.

————. 1990. "The Origins of the Debt Crisis," in Midnight Notes, *The New Enclosures*. Jamaica Plain, Massachusetts.

Cohen, Robin. 1987. *The New Helots: Migrants in the International Division of Labor*. Brookfield, Vermont: Gower.

————. 1991. *Contested Domains: Debates in International Labour Studies*. Atlantic Highlands and London: Zed.

Colatrella, Steven. 1997. "L'interazione tra famiglie immigrate e famiglie locali: la situazione nel Veneto." Paper presented at the ISPES sponsored conference, L'interazione tra famiglie immigrate e famiglie locali, April 17-18, Rome.

Comune di Padova. 1996. *Informazione Demografica sulla Populazione Rapporto 1995*. Padua: Comune di Padua.

Comune di Vicenza. 1996. *La presenza dei cittadini stranieri nella Provincia di Vicenza Rapporto 1995*. Vicenza: Comune di Vicenza.

Cornia, A. C., R. Jolly, and F. Stewart, eds. *Per un aggiustimento dal volto umano*. Milan: FrancoAngeli.

Coulon, Christian. 1988. "Women, Islam and Baraka," in Donal B. Cruise O'Brien and Christian Coulon, eds. *Charisma and Brotherhoods in African Islam*. Oxford: Clarendon Press.

Cox, Oliver. 1948. *Caste, Class and Race*. New York: Monthly Review.

Dal Lago, Alessandro. 1994. "La nuova immigrazione a Milano: Il caso del Marocco," in Giuseppe Barile, Alessandro Dal Lago, Aldo Marchetti, and Patrizia Galeazzo, *Tra due rive: la nuova immigrazione a Milano*. Milan: FrancoAngeli.

Dalla Costa, Giovanna Franca. 1978. *Un lavoro d'amore: La violenza fisica componente essenziale del trattamento maschile nei confronti delle donne*. Rome: Edizioni delle.

Dalla Costa, Mariarosa. 1974. *The Power of Women and the Subversion of the Community*. London: Falling Wall Press.

————. 1974. "Emigrazione e riproduzione," in *L'operaio multinazionale in Europa*. Milan: Feltrinelli.

Dalla Costa, Mariarosa, and Giovanna Franca Dalla Costa, eds. 1995. *Paying the Price: Women and the Politics of International Economic Strategy*. Atlantic Highland and London.

————, eds. 1996. *Donne, sviluppo e lavoro di riproduzione.* Milan: FrancoAngeli.

Danaher, Kevin, and Muhammad Yunus, eds. *50 Years is Enough: The Case against the World Bank and the International Monetary Fund.* Boston: South End Press.

Davis, David Brion. 1996. *The Problem of Slavery in Western Culture.* Ithaca: Cornell University Press.

della Porta, Donatella. 1996. "The System of Corrupt Exchange in Local Government," in Stephen Gundle and Simon Parker eds. *The New Italian Republic.* London: Routledge.

Di Liegro, Don Luigi. 1997. *Immigrazione: un punto di vista.* Rome: Sensibili alle Foglie.

Diop, Abdoulaye-Bara. 1977. *La Société Wolof.* Paris: Karthala.

Dominelli, Lena. 1986. *Love and Wages: The Impact of Imperialism, State Intervention and Women's Domestic Labor on Workers' Control in Algeria 1962-1972.* Norwich: Novata Press.

Dowty, Alan. 1987. *Closed Borders: The Contemporary Assault on Freedom of Movement.* Binghamton: Twentieth Century Fund.

DuBois, W.E.B. 1969. *The Suppression of the African Slave Trade to the United States of America 1638-1870.* New York: Shocken Books.

————. 1973. *Black Reconstruction in America.* New York: Atheneum.

Duggan, Christopher. 1994. *A Concise History of Italy.* Cambridge: Cambridge University Press.

Dwyer, Kevin. 1994. *Arab Voices: The Human Rights Debate in the Middle East.* New York and London: Routledge.

The Ecologist. 1992. *Whose Common Future?* London: The Ecologist.

Eder, Klaus. 1993. *The New Politics of Class: Social Movements and Cultural Dynamics in Advanced Societies.* London: Sage.

Ehrenreich, Barbara, and Anna Fuentes. 1983. *The Global Assembly Line.* New York: Monthly Review.

Elbadawi, Ibraham A. 1992. *Adjustment Lending and Economic Performance in Sub-Saharan Africa in the 1980s.* Washington: World Bank.

Evans, Peter, Dietrich Reushemeyer, and Theda Skocpol. 1985. *Bringing the State Back In.* New York: Cambridge University Press.

Evans, Robert. 1976. *Life and Politics in a Venetian Community.* Notre Dame: University of Notre Dame.

Eviota, Elizabeth Uy. 1992. *The Political Economy of Gender: Women and the Sexual Division of Labour in the Philippines.* Atlantic Highlands and London: Zed.

Federici, Silvia, and Leopoldina Fortunati. 1984. *Il Grande Calibano: Storia del corpo sociale ribelle nella prima fase del capitale.* Milan: FrancoAngeli.

Federici, Silvia. 1990. "Inscrutible China," in Midnight Notes, *The New Enclosures.* Jamaica Plain, Massachusetts.

————. 1992. "Development and Underdevelopment in Nigeria," in Midnight Notes, *Midnight Oil: Work, Energy, War 1973-1992*. Brooklyn: Autonomedia.

————. 1995. "Economic Crisis and Demographic Policy in Sub-Saharan Africa: The Case of Nigeria," in Mariarosa Dalla Costa and Giovanna Franca Dalla Costa, eds., *Paying the Price: Women and the Politics of International Economic Strategy*. Atlantic Highlands and London: Zed.

————. 1996. "Riproduzione e lotta feminista nella nuova divisione internazionale del lavoro," in Mariarosa Dalla Costa and Giovanna Franca Dalla Costa, eds., *Donne, sviluppo e lavoro di riproduzione*. Milan: FrancoAngeli.

Ferencz, B. B. 1979. *Less Than Slaves: Jewish Forced Labor and the Quest for Compensation*. Cambridge: Harvard University Press.

Fondazione Cariplo per le Iniziative e lo Studio sulla Multietnicità (ISMU). 1996. *Primo rapporto sulle migrazioni 1995*. Milan: FrancoAngeli.

————. 1997. *Secondo rapporto sulle migrazioni 1996*. Milan: FrancoAngeli.

Fondazione Corazzin. 1992. *La Società Veneta 1991*. Venice: CEDAM.

————. 1993. *La Società Veneta 1992*. Venice: CEDAM.

Fortunati, Leopoldina. 1996. *The Arcana of Reproduction*. Brooklyn: Autonomedia.

Franzina, Emilio. 1994. "Veneto: una società dinamica al bivio tra globalizzazione e leghismo," in Paul Ginsborg, ed., *Stato dell'Italia*. Milan: Il Saggiatore.

Freid, E. R., and Philip H. Trezise, eds. 1989. *Third World Debt: The Next Phase*. Washington: Brookings Institute.

Furlong, Paul. 1996. "Political Catholicism and the Strange Death of the Christian Democrats," in Stephen Gundle and Simon Parker, eds., *The New Italian Republic: From the Fall of the Berlin Wall to Berlusconi*. London and New York: Routledge.

Gabaccia, Donna. 1988. *Migrants and Militants: Rural Sicilians Become American Workers*. New Brunswick: Rutgers University Press.

Gambino, Ferruccio. 1992. "The Imaginery Acceptance of Immigrants in an Italian City." Photocopy of unpublished article.

Genovese, Eugene. 1976. *Roll Jordan Roll: The World the Slaves Made*. New York: Random House.

George, Susan. 1988. *A Fate Worse Than Debt*. New York: Grove.

Ginsborg, Paul. 1985. *A History of Contemporary Italy: Society and Politics 1943-1988*. London: Penguin.

————, ed. 1994. *Stato dell'Italia*. Milan: Il Saggiatore.

Goodman, Edward. 1989. "Introduction: The Political Economy of the Small Firm in Italy," in Edward Goodman, Julia Bamford, Peter Saynor, eds., *Small Firms and Industrial Districts in Italy*. New York: Routledge.

Goodno, James B. 1991. *The Philippines: Land of Broken Promises*. Atlantic Highlands and London: Zed.

Gould, Stephen Jay. 1997. "A Humongous Fungus Among Us," in Stephen Jay Gould, *Dinosaur in a Haystack: Reflections in Natural History*. London and New York: Penguin.

Gorz, Andre. 1983. *Farewell to the Working Class*. Boston: South End Press.

Gramsci, Antonio. 1989. *Selections from the Prison Notebooks*. New York: International Publishers.

Gundle, Stephen, and Simon Parker, eds. 1996. *The New Italian Republic*. London: Routledge.

Gundle, Stephen, and Simon Parker. 1996. "Introduction," in Stephen Gundle and Simon Parker, eds., *The New Italian Republic*. London: Routledge.

Haggard, Stephen, Jean-Dominique Lafay. and Christain Morrisson. 1995. *The Political Feasibility of Adjustment in Developing Countries*. Paris: OECD.

Hammar, Thomas. 1990. *Democracy and the Nation-State: Aliens, Denizens, and Citizens in a World of International Migration*. Aldershot: Averbury Press.

Hammond, Ross, and Lisa McGowan. 1994. "Ghana: The World Bank's Sham Showcase," in Kevin Danaher and Muhammad Yunus, eds., *50 Years is Enough: The Case against the World Bank and the International Monetary Fund*. Boston: South End Press.

Harvey, David. 1989. *The Condition of Postmodernity*. Cambridge: Blackwell.

Havnevik, K. J., ed. 1987. *The IMF and the World Bank in Africa*. Uppsala: Scandanavian Institute of African Studies.

Herbert, Ulrich. 1990. *A History of Foreign Workers in Germany 1880-1980: Seasonal Workers/Forced Laborers/Guest Workers*. Ann Arbor: University of Michigan Press.

Heyzer, Noeleen, Geertje Lychlama à Nijeholt, and Nedra Weerakoon. 1992. *The Trade in Domestic Workers: Causes, Mechanisms and Consequences of International Migration*, Vol. 1. Atlantic Highlands and London: Zed.

Hicks, J. R. 1932. *The Theory of Wages*. London: MacMillan Press.

Hindess, B., and P. Q. Hirst. 1977. *Modes of Production and Social Formation*. London: MacMillan.

Holmes, Douglas R. 1989. *Cultural Disenchantments: Worker Peasantries in Northeast Italy*. Princeton: Princeton University Press.

Homse, E. L. 1967. *Foreign Labor in Nazi Germany*. Princeton: Princeton University Press.

Hudson, Ray, and Jim Lewis, eds. 1985. *Uneven Development in Southern Europe: Studies of Accumulation, Class, Migration and the State*. New York: Metheun.

Hutchfel, Eboe, ed. 1987. *The IMF and Ghana: The Confidential Record*. Atlantic Highlands and London: Zed.

International NGO Forum. 1994. "World Bank and IMF Lending in the Philippines," in Kevin Danaher and Muhammad Yunus, eds., *50 Years is Enough: The Case against the World Bank and the International Monetary Fund*. Boston: South End Press.

Iraci, Fedeli L. 1990. *Razzismo e immigrazione: Il caso Italia*. Milan: Acropoli.

Istituto Ricerche Economico-Sociale del Piemonte. 1993. *Uguale e Diversi: Il mondo culturale, le reti di rapporti, i lavori degli immigrati non europei a Torino*. Turin: Rossenberg and Schiller.

James, C.L.R. 1970. *The Black Jacobins*. Vintage: New York.

Jeffries, Richard. 1978. *Class, Ideology and Power in Africa: The Railwaymen of Sekondi*. Cambridge: Cambridge University Press.

Jennings, Francis. 1988. *The Invasion of America*. New York: Cambridge University Press.

Jessop, B. 1991. "Thatcherism and Flexibility: The White Heat of a Post-Fordist Revolution," in B. Jessop, H. Kastendiek, K. Neilsen, and O.Pedersen, eds., *The Politics of Flexibility*. Aldershot: Edward Algar.

———. 1994. "Post-Fordism and the State," in Ash Amin, ed., *Post-Fordism: A Reader*. Cambridge: Blackwell.

Jones, Maldwyn Allen. 1992. *American Immigration*. Chicago: University of Chicago Press.

Kang, Su Dol. 1996. *Globalization of the Labor Market: Foreign Labor Issue in Korea*. Seoul: Labor Institute.

Kapur, Ishan, Michael T. Hadjimichael, Paul Hilbers, Jerald Schiff, and Phillippe Szymczak. 1992. *Ghana: Adjustment and Growth 1983-1991*. Washington: IMF.

Katznelson, Ira. 1986. "Working Class Formation: Constructing Cases and Comparisons," in Ira Katznelson and Aristide Zolberg, eds., *Working Class Formation*. Princeton: Princeton University Press.

Kelley, Robin D. G. 1994. *Race Rebels: Culture, Politics and the Black Working Class*. New York: The Free Press.

Khouma, Pap. 1990. *Io, Venditore di elefanti*. Milan: Garzanti.

King, Russell. 1985. *The Industrial Geography of Italy*. London: Croom Helm.

King, Russell. 1989. "Return Migration and Regional Economic Development: Overview," in Russell King, ed., *Return Migration and Regional Economic Problems*. London: Croom Helm.

Kocka, Jurgen. 1986. "Problems of Working-Class Formation in Germany: The Early Years, 1800-1875," in Ira Katznelson and Aristide Zolberg, eds., *Working Class Formation*. Princeton: Princeton University Press.

Kojo, Arthur. 1983. *Ghana's Food Crisis: Alternative Perspectives*. Philadelphia: Africa Research and Publications Project Inc. Working Paper #16.

Kojo, Sebastian Amanor. 1994. *The New Frontier: Farmer's Response to Land Degradation, A West African Study*. Atlantic Highlands and London: Zed.

Koptiuch, Kristin. 1992. "The Egyptian Petty Commodity Sector," in M. Blim and A. Rothstein, *Anthropology and the Global Factory*. New York: Praeger.

Korner, Peter, ed. 1986. *The IMF and the Debt Crisis: A Guide to the Third World's Dilemma*. London: Zed.

Kuhn, A, and A. Wolpe, eds. 1978. *Feminism and Materialism: Women and Modes of Production*. London: Routledge & Kegan Paul.

Kurzwell, Edith. 1983. *Italian Entrepreneurs: Rearguard of Progress*. New York: Praeger.

Kwesi, Jonah. 1989. "The Social Impact of Ghana's Adjustment Program 1983-1986," in Bade Onimode, ed., *The IMF, the World Bank and the African Debt: The Social and Political Impact*, Vol.2. Atlantic Highlands and London: Zed.

Kwong, Peter. 1992. *The New Chinatown*. New York: Hill & Wang.

Laclau, Ernesto. 1990. *New Reflections on the Revolution of Our Time*. London: Verso.

Lane, Frederick. 1973. *Venice: A Maritime Republic*. Baltimore: Johns Hopkins University Press.

Lapidus, Ira. 1990. *A History of Islamic Societies*. New York: Cambridge University Press.

Lash, S., and J. Urry. 1987. *The End of Organized Capitalism*. Madison: University of Wisconsin Press.

Lawless, Richard. 1989. "Return Migration to Algeria: The Impact of State Intervention," in Russell King, ed., *Return Migration and Regional Economic Problems*. London: Croom Helm.

Lawrence, Peter, ed. 1986. *World Recession and Food Crisis in Africa*. London: James Currey.

Lee, Everett. 1969. "A Theory of Migration," in J. A. Jackson, *Migration*. Cambridge: Cambridge University Press.

Le Goff, Jacques. 1988. *Your Money or Your Life: Economy and Religion in the Middle Ages*. New York: Zone Books.

Leonardi, Robert, and Douglas A. Wertman. 1989. *Italian Christian Democracy: The Politics of Dominance*. London: MacMillan.

Lewis, Sasha. 1979. *Slave Trade Today: America's Exploitation of Illegal Aliens*. Boston: Beacon Press.

Linebaugh, Peter. 1990. "Jubilating: How the Atlantic Working Class Used the Biblical Jubilee with Some Success," in Midnight Notes, *The New Enclosures*. Jamaica Plain, Massachusetts.

———. 1993. *The London Hanged*. London: Penguin Books.

Locke, Richard. 1995. *Remaking the Italian Economy*. Ithaca: Cornell University Press.

Lohmann, Larry. 1995. "Against the Myths," in Marcus Colchester and Larry Lohmann, eds., *The Struggle for Land and the Fate of the Forests*. Atlantic Highlands and London: Zed.

Lopreato, Joseph. 1967. *Peasants No More*. San Francisco: Chandler San Francisco.

Lovell, George W. 1985. *Conquest and Survival in Colonial Guatemala*. Montreal: McGill-Queen's University Press.

Lowry, I. S. 1966. *Migration and Metropolitan Growth: Two Analytical Models*. San Francisco: Chandler.

Lumley, Robert. 1991. *States of Emergency: Social Movements in Italy 1968-1978*. London: Verso.

Lupo, Salvatore. 1996. "The Changing Mezzogiorno: Between Representations and Reality," in Stephen Gundle and Simon Parker, eds., *The New Italian Republic*. London: Routledge.

Macioti, Maria Immacolata, and Enrico Pugliese. 1991. *Gli immigrati in Italia*. Bari: Editori Laterza.

Mageean, Deirdre M. 1991. "From Irish Countryside to American City: The Settlement and Mobility of Ulster Migrants in Philadelphia," in Colin G. Pooley and Ian D. Whyte, eds., *Migrants, Emigrants and Immigrants: A Social History of Migration*. London: Routledge.

Mangione, Jerry, and Ben Morreale. 1992. *La Storia: Five Centuries of Italian-American Experience*. New York: HarperCollins.

Marini, Daniele. 1993. *Vale più la pratica o la grammatica? una indagine sui bisogni formativo-professionalidegli immigrati extracomunitari: l'opinioni dei datori di lavoro*. Venice: Fondazione Corazzin.

Martin, Philip. 1988. "Network Recruitment and Labor Displacement," in David E. Simcox, ed., *U.S. Immigration in the 1980s: Reappraisal and Reform*. Boulder: Westview Press.

Martin, Tony. 1976. *Race First: The Ideological and Organizational Struggles of Marcus Garvey and the Universal Negro Improvement Association*. Westport: Greenwood Press.

Marx, Karl. 1977. *Capital*, Vol. 1. New York: Vintage.

———. 1981. *Capital*, Vol. 3. London: Penguin.

Marx, Karl, and Frederich Engels. 1992. *The Communist Manifesto*. Oxford and New York: Oxford University Press.

Douglas Massey, Rafael Alarcon, Jorge Durand, and Humberto Gonzales. 1987. *Return to Aztlan: The Social Process of International Migration from Western Mexico*. Berkeley Los Angeles and London: University of California Press.

Mauri, L, and L. Breveglieri. 1993. *Da lontano per lavoro: Indagine sull'inserimento lavorativo degli immigrati nel territorio padovano*. Milan: FrancoAngeli.

McCarthy, Patrick. 1997. *The Crisis of the Italian State: From the Origins of the Cold War to the Fall of Berlusconi and Beyond*. New York: St. Martin's Press.

Melotti, Umberto. 1994. *L'Immigrazione: Una sfida per L'Europa*. Milan: Molisv Edizioni Associate.

———. 1997. "International Migration in Europe: Social Projects and Political Cultures," in Tariq Modood and Pnina Werbner, eds., *The Politics of Multiculturalism in the New Europe*. Atlantic Highlands and London: Zed.

Meltzer, Milton. 1993. *Slavery: A World History*. New York: Da Capo.

Menchu, Rigoberta. 1984. *I, Rigoberta Menchu: A Guatemalan Indian Woman*. London and New York: Verso.

Midnight Notes. 1990. *The New Enclosures*. Jamaica Plains, Massachusetts.

————. 1992. *Midnight Oil: Work,Energy, War 1973-1992*. Brooklyn: Autonomedia.

Midnight Notes Collective. 1992. "Oil, Guns and Money," in Midnight Notes, *Midnight Oil: Work, Energy, War 1973-1992*. Brooklyn: Autonomedia.

Mihevc, John. 1995. *The Market Tells Them So: The World Bank and Economic Fundamentalism in Africa*. Atlantic Highlands and London: Zed.

Miles, Robert. 1987. *Capitalism and Unfree Labor: Anomaly or Necessity?* New York: Tavistock Publishers.

Ministero del Lavoro Regione Veneto. 1996. *Il mercato del lavoro nel Veneto 1995 Report*. Milan: FrancoAngeli.

Model, Suzanne W. 1990. "Work and Family: Blacks and Immigrants from South and East Europe," in Virginia Yans-McLaughlin, *Immigration Reconsidered: History, Sociology and Politics*. New York: Oxford University Press.

Moore, Barrington. 1966. *Social Origins of Dictatorship and Democracy*. London and New York: Penguin.

Morgan, Edmund. 1975. *American Slavery, American Freedom*. New York: Norton.

Mori, Giorgio. 1977. *Il capitalismo industriale in Italia*. Rome: Editori Riuniti.

Morris, Richard B. 1946. *Government and Labor in Early America*. New York: Harper & Row.

Mottura, Giovanni, and Pietro Pinto. 1996. *Immigrazione e cambiamento sociale: strategie sindicali e lavoro straniero in Italia*. Rome: Ediesse.

Munck, Ronaldo. 1988. *The New International Labour Studies: An Introduction*. Atlantic Highlands and London: Zed.

Musgrave, Peter. 1992. *Land and Economy in Baroque Italy: Valpolicella 1630-1797*. London: Leicester University Press.

Nanetti, Raffaella Y. 1988. *Growth and Territorial Policies: The Italian Model of Social Capitalism*. New York: Pinter.

Nash, June, and M. P. Fernandez-Kelly. 1983. *Women, Men and the International Division of Labor*. Albany: SUNY Press.

Ndiaye, Abdoulaye. 1994. "Food for Thought: Senegal's Struggle with Structural Adjustment," in Kevin Danaher and Muhammad Yunus, eds., *50 Years is Enough: the Case against the World Bank and the International Monetary Fund*. Boston: South End Press.

Nelli, Humbert S. 1971. *Italians in Chicago 1889-1930*. New York: Oxford University Press.

Nevins, Allen, and Henry Steele Commager. 1986. *A Pocket History of the United States*. New York: Washington Square Press.

Nicaso, Antonio, and Lee Lamothe. 1995. *Global Mafia: The New World Order of Organized Crime*. Toronto: MacMillan.

Nielsen, K. 1991. "Towards a Flexible Future: Theories and Politics," in B. Jessop, H. Kastendiek, K. Nielsen and O. Pedersen, eds., *The Politics of Flexibility*. Aldershot: Edward Elgar.

Nolan, Mary. 1986. "Economic Crisis, State Policy, and Working Class Formation in Germany, 1870-1900," in Ira Katznelson and Aristide Zolberg, eds., *Working Class Formation*. Princeton: Princeton University Press.

O'Brien, Donal B. Cruise. 1971. *The Mourides of Senegal*. Oxford: Clarendon Press.

————. 1988. "Charisma Comes to Town: Mouride Urbanization 1945-1986," in Donal B. Cruise O'Brien and Christain Coulon, eds., *Charisma and Brotherhoods in African Islam*. Oxford: Clarendon Press.

Onimode, Bade, ed. 1989. *The IMF, the World Bank and the African Debt*. London: Zed.

Organization for Economic Cooperation and Development (OECD). 1978. *The Migratory Chain*. Paris: OECD.

————. 1973. *Romania: An Economic Assessment*. Paris: OECD.

————. 1976. *Development Strategy, Employment and Migration: Insight from Models*. Paris: OECD.

Paci, Massimo. 1973. *Mercato del lavoro e classi sociali in Italia*. Bologna: Il Mulino.

————. 1978. *Capitalismo e classi sociali in Italia*. Bologna: Il Mulino.

Pasti, Vladimir. 1997. *The Challenges of Transition: Romania in Transition*. New York: Columbia University Press.

Patterson, Orlando. 1982. *Slavery and Social Death: A Comparative Study*. Cambridge: Harvard University Press.

Payer, Cheryl. 1974. *The Debt Trap*. New York: Monthly Review Press.

————. 1982. *The World Bank*. New York: Monthly Review Press.

Pederson, Poul Ove, Arni Sverrisson, and Meine Pieter Van Dijk. 1994. *Flexible Production: The Dynamics of Small-Scale Industry in the South*. London: IT Publications.

Petras, Elizabeth. 1981. "The Global Labor Market in the Modern World Economy," in M. Kritz, C. Keely and S. Tomasi, eds., *Global Trends in Migration*. Staten Island: Center for Migration Studies.

Pinto, Diana, ed. 1981. *Contemporary Italian Sociology: A Reader*. New York: Cambridge University Press.

Piore, Michael. 1980. *Birds of Passage: Migrant Labor and Industrial Societies*. New York: Cambridge University Press.

Piore, Michael and Charles Sabel. 1984. *The Second Industrial Divide: Prospects for Prosperity*. New York: Basic Books.

Pizzorno, Alessandro. 1978. "Political Exchange and Collective Identity in Industrial Conflict," in Crouch, Colin, and Pizzorno, eds., *The Resurgence of Class Conflict in Western Europe Since 1968*. London: MacMillan.

Polanyi, Karl. 1944. *The Great Transformation*. Boston: Beacon Press.

Popul Vuh. 1985. Translated by Dennis Tedlock. New York: Simon & Schuster.

Portes, Alejandro, and John Walton. 1981. *Labor, Class and the International System*. New York: Columbia University Press.

Portes, Alejandro, and Robert Bach. 1985. *Latin Journey*. Berkeley: University of California Press.

Potts, Lydia. 1990. *The World Labour Market: A History of Migration*. Atlantic Highland and London: Zed.

Presidenza del Consiglio dei Ministri (Italian Prime Minister's Office). 1991. *Atti della Conferenza Nazionale dell'Immigrazione Rome June 4-6, 1990*. Rome: Consiglio Nazionale dell'Economia e del Lavoro Rome.

Prigogine, Ilya, and Isabelle Stengers. 1984. *Order Out of Chaos*. New York: Bantam.

Putnam, Robert D. 1993. *Making Democracy Work: Civic Traditions in Modern Italy*. Princeton: Princeton University Press.

Race Today Collective. 1983. *The Struggles of Asian Workers in Britain* (pamphlet). London.

Rawick, George. 1972. *From Sundown to Sunup: The Making of the Black Community*. Westport: Greenwood.

Reyneri, Emilio. 1996. *Sociologia del mercato del lavoro*. Bologna: Il Mulino.

Richards, Charles. 1997. *The New Italians*. London: Penguin.

Rifkin, Jeremy. 1992. *Biosphere Politics: Enclosing the Global Commons*.

Rimmer, Douglas. 1984. *The Economies of West Africa*. London: Weidenfeld & Nicholson.

———. 1992. *Staying Poor: Ghana's Political Economy 1950-1990*. New York: Pergamon Press.

Robinson, Cedric. 1983. *Black Marxism: The Making of the Black Radical Tradition*. Atlantic Highlands and London: Zed.

Rodgers, Allan. 1979. *Economic Development in Retrospect: The Italian Model and its Significance for Regional Planning in Market-Oriented Economies*. Washington: VH Winston.

Rodney, Walter. 1972. *How Europe Underdeveloped Africa*. London: Bogle-Ouverture Publications.

Sabel, Charles. 1988. "Flexible Specialization and the Re-emergence of Regional Economies," in Paul Hirst and Jonathan Zeitlin, eds., *Reversing Industrial Decline*. Oxford: Oxford University Press.

Sachs, J. D. 1989. *Developing Country Debt and Economic Performance*. Chicago: University of Chicago Press.

Sachs, Wolfgang. 1992. *The Development Dictionary: A Guide to Knowledge as Power*. Atlantic Highlands and London: Zed.

Sandbrook, Richard, and Robin Cohen, eds. 1975. *The Development of an African Working Class*. London: Longman.

Saro-Wiwi, Ken. 1995. *A Month and A Day*. London: Penguin.

Sassen, Saskia. 1984. "The New Labor Demand in Global Cities," in M. P. Smith, ed., *Cities in Transformation*. Beverly Hills: Sage.

———. 1992. *The Global City*. New York: Cambridge University Press.

———. 1988. *The Mobility of Labor and Capital*. New York: Cambridge University Press.

Saxton, Alexander. 1971. *Indispensible Enemy: Labor and the Anti-Chinese Movement in California.* Berkeley: University of California Press.

Schmidt di Friedberg, Ottavia. 1995. *Islam, solidarietà e lavoro: i muridi senegalesi in Italia.* Turin: Fondazione Agnelli.

Schonfield, Andrew. 1965. *Modern Capitalism: The Changing Balance of Public and Private Power.* New York: Oxford University Press.

Schultz, Juergen. 1991. "Urbanism in Medieval Venice," in Anthony Molho, ed., *City-States in Classical Antiquity and Medieval Italy.* Ann Arbor: University of Michigan Press.

Schumpeter, Joseph. 1942. *Capitalism, Socialism and Democracy.* New York: Harper.

————. 1964. *Business Cycles: A Theoretical, Historical and Statistical Analysis of the Capitalist Process.* New York Toronto and London: McGraw Hill.

Sender, John, and Sheila Smith. 1986. *The Development of Capitalism in Africa.* London: James Currey.

Sergi, N. 1987. *L'Immigrazione straniera in Italia.* Rome: Edizioni Lavoro.

Shefter, Martin. 1986. "Trade Unions and Political Machines: The Organization and Disorganization of the American Working Class in the Late Nineteenth Century," in Ira Katznelson and Aristide Zolberg, eds., *Working Class Formation.* Princeton: Princeton: University Press.

Simcox, David. 1996. "The Nigerian Crime Network: Feasting on America's Innocence and Slipshod I.D. System," in John Tanton, Denis McCormack and Joseph Wayne Smith, eds., *Immigration and the Social Contract: The Implosion of Western Societies.* Brookfield, Vermont: Avebury.

Sivanandan, A. 1992. *A Different Hunger.* London: Verso.

————. 1990 *Communities of Resistance.* New York and London: Verso.

Skocpol, Theda. 1982. *States and Social* Revolutions. Chicago: University of Chicago Press.

Smith, Adam. 1976. *The Wealth of Nations.* Chicago: University of Chicago Press.

Smith, Denis Mack. 1969. *Italy.* Ann Arbor: University of Michigan Press.

Southall, Roger, ed. 1988. *Labour and Unions in Asia and Africa: Contemporary Issues.* New York: St. Martin's Press.

Spotts, Frederic, and Theodor Wieser. 1986. *Italy: A Difficult Democracy.* New York: Cambridge University Press.

Stahl, Charles V. 1986. *International Labor Migration: A Study of the ASEAN Countries/* Staten Island: Center for Migration Studies.

Stalker, Peter. 1994. *The Work of Strangers: A Survey of International Labor Migration.* Geneva: International Labor Office.

Stedman-Jones, Gareth. 1983. *Languages of Class: Studies in English Working Class History 1832-1982.* New York: Cambridge University Press.

Stella, Gian Antonio. 1996. *Schei: Il mitico nordest.* Milan: Baldini & Castoldi.

Strassoldo, Raimando. 1992. "Globalism and Localism: Theoretical Reflections and Some Evidence," in Zdradvko Mlinar, ed., *Globalization and Territorial Identities*. Brookfield, Vermont: Avebury.

Suret-Canale, Jean. 1971. *French Colonialism in Tropical Africa 1900-1945*. New York: Pica Press.

Susi, Francesco. 1988. *I bisogni formativi e culturali degli immigrati stranieri*. Milan: FrancoAngeli.

Tabacco, Giovanni. 1989. *The Struggle for Power in Medieval Italy*. New York: Cambridge University Press.

Tarrow, Sidney. 1981. *Democracy and Disorder: Protest and Politics in Italy 1965-1975*. Princeton: Princeton University Press.

Tawney, R. H. 1969. *Religion and the Rise of Capitalism: A Historical Study*. London: Penguin.

Thompson, E. P. 1963. *The Making of the English Working Class*. New York: Vintage.

Tilly, Charles. 1985. *Big Stuctures, Large Processes, Huge Comparisons*. New York: Russell Sage Foundation.

———. 1990. "Transplanted Networks," in Virginia Yans-McLaughlin, ed., *Immigration Reconsidered*. New York and Oxford: Oxford University Press.

Toffler, Alvin. 1991. *Powershift*. New York: Bantam.

Trigilia, Carlo. 1991. "Small-Firm Development and Political Subcultures in Italy," in Edward Goodman, Julia Bamford, and Peter Saynor, eds., *Small Firms and Industrial Districts in Italy*. London and New York: Routledge.

Udovicki, Jashminke, and Ridgeway, James. 1995. *Yugoslavia's Ethnic Nightmare*. Westport: Lawrence Hill.

Unione Regionale delle Camere di Commercio Industria Artiginato e Agricoltura del Veneto. *Fascicolo di Aggiornamento alla relazione sulla situazione del Veneto nel 1995 Import/Export 1993-1995*. Venice: Camere di Commercio del Veneto.

Volpato, Chiara. 1993. "Gli immigrati extracomunitari in Provincia di Vicenza," in Ubaldo Alifuoco, ed., *Verso una società multietnica*. Bologna: Quaderni della Fondazione Istituto Gramsci n. 13.

Wallerstein, Immanual. 1974. *The Modern World System: Capitalist Agriculture in the Sixteenth Century*, Vol. 1. Orlando: Academic Press.

Wallerstein, Immanual, Giovanni Arrighi, and Samir Amin. 1990. *Anti-Systemic Movements*. New York: Verso.

Ward, Katherine, ed. 1992. *Women Workers and Global Restructuring*. Ithaca: ILR Press.

Weatherford, Jack. 1992. *Native Roots*. New York: Fawcett.

———. 1994. "Tribal Technology," in Jack Weatherford, *Savages and Civilization*. New York: Ballantine.

Weber, Max. 1968. *The Protestant Ethic and the Spirit of Capitalism*. London: Unwin University Books.

Weiss, Linda. 1988. *Creating Capitalism: The State and Small Business since 1945*. New York: Blackwell.

Williams, Eric. 1984. *From Columbus to Castro: A History of the Caribbean 1492-1969*. New York: Random House.

———. 1964. *Capitalism and Slavery: The Caribbean*. London: Trafalgar Square-David & Charles.

Wood, Ellen Mieksins. 1986. *The Retreat From Class*. London: Verso.

———. 1988. *Peasant, Citizen, Slave*. New York: Verso.

World Bank. 1981. *Accelerated Development in Sub-Saharan Africa*. Washington: World Bank.

———. 1984. *Ghana: Policies and Programs for Adjustment*. Washington: World Bank.

———. 1989. *From Crisis to Sustainable Growth: A Long-Term Perspective*. Washington: World Bank.

———. 1989. *World Development Report*. Oxford: Oxford University Press.

———. 1995. *World Development Report 1995*. Washington: World Bank.

Zamagni, Vera. 1993. *The Economic History of Italy 1860-1990*. Oxford: Clarendon Press.

Zig, Henry-Layton. 1990. *The Political Rights of Migrant Workers in Western Europe*. London: Sage.

Zolberg, Aristide. 1981. "International Migrations in Political Perspective," in M. Kritz, C. Keely and S. Tomasi, eds., *Global Trends in Migration*. Staten Island: Center for Migration Studies.

———. 1986. "How Many Exceptionalisms?" in Ira Katznelson and Aristide Zolberg, eds., *Working Class Formation*. Princeton: Princeton University Press.

Zolberg, Aristide, Astri Suhrke and Sergio Aguayo. 1989. *Escape from Violence: Conflict and the Refugee Crisis in the Developing World*. New York: Oxford University Press.

THESES AND DISSERTATIONS

Bazzana, Manuela. 1994-95. *Carcere e detenzione in Veneto e in Italia: Un analysi comparativa*. Laurea Thesis Faculty of Political Science, University of Padua, Padua, Italy.

Colatrella, Steven. 1989. *We Want Everything: The Rise and Decline of the Autonomous Left in Italy from the 1950s to the 1970s*. Unpublished M.A. Thesis, New School for Social Research, New York.

Gasparini, Ilaria. 1992-93. *Le condizioni dei lavoratori stranieri immigrati in Provincia di Treviso*. Laurea Thesis Faculty of Political Science, University of Padua, Padua, Italy.

Rui, Irene. 1995-96. *L'Operaio in una media industria del Veneto orientale*. Research term paper for seminar of Professor Ferruccio Gambino on Sociology of Work, Department of Sociology, University of Padua, Padua, Italy.

Leonardi, Giulia. 1997-98. *Il lavoro delle donne filippine a Padova*. Research term paper for seminar of Professor Ferruccio Gambino on Sociology of Work, Department of Sociology, University of Padua, Padua, Italy.

JOURNAL ARTICLES

African Research Bulletin. July 1989. Devon, England.

Appadurai, Arjun. 1990. "Disjuncture and Difference in the Global Cultural Economy." *Public Culture* 2.

Bach, Robert. 1978. "Mexican Immigration and the American State." *International Migration Review* 12:536-558

Baubock, R. 1991. "Migration and Citizenship." *New Community* 18: 64-83.

Belotti, Valerio. 1992. "La rappresentanza politica locale delle Leghe." *Polis* 6.

Blim, Michael. 1990. "Economic Development and Decline in the Emerging Global Factory: Some Italian Lessons." *Politics and Society* 18: 143-63.

Bonacich, Edna. 1973. "A Theory of Middleman Minorities." *American Sociological Review* 38: 583-94.

Borjas, George. 1989. "Economic Theory and International Migration." *International Migration Review* 23: 457-85.

Bruno, Sergio. 1979. "The Industrial Reserve Army, Segmentation and the Italian Labour Market." *Cambridge Journal of Economics* 3: 131-52.

Brusco, Sebastiano. 1982. "The Emilian Model: Productive Decentralization and Social Integration." *Cambridge Journal of Economics* 6: 167-84.

Brusco, Sebastiano, and Ezio Righi. 1989. "Local Government, Industrial Policy and Social Consensus: The Case of Modena (Italy)." *Economy and Society* 18: 405-24.

Burawoy, Michael. 1976. "The Functions and Reproduction of Migrant Labor: Comparative Material from South Africa and the United States." *American Journal of Sociology* 81: 1050-87.

Campani, Giovanna. 1993. "Immigration and Racism in Southern Europe: The Italian Case." *Ethnic and Racial Studies* 16 : 507-35.

Cerase, Francesco. 1974. "Expectations and Reality: A Case Study of Return Migration from the United States to Southern Italy." *International Migration Review* 8: 245-64.

Colatrella, Steven. 1984. "The Working Class Waves Bye-Bye: A Proletarian Response to Andre Gorz." *Midnight Notes* 7.

Committee Against Repression in Italy. 1979-1985. *CARI Bulletin.* New York.

Commitee for Academic Freedom in Africa. 1991-1997. *CAFA Newletter* 1-12. New York.

Corrigan, P. 1977. "Feudal Relics or Capitalist Monuments? Notes in the Sociology of Unfree Labor." *Sociology* 11: 435-64.

Dell'Aringa, C., and F. Neri. 1987. "Illegal Immigrants and the Informal Economy in Italy." *Labour* 2: 262-77.

Diamanti, Ilvo. 1991. "La mia patria è il Veneto: i valori e la proposta politica delle leghe." *Polis* 1.

Dooley, Michael P., and C. Maxwell Watson. September 1989. "Reinvigorating the Debt Strategy." *Finance and Development.*

Fei, J.C.H., and Gustav Ramis. 1961. "A Theory of Economic Development." *American Economic Review* 51: 533-65.

Gabaccia, Donna. 1994. "Worker Internationalism and Italian Labor Migration 1870-1914." *International Labor and Working Class History* 45: 60-79.

Gambino, Ferruccio. 1996. "A Critique of the Fordism of the Regulation School." *Common Sense* 19.

Hammar, Thomas. 1985. "Dual Citizenship and Political Integration." *International Migration Review* 19: 438-50.

Humphreys, Charles, and William Jaeger. 1989. "Africa's Adjustment and Growth." *Finance and Development* 26: 6-8.

La Mendola, Salvatore. 1991. "I rapporti di parentela in Veneto." *Polis* 1.

Lazerson, Mark. 1988. "Organizational Growth of the Small Firms: An Outcome of Markets and Hierarchies. *American Sociological Review* 53: 330-42.

Lewis, W. A. 1954. "Economic Development with Unlimited Supplies of Labour." *Manchester School of Economic and Social Studies* 2: 139-91.

Linebaugh, Peter. 1982. "Karl Marx and the Theft of Wood." *New York University Law Journal.*

———. 1982. "All the Atlantic Mountains Shook." *Labour/Le Travail.*

Locke, Richard M. 1990. "The Resurgence of the Local Union: Industrial Restructuring and Industrial Relations in Italy." *Politics and Society* 18: 347-79.

Lovell, George W. 1986. "Rethinking Conquest: The Colonial Experience in Latin America." *Journal of Historical Geography* 12: 310-17.

Maldondo, E. 1979. "Contract Labor and the Origin of the Puerto Rican Communities in the United States." *International Migration Review* 13: 103-21.

Mattera, Philip. 1980. "Small Is Not Beautiful: Decentralized Production and the Underground Economy in Italy." *Radical America* 14: 67-76.

Moretto, Mauro. 1996. "Una zona di esportazione di rango alto e precario." *Altreragioni* 5.

Morokvasic, Mirjana. 1984. "Birds of Passage Are Also Women." *International Migration Review* 18.

Mungiello, Rossana. 1997. "Lavoro coatto a fine secolo in quattro grandi aree economiche." *Altreragioni* 6.

Murray, Fergus. 1987. "Flexible Specialization in the Third Italy." *Capital and Class* 33: 84-95.

Pollert, Anna. 1988. "Dismantling Flexibility." *Capital and Class* 34: 42-75.

Portes, Alejandro. 1976. "Determinants of the Brain Drain." *International Migration Review* 10: 489-508.

Portes, Alejandro. 1978. "Migration and Underdevelopment." *Politics and Society* 8: 1-48.

Portes, Alejandro, and Julia Sensenbrenner. 1993. "Embeddedness and Immigration: Notes on the Social Determinants of Economic Action." *Journal of American Sociology* 98: 1320-50.

Ravenstein, Ernst Georg. 1885. "The Laws of Migration." *Journal of the Royal Statistical Society* 48: 167-227.

————. 1889. "The Laws of Migration." *Journal of the Royal Statistical Society* 52: 241-301.

Rodriguez, Nestor. 1996. "Battle for the Border: Autonomous Migration, Transnational Communities and the State." *Social Justice* 23.

Sabetti, Filippo. 1996. "Path Dependency and Civic Culture: Some Lessons From Italy About Interpreting Social Experiments." *Politics and Society* 24: 19-44.

Sacchetto, Devi. 1996. "Nodi di autonomia controllata: il tessile e abbigliamento nel Veneto." *Altreragioni* 5.

Seccombe, W. 1974. "The Housewife and Her Labour under Capitalism." *New Left Review* 83: 33-47.

Segatti, Paolo. 1992. "L'offerta politica e i candidati della Lega alle elezioni amministrative del 1990." *Polis* 6.

Shearer, J. 1966. "In Defense of Traditional Views of the Brain Drain Problem." *International Educational and Cultural Exchange.*

Silver, Beverly J. 1995. "World Scale Patterns of Labor-Capital Conflict." *Review* 18.

Summers, Lawrence H., and Lance H. Pritchett. 1993. "The Structural Adjustment Debate." *American Economic Review* 83: 383-89.

Taplin, Ian. 1989. "Segmentation and the Organization of Work in the Italian Apparel Industry." *Social Science Quarterly* 70: 408-24.

Todaro, M. and J. Harris. 1970. "Migration, Unemployment and Development: A Two-Sector Analysis." *American Economic Review* 60: 126-42.

Veugelers, John W. P. 1994. "Recent Immigration Politics in Italy: A Short Story." *West European Politics* 17: 33-49.

NEWSPAPER ARTICLES

"Immigrati a Firenze sciopero della fame." *L'Unità*, 12 March 1990.

"Nero, la polizia non ti fermerà." *L'Unità*, 12 March 1990.

"Bisogno d'immigrati." *L'Unità*, 22 March 1990.

"Gli immigrati alla Cgil: 'non siamo straccioni'." *Il Sole-24 Ore*, 30 March 1990.

"Un tranquillo week-end di paura: A Castelvolturno fra 300 negri assediati." *L'Unità*, 30 April 1990.

"Cacciati dai loro connazionali 6 immigrati sospettati di spaccio." *L'Unità*, 1 May 1990.

"Milano, immigrati al rogo." *Il Manifesto*, 11 May 1990.

"Vicenza offre lavoro, ma si dorme all stazione." *Il Manifesto*, 11 May 1990.

"La griffe del vu' comprà per firma un cammello." *L'Unità*, 28 May 1990.

"150 Pakistani invisibili." *Il Manifesto*, 14 August 1990.

"Villa Litorno: Arriva la Croce rossa." *Il Manifesto*, 18 August 1990.

"Padova: Per un pugno di letti." *Il Manifesto*, 23 August 1990.

"Sindaco senza memoria." *Il Manifesto*, 24 August 1990.

"I tappetini nella 'T': revocati 40 permessi." *L'Unità*, 4 September 1990.

"Bologna: La giunta alla prova immigrati." *L'Unità*, 11 September 1990.

"I neri all'assolto delle case." *La Repubblica*, Bologna edition, 11 September 1990.

"Drama casa immigrati: Moruzzi apre il dialogo." *Bologna*, supplement to *L'Unità*, 13 September 1990.

"Sciopero bianco." *Il Manifesto*, 10 May 1991.

"La Pantanella dei somali." *Il Manifesto*, 16 May 1991.

"In corteo per i diritti." *Il Manifesto*, 17 May 1991.

"Il comune di Bologna sgombera 300 immigrati." *Il Manifesto*, 21 July 1991.

"Brescia: La spina nel fianco della Lega." *L'Unità*, 15 January 1992.

"Immigrati: In piazza a Brescia per i permessi di soggiorno." *Il Manifesto*, 18 January 1992.

"Un metro quadro a Casablanca." *Il Manifesto*, 18 January 1992.

"Immigrati: 300 associazioni in tutta Italia. Un primo identikit." *Il Manifesto*, 30 January 1992.

"La nuova schiavatù sommersa." *L'Unità*, 7 August 1992.

"Aliens Find a European Gateway at Spain's Coast." *New York Times*, 18 October 1992.

"Alloggi agli immigrati, è guerra." *Corriere della Sera*, 2 February 1994.

"Milano: Demolito il terzo centro per immigrati." *Il Manifesto*, 15 September 1994.

"Via i neri, causa dei nostri mali." *Corriere della Sera*, 25 September 1994.

"Naufraga la nave degli schiavi." *Il Manifesto*, 1 October 1994.

"Schiavi dell'est a Piacenza, Arrestati 5 imprenditori." *Il Manifesto*, 21 October 1994.

"Royal Seal: The Case of Saudi Prince, Maids in Texas Tests Issue of U.S. Immunity." *Wall Street Journal Europe*, December 28, 1994.

"Darkness Hides Migrant Flood into Italian Underworld." *Independent*, 8 January 1995.

"Il quinto stato." *Il Manifesto*, 26 February 1995.

"Ramos is Assailed at Rites for Maid." *International Herald Tribune*, 20 March 1995.

"I nuovi eroi del lavoro." *Il Manifesto*, 13 April 1995.

"A Grisly Market for Organs in India." *International Herald Tribune*, 5 May 1995.

"A Market for Human Organs." *International Herald Tribune*, 6-7 May 1995.

"Nordest: economia in crescita." *Il Gazzettino*, Padua 25 June 1995.

"Spaghetti Apartheid." *Il Manifesto*, 15 September 1995.

"Philippine Maid Hoping for a Pardon." *International Herald Tribune*, 18 September 1995.

"Immigrati, c'è l'accordo." *La Repubblica*, 15 November 1995.

"Via Anelli, blitz all'alba." *Il Mattino*, Padua 15 November 1995.

"Muscoli in vista rassicuranti e spettacolari." *Il Mattino* (Padua), 15 November 1995.

"19 November: A Torino contro il decreto." *Il Manifesto*, 15 November 1995.

"Extracomunitari, nuove regole." *Il Sole-24 Ore*, 19 November 1995.

"Arrivano le prime espulsioni." *La Repubblica*, 21 November 1995.

"Decreto immigrati, è il caos." *La Repubblica*, 25 November 1995.

"A Roma 15 mila contro il decreto." *La Repubblica*, 4 February 1996.

"Una larga intesa." *Il Manifesto*, 4 February 1996.

"L'esercito contro i clandestini." *Il Manifesto*, 8 October 1996.

"Belgians Uncover Asian Labor Scam." *International Herald Tribune*, 7 November 1996.

"Io, schiava della 'mafia nera'." *Il Gazzettino* (Padua), 15 November 1996.

"Nigeriano molesta tre bimbe." *Il Mattino*, Padua 20 November 1996.

"La mafia cinese ora è vicino." *Il Mattino*, Padua 7 December 1996.

"Storia di Claudia, lolita per forza." *Il Mattino*, Padua 13 December 1996.

"Un'altra storia di ordinaria schiavatù." *Il Gazzettino*, 13 December 1996.

"Economia, nell Alta tiene." *Il Gazzettino*, Padua 13 December 1996.

"Sbattuta sul marciapiedi a sedici anni." *Il Gazzettino*, Padua 20 December 1996.

"I cinesi 'mercanti di schiavi'." *Il Gazzettino*, 20 December 1996.

"Rapina su commissione: Banda di slavi in Italia da una settimana." *Il Mattino* (Padua), 28 December 1996.

"Due arresti su tre sono immigrati." *Il Manifesto*, 3 January 1997.

"I fantasmi del Mediterraneo." *Il Manifesto*, 5 January 1997.

"La prima lista di naufragi." *Il Manifesto*, 10 January 1997.

"Romania Seeks Large IMF Loan." *International Herald Tribune*, 3 February 1997.

"Immigrati, si volta la pagina." *La Repubblica*, 15 February 1997.

"Child Labour Common in Naples' Underground Economy." *The European*, 8 March 1997.

"Un'intervento colonialista." *Liberazione*, 9 April 1997.

"Immigrants turn tables on Ireland." *International Herald Tribune*, 16 June 1997.

"Sul marciapiedi col diploma." *Il Gazzettino* (Padua), 27 June 1997.

"Slave Trade in Children Grows in West Africa, Based on Recent Arrests." *International Herald Tribune*, 12 August 1997.

"I disperati del mare." *La Repubblica*, 28 December 1997.

"Il grande sbarco dei curdi." *La Repubblica*, 28 December 1997.

"Bande senza scrupoli, la Turchia le fermi." *La Repubblica*, 28 December 1997.

"Viva Soverato." *Il Manifesto*, 28 December 1997.

"Braccio Aperte." *Il Manifesto*, 28 December 1997.

"Italy's Open Borders Irk Neighbors." *International Herald Tribune*, 3-4 January 1998.

"Clandestini: rivolte e un morto." *Corriere Della Sera*, 2 August 1998.

"Immigrati, ora e' assedio." *Corriere Della Sera*, 9 August 1998.

"Sicilia: nuovi sbarchi di immigrati." *Corriere Della Sera*, 3 August 1998.

"I centri scoppiano." *Corriere Della Sera*, 3 August 1998.

PERSONS INTERVIEWED

Grazia Bellini, Immigrant Office, CGIL labor federation, Padua, February 22, 1997.

Valerio Belotti, Fondazione Corazzin, author, Mestre, March 8, 1995.

Gabrielle Brunetti, Municipal Office of Immigrant Welcome, Vicenza, March 12, 1997.

Silvano Cogo, organizer, CGIL labor federation, Padua, March 10, 1995, followed by virtually weekly meetings during various periods 1995-1997; interview April 4, 1997.

F., Nigerian metalworker, Padua, December 27, 1997.

Michele Fassina, President, Associazione Immigrati Extracomunitari, Padua, November 22, 1994; February 14, 1995; at certain periods, weekly meetings, 1995-1997.

Gianpaolo Feriani, ex-Director of the Asilo Notturno, Padua, February 16, 1995.

G., Eritrean-Italian man, Padua, December 10, 1996.

H., Senegalese man, Padua, January 27, 1997.

Suor Lia, Cucina Popolare, Padua, January 22, 1996.

M., Albanian man, Padua, February 7, 1997.

R., Zimbabwean man, Padua, December 10, 1994.

Giorgio Maschio, Scalibrini Brotherhood Welcome Center, Bassano del Grappa, March 15, 1997.

Mortesà, Municipal Office of Immigrant Welcome, Vicenza, March 8, 1996.

Muhammad, CGIL Immigrant Office, Montebelluna, April 23, 1997.

Professor Oblek, Office of Social Interventions of the City of Padua, Padua, March 11, 1997.

Paul Ocoye, President, National Union of Nigerian Citizens in Italy, Padua, February 17, 1995, and March 17, 1996.

Rev. Minister Simmons Odame, Pastor of Assembly of God Church, Vicenza, January 13, 1997.

Marco Paggi, Immigration Lawyer, Padua, February 15, 1997 and February 24, 1997.

Signora Pase, Unica Terra (Catholic non-profit cooperative), Padua, March 14, 1997.

S., Senegalese man, Padua, February 7, 1997.

Assessore Santone, Padua Municipal Government, April 15, 1997.

Giovanni Scattolin Ragioniere, Padua Chamber of Commerce (Camera di Commercio) Padua, Office of Foreign Trade (Sportello di Commercio Estero), Padua, November 2, 1996.

Three Moroccan men, Montebelluna, April 14, 1997.

Three Bosnian-Serb men, Padua, March 2, 1997.

Five Senegalese families, province of Padua, March 19, 1997.

Index